THE

ESSENE CHRIST

A Recovery of The Historical Jesus

Plate 1   From a painting by Upton C. Ewing

From a life size painting
by the Author
Courtesy of First Presbyterian Church
Coral Gables, Florida

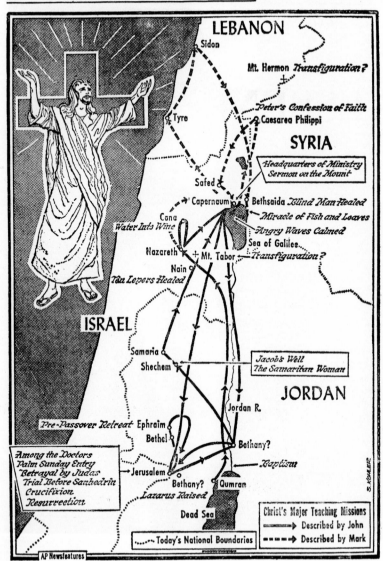

Plate 2

Note here that the path walked by Jesus begins at Qumran, or the Essene monastery, and leads first to Nazareth. Our evidence refers to Nazareth as an Essene community.

THE
ESSENE CHRIST

A RECOVERY OF
THE HISTORICAL JESUS
AND THE
DOCTRINES OF PRIMITIVE CHRISTIANITY

by

Upton Clary Ewing

PHILOSOPHICAL LIBRARY
NEW YORK

5/95

Library of Congress Catalog Card No. 61-10608

Printed in the United States of America

Gift
G. J.

This book is dedicated to all peoples in their strivings towards a bringing to pass of the "prophetic vision": to that peaceful state in which all life, all creatures, are to share: to the future great church and the fulfillment of "Thy will be done on earth."

viii CONTENTS

Page

Chapter 9—The Conception of John the Baptist
His Childhood Tendencies 106
Chapter 10—The Holy 107
Chapter 11—The Baptist Admonishes the Multitudes
The Baptism of Jesus 108
Chapter 12—The 111
Chapter 13—Jesus Becomes Aware of His Mission
.... 114

Chapter 117
The Prophecy of Blood
Let the Dead Bury Their ....
The Stone 121
Chapter 18—The Extreme of Jesus Dwells Here ....
Chapter 19—The Marriage Feast—Water
Mary and Not Self Denial ....
Chapter 21—The Parable 120
Chapter 22—....................................
Chapter 23—The Divorce Act ....
Chapter ....
Chapter Jesus Heals Through Prayer ....
....
Chapter 26—The Dead Are the Living ....
Advises the Rich ....
Chapter 181
.... Acquittal
Chapter 29—The Light of the World, Jesus Explains
"Follow Me" 186

CONTENTS

— BOOK ONE —

Page

— BOOK TWO —
The Covenant of Love

— BOOK THREE —

COMMENTARY ON THE GOSPEL OF THE COVE-
NANT OF LOVE

Page

FOREWORD

The intent of this four part volume is to recover, evaluate, and to promulgate the ethical criteria of a "pure religion."

First, however, let it be understood that the terms used in the development of this work are for the most part theological and tend to be specifically Christian in expression.

If the reader is inclined, from a liberal point of view, to resent this kind of terminology the author solicits his forbearance in the realization that language is merely an arrangement of symbols to convey a message, which usually is understood in a different manner by different people. It is therefore hoped that one might consider the underlying intent of the message contained herein even though the means used to convey it may be somewhat archaic to the modern thinker.

However, the fact that the theme of this entire work is based upon the ethical mysticism of the Old Testament and its influence upon the four gospels, the use of archaic terminology is not only preferable but necessary.

The most astonishing revelation which comes through a study of Old Testament ethics is the fact that both Jew and Christian alike, carefully avoid referring to the several Bible verses which are, in fact, more ethical than self indulgent, and more spiritual than sensate. Many of the great ethical messages of scripture are in consequence seldom, if ever, read from the pulpit, for the simple reason that, first they are contrary to doctrine and, second, that they would tend to annoy the self-righteous conscience of the conformer.

On the other hand, even though a multitude of liberal religionists reject the several customs and beliefs of the various orthodoxies, they still hold fast to the same Sybaritic practice which was especially emphasized, and most lustfully so, by the founding priests of the Judaeo-Christian tradition. As this practice was made to do duty for the superfluities of indulgence it consequently opposed the recovery of a higher ethical manhood wherein the nobility of spirit transcends the predacious instincts of the beast. Pure religion must first pass the tests of human dignity and responsibility. It must be ethical not only in its "world view" but in its relation to the universe: i.e., it must stress *Life's responsibility to life* and to the creative force which makes life possible. In short "pure religion" must be synonymous with an uncompromised "will to love."

However and notwithstanding, "it is fair to say that somewhere, somehow, hidden beneath the dogmas and the creeds, and standing, perhaps above the theological conflicts and inconsistencies, there is, or has been, in Christianity a core of meaning which touches the human heart and moves it to intuitive response. If this element could be given pure definition, then we should have pure religion, but at present, very likely, all that will win common assent is the ideal that some such primordial reality or truth exists in every great religion, and that strenuous search is involved in finding it out." [1]

It seems that the term "pure religion" more fittingly applies to a faith in the existence of truth unalloyed and uncompromised by traditional beliefs, collective habits, or formalized practices, for indeed these might well be viewed as the "antitheses" of a primordial reality.

Therefore to find, or recover, the truth of a primordial reality, of "pure religion," one must first scrutinize "acquired behaviors" with a critical eye, posing, if you will, the pure spirituality of an ethical mysticism against the sensual compromises of collective pietism.

The great mystics of the past courageously opposed these same "antitheses." To them was revealed the basic criteria of a "pure religion": i.e., a way and a means of behavior as of and between the life which is "God" and the life which inhabits the universe.

According to rather obscure but most impressive of records, the great Hebrew mystic, Moses, appears to have been truly the founding father of "pure religion." And this can be substantiated in principle in spite of the many myths which in effect have made his otherwise gentle character do duty for the carnal ideas and practices of his self appointed interpreters.

According to what seems to be the most ethical and, therefore, the most reliable of the literary texts, we find that Moses set forth in a very simple but extremely significant pair of ordinances the criteria of a universal ethic or of a "pure religion": i.e., the sixth commandment and its companion ordinance, Genesis 1:29 *¹

These—each an antitype of the other, were the keynotes *² of an ethical mysticism essential to the veneration of life, or to the making of a covenant between the author of Love, and the life which is of His creation.

In accord therewith, all creatures, great and small, were to dwell in peace together. There was to be no harm nor destruction: no need to kill, for all the green herbs, golden grains, and the rich fruits of the earth were given for food.

These prime requisites as they were first conceived by Moses were subsequently acknowledged by the great Persian mystic Zoroaster, by the august fathers of old China, Laotse and Confucius, and again by the immortal Buddha, Mahavira, Asoka, and other apostles of the author of Love and the endower of all life.

But alas, even though the great law giver was "God's first choice" among men to promulgate the way and the means of insuring the peaceful co-existence of all creatures, lying priests and vain scribes were the first to bring about its corruption.

In consequence, much of the texts of the Old Testament

*¹ During the Persian period Jewish scribes proclaimed Mosaic authorship of Genesis. It can hardly be doubted therefore, that the great law giver was at least one of its many authors.
*² The foundation stones of Schweitzer's "Reverence for Life."

are reminiscent of the lusts of the priests which are in glaring contrast to the prophets' and the Psalm writers' pleas for justice and mercy.

But the pure law of Moses was not to be denied for during the latter part of the First Century B.C. there came forth from among the Hebrews a remnant whose purpose was to recover the true covenant: to deliver it from the realms of darkness in which it had been engulfed.

These holy ones, called by the Greeks Essenes, believed that one would receive the truth of the voice of scripture only when he was correctly attuned, or had received the inner enlightenment.

"The acquisition of that light, however, was not attributed to any sudden spontaneous act of grace. Rather was it the result of man's own voluntary exercise of that power of discernment which God placed in every creature at the moment of its creation. All things, it was affirmed . . . had been endowed by God with sensate knowledge, though the choice of using it or ignoring it had been left, in the case of man, to his individual will. If he headed the gift, he achieved harmony with the eternal cosmic scheme and broke the trammels of his mortality. Automatically he was embraced in the communion of eternal things; he became one with the great forces of the universe . . ." [2] In other words they believed that all creatures being endowed by God with sensate knowledge were, even as man, part of the great cosmic scheme. Illumination, therefore, came through achieving harmony with the whole of life, which in effect, is becoming one with the universe and, or, one with the Author of all life. * (See footnote)

This is "pure religion" as it first enlightened the soul of Moses and caused him to set forth the great spiritual axiom which was subsequently acknowledged in the life and works of the founders of the ethical systems of the eastern world.

In accordance with Essene scriptures we find that "the

* Compare with p. 146. Ye are the city, also, with Job. 12:7-10.

Torah—that is, the Divine Teaching as revealed to Moses—had, it was held, been successively garbled and perverted by false 'expositors'. The community's main purpose was to exemplify and promulgate the true interpretation." [3]

In accord therewith, there came from out of this Hebrew remnant "One" whose purpose was to exemplify in person, to fulfill the pure covenant as it was first given to Moses: to complete the work of the Prophets. "Till heaven and earth pass, not one jot or one tittle of the true law shall be taken away. I am come to fulfill," cried Jesus.

Thus each of the world's great religious reformers was in turn inspired by the same pure source: a source which must necessarily oppose any word or any act, however piously conceived or interpreted, which is contrary or inconsistent with the "Will-to-Love."

But alas! again the covenant was "made of none effect." Much of what the Master taught was not recorded, and that which was later reconstructed from memory, and put into writing, has not come down to us in its original form.

In consequence "pure religion," even though it is still retained in part by followers of the great eastern mystics, was, as far as traditional Judaeo-Christian doctrines are concerned, buried in the rubble of Sinai, or, left hanging upon a tree at Golgotha.

The following work represents an interpretation of the ethical mysticism of the Old Testament wherein is preserved the simple purity of the first law of "God" and of Life. It is an attempt to recover the covenant as it was first conceived by Moses and later reclaimed and restated by the "Son of Man."

As the reader will note, the necessary approach was first to recover the historical Jesus from out of the maze of conflicting testimonies, opinions, and beliefs concerning his character: only thereby could the original "'Covenant of Love" again be recovered and revealed: i.e., as of and through the word and the way of life of Jesus called the "Christ."

Every man seeks and needs an ideal to look up to: an example to turn to for moral and spiritual guidance: a truly humane and sincerely ethical character, and, above all, one whose acts and purposes are not beyond the reach of human reason, human needs and human accomplishment.

Christianity's greatest error was when the gospel writers dramatized Jesus as a doer of miracles rather than as a symbol or an example of ideal manhood.

The Jesus of the "Covenant of Love" is such an example. He stands free, pure and uncompromised before the bar of human judgment: to exemplify if you will, stripped of the trammels of inconsistency and the grave clothes of dogma, the true Spirit of "Divine consciousness."

> "And the word of God became man that you
> also may learn from a man how a man be-
> comes a god." [4] *(Clement of Alexandria)*

FOREWORD

1 **Manas.**

2, 3 Theodore Gaster, *The Dead Sea Scrolls*. Doubleday & Company Inc., New York, N. Y.

4 Victor Gollancz, *Man and God*, Houghton Mifflin Company, Boston.

BOOK ONE

THE ESSENE CHRIST

PREFACE

The Covenant of Love is a Fifth Gospel of Jesus Christ: a reconstructed and expanded version of the four Gospels. Its message is synonymous with the highest ethical principles of ancient scriptures and is supported in kind by the authors of the "Dead Sea Scrolls" and by the fragmentary but significantly revealing records of primitive Christianity as it was taught and practiced both before and for some time after the four Gospels became the criteria of church authority.

The purpose of its writing is to recover the "Essene Christ"; the transcended spirit of the one and only historical Jesus: to censure the many compromises and inconsistencies that have, down through the centuries, crept into the New Testament writings and which to a considerable extent have obscured His true character.

"There is no historical task," writes Albert Schweitzer, "which so reveals a man's true self as the writing of a Life of Jesus. It has no vital impact unless a man breathes into it all the love or all the hate of which he is capable." [1]

Referring to the latter it is the writer's opinion that most of the so-called lives of Jesus which bear the mark of hate are but contentious devices wherein Jesus is made the "scape-goat" for a blast against ecclesiastical authority.

The Gospels which supply the greater part of source data contain many ambiguous references which one may

1

presumably interpret in a manner most suitable to his particular purpose.

The common knowledge that the Gospels were mostly written through "hear say" by men who never saw Jesus, should move the incredulous writer, providing he has no axe to grind, to reflect before making any derogatory statements concerning the character of the Nazarene. The researcher should also be reminded that the character of Jesus even as it appeared in the lost originals was necessarily subject to, and interpreted through, the particular complexes or characteristics of the men who made Him to conform to their own purposes. Also, one can not overlook the evidence that the many copies leading up to our present records were successively arranged and interpolated to satisfy the needs of their day, and to comply with the early century growth and development of both the Church's ritual and its doctrine.

The authority of the Christian belief is based upon the greatness of Jesus called the "Christ." This greatness is supported more intensively by a variety of eschatological expediencies, combined with an over emphasized sensationalism, than by a prescribed way of life, which stresses the dignity of character and the ethical teachings of Jesus. While leanings to the former have served the Church for purposes of indoctrination, they seem today to be yielding more to doubt than to belief. This tendency appears increasingly more prevalent among the clergy than among the lay members of the Church: a fact which challenges traditional Christianity to adopt a more realistic approach to an understanding of the "Christ example."

The conflict going on in the minds of men within the Church is a natural reaction of the historical conflict between the authority of the Church and the authority of Jesus Christ.

"In religion," says Albert Schweitzer, "there are two different currents: one free from dogma and one that is dogmatic. That which is free from dogma bases itself on the preaching of Jesus: the dogmatic bases itself on the creeds of the early church and the reformation. The religion free from dogma . . . is ethical . . . and endeavors . . . to remain on good terms with thinking. It wants to realize something of the Kingdom of God in the world. All efforts of historical theological science . . . are . . . proving that Christian dogma began with St. Paul and that the religion of Jesus is non-dogmatic . . ." [2]

"Ethics and theology do not stand for us in the same live relationship as they do with Jesus. The vividness of the absolute ethical idealism has been faded by history. To render the ethics of Jesus unconditional and self-sufficing is not only unhistorical, but it means also the degradation of his ethical idealism." [3]

"It is because Jesus does not think in a utilitarian way," continues Schweitzer, "but only according to the absolute ethic of, 'not being conformed to the world' that there is such a remarkable contrast between His thoughts and our modern views. Only when we experience this contrast, *through a reverence for life,** have we entered into relationship to the true Jesus. . . . His significance for us is that He fights against the spirit of the modern world, forcing it to abandon the low level on which it moves, even in its best thoughts, and to rise to the height whence we judge things according to the superior will of God which is active in us, and to think no more in terms of human utilitarianism but solely in terms of doing God's will— becoming forces of God's ethical personality." [4]

"The renewing of Christianity which must come will be a return to the immediacy and intensity of the faith of early Christianity," [5] affirms Schweitzer. "To dare to go back to the original fountainhead and keep alive true Christianity as it came fresh and sweet and clean from the heart of Jesus himself." [6]

Schweitzer, discussing Albert Kalthoff, writes: "His quar-

* Italics by author.

rel with the historical Jesus of modern theology was that
he could find no connecting link betwen the life of Jesus
constructed by the latter and primitive Christianity.
Modern theology he remarks, and with great justice, finds
itself obliged to assume, at the point where the history
of the Church begins 'an immediate declension from, and
falsification of, a pure original principle,' and that in
so doing 'it is deserting the recognized methods of historical
science.' If then we cannot trace the path from its beginning onwards, we had better try to work backwards,
endeavoring first to define in the theology of the primitive
Church the values which we shall look to find again in
the life of Jesus." [7] In other words, according to Schweitzer,
one should look to find the true doctrine of Jesus reflected
in the values taught and practiced by the old apostles and
by the primitive church. To put it in another way, if the
spiritual measure of Jesus, his moral and ethical attitude,
were exhibited in his behavior, his teachings and in the
practices of his daily way of life, would they not also be
similarly practiced in the way of life, and included in the
doctrines of His immediate followers? A positive answer
to this question, being the likely one, represents the approach
needed to recover a much needed portion of the subject
matter pertaining to the ethical teachings of Jesus.

However, and in recognition of the many more or less
critical as well as damaging analyses of the life of Jesus,
which, in a large measure, merely reflected the character
and the purpose of those who wrote into the books of the
New Testament, it is evident that an unbiased quest must
be based, in part, more upon the approach previously
described than upon the gospels themselves, if the true
nature of the Nazarene is to be recovered.

In view of the belief that Jesus was more than an
ordinary man it seems necessary to seek other than ordinary means of verifying his character. In other words, if
the character, the teachings and the way of life of Jesus
were as pure, honorable, just, and as ethical as Christians

seem to believe then it seems both plausible and necessary to direct our search accordingly.

As a preface to later more intensive expositions of this particular approach I quote in part from a writing by the Reverend Herold Kemmis of the Anglican Church: "Most disturbing of all to the would-be reverent disciple of the Master, is the fact that some of the sayings and doings attributed to Him are harsh, glamorous, unbeautiful in one way or another, and therefore unworthy of imitation. The student is constrained to ask: Was the Master, after all, not as stainless, humble and beautiful as we have been told? If so, the Christian world has indeed been led astray. Or can it be that the Gospels as they now stand, are seriously unreliable, having been changed from their original form; changed, not inadvertently, but deliberately, by people who desired to present a different picture of the Master from that found in the original documents?

"Here is indeed for the orthodox Christian a challenging dilemma. Have Christians been misled in reverencing the Master as a perfect manifestation of the Divine Nature? Have they been worshipping a merely imaginary figure, while the real Jesus was not only as human as themselves, but actually faulty in some important respects? The honest seeker for truth will not flinch from this question, even though it is most unwelcome to him, and pains his sensibilities. If the Christ-Soul was not altogether holy, saintly, loving, God-like, then Christians are utterly mistaken in their claims concerning Him, and must sorrowfully confess that they have been deceived, and have followed cunningly-devised fables.

"But if on the other hand He was as noble and Divine in His words and deeds as we have always supposed, then the Gospels are faulty in their presentation of Him, and give to us a portrait which is not only incomplete but distorted; and we ought to recognize this as a fact, and be willing to acknowledge it, and learn as best we can to distinguish the true from the false, the pure gold from the base metal which is mingled with it." [8]

In the Midmonth Magazine for Methodist Families Dr. Otto Nall writes: "In a calloused and brutal time the miracles of Jesus were deeds of pity and mercy, usually dependent for their effectiveness on the faith of those helped. We may be sure that any miracles lacking these qualities have been imperfectly or incompletely reported to us. *If out of character they are suspect.*" [9]

In a similar vein of thought the Reverend Holmes-Gore of the Anglican Church writes: "If we read in the gospels that the Master did something that was unworthy of Him, then we should know that the gospels give a false picture of Him." [10]

It is important to note here, that in the quest of the Historical Jesus, Schweitzer allocates considerable space to those scholars who were particularly critical of the trustworthiness of the gospel records. In this connection one is drawn to suppose that Schweitzer's purpose in the writing of the "Quest" was first to verify the historicity of Jesus in relation to the several recorded events and second, to reveal their improper or inaccurate reporting.

Schweitzer fully agrees with the common judgment that the older synoptic tradition is too fragmentary to reveal the fullness of the life and doctrine of Jesus.[11] "We are in danger," he says, "of acknowledging a Jesus who is too little (too insufficient) because we have forced him into man's measure* and into the mold of average human psychology . . . (behavior) . . . We make Him speak with our time another language than that which passed his lips." [12] Schweitzer concludes, "that our knowledge of the historical Jesus is more extensive and certain than modern theology dares to assume in its exposition of the gospel accounts." [13]

"What Christianity needs," says Schweitzer, "is that it

Above parentheses by author
* Here Florens Tertullian 1st C. Church Father would add "Made Him to come eating and drinking into the service of your lusts." (De Juniis Adversus Psychicos.)

shall be filled to overflowing with the spirit of Jesus, and in the strength of that shall spiritualize itself into a living religion of love. Only as such can it become the leaven in the spiritual life of mankind. What has been passing for Christianity during these nineteen centuries is merely a beginning, full of weakness and mistakes, not a full-grown Christianity springing from the spirit of Jesus." [14]

"Christianity . . . . . must insist on the fact that the ethical is the highest type of spirituality and that it alone is living spirituality. Thus Christianity shows itself as the religion which, penetrating and transcending all knowledge, reaches forward to the ethical living God. . . . . . " [15]

However, "ethics has not only to do with mankind," continues Schweitzer, "but with the animal creation as well. This is witnessed in the purpose of St. Francis of Assisi. The explanation which applies only to man must be given up. Thus we shall arrive at saying that ethics is—reverence for *all* life. [16] This is the ethic of Love widened into universality. It is the ethic of Jesus now recognized as a necessity of thought." [17]

"The essential element in Christianity as it was preached by Jesus . . . is this," continues Schweitzer, "that it is only through Love that we can attain to communion with God. All living knowledge of God rests upon this foundation, that we experience Him in our lives as Will-to-Love". [19]

"God is Life" and "God is Love" (Jo.1:4) (1.Jo.4:8). This is a spiritual axiom which verifies the nature of God. "Reverence for Life", is in truth "Reverence for God".

Therefore, "one last conclusion must be drawn from the principle of devotion," says Schweitzer, "it no longer allows us to concern ourselves only with other human beings. We must behave in exactly the same way towards all living creatures, of whatever kind, whose fate may in some way be our concern. They too are our kith and kin, inasmuch as they too crave happiness, know the meaning of fear and suffering, and dread annihilation." [20]

"However much it struggles against it, ethics arrives at

the religion of Jesus. It must recognize that it can discover
no other relationship to other beings as full of sense as the
relationship of love.* Ethics is nothing else than reverence
for life. All spiritual life meets us within natural life. Reverence for Life, therefore, is applied to natural life and
spiritual life alike. In the parable of Jesus, the shepherd
saves not merely the soul of the lost sheep but the whole
animal."[21]

"Only a universal ethic which embraces every living
creature can put us in touch with the universe and the Will
which is there manifest."[22]

In accord with this great truth the legitimacy of Jesus
in terms of the "Cosmic Christ" necessarily depends upon
proof that His doctrine of love and mercy concerns the
peace and contentment of every living creature—all of God's
creation: otherwise and unconditionally the Christian doctrine of "divine kinship" cannot possibly be justified.

My purpose in writing the Covenant of Love is to reveal
and to expound the existing evidence which indicates that
the ethical system of Jesus was far more extensive than is
generally known.

In consequence, even though my intent is neither to
affirm nor deny the question of "divinity", the case as presented in the following chapters removes the paradox and
annuls the most devastating of all circumstances contrary
to the Christian viewpoint, while supplying the only realistic premise upon which the validity of Jesus as the "Cosmic Christ" can be maintained.

Knowledge pertaining to the humane teachings of Jesus
was much more available to the church fathers of the early
centuries than it is today. In fact, the greater part of what
little is available to the modern seeker was discretely preserved in one way or another, probably in the hope that

---

* Schweitzer admits that Jesus' weltanschauung (ideology) is identical with his own. St. Francis and many of the Saints before him
had demonstrated similar conclusions. To what knowledge not of
common interest did they have access? An answer to this question
is the purpose of this book.

Christians of another day might understand the message they contain.

Those among the less informed who have long wondered why the more truly spiritual among the church fathers abstained from any practice which might interfere with the peace and security of even the meanest of God's creatures, will find in the Covenant of Love the authority which both inspired and directed them.

The purpose of St. Francis, according to the Catholic encyclopedia, was to "imitate the example of Christ as literally as it was in him to do so".

Our own beloved Dr. Schweitzer has in our day followed a similar path.

Certainly both of these men were favored with a particularly revealing insight, but, also, both had delved deeply into the available source writings, extra to the canonical literature, seeking the key to the way of life of the Master. Both arrived at the same conclusion: that "the ethic of reverence for *all life* is the ethic of Jesus."

One does not necessarily have to be gifted with the insight of a Francis, a Schweitzer or that of the Saints of old to find for himself the "Christ" who filled the souls of these great men so full of love for all creatures great and small. The knowledge that came to them is clearly set forth in the Covenant of Love for all who are ready to receive it.

In all fairness to both the reader and the author of this work, one should hesitate to appraise any portion of it without having first reviewed it as an entirety. The contents are divided into four books which should be read consecutively and with an open mind if one is to grasp the great spiritual reforms conveyed therein. From the introduction to the last word of the appendix the author has endeavored to interpret the "will of God" as it seems to have been both expressed and demonstrated down through the centuries by the purest and most noble of the human family.

If the spiritual attitude of the reader is such that it is

reaching out toward more soul satisfying fields of learning it cannot help but see revealed herein the criteria of a higher, purer, more honorable, and more dignified approach to the meaning of "salvation."

Instead of limiting the "means and the way" to the narrowness of a world consciousness concerned only with human relationships, the "Covenant of Love" removes all limitations. Herein the merciful arms of a loving God reach out to embrace the entire universe of life. In consequence the "spirit life" of man is released from its own cloistered disunity with the "spirit life" of the universe and in turn becomes a living addition to the immortal whole.

The ethical idealism upon which this work is founded represents a rational interpretation of the life and purpose of Jesus Christ. As the reader will find, the whole work is built entirely upon a foundation of Love, for on such a foundation a house is unassailable.

"And the rains descended and the floods came, and the winds blew and beat upon that house: and it fell not for it was founded upon a rock" (Matt. 7:25).

BOOK ONE

References
Introduction

1 Albert Schweitzer, paraphrased from *The Quest of the Historical Jesus*, Macmillan Co., N. Y.

7

2 Chas. R. Joy, Albert Schweitzer, *An Anthology*. Adam and Chas. Black, London. Beacon Press, Boston.

4 *Ibid.*

5 *Ibid.*

14 *Ibid.*

15 *Ibid.*

16 *Ibid.*

21 *Ibid.*

3 Albert Schweitzer, *The Mystery of the Kingdom of God*. Macmillan Co., N. Y.

12 *Ibid.*

6 Rev. C. Edward Park, *Christianity*, Beacon Press, Boston.

8 Rev. Harold Kemmis, *Searchlight on the Gospels*. The Order of

the Cross, Publications.
(a) Dr. Otto Nall, *Midmonth Magazine for Methodist Families.*
10 Rev. Holmes-Gore, *These we have not Loved,* C. W. Daniel Co. Ltd., Ashington Rochford, Essex, England.
13 Martin Werner, *Essay on Albert Schweitzer,* Friends of Albert Schweitzer, Edited by Dr. H. A. Jack.
13 quote deleted, 11 paraphrased.
17 Albert Schweitzer, *Out of my Life and Thought,* Henry Holt & Co., N. Y.
20 Albert Schweitzer, *The Problem of Ethics in the Evolution,* Friends of Albert Schweitzer, Edited by Dr. H. A. Jack.
22 *Ibid.*
19 Dr. George Seaver, *Albert Schweitzer The Man and His Mind,* Harper, N. Y.

CHAPTER ONE

Pertaining To Historical Narratives

From the First Century on down to the present day, various writers have brought forth a continuous supply of works based upon the life and teachings of Jesus of Nazareth. Even up to the beginning of the Fourth Century there were already thousands of papers, epistles, gospels, and books written, all of which proclaimed the truth of the person and the ministry of the Son of man.

During the past century much effort was expended to arrange and catalogue these works, many of which no longer exist. Historians, archeologists, and theologians have worked diligently, examining old documents and antique writings to the end that students of Bible literature today may obtain broader understanding of Christian beginnings.

To roughly classify the various types of writings available to the reader today on the life and teachings of Jesus Christ, one would probably first set aside the traditional or canonized literature of the New Testament. It is upon this source that the popular narrative form of writing on the life of the Nazarene depends.

Next, we have the historical writings. Among these are the scholarly works pertaining to the cataloging of ancient manuscripts: i.e., who wrote them, when, and for what purpose, etc. Among these are also the works of the critics —those who attempt to rationalize and explain away the miracles as well as describe the character and behavior of the Jesus of history.

It seems, however, that nearly all the historical writings with the probable exception of those of a scientific or archaeological nature are more or less prejudiced, either in favor of, or against the traditional Christian point of view. Being aware of this fact is somewhat of an advantage to the middle of the road search for the true character of the "man of destiny." It may truthfully be said that much of what the rationalist or critical analyst has to say is based upon the much edited and many times copied writings of men who never saw or knew Jesus, and who interpreted him in part to conform to their own ends and purposes. It seems, therefore, that the critical analyst does not actually examine the character of the principle in question but instead merely analyzes the opinions and purposes of those who wrote about him. In view of this fact a severely critical or unsympathetic attack on the character of the historical Jesus is most unfair if not downright distasteful.

"The primary need is to discover, behind the phenomenal, the real character of the personality and preaching of Jesus. The starting point must therefore be the simple fact that Jesus came as a living man into a dead world. He is living because, in contrast with the people of his day, he has a living idea of God." [1]

"The Christian tradition must be explained by the inner truth of Christianity, and no written traditions can give it that inner truth if it does not possess it." [2] "In proportion as we have the spirit of Jesus, we have the true knowledge of Him." [3]

"When we go back to the headwaters of the mighty stream of Christianity we find, not the formulation of a set of doctrines, not the founding of a new ecclesiastical organization, nor the formulation of a new ritual, but we find a radiant and illuminating personality who made God mean more than He has meant before and who exhibited a new quality of life altogether." [4]

Chapter One

1 Dr. Albert Schweitzer, *The quest of the Historical Jesus.* Macmillan Co., N. Y.
2 *Ibid.*
3 *Ibid.*
4 Rufus M. Jones, *Religious Foundations*, Macmillan Co., N. Y.

CHAPTER TWO

On the Historicity of New Testament Writings

"The New Testament consists of twenty-seven short books by an inexactly known number of authors having different temperaments, backgrounds, outlook, and objectives. These books were addressed to people living under different conditions in scattered parts of the Roman Mediterranean world . . . "[1]

"Although it was born in Aramaic-speaking Palestine, Christianity came into the Roman world as a Greek-speaking religion; all of its books were written in Greek. When Paul wrote to the Christians in Rome he wrote not in Latin but in Greek."[2]

"The fact is that the original books themselves, technically known as autographs, are not known to be in existence. In their place are thousands of copies, many in Greek as well as in other languages into which at different times the Greek had been rendered."[3]

"Many scholars, including Goodspeed, believe that the first group of collected writings these New Testament—or so-called Pagan—Christians received was probably Paul's Letters to the Ephesians. The New Testament writers were evangelists, apologists, and missionaries before they were authors. The New Testament did not shape the early church; it was made by the church. Even before the earliest New Testament Epistles had been written (I and II Thessalonians C.A.D. 50 and Galatians 51 or 49), or the basic gospel of Mark reduced to writings (C. 65-67), there existed written matter, since lost, dealing with Jesus and his sayings."[4] Some of these lost writings no doubt appeared as part of what was classified as Apocrypha. In their original Aramaic form they probably contained a list of notes of

14

sayings of Jesus made probably by those in direct contact with him. "Jesus himself did not commit his teachings to writings, but contented himself with uttering them orally, subject to misunderstanding, garbling, and oblivion through faulty human memories." [5]

"So-called 'criticism' (more accurately, examination) has done service to students of the New Testament by putting personalities and events in their proper historical perspective by attempting to determine which of the several strands making up the narratives are the most trustworthy, and by making it clear that the writings as we now read them are in part based on earlier brief documents which may account for the survival of some traditions and the deletion of others." [6]

"The gospel traditions were crystallized in Aramaic-speaking communities in Palestine and were not written down in Greek until the revolt of A.D. 66-70 against Rome had widely dispersed the Jewish Christians of Palestine and thus broken the chain of oral tradition which ties Jesus to the Apostolic circles by means of firsthand narrations of his deeds and words as witnessed by his disciples." [7]

"Although the ministry of Jesus has been estimated as covering as much as 550 days, the days identifiable by specific events narrated in Mark account for only twenty-three. The Synoptists draw part of their material from the basic gospel of Mark, dealing chiefly with the Galilean ministry of Jesus, and using material seldom paralleled in John. None of them gives a complete list of events in the life of Jesus." [8]

"Today we recognize that we cannot hope to reconstruct the early days of the Christian beginnings by an uncritical reading of the four gospels and book of Acts. The authors, not one of whom was himself an eyewitness to the events he recorded, had to depend upon earlier sources, written or oral, for their information." [9]

"According to tradition Paul wrote fourteen Epistles. But the Epistle to the Hebrews is positively not from him;

Second Thessalonians is almost certainly Apocryphal. So is the Epistle to the Ephesians. Many hold that the Epistles to Timothy and to Titus, in their main content, cannot be his.

"There is strong reason to think that the church deemed it necessary to include in the Canon, as pendant to Paul's Epistles, a number of others bearing the names of reputed Apostolic persons other than he, notably Peter, John, and the two 'brothers of the Lord,' James and Jude. Not one of these Epistles goes back to the first Christian age. The Second Epistle of Peter is a forgery. The First is no more authentic. The three Epistles attributed to John were composed in the course of the same century to accompany the fourth gospel when its claims were being pressed among the Asiatic churches. They are no more the work of the Apostle John than is the gospel itself." [10]

"Were the documents to be taken in strict order, the Pauline Epistles would come before the Synoptic Gospels. Matthew and Luke incorporated not only the greater part of Mark but also another document known as 'Q,' the sources of which are at least as early as those of Mark.

"The results of fifty years of investigation would be to give us three Synoptic Gospels—Matthew, Mark, and Luke —each embodying with modifications of its own, one or more of three earlier sources." [11]

"As has already been said, during the centuries that elapsed between the time of composition and the appearance of our earliest manuscripts, the writings had been frequently copies. As a result numerous changes had been made, both intentional and accidental.

"Many scholars are of the opinion that II Corinthians is not in the form in which Paul composed it.

"It is universally recognized that Mark 16: 9-20 is not a part of the original gospel, but was added by a later hand many years after the evangelist had finished." [12]

Mark

"John Mark (Acts 12:12,25 and 15:37) designated sometimes only as John, was a Jerusalem Jew and a kinsman of Barnabas (Col 4:10). He accompanies Barnabas and Paul to Antioch (Acts 12:25, 13:1) and later served as their attendant on the First Missionary Journey (13:5) but for some reason Mark deserted the missionary party at Perga and hurried home (13:13). Because of this Paul thought it unwise to take Mark on the Second Journey (15:38). This caused a disagreement between Paul and Barnabas and the end of their missionary partnership. Barnabas gave Mark another chance and took him to Cyprus as a companion.

"After ten years Mark is next heard of with Paul. Tradition declares that Mark was the founder of the church in the great Jewish Greek city of Alexandria where he is believed to have died and been buried." [13]

" . . . the view taken of our almost sole authorities, the Four Gospels, is that Mark is not merely the oldest but that it was the actual source used by Matthew and Luke. Matthew may be characterized as a second edition of Mark, revised and enlarged." [14]

"In popular favor Matthew and Luke supplanted Mark. But Mark was not discarded as were other early records which were used as sources and then allowed to disappear." [15]

What other information had these discarded records contained? Could it be that certain disciplines set forth therein might have offended the free living self indulgent natures of the heathen candidates? Further discussion of these source writings may supply an answer.

"In addition to documentary sources Mark must have used the oral traditions which Papias, in the Second Century, declared he preferred to the written records. The oral tradition would have supplied material expanding or modifying the documentary sources. The end of the gospel

(16:9-20) which is lacking in the two oldest Greek manuscripts and other authorities, is a later addition. Possibly the original manuscript may have suffered mutilation at the end of the scroll." [16]

"This gospel—and the same is true of the other three—is anonymous. Not only is there no statement of authorship, but there are also no hints. Thus they are not to be called pseudonymous despite the titles, 'According to Mark,' 'According to Matthew,' etc., which stand regularly in the manuscripts of modern editions. These titles are not part of the original writings, but were prefixed apparently at a time when a collection of gospels was being made, and it thus became necessary—as it had not been earlier—to distinguish between them.

"Eusebius, quoting Papias, an early bishop of Hurapolis, who wrote some time before 160 A.D., says—'and the presbyter used to say this: "Mark wrote what he remembered not to be sure in order of the things said or done by the Lord for he had neither heard the Lord nor followed him . . .'

"It would appear to me more probable that he (Papias) is contrasting this gospel with some other writing and (is) attempting to excuse the contrasts." [17]

In St. Catherine's Library, June 12, 1950, Professor Atiya discovered a dictionary of the Pauline Epistles which "contains a number of interesting variants from the authorized Greek version, also in Arabic, and the more ancient contains one of the oldest gospel translations in existence; . . . investigation reveals remarkable variations in the text of the gospel of Mark as compared with the Fifth Century Peshitta text." [18]

As to Matthew, Luke, and Mark: "any theory which denies literary dependence of the two upon the third is unthinkable." [19]

"It may be accepted today as a certain result of the industrious gospel-research of the last century, that Mark is the oldest of the Canonical gospels and is the groundwork for Luke and Matthew. Also, that aside from Mark, there did exist a source-book written in Aramaic, which was part of the groundwork of the other gospels. Did this Aramaic source contain merely a collection of the sayings of Jesus, or were there narratives also in it, so that it might be termed 'the earliest gospel?' Was this one of Mark's sources aside from oral tradition?" [20] Later readings herein may provide an answer.

"Mark as the pupil of Paul is most evident in the speeches which the Evangelist did not find in his sourcebook or in the Palestinian tradition, but created independently, and for the first time fitted into the traditional material as the leading religious motives for the judgment of the history of Jesus.

"It seems that those important points in Mark which are peculiar and historically impossible are to be attributed to the doctrines taught by Paul." [21]

"Mark consists more of invention and of compiler's arrangement than of tradition in the strict sense. The same is true of the others, and of Matthew in the first place, which has, moreover, even more distinctly than Mark, the character of a compilation. The evidence is unmistakable that the latest revision of Mark has been absorbed, almost entire, into Matthew, though not without a partial dislocation of the material. Numerous discourses, largely common to Matthew and Luke, have been inserted, and just as Mark reveals a long process of editorial operations, so the collection or collections of these discourses are progressively constructed compilations." [22]

Matthew

"An early Christian writer, Papias (A.D. 140), speaks of Matthew's composing the *Sayings* in the Aramaic language and 'each one translating them as best he could.'

"While this elusive primitive gospel must have had a great influence on Christian preaching, and through it indirectly upon the gospels that were later written, we cannot recover it, or even describe it in any detail. It contained some characteristic pieces of Jesus' teaching, with accounts of that Last Supper, the Crucifixion, and Resurrection experiences. We might expect relics of it to survive in Luke or in Matthew, but if so, they cannot be identified.

"It is true the written gospels when they appeared sprang up under its shadow, and not so much to reproduce it as to supplement it.

"A full generation was to pass before Christians thought of writing gospels, and then they were to arise in Greek, not Aramaic, and in circles far removed from Jewish Palestine." [23]

"The author of our present Matthew has used sources, probably more completely than has often been admitted, but he clearly felt perfectly free to interpret, to rearrange, to rewrite drastically, and to suppress. Though his readiness to rearrange is everywhere evident, his fondness for preserving the exact phraseology of his several sources, if at all possible, is equally noticeable." [24]

"Self evident it is that the author of this gospel could not have been the Apostle Matthew. We do not know who it was although it is scarcely the work of a single author, but the work of various hands; yes, generations of early Christians worked at it; it grew with and out of the Church." [25]

Luke

"The gospel of Luke is a regular composition, founded on anterior documents. It is the work of a man who selects primes and combines." [26]

"He is guided by a decided apologetic purpose in the selection and manipulation of his material. He wrote for heathen Christians and wished to awaken or confirm the conviction that Jesus of Nazareth was proven to be the Christ and the Son of God by wonders and signs of every kind." [27]

"The reluctance of Matthew to represent Jesus as moved

by human emotions—as sorrow, anger, love—and his frequent omission of those touches in his revision of the Markan account have already been noted. An even more careful pruning of these is to be seen in Luke, who cancels several which had not offended Matthew.

"The so-called 'external tradition' about the author—that is, the observations of the early writers—is singularly inconclusive despite the fact that from the later half of the Second Century it is regularly stated that both 'gospel' and 'Acts' were composed by Luke, the physician and friend of Paul. The famous Muratorian fragment provides the earliest statement of this tradition. All the later writers—Irenaeus, Clement of Alexandria, Tertullian, Origen, Eusebius, and Jerome—simply attest in essence the same view.

"The third book of the gospel according to Luke, that physician, after the ascension of Christ, when Paul had taken him with him a devoted helper, composed in his own name from hearsay. Yet he himself did not see the Lord in the flesh and therefore as he could follow, so he set them down and began to speak from the nativity of John . . . But the Acts of all the apostles were written in one book. Luke compiled for 'most excellent Theophilus' the several events." * [28]

However, another historian says: "Luke wrote neither the third gospel nor Acts. He wrote only passages of the later book and we are compelled to recognize at least two steps in the composition of both books." [29]

"The gospel of Luke was probably written at the beginning of the Second Century by an unknown heathen Christian who was conversant with the literary culture of his time and probably versed in the works of the Jewish historian, Josephus. Because he made use of the journey of Luke, the pupil of Paul, in his *Acts of the Apostles,* church tradition used the name 'Luke' to designate the author of the gospel and the Acts." [30]

---

* From the Muratorian fragment.

John

"The Fourth Gospel, written possibly as late as 95-125, uses a very different viewpoint, stressing the metaphysical and mystical concepts growing out of the Hellenistic philosophy of the Logos or word of God." [31]

"Many are of the opinion that not one of the gospels is the work of the apostolic person whose name it bears, and that the apostle John, in particular, had nothing whatever to do with writing the gospel attributed to him." [32]

"While Mathew, Mark, and Luke stand so close together, despite their many differences, that the thoughtful reader, even without any technical knowledge of Synoptic criticism, is struck by their similarity of expression and choice of material, the gospel of John—or as many writers prefer to call it, 'the Fourth Gospel'—is widely different. More than ninety percent of its material falls outside the Synoptic tradition.

"Clement of Alexandria (ca 200 A.D.) said: 'But that John last of all, aware that bodily facts had been revealed in the gospels (of Mark, Matthew, and Luke) was urged on by his acquaintances, and, under the inspiration of the Spirit, wrought a spiritual gospel.' " * [33]

"The much debated question as to the authorship of the gospel and the first epistle of John has not yet been solved: also did the author mean to write history or something else? The Synoptic gospels place the scene of the Ministry mainly in Galilee, John mainly in Judea."*[34] (See map plate 2)

The Fourth Gospel has been highly considered by many theologians, historians, and archaeologists as an Essene document.

"Professor Brownlee remarks . . . the language and ideas of the Fourth Gospel are so closely connected with Essene thought as represented in Qumran documents that 'one may suppose that in John's portrayal of Jesus we have the Essene Christ.' " [35]

---

* Quoted from the Hypolyposis, by Eusebius, His. Eccl. VI: 14,7.
* See map plate 2—Jesus Ministry begins at Qumran.

"Certainly the writer of the prologue of John found himself in agreement with the Essenes, who could not conceive of any created reality which does not derive from God. **
Similarly, for the writer of the Fourth Gospel and for the Essenes, light and darkness, which are in antithesis of each other, are things that men walk in and by which they are guided.

"It seems likely that John wrote under the impact of an ethical dualism found in the Essene documents, and that his system finds its appropriate place as we set his gospel beside them." [36]

Peter

"In the case of the First Epistle of St. Peter, indeed this seems to be distinctly stated, for the words *Sia Eixouayou* 'by Silvanus' in Ch. V. 12, are best understood as implying that Silvanus was the actual scribe of the Epistle.

"In the same way tradition of the Fourth Gospel says that St. John dictated his gospel to his disciple Prochorus." [37]

"The most striking thing in this writing (Peter) is its dependence upon Paul. It is not an overstatement to say that it is saturated with Pauline ideas. In fact, it actually stands closer to Paul's thought than do some letters which bear his name.

"Then again, there is an almost complete absence in the epistle of those references to the sayings and doings of Jesus which, according to Papias as quoted by Eusebius, were wont to form the burden of Peter's preaching. But since the epistle itself does not appear to be earlier than 100 A.D., this courageous skepticism appears unnecessary. By that date Peter was presumably neither dictating nor approving letters." [38]

"The Roman church, in looking about for some church that needed instruction, saw that the churches of Asia needed to be reminded to love their enemies and respect the

** "Thou are the Prince of Gods, apart from Thee nothing was made." (Essene)
"The same was in the beginning with God, without Him was not anything made that was made." (John 1:2,3)

Emperor—and wrote I Peter to convey this corrective. As the revelation had claimed the authority of a Christian prophet, writing in the name of Jesus himself, the Roman church wrote in the name of the chief of the apostles, as it could do—the ancients thought—since it was the custodian of his tomb and so of his memory and teachings." [39]

James

"But be ye doers of the word, and not hearers only, deceiving your ownselves." (James 1:22) " . . . there is one emphasis which recurs throughout the writing and which serves more or less to hold the various admonitions together, namely, a vigorous and blunt hatred of sham and smug pretense. One's profession and one's conduct must square as opposed to 'faith without works' or being hearers of the word but not doers. It is only as one keeps his feet solidly on the ground and shows his genuine acceptance of the law of God by his conduct that he can hope to draw nigh to God and thus keep himself 'unspotted from the world.' " [40]

"Endurance in temptations—which are never to be ascribed to God, but always to the enticing power of man's own lusts—bring the crown of life which has been promised by God. (1:28)

"James shows no comprehension of Paul's doctrine of salvation through faith. For him faith and works are inseparable. (James 1:3, 2:1) It is not that he is denying the need of faith, but that he is attacking those who were excusing themselves from works on the flimsy pretense of having faith. Faith without works is dead. 'But wilt thou know, O vain man, that faith apart from works is barren?' (James 2:20)

"The identity of this James was expressed by Origen in the early part of the Third Century as James, the brother of Jesus. He was the head of the Jerusalem church. Furthermore, traditions of James are preserved both by Josephus and Hegesippus that he appears to have been *highly honored in Ebionite circles*." [41]

On the Editing of New Testament Writings

"Brief mention has already been made of the reason for the study of the text of the various New Testament writings, namely, the fact that the original books themselves—technically known as autographs—are not known to be in existence and that in their place are thousands of copies, many in Greek as well as in other languages into which at different times the Greek had been rendered.

"If we had the original copy today . . . the autograph—of each of these books, there would be no reason for textual criticism. But these have long since disappeared and in their place we have thousands of copies both in Greek and in various dialects into which the Greek was translated, and no two of these copies exactly agree." [42]

However, it was in the Third Century that a great multiplicity of translations, along with a variety of Apocryphal writings, induced the church to select, revise, or discard many of these writings to bring them in conformity with doctrinal prerogatives.

"From one translation, or as many would prefer to say, from several independent translations, there soon arose a medley of variant readings. As Jerome phrased it, in his day there were almost as many types as there were Latin manuscripts. And Augustine a little later gave caustic expression to the confusion of the text which had now come to be in general use: 'Whenever in earlier days a Greek manuscript came into any man's hand, provided he fancied he had any skill at all in both languages, he did not hesitate to translate it.'

"Toward the end of the Fourth Century, Damasus, then the Roman Pontiff, (366-384 A.D.) decided to bring order out of chaos. He directed his secretary, Jerome, to revise the existent texts and to produce one which could be used by all. Jerome apparently reluctantly complied. By 383 or 384 he had finished the text of the gospels, and in the next year, the rest of the New Testament. This was not a new translation but a revision of the Latin texts on the basis of the Greek manuscripts which appeared to him the best witnesses to the original text.

"Probably in official circles Jerome's revision was at once received. But in many circles conservative souls were lacerated. Augustine, who apparently himself accepted it, was aware of opposition to it and told Jerome of one bishop who was put into an awkward position by his flock, who were outraged at the effrontery of one who would change God's holy word." [43]

In evaluating the contents of the preceding pages, one may recognize a decided conflict between what is considered historically valid by the researcher, and what is also accepted as historically valid by religious orthodoxy. However, the basic demand is not whether the gospel writings are fitting historically, but whether they are fitting spiritually; that is to say, not whether the accumulated data of the various narratives are either factual or fictional, but whether they serve to promote the moral welfare and spiritual dignity of humanity, for it is less necessary that they constitute a chronological record of precise words and incidents than that they represent spiritual truths which are timeless.

The important question seems to be not particularly *who* wrote the Canonized gospels, or *how* they were written, but what they contain or convey as well as *what they do not* contain or convey; i.e., what has been either added to, overlooked, or purposely omitted from the records. It is this writer's opinion that these interpolations or omissions, which later in this work will be discussed at length, are major obstacles to a more fully flowered Christian religion.

CHAPTER TWO REFERENCES

1   Madeleine S. and J. Lane Miller, Harpers Bible Dictionary, Harper & Brothers, N. Y.
4   *Ibid.*
6   *Ibid.*
7   *Ibid.*
8   *Ibid.*
13 *Ibid.*
15 *Ibid.*
16 *Ibid.*
31 *Ibid.*
2   Prof. Morton Scott Enslin, *Christian Beginnings* (Harper, N. Y.) (35, Eusebius Hist. Eccl. VI, 14, 7)
3   *Ibid.*
9   *Ibid.*
12 *Ibid.*
17 *Ibid.*
19 *Ibid.*
24 *Ibid.*
28 *Ibid.*
33 *Ibid.*
38 *Ibid.*
40 *Ibid.*
41 *Ibid.*
42 *Ibid.*
43 *Ibid.*
5   Dr. Kenneth Scott Latourette, *History of Christianity,* (Harper, N. Y.)
10 Dr. Alfred Loisy, *The Origin of the New Testament.* (Macmillan Co.)
22 *Ibid.*
29 *Ibid.*
32 *Ibid.*
11 Rev. Charles Scott, D.D., *The Theology of the New Testament* from *History of Christianity in the Light of Modern Knowledge.* (Harcourt Brace, N. Y.)
34 *Ibid.*
14 Francis Burkett, T.B.A.D.D. *Life of Jesus History of Christianity in the Light of Modern Knowledge.* (Harcourt Brace)
37 *Ibid.*
18 Wendell Phillips, *Exploring the Ancient Spice Routes of Africa.* (Harcourt Brace, N. Y.)
20 Otto Pfleiderer, *Christian Origins.* Translated from the German by Daniel A. Huebsch, Ph.D. (B. W. Huebsch, N. Y., 1906).
21 *Ibid.*
25 *Ibid.*
27 *Ibid.*
30 *Ibid.*
23 Dr. Edgar Goodspeed, *A History of Early Christianity.* (University of Chicago Press)
26 Ernest Renan, *Life of Jesus.* (Carlton House, N. Y.)

35   Charles T. Fritsch, *The Qumran Community*. (Macmillan Co.)
36   Bible Archaeologist, Dec. 1954, The American Schools of Oriental
      Research, New Haven, Conn.
39   Dr. Edgar Goodspeed, *History of Early Christian Literature*.
      (University of Chicago Press)

CHAPTER THREE

On The Mostly Lost Scriptures

There were many gospels written during the early centuries that contained sayings of Jesus. Some of these were written before the canonized gospels and even before the first Epistle written by Paul. Gospels bearing the names of Andrew, Bartholomew, James, John, Jude, Matthew, Peter, Thomas etc., have been spoken of and parts of them quoted by the early Christian fathers. One cannot help but wonder why these manuscripts were not preserved or at least copies of them made for future reference. As it is, not a single record of the ministry of Jesus as written or dictated by any of the Apostles who walked, talked or prayed with him in the flesh, exists today but, in their place are a collection of writings authored by men who, according to scholarly authority, never saw Jesus or heard him speak.

There is but one exception, however. Most scholars today seem to agree that the epistle of James is from the writings of the Lord's brother.

However, even though various evidences and circumstances detract somewhat from the historical accuracy of the four gospels, they are indeed our most valuable, if only partial, records of the ministry of the Son of man.

It is most unfortunate that much of the great ethical teachings of Jesus were lost to our present day.

As thorough as he was, for example in the portion of the Sermon on the Mount that has come down to us in Matthew, it would be unthinkable not to credit his teachings as covering every phase and condition of life wherein the peace, happiness and spiritual welfare of every man is concerned.

Surely the great reformer, the unparalleled teacher, the

criterion himself of all that is equitable, humane, pure and good, would not have been remiss in his instruction. He would not have evaded or failed to denounce the institutions of war and slavery just as he did not evade or fail to denounce the custom of animal sacrifice. Neither would he also have failed to caution his listeners on the hazards of indiscriminate eating and drinking. Certainly, his great compassionate heart pitied the dumb innocent creatures of God's creation and he must have wept many times as he witnessed their sufferings in the hands of man. Surely, his intense awareness of love and mercy must have induced him to teach kindness and consideration toward all creatures.

Yet, the four gospels are mostly silent on these four great moral issues which have plagued the welfare of life upon this earth for centuries, both before and after the appearance of the great teacher.

It seems, therefore, that in order to discover the full measure of ethical responsibility which was of the person of Jesus, one must search both within as well as beyond the present New Testament records. We must bring Jesus as the highest ideal of moral and spiritual supremacy up to our present day and times.

Today in our swaddling clothes concept of a God of love and mercy, we look back with horror at the God who demanded the firstborn of its mother's womb, or the God that administered justice through vengeance, and obedience through the spilling of blood. Christians no longer approve of slavery even if the New Testament does in part seem to provide for its acceptance.

Even though we find little in the gospels to verify the Son of man's denunciation of the institution of war, all men are earnestly hoping that some miracle in the affairs of nations will release them from their political ties to military institutions. This is still a major obstacle which Christians must eventually overcome in order to approach the high standard of morality as taught by the Master.

Many thinkers today, both within the church as well as

those outside the church, are beginning to hear the "wee small voice" demanding that the heart yield to the Commandment, "Thou shalt not kill," which according to Isaiah applies to man and his fellow creatures alike.

They are beginning to realize that only in a broader form of obedience to this fundamental commandment can man ever hope to find peace upon this earth.

Thus, it seems in lieu of the incompleteness of Testament literature, that the pleading voice of a merciful God is even now coming through to man across the dark centuries separating our day from the day when Jesus walked upon the earth teaching the fullest of God's love.

The viewpoint that Jesus is not of our day but of his own time is agreeable only if we accept as final the traditional means of knowing him. It is quite obvious that these means supply us with only a partial picture of the character and teachings of the Jesus of history.

To bring back to our present day the sublimely ethical Jesus of the old apostolic age is indeed a challenge to modern thought.

Certainly, the evidence of his character is not as complete today as it was in the early centuries but, even so, the intervening years have not set up an impenetrable barrier. We still have access to ancient writings which, when considered along with recent archeological discoveries, should reveal an astonishingly clear likeness of the ethical Jesus of history.

"In the early Christian centuries there were many gospels in circulation other than those which are in the New Testament.

"*It is obvious that the canonical gospels tell us only a small part of what might have been narrated of Jesus, and it may be assumed that there were current in early days not only sayings of our Lord but also stories dealing with his ministry, which either were unknown to the four evangelists or were passed over by them as unsuitable for their purpose.*

"The most primitive of the uncanonical gospels, the gospel of the Nazarenes, was in use up to the end of the Fourth Century in a community which set special store by it; another, a gospel of Peter, which was episcopally condemned at the close of the Second Century, was found in an Egyptian grave.

"One of the most important of the noncanonical writings is the gospel of the Nazarenes. Most of our information regarding it is derived from Jerome, who states that he found it in use among the Nazarenes, a Jewish-Christian community in Northern Syria,* and that it was written in Aramaic.

"It is interesting to note that Jerome, who accepted the view prevalent in the early church that St. Matthew's gospel was originally written in Hebrew, was at first disposed to think that in the Nazarene gospel he had discovered the lost original of the canonical book.

"The Nazarene gospel belongs to an early stage of evangelic literature. Some scholars believe that it was earlier than the canonical Matthew, which was simply a revised version of it.

"In seeking to gain some idea of the gospel of the Nazarenes we are under the disadvantage of having only fragments to deal with." [1]

Renan writes: "I have been very attentive to collect the shreds preserved by the Fathers of the Church, of the ancient gospels which formerly existed parallel with the canonical gospels, and which are now lost—such as the gospel according to the Hebrews, the gospel according to the Egyptians, the gospel styled those of Justin, Marcion and Tatian. The first two are principally important because they were written in Aramaic, like the Logion of Matthew, and appear to constitute one version of the gospel of the apostle, and because they were the gospels of the Ebionites —who appear in some respects to have followed the course

* The Nazarenes settled in northern Syria following the flight from Jerusalem A.D. 66-70 (Enclp. Britt.)

marked out by Jesus." [2]

"The 'Gospel of Judas' is mentioned by Irenaeus (A.D. 181-89) as a production of the Cainites whom he describes as a variety of Valentinian Gnostics. It embodied the view that Judas had a deeper knowledge of the truth than did others, which led him to betray Jesus. The book was also mentioned by Epiphanius.

"The 'gospel of Truth' was another epistle of the Valentinians according to Irenaeus.

"A 'Gospel of Philip,' the holy disciple, is mentioned by Epiphanius about A.D. 376.

"A 'Gospel of Bartholomew' is spoken of by Jerome in the prologue of his commentary on Matthew. He also mentions a 'Gospel of Thomas.'

"Eusebius said, (Church History V. 10.3) that Bartholomew on his mission to India found there an Aramaic form of the Gospel of Matthew.

"A 'Gospel of Andrew' is mentioned by Augustine as having existed." [3]

"Clement of Alexandria, writing early in the Third Century, quotes a very curious saying of Jesus which, he says, is found in the Gospel of the Hebrews: 'He will not cease seeking until he finds; and when he finds he will be amazed; and when he is amazed he will reign, i.e., enter the *Kingdom.*'

"Exactly this saying has been found in the Papyrus fragment of Jesus' sayings at Oxyrhynchus in 1903.

"Eusebius lists this gospel among the 'disputed'—or nonconforming books. Jerome, toward the close of the century, could not find a Greek copy of it but saw an Aramaic text of it in Palestine, which, he says, he translated into Greek and Latin, probably meaning for the parts he wished to copy or use in his works. This Aramaic version, so often regarded as the original, was probably made for the use of the Jewish Christian sects—perhaps Ebionites, more probably Nazarenes—who in the Third Century were using the book, and finally gave their name to it, so that it came to be known as the 'Gospel of the Nazarenes.' Epiphanius says that the 'Nazarenes,' or Gnostic Jewish Christians, used a gospel resembling Matthew, which they call, 'According to the Hebrews.' This gospel disappeared probably some time during the latter part of the Third or early part of the Fourth Century." [4] Wouldn't this be about the time that Jerome reconstructed the gospel writings?

"Among the various Christian sects which arose in the Second Century, the most Jewish were the Ebionites—or 'poor.' They seem to have been the successors of those Jewish Christians of Palestine, and especially of Jerusalem, who had not accepted Paul's views and letters. They did not accept the Pentateuch or practice animal sacrifice. We hear of them first from Irenaeus in the Second Century, from Origen and Pippalytus in the Third, and from Epiphanius in the Fourth, when they had revived some of the ways and views of the old Jewish monastic order of the Essenes.

"They produced or read from a gospel written in the first person, Matthew being the spokesman in the singular, and the Twelve Apostles speaking in the plural. This led to its being called, especially by Epiphanius, by such names as 'According to Matthew,' the 'Gospel of the Hebrews,' 'Gospel of the Twelve,' (and) the 'Gospel of the Ebionites.'

"From the quotation from it preserved in Epiphanius, it is clear that the gospel of the Ebionites opposed animal sacrifice and advocated vegetarianism.

"This gospel described the food of John, the Baptist, as wild honey and cakes made with oil and honey.

"The Greek word for oil cake is 'enkris;' the Greek word, 'locust,' is 'akris.' * (Mark 1:6)" [5]

If this was the gospel that both our Matthew and Luke are transcribed from, then the original teaching of Jesus in regards to animal sacrifice and the eating of flesh was purposely deleted.

"Symmachus, the first Christian translator of the Old Testament into Greek, in the days of Marcus Aurelius (A.D. 161-80) was an Ebionite; in fact he made his translation for the Greek-speaking Jewish Christians of that sect." [5a] It was probably he who translated from the Aramaic certain sayings of Jesus that had been overlooked or omitted by others.

"Origen is the earliest writer to mention the 'Gospel of the Twelve,' as he called it (Homily 1 on Luke), and it was probably written in Greek (about the time that Luke was written). Except for a few fragments preserved by Epiphanius the work has disappeared, but it is one of the early Christian books that learning hopes may yet come to light." [6]

"Another book, called the 'Acts of Peter,' was used in the early centuries. Eusebius himself says that the 'Acts of Peter' was not accepted by the church (Church History III 3.2) but it does not seem to have been definitely disapproved until sects like the Manicheans made so much of the ascetic elements in it." [7] (i.e., such as in the obeying of Genesis 1:29)

"The Gospel of Thomas is reported to have probably been written between 150-300 A.D. Some scholars argue that it was written about the same time as John.

" 'The Acts of Thomas' was used by the Gnostics and, according to Epiphanius, by the Encratites and the Apostolics. Augustine says it was used by the Manicheans, Turrebins, and by the Priscillianists.

"The ascetic ideal of the Acts is presented in the description of Thomas himself. He continually fasts and prays, wears the same garment in all weather; accepts nothing from anyone; gives what he has to others, and abstains from meat and wine.

"Eusebius speaks of Acts of Andrew and John. His reference (in III. 1. 1,2 Church History III 25.6) to Origen's account, now lost, of the labors of these apostles—John in Ephesus and Andrew in Scythia—may imply that Origen knew Acts of each of them.

"Epiphanius in Heresies 47 says that the Acts of Andrew, as well as those of John, Thomas, and others, was appealed to by the Encratites, who were vegetarians and total abstainers, as well as by the self-styled Apostolics and the Origenians." [8] Origen himself abstained from eating the flesh of animals.

"The earliest Christian book in this field was the so-called 'Preaching of Peter.' Peter appears in the Acts as the first Christian preacher. The book itself has long since disappeared but quotations from it in Clement of Alexandria and in Origen give us some substantial information about it. It attacked the Greek ways of worshiping God, as well as those of the Jews, which meant temple ritual, sacrifice, feast days, etc. For twelve years, the Apostles were to labor among the Jews, and then they were to go forth into the world to preach to all men the one God.

"About the middle of the Second Century lived a man named Tatian; Clement of Alexandria calls him a Syrian. (Miscellanies III:12)

"Tatian wrote a book on animals but nothing is known about it. He became a pupil of Justin. There he must have written the book of Problems which Eusebius knew of from the mention of it by Rhodo, an Asian writer of the time. In it, Rhodo said, Tatian promised to explain the obscure and hidden parts of the scriptures. (Church History V: 13-8) After the death of Justin, Tatian broke with the church and became the leader of the Encratite sect.

"Clement of Alexandria mentions another book written by Tatian, 'On Perfection according to the Savior.'" [9]

The disclosure that Tatian broke with the Pauline branch of the Christian Church and became a leader of the Encratite Christians who were opposed to war, slavery, and the slaughter of animals for food, indicates quite clearly that this evangelist had knowledge of the humane Christ when he wrote his book, 'Perfection according to the Savior.'

"Tatian's great work was his *Diatessaron*, or interweaving of the Four Gospels into one. The Syriac version into which Tatian put it had a remarkable success; became the first Christian scripture of the Syriac-speaking Christians.

Tatian, with his Syriac *Diatessaron,* seems to have been the founder of Syriac Christianity.

"Theodoret, Bishop of Cyprus, in his 'Epitome of Heresy,' written about A.D. 453, relates (1:20) that he found, held in honor among the churches, more than two hundred copies of the *Diatessaron,* which is gathered up and replaced with the gospel of the four evangelists. Not a single copy of the *Diatessaron* in Syriac has yet been found.

"Tatian has been called both an apologist and a heretic by numerous early Christian writers." [10]

There is quite an agreement among scholars that much of the existing writings attributed to Paul were not authored by him. It has been pointed out that our present day records of these are, at best, incorrect similes of the Greek originals which no longer exist.

"This voluminous literature—letters of Paul and writings of other early Christian writers—broke conveniently for us at the Council of Nicaea in 325, for the actions there taken so colored the literature that followed, that it can hardly be mistaken; every page of it bears their stamp. An even more practical terminus is afforded by the Church History of Eusebius, published in A.D. 326, for that book is in no small degree a history of early Christian literature and Eusebius gives us information on not a few books which he had examined but which are now lost." [11]

The following is a list of the gospels mentioned by writers of the first four centuries and which no longer exist:

The Acts of Andrew
The Gospel of Andrew
The Gospel according to the Twelve
The Writings of Bartholomew
The Gospel of Bartholomew
The Gospel according to the Egyptians
The Acts of the Apostles made use of by the Ebionites
The Gospel of the Ebionites
The Gospel of the Encratites
The Gospel according to the Hebrews

The Book of James
The Acts of John
The Gospel of Jude
The Acts of the Apostles used by the Manichees
The Gospel of Marcion
Book of Matthew
The Gospel of Matthias
The Gospel according to the Nazarenes who used the
    Gospel according to the Hebrews
The Gospel of Peter
The Acts of Thomas

According to historical records, it appears that most, if not in fact all, of these gospels were used by various followers of "The Twelve." They were, as history shows, the sects who opposed both slavery and animal sacrifice, and who abstained from eating flesh and drinking wine.

On these principles they differed from the Pauline branch of the Christian faith.

But we seem to be a little ahead of ourselves. First, suppose we examine what appears to have been the actual cradle, morally and spiritually speaking, from which a character such as Jesus of Nazareth might have come forth. The most convincing of evidences point to an honorable and highly spiritual Hebrew sect that dwelt in the various towns and villages of Judea, supporting a central mission not far from Jericho on the shores of the Dead Sea. Of the several sects that inhabited the country wherein Jesus talked and preached, these people alone appear to have been equal to the bringing forth or the influencing of a person of his character.

Even though some Christian authorities are more or less indifferent to this possibility, the evidence from a theological point of view identifies the Qumran community as the end of the "Highway made straight for the coming of the Lord." Indeed, one might add here an entirely new chapter to the scriptures, not previously considered by the church.

The writer will later attempt to point out that the church can hardly afford not to recognize an Essenic background for Christianity if it is to present a convincing defense of the uniqueness of Jesus.

CHAPTER THREE REFERENCES

1 Rev. Adam Findlay, M.A.D.D. *The Apocryphal Gospels* from *The History of Christianity in the Light of Modern Knowledge.* (Harcourt Brace)
2 Ernest Renan, *The Life of Jesus.* (Carlton House, N. Y.)
3 Dr. Edgar Goodspeed, *History of Early Christian Literature.* (University of Chicago Press)
4
5-5a
6
7
8
9
10
11

CHAPTER FOUR

The Essenes of the Dead Sea Scrolls

Before we attempt to evaluate further the historical background of Christianity in anticipation of the recovery of more complete knowledge of the doctrine of the Son of Man, it would be well to begin our search back in the "pre-manger" days of the Christian era. At no other time or place among people could one possibly look for a more promising starting place for such a quest than that which has been pointed out through the discovery of the Dead Sea Scrolls.

It would indeed be quite presumptuous for one to attempt to cover in this limited space a formidable portion of what the Dead Sea Scrolls mean to the student of religious theory.

Many books and papers have been written on the finding and the interpretation of these musty old documents since they were first returned to the world of knowledge in the spring of 1947, and it is both a pleasure and a privilege for this writer to quote from some of the most outstanding of these.

The discovery of a treasury of ancient manuscripts in an isolated cave high up on the stony slope of a cliff not far from the shore of the Dead Sea has added a new chapter to our knowledge of Bible times.

One might say that the retelling of the finding of these scrolls sounds much like the reading of a passage of scripture. The unusual manner in which they were found tempts one to ponder again the age old doctrine of fore-ordination. In referring to the story as told, was it mere coincidence that a wandering shepherd boy happened to throw a stone through a narrow opening in the rocks, high up on the side of a cliff? Was it merely by chance that the stone happened to strike a clay jar? Was the resulting clatter of broken pieces merely an incidental sound or were they vibrations of Providence leading the mind of man on towards the discovery of new knowledge? Whatever the underlying cause may be, ordinary or extraordinary, the sudden unexpected sound did, according to the story, frighten the lad and he ran away; but later he returned with another boy to explore the cave. The stone jars they found inside, along with their precious contents, have since been the cause of no little interest and excitement among both scholars and laymen all over the world.

For almost 2,000 years the relentless elements of time seem to have been especially kind towards this little cache of documents. The fact that they were somehow miraculously preserved down through the centuries might suggest the still further interest of Providence. Certainly the time had not been right for their discovery during the past several centuries, for much of their contents would probably have been relegated to oblivion by those with the power to enforce the charge of heresy. However, in this Twentieth Century man can write, read, and voice his personal opinion on Christian beliefs without the fear of being tortured or burned at the stake. *

One might say then, that the time was most opportune for their finding; also that they had not been preserved merely to be interpreted as inconsequential to Christian interests. Indeed, the fact that they were brought to light at a time when Christians are free to consider and discuss their historical significance seems in itself to promise a most rewarding interpretation of their contents.

However, to date, the unprejudiced scholarly evaluation of the contents of these scrolls and their obvious relation-

* Today the Christian Church has no fear of truth even though at times it hesitates to apply it in a broad sense to freedom: i.e., to acknowledge the equal interest of God in both the dignity of man and the dignity of the church, without, as well as within, its jurisdiction.

ship to Christian origins has caused no little concern among church leaders and laymen alike. In fact, as Dr. Davies points out, "many people will feel deprived because of the new knowledge since it seems to take away much that has been thought dependable." [1]

However, any feelings of this kind should be only temporary. The present confusion among Christians has been to some extent brought about through a misunderstanding of what the scrolls convey.

Indeed, the Essenic background of Christianity as revealed through the scrolls re-identifies the very foundation of the church—a foundation laid upon the highest and purest of ethical concepts, consistent with a kind, merciful, dignified, trustworthy, and just God. In this the Christian should rejoice for his faith in the Most High can now broaden out in full complement with the pure teaching of Jesus and the old apostles of the primitive church. Today's Christianity need no longer be embarrassed by the inconsistency of its heathen lineage. For example, the Christian knows within his heart, even though he may be reluctant to admit it openly, that the doctrine of Paul is, in regards to slavery for example, as incompatible with our present day concepts of human dignity and brotherly love as it must have been (thanks to our knowledge of Essenic doctrine) to Jesus, and later to the Apostles of the Primitive church of Jerusalem.

To be sure, an Essenic background for Christianity seems to point towards both a re-evaluation of ethical concepts as well as a partial reconstruction of the gospel framework. This should not in any way embarrass the Christians' faith: on the contrary, it should make it more secure, spiritually as well as historically. A theology conforming with the Essenic tradition is astonishingly timely and exceptionally complementary to gospel narratives of both the birth and the baptism of the Son of Man, as well as to the uniqueness of Christian eschatology.

"Theological scholars have known for a long time that

the traditional view of Christian origins is not supported by history so much as by theology. Unlike the layman, they are familiar with New Testament historical problems to which it has never been possible to find historical solutions. Dogmatic solutions are another matter. But what the layman thinks he is dealing with in trying to grasp the meaning of the Scrolls is not theology but history, not dogma but fact.

"Theological students have known for some time that there were important resemblances between Essenic organization and that of the early Christian church, and have had reason to suspect that the two may have been organically connected." [2]

"Dupont Sommer holds rigidly that the Jewish sect of the Covenant 'directly and immediately prepared the way for the Christian Church' and that it helped to shape both the Church's soul and its body." [3]

"There takes shape a whole missing chapter for the history of the growth of religious ideas between Judaism and Christianity—a chapter which as Albright has said in his postscript of 1951 to Brownlee's translation of the Manual of Discipline 'bids fair to revolutionize our approach to the beginnings of Christianity.' " [4]

"The interest of the Qumran scrolls on the part of New Testament scholars may be expected to grow with mounting crescendos in the years that lie ahead. The high estimate of the Dead Sea Scrolls for the light they shed upon the New Testament will not be a passing fad of our generation, but after the intense excitement is over, the emerging New Testament criticism will be so profoundly affected that everyone will know that a new era of New Testament science (or theology)* has been born."[5]

"In any case, as we look now at Jesus in the perspective supplied by the scrolls, we can trace a new continuity and, at last, get some sense of the drama that culminated in Christianity." [6]

* Parentheses by U.C.E.

"The evidence for linking the Essene movement with the beginnings of the Christian Church is both voluminous and impressive. This relationship cannot be separated from the relationship between Jesus Christ and the Essenes.

"If the parallels in the gospels between Jesus and the Essenes do not prove a connection between them, then the parallels must prove a connection between the Essenes and the early church which produced the gospels." [7]

"But we should not minimize the fact that our picture is limited. Only a decade ago we had very little to go on. Until the discovery of the Dead Sea Scrolls, the Essenes were dismissed by our ablest scholars as a shadowy sectarian group of ascetics in Israel in the time of Jesus. Now we know that Christianity germinated, took root, and enjoyed it first growth in Essene soil. And we know that Christianity itself, in the beginning, was Essenic in Character." [8]

"The profound Messianic teachings of the Essenes must have been known by Jesus. There is little doubt that His own Messianic consciousness was strongly influenced by their interpretation of the Old Testament prophets.

"Professor K. G. Kuhn, of the University of Gottingen has recently shown that the Essene communal meal, as described by Josephus and the newly discovered Manual, throws light upon the origins and meaning of the Christian Sacrament of the Lord's Supper. The fact that Peter beckoned to John "that he (John,) should ask who it should be to whom he spoke," (John 13:24) may now be understood in the light of the practice of the Essenes when they met together in sessions. 'Nor shall a man speak in the midst of the words of his neighbor, before his brother finishes speaking. Neither shall he speak before his proper order.' Evidently John, who sat next to Jesus, held a higher rank in the group than Peter, and was the one to address the question to Jesus. More important are the actual parallels between the Essene communal meal and the Lord's Supper of the New Testament. In both cases

Plate 3

They shall not hurt nor destroy each other, for the earth shall be full of the knowledge of the Lord as the waters cover the sea. (Is. 11:6-10)

FEEDERS ON INSECTS include the most numerous and the most grotesque. Among them (*l* to *r*) are: the long-fingered *Miniopterus*; sheath-tailed *Emballonura*; golden-haired *Kerivoula*; world-wide *Pipistrellus*; the scarce *Tadarida*; and three "horseshoe bats," *Ascelliscus, Rhinolophus* and *Hipposideros diadema*. Nose-leaves may aid echolocation.

COURTESY OF MUSEUM OF
NATURAL HISTORY

Plate 4   CARNIVORA OR FLESH FEEDERS

only men participated. In both groups the recognized leader presided over the meal. Finally, the leader blessed both the bread and the wine. Because of these close parallels, Professor Kuhn believes that the background of the Lord's Supper must be sought in the communal meal of an Essenian group rather than in the Passover meal, which is definitely a family rite over which the father of the family presides." [9]

"As we have seen earlier, it is difficult to know when the New Testament is giving us actual history and when it is giving us history that doctrine has elaborated.

"Since the Essenes were predecessors, as well as contemporaries of the Palestinian Christians, it is immediately evident which group derived its sacred meal from the other. There is only one alternative possibility: If the Christians did not derive their sacred meal from the Essenes, then the Christians were themselves a sect of the Essenes." [10]

"What we know now with a probability which for all practical purposes we may as well call certainty, is that a sect existed in the centuries just before the emergence of Christianity which was organized in ways that suggest a relationship to the early Christian Church; that this community had scriptures upon which Christian writers drew in composing their own scriptures; that there were practices, including sacraments, which foreshadow Christian practices; that there was an expectation of a Messiah to whom the sect looked forward." [11]

"No less interesting and perhaps more exciting than their connection with the Essenes are the many parallels which these texts afford with the organization of the primitive Christian Church. The community calls itself by the same name (*Edah*) as was used by the early Christians of Palestine to denote the Church. The same term is employed to designate its legislative assembly as was used by that community to denote the council of the Church. There are twelve 'men of holiness' who act as general guides of the community—a remarkable correspondence with the twelve Apostles. These men have three superiors, answering to the designation of John, Peter and James, as the three pillars of the Church (Galatians 2:9f). There is a regular system of *mebaggerim* or 'overseers'—an exact equivalent of the Greek *episkapoi* or 'bishops' (before they had acquired *sacerdotal* functions) and the Brotherhood describes itself as 'preparing the way in the desert'—words which John the Baptist likewise quoted from the Old Testament in defining his mission (John 1:23).

"If we translate the documents relating to the organization of the Primitive Church from Greek back into Hebrew or Aramaic we shall find that they show quite a remarkable correspondence to the Qumran texts." [12]

"The first Christians thought of themselves as the people of the 'New Testament' or 'New Covenant.' The Essenes thought of themselves as being under a 'New Covenant' that had replaced the old covenant between Yahweh and Israel. This concept is found nowhere else in Judaism. Furthermore, both the Essenes and the Christians describe themselves as 'the poor in the world,' 'the children of light,' 'the Elect of God who shall judge the nations at the end of days.'" [13]

"Let us again notice that those to whom the name *Essene* is given did not use that name in speaking of themselves. Nor was the name *Christian* used by those who are called the early Christians. The people who came to bear these names called themselves 'the saints,' 'the brethren,' 'the elect,' 'they that believe,' 'they that are in Messiah,' 'they that are of the Lord,' 'the Sons of light,' 'of peace,' 'the disciples,' 'the poor,' 'they that are of the way,' etc. They were known as the Messianists, which word in Greek means 'Christianoi' or Christian. The names that applied to the Essenes are the same as those used by the 'Christianoi.'" [14]

"By far the most common expression used by New Testament writers to denote Christians is 'brethren' (Adelphoi).

The word is found, without exception, in every book of the New Testament. In fact, to judge from Mark, Luke, Matthew and John, it certainly seems that the usage was traceable to our Lord's own language." [15] The Lord's own language was full of Essenic expressions. They spoke of one another as "brethren." *

"Especially illuminating is a comparison of the Dead Sea Scrolls with the general Epistle of James, the earliest of all the epistles contained in the New Testament.

"It is now generally agreed that this document, addressed to the twelve 'tribes' in the dispersion, was written between 40 A.D. and 50 A.D., that its author was James, the 'brother' of Jesus, who occupied a leading position among the Jewish Christians in Jerusalem (Acts 12:17; 15:13; 21:13).

"It is possible to detect in the Epistle of James several direct echoes of ideas and expressions prominent in the Qumran texts.

"At one place James 4:15 seems to refer quite definitely to the Dead Sea Scriptures. He declares, 'Do ye think that the scriptures saith in vain: *The spirit which God made to dwell in us lusteth to envy?*' The scripture he refers to cannot be our traditional books, for nowhere in them can such a statement be found. There is, however, a fitting parallel for this saying in the Manual of Discipline, i.e., 'God has made two spirits to dwell in us, each rivaling the other; the evil one lusteth and envies the good.'" [16]

"One of the most impressive similarities between the practice of the Essenes and that of the early church is the following passage from Matthew: 'If your brother sins against you, go and tell him his fault between you and him alone. If he listens to you, you have gained your brother. But if he does not listen, take one or two others along with you, that every word may be confirmed by the evidence of two or three witnesses. If he refuses to listen to them, tell it to the Church; and if he refuses to listen

* Manual of Discipline VI, 13-23, Dead Sea Scrolls.

to the Church, let him be to you a Gentile and a tax collector.'

"It has long been questioned whether this passage represents the true words of Jesus, since no 'church' existed in his time.

"Now we know that this passage contains a set of Essene rules which somehow came to be attributed to Jesus some time before the gospel of Matthew was written. The same formula is found in the Manual of Discipline, and it occurs nowhere else in Judaism.

"The phrase in Luke, 'Peace on earth, good will towards men,' more accurately translated from the Greek, would read, 'Peace on earth among men of God's favor,' or 'among those who, by God's gracious election, find themselves members of the Eschatological community.' This same phraseology appears in the Manual of Discipline, * but is to be found nowhere else in Judaism." [17]

"False Christs and false prophets will rise and show signs and wonders to lead astray if possible the elect. Again, the elect seem to constitute a special group, not all Israel. The words from the Sermon on the Mount, 'Ye are the salt of the earth;' 'Ye are the light of the world;' appear to mean the same thing." [18]

John the Baptist

The theory of the relationship of the Essenes and John the Baptist has been considered for well on to one hundred and fifty years. Much has been written on the subject ** but until the discovery of the Dead Sea Scrolls, the evidence has not been clear. Today however, scholars, after studying these manuscripts, are more or less in agreement that John actually was an Essene.

"What are we to say, for instance, in the light of our new knowledge, of John the Baptist who the gospels tell us was brought up in the desert, the wilderness of Judea? Can we any longer imagine him wandering about (from

* Manual of Discipline III, 13-IV, 26, Dead Sea Scrolls.
** See Hastings Bible Dictionary.

childhood) sustaining himself somehow in solitude in the unrelieved desolation of this wilderness and then coming forth and preaching a doctrine that is only coincidentally similar to that of the covenanters whose monastery was in the area where John is reported to have lived? Where did John get his ideas? And his ascetic practices? And his baptism?

"Where else shall we look when the evidence points so plausibly to the Qumran monastery? That John was, in the broader sense of the term, an Essene can scarcely be doubted. In this same broader sense were not his followers also to be numbered with the Essenes?" [19]

"There is little doubt that John the Baptist was a key figure through whom many of the practices and teachings of the Qumran sect found their way into early *Christianity*. As a lad he left home and dwelt in the desert of Judea 'until the day of his showing into Israel.' It is suggested that he passed this period with the Essenes, for Josephus tells us they chose out other person's children, while they are pliable and fit for learning, and esteemed them to be their kindred." [20] Brownlee suggests that the Essenes may have adopted John as a boy, as was their custom.

"It may well be, in view of John's acquaintance with Essene thought, that he lived with the ascetics during his early years and learned of their manners and doctrines.

"It was in this same wilderness of Judea, of course, that the Qumran community had settled in accordance with its interpretation of Isaiah 40:3. 'Now when these things come to pass in Israel to the community, according to these rules, they will separate themselves from the midst of the sessions of perverse men to go to the wilderness to prepare there the way . . . make level in the desert a highway for the Lord.' (1 QS VIII 12-14. Manual of Dis.)" [21]

Like the Essenes, John was devoted to the preparing of the way of the Lord in the wilderness. Like the Essenes, he insisted that without previous spiritual cleansing, bathing in water cannot remove guilt. Having succeeded in purifying his own soul through the "Holy ones" custom of abstaining from eating flesh and drinking strong drink as well as abstaining from all things adverse to God's commandments, he now brought himself forward to admonish and encourage others to do likewise. "Repent," said he, "for the Kingdom of God is even now at hand." Repentance was of course important to the Qumran theology, for the members of the sect believed that they belonged to a "covenant of repentance." (CDC. IX 15. Zadokite Doc.)

"Professor Brownlee remarks in his definitive study of John the Baptist and his relation to the Essenes, 'the most astonishing result of all is the validation of the Fourth Gospel as an authentic source concerning the Baptist.' But more than this, the language and ideas of the Fourth Gospel are so closely connected with Essene thought as represented in the Qumran documents that 'one may suppose that in John's portrayal of Jesus we have the Essene Christ.'" [22]

"We find the answer in belief both of the Essenes and of John that the kingdom was at hand and the Messiah was soon to come. Both expected the end of days and the coming of the Messiah." [23]

"There is a strong tradition that the Fourth Gospel was written at Ephesus, which could explain how the evangelist came to know so much about John the Baptist and the Essene covenanter background out of which he came." [24]

"According to John, the Messiah will baptize (or anoint) his followers with the Holy Spirit. Likewise, according to the Manual of Discipline IV, 21, the time is coming when God will 'cleanse' man through the Holy Spirit from all wicked practices, sprinkling upon him a spirit of truth as water for impurity (to cleanse) from all untrue abominations. According to the Manual of Discipline, it is 'through His Messiah' that God will make the 'remnant' of his people 'know His Holy Spirit.'" (2:10) [25]

Jesus and the Essenes

"It may seem as though we are assuming too much in

supposing that Jesus was brought up as an Essene. But he was certainly not brought up as a Sadducee; and in view of his hostility to the Pharisees, it is not likely that he had been brought up by that sect either.* So it was the Essenic sect or nothing. As Jesus obviously knew the scriptures well, it is impossible that he belonged to no sect at all. Thus even by a process of elimination, we see the strong probability that his education was Essenic, and as we know from previous sections, his teachings and his entire outlook relate him to the Essenes.

"Jesus was baptized by John the Baptist. Some of his disciples were drawn from John's following. Can Jesus any more than John be thought of as having been unconnected with Essenic communities before he decided that John's version of the Messianic faith was the one he was ready to adopt?" [26]

The Scriptures tell us that the boy John the Baptist was in the desert until the day of his showing in Israel. This seems to represent in his life an age span of somewhere between twelve and thirty.

The Scriptures are also vague as to the whereabouts of Jesus during this same period of years.

Now both Jesus and his cousin John were about the same age which brings up the question: Why is it that the same period in time, paralleling the ages and activities of both John and Jesus, has not been accounted for in the Scriptures? The only plausible answer to this question is that the early makers of church doctrine did not want to identify them with the Essenes' system of ethics.

Josephus writes that the Essenes adopted children and brought them up in the ways of God. He probably means that they accepted certain precocious youths which they raised up in their monastery as teachers or Rabbis to lead the services in their synagogues for, as he says, there were

---

* Josephus emphasized in three different places in his writings that there were but three sects among the Jews. (Ant. G.XIII,1,2) (Ant. B.XIII,V,9) (Wars B.II,VIII,2).

communities of Essenes in all the cities of Judea. According to the gospels both John the Baptist and Jesus were known and addressed as Rabbis.

According to the law of the fathers a student must reach his thirtieth birthday before he can qualify as a priest or rabbi. Both Jesus and John conformed almost to the day with this requirement. John being a few months older than Jesus was the first to begin to preach, and it may be assumed that Jesus followed his example the very day he turned thirty.

The title of Rabbi was conferred by the priests of the synagogue or temple.

We know that neither Jesus nor John received this honor from either the Pharisees or the Sadducees, which again leaves only one other source—the Essene monastery.

It seems that one may find in these several references an answer to the age old question concerning the missing years in the life of Jesus even as our new knowledge apparently reveals the whereabouts of John the Baptist during this same period of time.

"The followers of both Jesus and John had close connections with the Essenes. The difference, then, must be found in the two men—in their lives, in their teachings, and in the quality of followers they were able to draw about them. The data that has come to us through the Dead Sea Scrolls, together with the information we already possessed, lead to the conclusion that in the person of Jesus is to be found the explanation of Christianity's special qualities." [27]

"Jesus' attitude towards riches is similar to the condemnations, characteristic of the Essenes, 'Blessed are the Meek,' 'Blessed are the poor in Spirit,' 'Go sell all thou has't and give to the poor.' These qualities are not emphasized among the Pharisees nor elsewhere in Judaism except among the Therapeutae in Egypt, who may have had some relationship to the Essenes." [28]

On one occasion Jesus asked, "And will not God vindicate his elect who cry to him day and night? Will he delay long over them? I tell you He will vindicate them speedily."

It was the custom of the Essenes, the "Elect" to provide a constant vigil to God; day and night several of the brethren read the Torah and prayed.

"The Essenes were strict determinists who believed that God's purpose was to establish the Teacher of Righteousness in order that he might build the congregation of the Elect." [29]

"The teaching of Jesus was prophetic in character, resulting from direct inspiration, and not based upon tradition like that of the Pharisees. In this respect he was in line with the Teacher of Righteousness to whom God had made known all the mysteries of the word of his servants the Prophets." [30]

According to Essene scripture: The wrath of God will be kindled against Israel *about* forty years after the death of the Teacher of Righteousness.

The destruction of Jerusalem, as was also prophesied by Jesus, did come to pass very near or *about* forty years after *his* death, thus fulfilling a "fourfold" prophesy consistent in time with the place, the event and the identity of the principals, or principal concerned.

Dr. Wm. H. Brownlee in the Bulletin of the American Schools of Oriental Research, December 1953, p. 9, writes, "The very original French orientalist, A. Dupont-Sommer, caused a sensation in Paris at the Academie des Inscriptions et Belles Lettres, May 26, 1950, when he presented his dramatic paper dealing with the historical allusions of the Habakuk Commentary (or Midrash). What evoked the most astonishment was his disclosure that the Teacher of Righteousness . . . . was in some respects an exact prototype of Jesus, particularly as a martyred prophet, revered by his followers as the suffering servant of the Lord in Isaiah. Like Jesus, he said, the Teacher of Righteousness was believed by his disciples to be God's elect the Messiah, the redeemer of the world. Both the Teacher of Righteousness and Jesus were opposed to the Priestly party, the Sadducees; both were condemned and put to death; both proclaimed judgment on Jerusalem; both established communities where members expected them to return and judge the world."

Especially revealing however is the viewpoint which gives to the Teacher of Righteousness,* or, the one most favored by God, a mystical, or spiritual, rather than an historical existence.

"The Brotherhood representing the Scrolls, did not believe, as has been supposed, in a martyred Messianic Teacher of Righteousness . . . . whose second coming was awaited. The Brotherhood indeed looked forward to the advent of a prophetic and priestly Teacher before the Final Era . . . to usher in the golden age." [31] In other words the character called the Teacher, developed out of the prophetic insight of his successive biographers, as a Spiritual Ideal: one who had not heretofore existed in the flesh but who was to come to judge the world.

Again from a mystical point of view; if, as the Essene scriptures report, those among the brethren were the "Elect" the "Chosen Ones" whom God had appointed to make straight the highway in the wilderness for the coming of the Lord, *then they were also keepers of the word*, i.e., guardians of the "Divine" writings wherein "one who was to come" would accept for himself the message contained therein.

"Thou hast brought me into Thy covenant: words flow free on my tongue as it were trained by Thee" (Essene) i.e., "The Spirit of the Lord is upon me because he has anointed me to preach the gospel . . ." (Luke 4:18)

In complete accord with these and other more conclusive evidences to follow, one might justly believe that Jesus being exceptionally influenced and motivated by the prophetic contents of the Essene scriptures actually imagined, or if

* "In a gospel called *The Circuits of Peter*, probably written late in the First Century, Peter refers to Jesus with such Essene epithets as Teacher, Master, True Prophet, *The Teacher of Righteousness*, etc."[32]

you will "realized" himself to be the incarnated Spirit of the "One" who was to come: "that the scriptures might be fulfilled."

What a tremendous challenge was presented, and what an enduring reward was promised to the one whose spiritual fortitude qualified his acceptance, for the scriptures say:

"Until the consummation of the Age shall he be in the synagogues . . . and both his work and his word shall be inscribed in the holy books, and he shall be a chosen one of God forever." (Essene) [a]

Among the basic scriptures used by the Brotherhood were the *Revelations of Enoch* and *The Testaments of the Twelve Patriarchs*. The later was composed a hundred years or more before the Christian era, perhaps near or during the time of the writing of the Zadokite document. It probably grew up and along with the Essene movements, for indications are that several amendments were made about the year 63 B.C., or near the time of Pompey's conquest of Jerusalem.

The several verses in the *Patriarchs* which scholars assumed to be interpolations of early Christians, we now know to refer to one whose coming was anticipated by the Sect of the Scrolls. (See footnote)

"For the Lord shall raise up a Priest from Judah as it were a king, god and man. He shall save all the Gentiles and the race of Israel.

"For the Lord God shall appear on earth in the body of man. He shall sit and eat with men and save them." [b]

According to scholars, "this concept could not have been written by a Christian because the Apostolic Church never taught that Jesus was god . . . . it was however established among the Essenes that the ultimate judge of mankind would be both." [33] i.e., both God and man.

The remarkable conformity of the prophesies contained

Fragments of the Aramaic Levi were found containing the very paragraphs scholars have previously supposed to be of Christian origin.

in the various Essene texts with the later appearance of Jesus as reported in the gospels can not, by any stretch of the imagination, be considered coincidental.

For example from the texts: "And I saw that from Judah was born a virgin wearing a linen garment: (The Essenes wore white linen garments) and from her was born a lamb. The Lamb of God, who taketh away the sin of the world:* Who saveth all the Gentiles and Israel": (c) "And his star shall arise in heaven as a King: and there shall be peace in all the earth." (d) (See Matt. 2:9, 10 Luke 2:14)

"The Most High shall send forth His salvation in the visitation of an only begotten prophet:" (e) "And He shall speak to God as to a Father: And his priesthood shall be perfect with the Lord, and he shall arise for the salvation of the world:" (f) "for he is true and long-suffering, meek and lowly, and teacheth by his works ** the law of God." (g)

"In him shall be fulfilled the prophecy of heaven concerning the Lamb of God, and Savior of the world, and a sinless one shall die for ungodly men in the blood of the covenant (blood of the Passover) for the salvation of the Gentiles and Israel. He shall enter into the temple and there shall the Lord be treated with outrage, and He shall be lifted up upon a tree." (h)

In accord with this prophesy the Lord was to die in the blood of the covenant i.e., the blood which stained the hands of man at the paschal sacrifice (see Isaiah 1:11-16) His outraging was to begin with his entry into the temple i.e., in consequence of his denunciation of the practice of animal sacrifice.

It is quite obvious that these prophesies reverenced by the Brotherhood were directly concerned with the advent of the "Essene Christ."

But this is only a portion of what the Scrolls reveal, of the time, the place and the circumstances pertaining to the

---

* See John 1:29, also mentioned in Enoch.

** Note here the precedent for 'works' as later stressed in the epistle of James.

"Son of man's" immortal date with destiny.

Most of the Psalms and the Hymns of the Essene Scriptures are written in a subjective tense, wherein the reader himself becomes the subject concerned. This indeed adds considerably to our hypothesis that Jesus "read himself into the scriptures" so to speak. In fact the various realizations, motivations, and emotional stresses, which Jesus later endured along with the tremendous spiritual responsibilities which he accepted as his own were clearly premeditated in texts such as these:

"Thou has sheltered me O God in the face of all mankind and hidden Thy teachings within me, until it be shown unto me that the hour of Thy triumph is come And Thou O God of mercy has in Thy bounty given me place among those to whom Thou art pledged *Thou has't chosen me and sent me* as a Father to them Thou holdest dear and as a nurse* unto them whom Thou has't made exemplars of men" (i)

In these lines the word "Father" might be interpreted as an earthly prototype, or Son of the Heavenly Father: i.e., "I and my Father are one" (Jo. 10:30) Also the word "nurse" is better understood as one who comforts and quickens the life of a patient. This interpretation is verified by other lines from the Book of Hymns.

"Thou has't sent me as a banner in the vanguard of Righteousness a symbol of truth and understanding to all whose way is straight By the words of my mouth Thou has't set men's life to rights and to them that repent I am a source of healing." (j)

It is interesting to note here how the various parallels which appear in the Essene Scriptures of the phrase "Thou has't sent me" are repeatedly emphasized in the gospel of John.

As previously mentioned many of these texts were written in first person, as if to emphasize a most direct and personal means of preparing "A One" for His Messianic

* Moses also referred to himself as a nursing Father (Num. 11:12).

destiny. Consider the following examples.

> "Through me hast thou illumined the faces of full many:
> and countless be the times Thou hast shown Thy power
> through me: for Thou hast made known to me *Thy
> deep mysterious things; hast shared Thy secret with
> me,* and so shown forth Thy power: and before the
> eyes of full many this wonder stands revealed: Thy
> glory shown forth and all living known of Thy
> power." [k]

Here the secret of the mysterious things are revealed
only to "the One." In turn Jesus said to his Disciples "Only
to you is it given to know the mysteries of the kingdom of
Heaven." (Matt. 13:11)

Next we consider a verse which clearly refers to the
Sermon on the Mount and the Beatitudes.

> "In the mouth of Thy Servant Thou did'st open as it
> were a fount as a wellspring of truth: as a herald of
> Thy good tidings bringing cheer to the humble bless-
> ings to the wounded in spirit and joy everlasting to
> those who mourn." [l]

Another line from Psalm 37 of the Essene text also
parallels the beatitudes.

> "The meek shall inherit the earth and delight in peace
> abounding." [m]

It is quite meaningful to note that the Hebrew word for
"meek" as used here and as again repeated in the sermon
on the Mount is, *"aniyim* and in the Aramaic dialect of the
early Palestinian Christians the cognate term is used specifically in the sense of 'Ascetic' " * i.e., those who practiced
abstinence. The significance of this observation will be
further understood as the reader continues.

But now, another text from the Essene Scriptures which
appears quite prophetic in supporting the Christian doctrine
of the Messianic hope.

> "I am come to know Thou didst open the ear of one
> that He might hear Thy teachings and deliver Thy

* Translation by Gaster.

chosen people from the 'uncleanness' which surrounds them. And Thou didst send Thy light and Thy wisdom that he might announce Thy wonderous tidings, and reveal them to all who would hear. Thou didst encourage Him by Thy mighty strength that he might achieve renown, for Thy name, and triumph in glory."[n]

Note here that where the Messiah of the Old Covenant was to deliver the children of Israel from their oppressors, and to establish a political kingdom after David, the Messiah of the New Covenant was instead to deliver them from all "uncleanness." *The latter course as prophesied in the Essene Scriptures was the course followed by Jesus.*

And here again is a text that clearly sets forth the doctrine of the virgin birth, the doctrine of salvation and the doctrine of the resurrection.

"Thou alone it is that hath created the righteous One: *Preparing Him from the womb* for the time of Thy good pleasure to heed Thy covenant and walk in Thy ways. Thou hast lavished upon Him the abundance of Thy mercies, and opened *all of his soul to everlasting salvation. Thou hast raised His inner glory out of the flesh.*" [o]

Here God prepared *the righteous one* from the womb for the time of His good pleasure in accord with the Prophet Jeremiah who said: He shall be called the Lord our Righteousness." (Jer. 23: 5-6)

Several times in the Essene Scriptures "The One" refers to himself as the "son of God's handmaid."

For example:

"Reject not Thy servant, the son of Thine handmaid, for by Thine own words have I called upon Thee." [p]

This same idea is inferred again in the following text. Here also the words "or ever" seem to describe a remote dimension in time, such as, "In the beginning was the word; and the word was with God. (John 1:1) And then later "The word became flesh." (John 1:14)

"Or ever (or before) my father begat me Thou dids't know me. From the womb of my mother (Thine hand-maid) Thou dids't shower me with grace, and from her breasts Thou dids't sustain me, and from my youth up Thou has't enlightened me with understanding of Thy judgments, and caused me to delight in Thy Holy Spirit.[q]

One may clearly recognize in these several texts that the Christian idea of the "virgin birth" came out of the pro-phetic writings of those who made the "highway straight in the desert for the coming of the Lord." For if one parallels the words, "And the angel said to Mary the power of the Highest shall overshadow thee, and there shall be born of thee the son of God," (Luke 1:35) both the son born of a virgin as described in Luke and the son of God's hand-maid as set forth in the Essene texts are one and the same. In fact in Luke 1:29 Mary refers to herself as the "hand-maid" of the Lord.

The doctrine of the virgin birth is in consequence legiti-mately Christian of a "pre-manger" period rather than a reconstruction of ideas taken from the various mystery religions as some writers have proposed.

Next, as was noted before, the Essene texts say: "Thou has't lavished upon him the abundance of Thy mercies and opened *all his soul to everlasting salvation.*" This is to de-clare, that through the "One" upon whom the Father has lavished the fullness of his mercies may be found everlast-ing life for as the texts further state: "Thou hast raised his 'inner glory' out of the flesh," i.e., hast resurrected his soul out of the flesh, or, as according to St. Paul, has put off the corruptible and put on the incorruptible.

Again the same blessings of "grace" are set forth in the following text.

"Blessed art Thou O my God who hast opened the heart of Thy servant: directed all his works in right-eousness and vouchsafe into the son of Thy handmaid the favor which Thou hast assured to all mortal "elect." [r]

As this text reads, God, through "His son," or through the son of his handmaid, (one and the same) assures all mortal "elect" (meaning those who believe) of salvation.

Another verse from the Essene Scriptures refers to those who reviled Jesus (Matt. 11-19)

"Thou hast made me a reproach and a derision to them that live by deceit, but a symbol of truth and understanding to all whose way is straight. Through me Thou has kept Thy pledge. All them that challenge me Thou makest to stand rebuked, distinguishing through me the right from the wrong. Thou in Thy might hast shed upon me the perfect light. They that walk in the way Thou desirest have harkened unto me and rallied to Thy cause in the legion of the Saints." [s]

Let us consider another verse from Essene Scriptures which appears to be most astoundingly prophetic. Herein is actually foretold the deserting of Jesus that night in the garden by those with whom he consorted: by those who only a few hours before ate of his bread: by those who turned their backs upon him and fled, and by those, as did Peter, "deny him up and down."

"All that ate of my bread lifted their heels against me: all that shared of my table mouthed distortions about me, and they with whom I consorted turned their backs upon me and defamed (or denied) me up and down." [t]

According to (Matt. 26:74) Peter indeed mouthed distortions about Jesus when "he began to curse and to swear saying I know not this man." Thus Peter also defamed Jesus, and thrice denied him up and down. Considering the others with whom the Lord consorted and who turned their backs upon him and fled, one might very well assume that they likewise when challenged, mouthed distortions concerning Him.

It is to be noted that the first two lines of this Essenic text are practically identical to those recorded in John 13:18. The only difference is that the Essenic texts do not particularly incriminate Judas which contrary to traditional beliefs may be nearer the truth. (See the vindication of Judas p. 320).

It is well known that the writers of the four gospels and the Epistles borrowed extensively from these Essene scriptures. The question now is how much did they borrow?

There seems to be only one answer, to this question, the truth of which depends upon the most likely choice of two alternatives. (1) That, in accord with the preponderance of evidence as set forth herein, the gospel writers not only borrowed many of the devices and expressions from the Qumran texts, but they also borrowed much of the basic material which they in turn rewrote and attributed to the ministry of Jesus, or (2) That, Jesus being an extremely gifted one of the brethren, one whose extraordinary insight and will-to-love induced a feeling of oneness with the whole of creation, and one who would suffer, even as it was written, to become himself the evidence of everlasting salvation, was, in consequence, inspired divinely or otherwise to recognize himself as the incarnated Teacher of Righteousness, * and the "One" through whom "the prophesies needs be fulfilled."

The Baptism, where according to John, "The Spirit descended from heaven and abode upon Him," represents the full bloom of self realization. Henceforth Jesus is convinced of his responsibility as the incarnated "Teacher."

As the evidence of proof which we shall later present confirms all other particulars pertaining to the common beliefs and practices of both the Sect of the Scrolls and those of the Palestinean Christians, the second alternative is by far the most convincing. It both favors the historicity of Jesus as set forth in the gospels as well as conforming to a comprehensive approach to truth. This is to say, the hypothesis of the "realization" of Jesus, applies with equal favor to the opinions of both the believer and the non-believer: to those who refer to Jesus as a prophet, or an inspired Teacher and to those who believe Him to be the

---

* "He shall be called the Lord our Righteousness" (Jer. 23:6).

"Only Begotten Son." To those of the former however the word "imagination" would probably be more acceptable, than the word "realization": one favors opinion and the other belief, otherwise and in accord with either viewpoint my hypothesis appears to be quite sound.

In accord with the "realization" hypothesis, wherein Jesus recognized himself to be the object of "divine" intent, it might be assumed, from a theological viewpoint that the scriptures of the "Chosen Ones" were inspired by, or their authors directed by, the will of God, as it were, to forewarn and forearm the Son of Man in the choice he was to make.

Certainly if any man believes that a God bestowed special favors as well as responsibilities upon any man, or group of men, mentioned in our own cloistered collection of ancient writings, then to be honest and sincere in his opinions he cannot fail to recognize, with equal reverence, the will of this same God as it applies to those spoken of in the Dead Sea Scriptures.

"Thou hast acted for Thyself and for Thy glory and hast sent among mankind those to be schooled in Thy council to the end that they may indeed prepare the way; make straight in the desert a highway for the Lord." * (u)

How can one better prepare the way: make straight in the desert a highway for his coming than to provide for a favorable environment: an environment wherein to set forth "God's holy word" that it might open the ear of "One" to make straight in his mind the way he is to follow, to forearm and forewarn him of the choice he was to make. In other words, to make straight the highway for his coming: prepare him for the day he is to go forth to preach the "full knowledge of the Lord as the waters cover the sea."

And now in overwhelming support of all the other evidences presented herein your author proposes to further maintain beyond any reasonable question of doubt that the

* Dead Sea Scriptures.

Sect of the Scrolls and the early followers of Jesus Christ were one and the same people.

My concluding evidence of proof therefore is in the mutual adherence of both the sect of the scrolls and the early Christians to the following three great ethical principles which were practiced neither by the Pharisees, the Sadducees, nor by any other religious orthodoxy of the near eastern or western world.

1. Freedom for all men from the bonds of forced servitude.
2. (a) Rejection of the whole sacrificial system in favor of mercy and the knowledge of God.
   (b) Abstinence both from strong drink and the flesh of animals where life has been.
3. To do violence to no creature, nor to take up arms against one's brother but instead to teach that all men should love and be at peace with one another and with God.

It is upon the many documentary and circumstantial "evidences of proof" as set forth in later chapters of this work, which maintain that these three ethical principles were strictly adhered to by the early Esseno-Chrisitan communities. that the validity of the "humane Christ" of the Covenant of Love is sustained: for it is only through his knowledge of, his practice of, and his teaching of, these, among other kindred essentials, that his words "I and my Father are one" (Jo. 10:30) have any spiritual value whatsoever. That is to say, as demonstrating the concern, the mercy, the loving kindness, and the peaceful blessings of the "Father" towards all His creation.

On the Moral and Spiritual Evolution of the Chosen People

For many centuries the carnal habits and sensual desires of the ancient Hebrews were in constant conflict with their spiritual ideas and beliefs. The amelioration of these spiritual values had been a long and almost despairing fight against the evils of the flesh. Gradually, however, the light began dawning. The arising of the prophets brought forth new concepts of God. "Mercy!" was the prime word of their appealing cry as they denounced the sacrifice of the first-born of human flesh, and again the same word came forth as God implored man to approach him with thanksgiving instead of sacrificing the lives of his creatures.

"He hath showed thee, O man, what is good: and what doth the Lord require of thee, but to do justly, and to love mercy, and to walk humbly with thy God." (Micah 6:6) and again (Hosea 6:6): "For I desire mercy and not sacrifice; the knowledge of God more than burnt offerings."

Gradually the shadows of Sodom and Gomorrah were withdrawn. Greater accent was put upon the teachings of the prophets, and there arose among the people of Judea a sect that was destined to reach an all-time high plane of moral and spiritual consciousness.

These were the brotherhood called the "Saints," or the ones we now know of as the Essenes.

While these people had progressed almost to a point of moral and spiritual perfection up to the beginning of the First Century, they necessarily had to come a long way, even as had their lesser spiritual contemporaries, the Pharisees.

"It must be admitted that the Essenic party, whether its headquarters were at Qumran or not, almost certainly contained divisions varying from one another; . . . these were not static during the party's more than two centuries of existence, but were constantly changing and developing.

"The fact of change within the Essenic party may well be significant for the rise of Christianity." [34]

Gaster also recognizes this same spiritual growth and development. "One must remember," he writes, "that Philo and Josephus are describing conditions as they obtained in the First Century, whereas our documents (the Scrolls) may reflect an earlier state of affairs and may even ascend to the Hasîdim, Pious Ones, of Maccabean times, who were the spiritual forerunners of the Essenes." [35]

This ascension from an earlier date is clearly borne out upon comparing, for example, the Zadokite document with the Manual of Discipline. The latter seems to have been written some time before the beginning of the Christian era, while the former must have reached back through many generations of the Sect.

Note, for instance, the difference even in the mood of the opening paragraph of the Zadokite Document compared with the opening paragraph of the Manual of Discipline.

As to the former: "Now listen, all right-minded men, and take note how God acts: He has a feud with all flesh and exacts satisfaction from all who spurn Him." As to the latter: "Every one who wishes to join the community must pledge himself to respect God and Man; to live according to the communal rule, to seek God's truth."

In view of the similarity of some of the phrasing in both documents, it is quite evident that the author, or authors, of the later one used the former for reference. Josephus says that the Essenes, "take great pains in studying the writings of the ancients, and choose out of them what is most for the advantage of their soul and body."

Consider the following translation from the Zadokite document: "We have done wickedly, we and our fathers, because we have walked contrary to the statutes of the covenant." The same phrase is found in the Manual of Discipline but with an added emphasis: "We have done wickedly, we and our fathers * before us, because we have walked contrary to his statutes." Here the addition of the words, "before us," suggests that the writer of the Manual of Discipline was referring not so much to his past generation as he was to those of many generations before; i.e., those who followed the old standards contained in the Zadokite scripture; namely, Our fathers before us did those things which we even now still feel the guilt of. (See Ps. 106:6-15 RSV).

The evidence that the Zadokite document represented a much earlier phase of the spiritual development of the sect

* See Psalm 106:6-15 R.S.V. (they had a wanton craving).

is quite clear. For example, in reference to animal sacrifice: "No one is to present any offering upon the altar on the Sabbath except the statutory Sabbath burnt-offering" *— as the Scripture puts it, your Sabbath offering exclusively (Lev. 23:38). The custom of slavery, which also belongs to old covenant practices, is somewhat compromised in the Zadokite Document as follows: "No one is to sell to the heathen any of his male or female servants." This indicates that they considered their servants to be under the protection of the Order and that it would constitute an injustice to consign them to the mercies of the outside world.

Even at this stage in the spiritual evolution of the sect, one can observe a trend towards improvement. Along with a concern for the welfare of their servants is to be noted the small, almost incidental, reference in the Zadokite document regulating animal sacrifice. A pointing towards complete vegetarianism appears in their extending of the prohibition of swine's flesh to the prohibition of all animal flesh for food: "Let not a man make himself abominable with any living creature or creeping thing by eating of them." † However, the Zadokite document does permit the eating of fish. Whether or not this translation takes precedence over the eating of sacrificial flesh is not clear, for usually both animal sacrifice and flesh eating go hand in hand; the former is but a convenient means to the latter. Whenever animal sacrifice is abolished as a ritualistic practice, then the religious man harkens to the integrity of his God and likewise abhors the "erstwhile pleasant savor."

---

* Verification of this practice is found in the excavation of the bones of animals that appear to have been buried in a manner in keeping with a particular ceremonial observance. But this early custom of the Sons of Zadok was, as the latter Manual of Discipline and the Hymns of the Initiants verify, replaced by more dignified overtures to God. It must be remembered, also, that Qumran was inhabited some 200 years, during which time several reformations must have taken place. Thus the Essenes of the Manual and the Hymns, and those of Philo and Josephus, are found to be considerably more advanced morally and spiritually than the Essenes of the Zadokite Document.

† Translated by Millar Burrows.

(See sacrifice p. 303)

In examining the Manual of Discipline for reference to animal sacrifice, one finds that "atonement will be made more effectively by *an oblation of the lips*" than by any flesh or burnt-offerings or fat of sacrifices. In fact, in the Hymns of the Initiants they regard the law of Moses as requiring only a "free will" offering in the form of thanksgiving, a "blessing of the lips" as a tribute to God. They actually imply that the law of Moses had been successively "garbled." This will be discussed later in detail because of its most important theological significance.

The Essenes had now reached a state of enlightenment where they began to look back upon their forefathers' custom of animal sacrifice with a similar feeling of humiliation that probably annoyed the Pharisees as they looked back upon the evils of human sacrifice. Here one may observe the spiritual evolution of the Hebrews on the march, with the Essenes well in the lead. Even now, they were ready to advance still further that they might experience the insight that was Daniel's, for, along with their abolition of animal sacrifice, went also abolition of the slaughter of animals for food. Here the full force of the Prophets' pleas for mercy and loving kindness fell upon sympathetic ears, and for the first time in Judaism, a collective people realized the full and uncompromised meaning of the word "Love."

Considering that the law of Moses had been garbled by the Scribes, they selected those portions of scripture which were consistent with their conception of a just, merciful, and understanding God. In accord therewith, their eating pleasures were made to conform with the divine formula as set down in Genesis, which they acknowledged in their own scriptures.

"Thou hast created plants
for the service of man
and all things that spring from the earth
that he may be fed in abundance,

and to them that acknowledge Thy truth
Thou has also given insight
to divine Thy wondrous works." *

Epiphanius, a bishop during the Third Century, says that "the Essenes eschewed the flesh of animals." Josephus says the same thing in a more subtle manner, that: "they all sit down together to one sort of food, a settled measure of food as is abundantly sufficient for them." Josephus says that they "live the same kind of life as those whom the Greeks call Pythagoreans." [36] Philo says: "They live the longest lives, so that many of them exist above a hundred years, owing to the simplicity of their diet." Porphyrius also referred to their repast as a "single simple dish of pure clean food."

"St. Jerome expressed admiration for (the Essenes) 'those men who perpetually abstained from meat and wine and had acquired the habit of everyday fasting.' That habit, it is true, is attested by the Therapeutae, whose connection with the Essenes cannot be doubted." [37]

Voltaire writes, "It is well known that Pythagoras embraced the humane doctrine of anti-flesh-eating. There was a rivalry as to who could be the most virtuous—Essenes or Pythagoreans." [38]

"The Essenes' code of life was partly Greek—possibly Pythagorean." [39] They all wore white garments, probably to accentuate their purity. This also suggests a sort of spiritual kinship with oriental traditions.

"Robed in pure white I have born me clean
From man's vile birth and coffined clay
And exalted from my lips away
Touch of all meat where life has been." [40]

Most of the Essenes' scriptures were written upon parchment. One may suppose that the use of the skins of animals for this purpose may have been somewhat of a controversial subject among these devout vegetarians, for some of their

* Hymns of the Initiants X. 14-XI,2 Trans. by Gaster. Also see Gen. 1:29 and Dan. 1:9-30.

writings were done on thin copper sheets made up into rolls or scrolls.

If one should attempt to parallel this issue as it may have been discussed by the Essenes with the viewpoint of many of our ethical vegetarians today, one might suppose that they had arrived at similar conclusions.

The man who endorses a humane diet is none too happy at the idea of wearing leather shoes. But he finds partial consolation in the fact that animals are killed mainly for food and that their skins, being merely by-products, would go to waste if they were not used in the manufacture of leather goods. However, this explanation does not satisfy others who prefer not to be a party, either directly or indirectly, to the sacrifice of the animal's life or the use of the products resulting from it. These men and women do not wear or use any article made of leather.

One might suppose, then, that some of the more devout of the brethren had refused to record their thoughts on the skins of animals, using instead either papyrus or copper rolls to write upon.

Certainly copper was neither convenient to obtain in thin sheets, nor was it as pliable to handle or as easy to write upon as parchment. Also, through probable previous examination of other old writings handed down to them, they may have found parchment to be as durable if properly preserved as was sheet copper, and even more so, as the evidence today indicates.

It is probable that those who wrote on parchment considered their guilt absolved in view of the fact that through their hands the animals' skin was being made holy unto God. Of course, this is merely an assumption but it may in part, explain the existence of the copper scrolls among the discoveries at Qumran.

There is no mention in the Manual of Discipline about personal servants or slaves. It is evident that this custom had been abolished some time before the writing of this document. In fact, "They were the first society in the world to abolish slavery." (Enc. Brit. II Ed. VIN p. 779)

Philo says: "Not a single slave is to be found among them, but all are free, exchanging services with each other, and they denounce the owners of slaves, not merely for their injustice in outraging the law of equality, but also for their impiety in annulling the statutes of nature, who mother-like has born and reared all men alike, and created them genuine brothers, not in mere name, but in very reality . . . . they have shown themselves especially devout in the service to God, not by offering sacrifices of animals, but by resolving to sanctify their minds."

Josephus writes, " . . . Nor are they desirous to keep servants, thinking that this tempts man to be unjust . . . they do not offer sacrifices because they have more pure lustrations of their own; on which account they are excluded from the common court of the temple."

Again, Philo writes: The first thing about these people is that they live in villages, avoiding the big cities because of iniquities that become inveterate among city dwellers, for they know that their company would have a deadly effect upon their own souls, . . . some of them labor on the land and others pursue such crafts as cooperate with peace and so benefit themselves and their neighbors." "Blessed are the peacemakers for they shall be called the children of God." (Matt. 5:9) "As for darts, javelins, daggers, or the helmet, breastplate or shield," continued Philo, "you could not find a single manufacturer of them nor, in general, any person making weapons or engines or plying any industry concerned with war; nor, indeed, any of the peaceful kind which easily lapse into vice." (Compare Matt. 26:52) "They do not hoard gold and silver, or acquire great slices of land because they desire revenues therefrom, but provide what is needed for the necessary requirements of life. For, while they stand almost alone in the whole of mankind in that they have become moneyless and landless by deliberate action rather than by lack of good fortune, they are esteemed exceedingly rich because they judge frugality with con-

tentment to be, as indeed it is, an abundance of wealth."
(Compare Matt. 6:20)

"As for philosophy, they abandon the logical part to
quibbling verbalists as unnecessary for the acquisition of
virtue, and the physical to visionary praters as beyond the
grasp of human nature, only retaining that part which
treats philosophically of the existence of God and the creation of the universe. But the *ethical* part they study very
industriously, taking for their trainers the laws of their
fathers which could not possibly have been conceived by
the human soul without divine inspiration.

"In these they are instructed at all times, particularly on
the seventh day, for that day has been set apart to be kept
holy, and on it they abstain from all work and proceed to
sacred spots which they call synagogue." (Compare Matt.
4:23)

"They are trained in piety, holiness, justice, domestic
and civil conduct, knowledge of what is truly good, or evil,
and how to choose what is good through the love of God,
love of virtue, and love of men. Their love of God they show
by a multitude of proofs: by religious purity constant and
unbroken throughout their lives, by abstinence from oaths,
(Compare Matt. 5:43) by veracity, by their belief that the
godhead is the cause of all good things and nothing bad:
their love of virtue, by their freedom from the love of either
money (Compare Luke 18:22) or reputation or pleasure;
by self-mastery and endurance; again by frugality, simple
living, contentment, humility, respect for law; (Compare
Matt. 22:21) steadiness, and all similar qualities: their love
of men by benevolence and sense of equality, and their spirit
of fellowship, which defies inscription, though a few words
on it will not be out of place. First of all, then, no one's
house is his own in the sense that it is not to be shared by
all, for besides the fact that they dwell together in communities, the door is open to visitors from elsewhere who
share their convictions." (Compare Luke 10:5-8, Matt.
10:11-13, and Mark 6:10).

The reports of Josephus on the virtues of this people are equally impressive, both of which conform in a remarkable degree with the Manual of Discipline, the Hymns, Psalms, and other of the Dead Sea Scroll writings. Our records, therefore, clearly indicate that by the end of the First Century B.C., Judaïsm had achieved through the Essenic movement an extraordinarily high state of moral and spiritual enlightenment, the like of which is nowhere else in the history of mankind so voluminously illustrated. Is it any wonder that these good people were known as the "holy ones," the "saints," the "poor," the "Sons of Peace," the "elect," or the "chosen ones?"

Considering an affirmative answer to this question as the correct one, we find that there did come from among the ancient Hebrews a humble and sincerely ethical "remnant" who, after hundreds of years of seeking the good of God's nature, and of applying the knowledge gained thereby to themselves, seem to actually deserve the title of "God's chosen people."

Christians, therefore, are deeply indebted to the Jews, for it was from out of the "chosen ones" of their tradition that the Lord Jesus came forth to exemplify God's nature to the world.

Chapter Four

1 Dr. Powell Davies, *The Dead Sea Scrolls*. Signet Key Book (New American Library, N. Y.)
2 *Ibid.*
10 *Ibid.*
26 *Ibid.*
19 *Ibid.*
11 *Ibid.*
14 *Ibid.*
34 *Ibid.*
3 Charles T. Fretsch, *The Qumran Community*, (Macmillan Co., N. Y.)
20 *Ibid.*

21   *Ibid.*
22   *Ibid.*
24   *Ibid.*
 9   *Ibid.*
30   *Ibid.*
 4   Theodore H. Gaster, *The Dead Sea Scriptures.* (Doubleday & Company, Inc., N. Y.)
 *   i, j, k, l, m, n, o, p, q, r, s, t, u, from the Hymns, and Psalms. This author has taken the liberty to rearrange several lines of the original translation by Gaster. None of the words or the meaning of the texts were changed in so doing.
12   *Ibid.*
16   *Ibid.*
31   *Ibid.*—Interpretation expanded upon with apologies to Gaster.
35   *Ibid.*
 5   Dr. Wm. H. Brownlee, *Bulletin of the American Schools of Oriental Research,* Dec. 1953.
 6   Edmund Wilson (The Scrolls from the Dead Sea). Oxford University Press, N. Y.
 7   Duncan Howlett, An Interpretation of the Dead Sea Scrolls. (Harper & Brothers, N. Y.)
 8   *Ibid.*
23   *Ibid.*
29   *Ibid.*
28   *Ibid.*
13   *Ibid.*
17   *Ibid.*
18   *Ibid.*
27   *Ibid.*
25   Bible Archaeologist American Schools of Oriental Research.
15   Rev. T. G. Jalland, D.D., The Origin and Evolution of the Christian Church. (Hutchinsons University Library Hutchinson House, Stratford Pl., London)
 †   Millar Burrows, *The Dead Sea Scrolls.* (Viking Press, N. Y.)
32, 33   Martin A. Larson, *Religion of the Occident,* Philosophical Library, N. Y.
 a, b, c, d, e, f, g, h, The Testaments of the Twelve Patriarchs, † fragments of which were found with the Essene Scriptures. (a, e, h, Benjamin) (b, Simeon) (c, Joseph) (d, f, Levi) (g, Dan).
36   Josephus Chap. X, p, 471.
37   Geze Vermes, *Discovery in the Judean Desert,* p. 55. (Desclee Co., N. Y., Paris, Rome.)
38   Howard Williams, *Ethics of Diet.* (Albert Broadbent Manchester), (Richard J. James, London).
39   Rev. David Simpson, M.A.D. D., *History of Christianity in the Light of Modern Knowledge.* (Harcourt Brace Co., N. Y.)
40   Confession in the Cretans of Euripides of one initiated into the mysteries of Orpheus.
 †   *The Lost Books of the Bible,* World Publishing Company, Cleveland, New York.

CHAPTER FIVE
The First Christians
and
The Ethical System of Jesus

"The first church of Jesus came into existence in Jerusalem. We know that it baptized, celebrated the Eucharist, and practiced the laying on of hands to impart the Holy Ghost . . . . . We have every reason to believe that they insisted on . . . . vegetarianism. In short the new communion was patterned upon the Essene." [1]

Prominent among these Jewish Christians were those who charged openly that the law of Moses had been garbled by the scribes and priests. They decried the sacrificial system, as may be seen from the apology of Stephen.

"Did you offer me slain beasts and sacrifices,

"Forty years in the wilderness, O house of Israel?

"You stiff-necked people, uncircumcised in heart and ears, you always resist the Holy Spirit. As your fathers did, so do you. Which of the prophets did not your fathers persecute?" (Acts 6:8 to 7:53) This is Essenic doctrine spoken from the same high principled ethics as motivated those who made the "highway in the desert straight for the coming of the Lord."

Looking between the curtains of many windows, one can recognize in the behavior of the early Christian sects a carry-over or a continuation of the fundamental customs and beliefs which characterized the religious practice of the Essenes. In fact, as some scholars have pointed out, early Jewish Christianity was Essenic Christianity.

In tracing the ascetic practices of the former we find that they were paralleled nowhere else among the peoples of Judea, and they were unique in that area for their extreme virtue.

The Essenes were the first of the Hebrew people to collectively ban animal sacrifice: i.e., to replace the "pleasant savor" to the Lord with a covenant of justice. Thus were they also the first Hebrew sect to recognize the injustice of slaughtering animals for food.

"Blessed art Thou O God of compassion
for the greatness of Thy power,
the abundance of Thy truth,
the profusion of Thy mercies
over all Thy works." *

It is to be noted that the first principle of abstinence from flesh-eating is based upon humane prerogatives—justice, mercy, loving kindness, etc.—even as the abolition of animal sacrifice was the fruition of the Prophets' call for mercy.

In order to gain a full understanding of the Jesus of the following Fifth Gospel, it will be necessary first to review some of the doctrinal practices of the first Christians and the first Apostles.

The first Christians (Gr. Christianos Christos), i.e., "Messianists," were Jews. Jesus was a Jew and all of his twelve disciples were Jews. The multitudes that followed him and listened to his preaching were Jews. His religion was the religion of the Jews. He believed in the law of Moses, the pure law, the true law of the Prophets before him, and like them, He endeavored to resurrect it from out of the garbled interpretations of the scribes and the prerogatives of the Priestly Code. His was strictly a Hebraic mission among the Jews and for the Jews. He preached the current Jewish idea of repentance; that the Kingdom of Heaven was at hand, as did his fellow Jew, John the Baptist. In fact, they both preached this same gospel as they received it from the Jewish sect which the Greeks called *Esseni* (Holy Ones).

So in attempting to understand the true character of Jesus, we cannot delude ourselves by injecting into his way

* From the Essenes Book of Hymns.

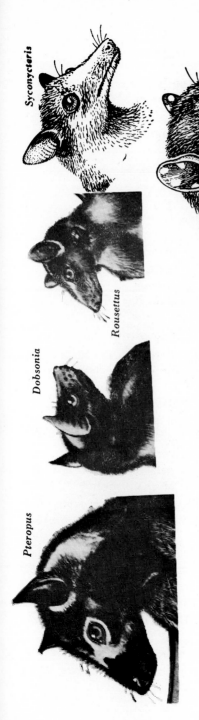

Pteropus

Dobsonia

Rousettus

Syconycteris

Nyctimene,

THIS BAT MAY BE
OMNIVOROUS

(See Note)

FEEDERS ON FRUITS AND BLOSSOMS include these five: (*l* to *r*) the large bat, *Pteropus*; the hoverer, *Dobsonia*; dog-faced *Rousettus*; the nectar-eating *Syconycteris*; and the solitary, tubed-nosed *Nyctimene*. All are of the family Pteropidae, suborder Megachiroptera ("great bats"), one of the six families of bats to have been found thus far in New Guinea.

FRUIT AND BLOSSOM FEEDERS

HERBIVORA OR VEGETARIANS

Plate 5

DR. ALBERT SCHWEITZER
modeled from life at his home in
Alsace, by the Author.

of life any heathen or gentile notions that pretend to supplement or suppress that which is so clearly obvious.

Christianity, in its purest state, was the doctrine taught by Jesus to his disciples and to the multitudes of Jews who followed him. Later the preaching of Peter, James, Andrew, Thomas, and others of the disciples were accepted in their fullness mainly by the Jews. Peter "preached in the circumcision," which was a colloquial way of saying he preached to the Jews.

According to the "Acts of Peter," the Apostles were to labor among the Jews for twelve years, and then were to go forth into the world to preach to all men the one God.

It probably was the intent of Jesus to convert first the Jewish people to the new "Essene Covenant" so that they would stand out as examples of the good life, thereby influencing the whole world to a full recognition of the God of justice, mercy, and loving kindness.

The first Christians, or "Messianists," were, as historical reference indicates, a Jewish sect known in their time as the "children of light," the "holy ones," or the "chosen ones." As a preponderance of evidence seems to suggest, Jesus grew up and received his religious instruction among these people. It is quite obvious that if he was to astound the learned doctors with knowledge of the Torah at the age of twelve, he would have necessarily had to be first schooled. According to what the gospels indicate, his background was anything but Sadducean. Also, in view of his apparent aversion to the practices of the Pharisees, it is not likely that he had been "mothered" or instructed by members of this sect.

In consequence, the only remaining source for his astounding knowledge of the scripture must have been the "Essenes," for as Josephus "thrice" emphasizes: "There were but three sects among the Jews." They were known for their industrious instruction and their zest for full knowledge of God's word.

These first "Christians," or "Messianists," appear to have

been the "chosen ones," those selected by God to "make the highway straight in the desert for the coming of the Lord," as well as to furnish a means through which the boy Jesus would grow up in full recognition of his future destiny.

It is to be particularly noted that the basic principles these people stood for were held neither by the Sadducees, the Pharisees, nor in fact by any of the heathen communities wherein St. Paul founded his religion. These principles involved the denouncing of war, slavery, animal sacrifice, and the consumption of superfluous meats and strong drinks. These were basic Christian prerogatives which quite obviously must have found a prominent place, both in the character and in the teachings of Jesus. Not to concede this point would be the same as suggesting that Jesus was woefully lacking in an understanding both of the nature of man and of his responsibility to the world of life around him: that he was indeed derelict in his duty as an interpreter of the good life, for actually these four major evils represent crimes against both nature and God: They directly and indirectly cause by far the major portion of all the hate, sorrow, ill health, pain, suffering, and death of living things upon this planet.

To be fair, therefore, to Jesus as a great teacher, who had a supreme knowledge of the good life, one need no longer question whether he pleaded for the welfare of the whole living man, that is, for an unrestricted and uncompromised awareness of God's mercy and loving kindness. Instead, from his Essenic background, we now know that he did.

"The fact that the Pharisees and Sadducees so often figure in the pages of the New Testament while the Essenes are never mentioned might plausibly be interpreted to show that the New Testament emanated from the side of the Essenes." (Encyp. Brit. V9: p. 781) But we do find names in the gospels such as "the Elect," "Children of Light," "the Poor," "Sons of Peace" etc., which are also found in the Essenic Scriptures. Some of these references also describe the early Christian name, "Ebionite." This name is from the Hebrew word, "ebionim," meaning "poor." "Probably," as Professor Latourette remarked, "harking back to the 'poor' of the Sermon on the Mount." The Essenes were also known as the "poor," thereby conforming to the definition, "Ebionite." [2]

Dr. Bartlet said that "the Ebionites probably fraternized with the kindred Jewish sect of the Essenes," which is the same as saying that those among the Jews with kindred thoughts, beliefs, and practices, fraternized, or were drawn together.

We find also that the names "Nazarene" and "Ebionite" are synonymous; that they actually represent the same sect. * It has been pointed out by scholars that the word "Nazarene" could be interpreted to mean "watch-tower."* *

The Essenes built a tower on their monastery which may have been used as a place of observation.

They were particularly devoted to preparing the way for the coming of the Messiah. They expected this to occur at almost any moment, living a life of constant anticipation. It might be supposed, therefore, that the building of the tower had a special significance. From such a vantage point one could maintain a constant search of the heavens for a sign, as well as scan the desert horizon for the coming of the anointed one from out of the wilderness. The name "watchers from the tower," "tower-watchers," or even "watch towers" could very well result as a common expression, conforming with a translation of the name, "Nazarene." The ordinary oriental name for Christian, or "Messianist," is "Nasara." Both of these explanations, however, suggest the naming of the town after the name of its inhabitants. It has been pointed out that of all the cities, towns, and villages named in the Old Testament, a place called Nazareth is nowhere indicated. It seems to have been

---

* See "Ebionite" (Encyc. Brit. 11th Edit.).
* * Dr. Powell Davies, *Dead Sea Scrolls*, Signet Books.

brought to our notice as the home neighborhood of Jesus which later got its name through its people, they being mostly "Essenes," "Nazarenes," later called "Ebionites." (See map Plate No. 2)

"The Ebionites were a party of Jewish Christians who saw in Jesus a man on whom the Spirit descended at his baptism to fit him for his mission. In practice they were vegetarians, looking with abhorrence on flesh as food and the slaying of animals for sacrifice." [3] These are basic Essenic practices.

"Jerome found the Nazarenes also dwelling in Peraea beyond Jordan, and classed them with the Ebionites; they held to the virgin birth and the Divine Sonship.

"Origen says that those Jews who have received Jesus as Christ are called by the name Ebionites." [4] What Origen reveals here is that *these Jews are the original children of the New Covenant and are direct followers of the Nazarene Jew, Jesus Christ, and his Jewish Apostles,* thereby conforming devotedly to the practices and customs taught by the Master: "Their most remarkable treatment of the Old Testament was their rejection of the whole sacrificial system. (See Essenes)* In their interpretation of Matthew's gospel (the unrevised original),* which gospel alone they accepted, they gave as one of the objects of his coming, the abrogation of the sacrificial system." [5] (Hoer XXX16) "They refused to partake of flesh or wine, taking as their pattern, St. Peter, whose food was bread and olives. (Hoer 15: cf. Clem. Hom JII.6)

"They also followed St. Peter in his custom of daily lustrations. The Lord's Supper they partook of with bread and water. (1b 16) Ebionism in the form we have described and as given in Epiphanius has assimilated elements from Essenism. Its asceticism in meat and drink, its persistent rejection of animal sacrifice, and its speculative elements have come through Essenism." [6]

Pliny, who was Governor of Bithynia, where Peter had

* Parentheses in 5 by author.

preached the gospel of Jesus Christ, wrote a letter to Trajan, the Roman Emperor, describing the early Christian practices: "They affirmed the whole of their guilt, or their error; they met on a day before it was light (before sunrise) and addressed a form of prayer to Christ as to a divinity, binding themselves by a solemn oath * never to commit any sin or evil and never to falsify their word, nor deny a trust, after which it was their custom to depart and to meet together again to take food, but ordinary and harmless ** food." [7]

It is quite obvious that this is an Essenic Christian custom. Josephus writes of the Essenes: "They assemble before sun-rising and speak not a word about profane matters, but put up certain prayers;—after this every one of them is sent away; . . . then they assemble together again . . . and sit down together each one to a single plate of one sort of food," i.e., "harmless" or "innocent" food. It might be noted here that these Christians spoken of by Pliny were not followers of Paul (Acts 16:7), for Pliny was the Governor of Bithynia, where Peter preached. (I Peter 1:1) This observation seems to verify other documentary evidence regarding the vegetarian practices and teachings of the Apostles who listened firsthand to the sublime words of the Master.

Pliny referred to Christianity as a contagious superstition, describing those under suspicion as abstaining from flesh food. Seneca also some forty years earlier referred to those under imperial suspicion as: "the foreign cultus or superstition who abstained from the flesh of animals." ***

The most revealing of all our evidence regarding the true way of life of Jesus and His Apostles is contained in what some scholars believe to be the original gospel: "the gospel

---

* "Commit myself by oath never to sin against Thee nor do ought that is evil." (Essene Scriptures).

** Some translators use here the word "harmless," others the word "innocent." However, they both refer to food that had suffered no harm or hurt; innocent or blood guiltless. (vegetarian)

***Seneca's letter to Lucilius, Ethics of Diet, p. 34.

according to the Hebrews. This name, however, cannot have been original, for the Hebrews themselves would not have used this designation. It may have been known simply as 'the gospel.' The language was western Aramaic, the mother tongue of Jesus and his Apostles." [8] It was regarded by many in the First Century as the Hebrew original of the Canonical Matthew. (Jerome in Matt. XII-13: Adv. Pelag 111, 1) It circulated among the Nazarenes in Syria and among the Ebionites. Parts of it are to be seen in the Canonical Matthew and other parts in Luke, which suggests that this was the original gospel from which the Canonical versions were taken.

"The Gospel of the Hebrews, or the 'Gospel' as used by the Nazarenes, was called by many the 'authentic Matthew.' (authenticum Mattholi Jerome ad. Matt. XII. 17) It was written in Aramaic words and Hebrew letters. (Hegesippus, A.D. 160) Eusebius, like Origen, implies that many reckon it Canonical, while Jewish Christians make use of this Gospel and take small account of the others." [9]

"Of some thirty fragments extant, Nichelson regards ten as independent of the Canonical Gospels. Handman thinks that twelve are nearest to St. Luke, eleven to St. Matthew, and six to St. Mark. Lessing (1784), the first to realize the importance of the Gospel of the Hebrews, finds here the original 'Hebrew Matthew' mentioned by Papias in A.D. 110 and the primal source of all the other Synoptic Gospels. Hilgenfeld calls it the 'Punctum Archimedis' of the whole Synoptic problem, taking the place usurped by St. Mark." [10]

"The Gospel according to the Apostles was used by the Ebionites. *Herein is found the 'Essene Christ.' He denounces sacrifice and the eating of flesh.* Jerome identifies this Gospel with the Gospel of the Hebrews. Lipsuis accepts the statement of Jerome and is of the opinion that this Gospel—in the form in which it was known to Epiphanius, Jerome, and Origen—was a copy of an older original written in Aramaic" [11]: i.e., the Gospel of the Hebrews, or *the true Gospel* of Jesus Christ used by the primitive church.

This Gospel appears to have contained many of the sayings of Jesus that for obvious reasons were not written into the Synoptic Gospels. The Pauline branch of the early church would not, for reasons to be discussed later, subscribe to the abolition of slavery or of the slaughter of animals for food.

From all of these references, the unprejudiced searcher for the "good and true" can feel assured that the original Aramaic Gospel of the Hebrews or, as (according to the apostles) used by the Nazarenes, or Ebionites (the poor), contained the pure uncompromised doctrine of the humanely ethical Jesus: the Jesus through whose awareness of, the wolf would lie down with the lamb and no one would harm or destroy the life of any creature upon the earth. (see Isa. 11:1-10)

The Hellenized Jew, Stephen, upheld the true Essenic and Nazarene traditions through challenging the priestly code and its garbled interpretation of the law of Moses (Acts 6:13-14) by openly denouncing the slaying of animals for sacrifice. (Acts 7:42) "But let justice roll down like waters, and righteousness like an everflowing stream." (from Stephen's reference Amos 5:24-25) Jeremiah also seems to be brought into the reference of Stephen wherein God speaks (sarcastically): "Put your burnt offerings into your sacrifices and eat flesh. For I spoke not unto your fathers nor commanded them in the day that I brought them out of the land of Egypt concerning burnt offerings or sacrifices. This I commanded them. Obey my voice, walk in the ways that I have commanded you, that it may be well with you." (Jer. 7: 22-3) Stephen was of the Hebrew Christian Church of Jerusalem and a true disciple of Essenic virtues.

About the Apostles

Now it goes without saying that Jesus, in selecting his disciples, would not have approached either a Sadducee or a Pharisee. Neither would they have approached him.

The Sadducees were more inclined to be atheistic than religious. They were men of the world: hypocrites and skeptics. The Pharisees were, in contrast, extremely devoted to the 'dyed in the wool' religious customs and practices of their fathers before them. Paul was a striking example of this inherited Phariseean influence for in spite of his 'spiritual illumination' he still publicly, if not within his own heart, subscribed to the temple sacrifices, the slaughter of animals for food, and the practice of slavery. All of these were contrary to the Essenic doctrine of justice and mercy as practiced by the Master and his immediate disciples. (see the justification of Paul, page 371)

As Josephus had thrice emphasized, there were three Sects among the Jews: the Sadducees, the Pharisees, and the Essenes. It seems, therefore, that a Hebrew either belonged actively to one of these three Sects or his sympathies were in accord with one or another of them. Ruling out both the Sadducees and the Pharisees, the Essenes, then, are the only remaining sect which alone, even if there were others to select from, could qualify for the way of life of one of Christ's Apostles.

Again, let us be reminded of the Essenic background from out of which the Apostles must have come. Circumstantial evidence, as set forth in the Four Gospels, supports the validity of this assumption. For example, in the various narratives wherein Jesus meets up with those who were to become his disciples, He usually is reported as saying merely, "Follow me," and they do so almost without hesitation. It is common sense to assume that these men must have had some previous briefing on the coming of the anointed one. The Essenes were the only people expecting this thing to happen, and at any moment. Being religiously schooled in the expectancy of such an event, any one of them might have been somewhat fearful not to obey the command of one whose manner and bearing indicated that he was not just an ordinary man. It seems therefore that only an Essene or one sympathetic to Essenic customs and beliefs would have reacted to the call of Jesus. Certainly no Sadducee or Pharisee would have.

Drawing even closer to the truly honorable and humane Son of Man, we find Him brought to witness in the personal practices of the Apostles who walked, talked, and prayed with him.

We learn from the church Father Eusebius, quoting Hegesippus (Circa 160 A.D.), that James, the brother of Jesus, was holy from his mother's womb—drank no wine nor strong drink, nor ate the flesh of animals.

"We shall be far nearer the truth," writes Dr. Bartlet, "if we relate the piety of James as of the Apostles in general to that which breathes in the Magnificat and Benedictus or lives in the pages of Philo and Josephus touching the Essenes." [12]

Indeed, Dr. Bartlet seems to be quite right in his paralleling the piety of James as of the Apostles in general. "Peter's food was bread and olives and herbs without the use of flesh or wine." (Hoer. 15 Clem. Hom X11.6) "Matthew lived upon seeds and nuts, fruits and vegetables without the use of flesh." (Clem. Instructor)

"The Acts of Thomas, which was probably a Second Century reconstruction of an original gospel, presents Thomas as fasting, wearing a single (probably white) garment, giving what he has to others, and abstaining from the eating of flesh and the drinking of wine." [13]

Thomas was also represented by a gospel which circulated among the Nazarenes and the Manichaeans, who adhered to a "merciful diet."

Andrew was represented by a gospel and an Acts. The Apostle Philip was also represented by a gospel. Both of these gospels were used by the Encratites and the Apostolic Brethren, who also ate only pure and "innocent" food. Andrew was Peter's brother. He was also a disciple of John the Baptist. It would be hard to believe that the same principles of abstinence held by these two were not also observed by Andrew.

According to the Fourth Gospel, two of the Baptist's disciples followed Jesus: One was Andrew and the other is not named. As John the Baptist was an Essene, so must have been his disciples.

Now Philip was probably a close neighbor of the brothers Peter and Andrew for they all came from the same community in Bethsaida which probably was Essenic.

"Papias, the pupil of John the Evangelist, told how John, the disciple of the Lord, related how the Lord would teach that when all creatures would use for food the products of the soil, they would become peaceable and in harmony with one another." [14] This teaching of Jesus describes the basic formula for a humane and God-loving way of life based upon Gen. 1:29-30. One cannot doubt, therefore, that a favorite Apostle of Jesus would live according to the teachings of the Master; i.e., according to the Divine Formula of Genesis.

So far, therefore, our evidence seems to verify that John the Baptist, James the Lord's brother, Matthew, Peter, Andrew, John, and Thomas all practiced the higher ethical way of life. It suggests, too, that Philip and the other disciples of the Baptist mentioned in John, were of the Essenic tradition. This accounts for a probable total of nine among those close to Jesus who favored mercy instead of sacrifice, and who, like their Essenic brethren, were consistent in their selection of "innocent" food.

That it was paramount to the qualification of a disciple that he abide by the Gen. 1:29 precedent is, indicated in the choosing of Matthias to fill the place in the twelve vacated by Judas (Acts 1:21-26) for his food was the same* as told of Matthew (in Clem. Alex. Paedag. ii.16).

Nothing much is known of the other Apostles but it is almost certain that their conduct would necessarily follow a similar pattern.

"The Apostolic Brethren of the Second to the Fourth

* In re: Ency. Britt. 11 Ed. XVII, p. 895.

Century professed an ascetic rigidity of morals. They sought to imitate the manner of life of the Apostles of Christ. They condemned individual property and abstained from wine and flesh meat." [15]

Further evidence of the mercy loving life as taught by the Master is brought to witness in the vegetarian practices of many early Christian sects. As we have seen, the first of these were the Essenes, also known as the Nazarenes, and again known later as the Ebionites. It was noted before that these holy ones used what has been considered to be the original Aramaic Gospel of Matthew along with a gospel of the twelve, and probably Epistles, Acts, or Gospels written by or under the dictation of Peter, James, John, Andrew, Thomas and Philip. The authenticity of these later gospels has never been established, although many believe them to have been copied from original notes and records of the Apostles whose names they bear.

It seems that one can hardly doubt this to be true if we consider the tremendous impression Jesus must have made on those whom he instructed. On the other hand, if His Apostles did not endeavor through every means possible to either record, or cause to be recorded, some of the words and the works of Jesus for posterity, then they must not have been sufficiently impressed to make the effort.

Not believing this to be true, one may rightfully assume that many of the gospels, Acts, etc., written in the early centuries, were actually copied from notes made by the Apostles and entitled accordingly. The main stream of the early century writings which followed the original Hebrew gospel of Matthew, the gospel of the Egyptians, and the gospel of the Twelve used by the Nazarenes and the Ebionites, included gospels of Peter, Andrew, Thomas, Philip, and the Acts of Peter, John, Andrew, Preaching of Peter, Protevangel of James, as well as Gospels of Bartholomew, Andrew and others used by the Gnostics. As was suggested before, the evidence points to the probability that these books were in some cases either copies of originals or gospels reconstructed through knowledge of such sources, even as were the Four Gospels that are now used by the church.

We find that these mostly no longer extant books were used, it seems, by the Nazarenes, Ebionites, Gnostics, Apostolics, Encratites, Manicheans, Turribins, Priscilianists, Origenians, Elkesaites, Montanists, Kathari, Marcionites, Cerdonians, Paulicians, Albigeois, Henrieans, and others.

The amazing and most enlightening observation to be made in this connection is that all of these Sects were strict abstainers from flesh-eating, holding it as evil to kill any living thing.

To further verify the true humanity of this Christ-honored principle, we find that the four great fathers of the early Roman Church—Tertullian, Clement of Alexandria, Origen, and St. John Chrysostum—knew of the sublimely ethical teachings of Jesus, for they not only abhorred the unholy practice of flesh-eating, but they also wrote extensively on the subject. Even Jerome, according to the tone of some of his critics, may also have been sympathetic in his private life.

This no doubt was the case of many of the early Church Fathers who had seen the original Apostolic writings. It might be said that some of them ate flesh only in public, to uphold the unfortunate position of church doctrine, while in their private lives they fasted and prayed to God for understanding. Thus we find the beginning of a later compromise between humane ethics and church doctrine, wherein abstinence becomes associated with penance, self-denial, mortification, etc.

It seems quite opportune to refer herein again to the saying of Jesus as was probably recorded in the original First Gospel used by his immediate followers: "He will not cease seeking until he finds; and when he finds he will be astonished."

The reader who has followed along with the author in his search for the truly "ethical Jesus" may begin to feel the force of these prophetic words.

The amazing thing is that practically all of the gospels and acts, written during the early centuries and bearing the names of the Apostles, were used exclusively by Christians who recognized in the character and practices of Jesus and his Apostles that the good life is a humane one; that purity of spirit demands purity of the whole body; that no man can ever be completely humane as long as he compromises his conscience with the horrors of the slaughter pen; that a body can never be both a tomb or a crematory for the corpses of dead animals and at the same time, a pure and holy temple wherein God may dwell.

Again, the amazing thing is that out of the seven or eight early Christian sects, it appears that only one of these was reluctant to give up the sacrifice of God's creatures for food. However, it is quite obvious in view of the fact that this surviving sect was rather violently separated into what are now over two hundred competing factions, that something of the original purity of the Primitive Church had been left behind and obscured from view.

Many Christians today look forward to the millennium: to a day when Christ will again return to found His kingdom upon the earth. But lest we deceive ourselves, His coming can only be in the moral and spiritual fulfillment of the Christ consciousness in man. Only as human nature progresses toward love in its "cosmic purity" will the wolf lie down with the lamb, will there be no more harm or hurt, and all men have full knowledge of the will of the Lord. It seems clear that where a world is lacking in love and consideration for any of its creatures, it will also be lacking in love and consideration for itself. Reverence for life begins at the bottom. It can never reach to its full height until it builds a kindly foundation to stand upon.

Christian ethics, therefore, can never become all-inclusive of "Christ" until they also become all-inclusive of "life." God is the living essence of a living universe: The cosmic Christ is the epitome of this same essence. Seek Him therefore not only through the love of man for man, but also through the love of God for all His creation. There only will you truly find Him.

*   *   *

In summarizing the many references in "Book One" pertaining to the uncertainties of the Gospel writings one is no longer reluctant to question either their accuracy or their completeness. In full accord with the last words of the Gospel of John: "there were many other things which Jesus did and said, which if we had records of them would fill many books," one can with the voluminous evidence now at hand begin to reconstruct in principle as well as with a considerable margin of fact much of the doctrine of the Master which is little known and untaught today.

Chapter Five

1 Martin A. Larson, The Religion of the Occident Philosophical Library, N. Y.

2 James Vernon Bartlet, M.A., The Apostolic Age. (Charles Scribner's Sons, N. Y.)

12

13

3 Rev. Adam Findlay, M.A., D.D., The Apocryphal Gospels from the History of Christianity in the Light of Modern Knowledge. (Harcourt Brace, N. Y.)

4 Hastings Encyclopedia of Religion and Ethics, V. 5, p. 143. (Charles Scribner, Sons, N. Y.)

5

6

9

10

11

7 Pliny "the younger" Gaius Plinius Secudus. 53-110 A. D. Governor of Bithynia under the Roman Emperor Trajan.

8 Encyclopedia Britannica, Vol. 2-p. 180, 11th Ed.

14 Edgar J. Goodspeed, Apostolic Fathers. (Harper Brothers, N. Y.)

15 Encyclopedia Britannica, Vol. 2, p. 204.

BOOK TWO

THE GOSPEL OF

THE COVENANT OF LOVE

FOREWORD

We are about to enter into the First Chapter of this Twentieth Century Gospel of Jesus Christ: a gospel based upon new evidence which seems to provide the long sought for environment favorable to the coming of the Lord Jesus Christ.

It is my fervent hope that what I have been privileged to write herein will go a long way towards strengthening the Christian's search within himself for the higher good. That this good does exist as a universal property apart from, as well as within, the scope of human behavior, is consistently illustrated herein by the sublimely humane character of the Son of Man.

I have written the following Gospel with a deep sense of having been directed to do so; probably by the same authority invested in the heart and soul of every man who would seek out the highest good, unhampered by the stringencies of custom and the dictates of his own sensual nature; that is, by the same authority of the "God within," who influences the writing of all that is morally and spiritually beneficial to mankind.

Those who read the Bible intelligently will find that many of the narratives therein were constructed to convey certain spiritual truths. It is not always necessary that they represent actual happenings. After all, words and phrases are merely symbols used to convey a message.

91

From the time that the first prophet set forth to preach, the favored means of teaching has been through allegory, or parable. Jesus himself originated many of the parables he used in his teaching to convey or stress certain moral or spiritual truths. The temptation of Jesus in the wilderness, as described in Matthew, is pure allegory. It illustrates Jesus as wrestling with a problem concerning only his own personal decision. In a similar allegory, the Jesus of the "Fifth Gospel" is portrayed. Also, in the accompanying commentary, the temptation of Jesus is again allegorically described, this time by the immortal Milton.

In the following Gospel the author makes use of the same privileges which were commonly used by the evangelists who wrote the traditional gospels. It was necessary in most instances for them to put words in Jesus' mouth to conform first, with their own manner of interpreting him and second, to convey certain sayings taken from an earlier gospel, or gospels, written in Aramaic.

In consequence, much of their original writings with certain exceptions followed quite closely the various experiences of the Master, copying and editing of later editions, notwithstanding. They not only recorded many of his actual sayings, but they also wrote down what he might have or would have said under certain circumstances.

The writer of this Twentieth Century version does a similar thing. Many of the speeches of Jesus herein set forth are supported in principle by historical reference, while others are from passages of scripture well known to Jesus. Under circumstances as herein described, Jesus could very well have spoken them. The same may be said for the speeches of John the Baptist. The historical evidence upon which this Gospel is founded seems to demand not only a more ethical interpretation of the things Jesus did and said, but also, that one contemplate in His nature the fullest of God's justice, mercy, and loving-kindness towards all creatures. In such a spirit only, can one recognize the Divine.

The many traditional acts and sayings of Jesus herein copied from the Four Gospels, as well as those which this writer finds necessary to either reconstruct or add to, may be considered by the reader as either historically valid or spiritually acceptable according to his own personal frame of thought.

With the probable exception of the symbolic or allegorical involvements of the first few chapters, much of the writings herein are founded upon documented historical evidence which seems to favor truth in principle as well as, to a large degree, in fact. However, since the entire scope of this gospel is concerned with spiritual truth, any other interpretation would be merely subordinate. In other words, since we are dealing with metaphysics, there seems to be only one pure truth: that which is manifested as the "all good." Thus, one might recognize various degrees of the good as extending from and through the lowest to the highest, or from the finite to the infinite.

In order to verify "truth," we first oppose it with "falseness," as we also verify "knowing" by opposing it with "ignorance." We recognize that falseness has an affinity for ignorance even as truth has an affinity for "knowing." In consequence, various degrees of "knowing" equal various degrees of truth even as various degrees of falseness equal various degrees of ignorance. The "all good" is therefore in the "all knowing." The various steps away from this infinite state are affected—or better to say, infected—by various degrees of falseness or ignorance. Thus it might be said that ill health is actually the result of our ignorance of natural prerogatives which are true. What we call "sin" or evil is ignorance of the good. Evil is therefore false, for it is opposed to truth, which exemplifies the all-good or the all-knowing.

When Thoreau said, "The only way to speak the truth is to speak lovingly," he recognized that truth in its pure essence parallels the all-good.

The all-good is therefore its own evidence of the nature

of God. In conformity, one might rightfully declare that any concept, written or oral, involving the nature of God, which violates this principle, may be considered both false in its construction as well as profane in its presentation.

In consequence, if Jesus was or is the true exemplification of divine consciousness—as the Christian believes— then He must necessarily have reflected the full and uncompromised nature of the all-good in His every act and deed.

In this connection it seems only fair, in consideration of the honor and integrity of the evangelists who wrote the gospels, to say that they, being human like ourselves, were subject to the same common frailties which sometimes take precedence over our better judgment. Indeed, one can readily understand through the medium of his own intimate experiences that good intentions do not always provide unblemished consequences.

The human minds of the gospel writers poured into their works all the enthusiasm and zeal a crusading evangelist is capable of. Their ambition was to convince the pagan community that Jesus Christ was vastly superior in every way to their traditional gods.

Hence, Jesus was made to snare tons of fish at the command of his voice; to cause a fig tree to wither and die with a barb from his tongue; to make a herd of swine rush madly into the sea with a nod of his head, and to turn gallons of water into barrels of wine with a wave of his hand.

Here it seems that the ambitious fire of the evangelists overcame their sense of moral equilibrium, and Jesus was made to do feats of magic which overwhelmed those of the pagan gods. In their enthusiasm, the writers completely lost sight of the extremely ethical and sublimely dignified character of Jesus—whom they otherwise referred to as humble, compassionate, pure, and completely free from any destructive thought or practice.

Realizing the contradictions which the construction of these narratives have unfortunately set up against the doctrine of the divinity of Jesus, Christian teachers have, down through the years, either avoided discussing them, or have attempted to explain them in a manner more fitting and proper to divine character.

However, after many centuries wherein both the silent as well as the outspoken protests of Christian teachers have resulted in compromise instead of decisive action it is now the purpose of the following gospel to correct rather than to compromise, to dignify the irreproachable through emphasizing the ethical rather than the sensational, thereby bringing the gospel narratives more sincerely into harmony with our new and more revealing evidence concerning the character of "the son of man."

Even though divinity in its purest state may transcend the comprehension of man it certainly cannot be less ethical, less honorable, less dignified and less consistent than it is characterized in the following gospel.

Those who consider the Lord Jesus Christ to be the epitome of all that is kind, merciful, just, humane, and good, will find herein the fulfillment of their trust. It is in full recognition of this, along with the purest evidence of God in man, that I now humbly present this Fifth Gospel of Jesus Christ, a gospel of the humane Christ, entitled The Covenant of Love.

*   *   *

"Howbeit when the Spirit of truth is come he will guide you into all truth; he shall glorify me for he shall receive of mine and show it unto you." (Jo. 16:13, 14)

THE COVENANT OF LOVE

CHAPTER I

The Creation and the Fall
The Divine Formula

1. God is the spirit and the flesh is of nature. God creates life and nature generates form. The law is of God and the means is of nature.

2. Thus the heavens and the earth came into existence. Thus were caused to grow upon the earth every green plant and every moving creature: And the will of God became the will to live in every living thing.

3. The Spirit of God and the means of nature selected and re-selected all manner of substances and forms and the body of man appeared. And God was pleased.

4. And man knew God, for out of His Spirit was he made.

5. And God gave man greater understanding than He gave the ape, even as He gave the ape g r e a t e r understanding than the ox, the ox greater than the fowls of the air and the fowls of the air greater than the fish of the sea; and He saw that this was good.

6. And God also gave man a greater power to choose and to reason that he might temper his superiority with consideration and kindness for those creatures beneath him.

7. He appointed man to rule in His place over all the living things of His creation. Thus were all creatures given into His care and mankind became the recipient of an unprecedented trust—a trust which bound the soul of man to God in mutual love and understanding.

8. And God said to man: "Behold! I have given you every herb bearing seed and every tree in the garden which is the fruit of the tree yielding seed; to you it shall be for meat." [1] Thus was the "Divine Formula" given to man.

9. And to every beast, fowl, and to everything that creepeth upon the earth gave He likewise these things for food.[2]

10. Thus did God prescribe the exact kind of nourishment to maintain the intricate mechanisms of flesh and bone, for He alone understood its exacting operation; He alone knew

[1-2] Gen. 1: 29-30.

the optimum requirements thereof for health, peace of mind, long life, dignity of spirit, knowledge, skill and understanding in all things. [3]

11. But alas! The flesh that was of nature became weak, and man soon lost his untarnished contact with the Divine.

12. The will of God was no longer obeyed. Divine principles were overcome by sensual desires, and the human will succumbed to a perverted power of choice.

13. The most sacred of trusts of all time was annulled by the lusts of appetite, and the blood of an innocent creature stained the hands of man.

14. The tree of life was rent with pain. Its leaves hung limp in sorrow its precious fruit fell to the ground in rot, and its stench deplored the sickening deed.

15. Fear and foreboding grasped the heart of every living creature. The bold became vicious and the meek fled in terror, and the carcasses of dead beasts became the abomination of carnal appetites.

16. Thus did the bold and the vicious fall, and the innocent suffer with the guilty.

17. But the fall of man was greater, for after the killing of his fellow creature did he slay his own brother.

CHAPTER II

The True God of Creation Succeeded by False Gods

1. Farther and farther man strayed from the truth of God. More and more did his power of choice become dominated by greeds and lusts. Weaker and weaker became his will to resist the cravings of the senses. Greater and greater grew the separation between the way of God and the way of man.

2. And the True Light was obscured by the denseness of man's own maleficent designs, and he no longer recognized the Divine presence.

3. Man thereafter began to invent his own god or gods. He created out of his own mind a creature equal to his wayward nature. He projected into cosmic dimensions his own emotional inconsistencies, his own lusts, desires, vanities, and passions, and considered them as an extraordinary means towards the fulfillment of his selfish ambitions.

4. He arranged a variety of lewd ceremonials and lurid dances to please the indulgence of a "sensuous God."

5. He spilled the blood of virgins, of children, and of the gentle lamb and the faithful ox upon the temple altars to satisfy a "lustful God."

6. He submitted to the ex-

[3] See Daniel 1:16, 17, also see Commentary Page 165.

travagances of the temple priests who provided spiritual remuneration in exchange for his material possessions. With hands soiled by the blood of war and coffers bulging with the loot of conquest, he stood before compromising authority and received the blessings of a "covetous God."

7. Dominating the bodies of thousands of sickening slaves, he constructed great temples of costly marble. Arraying himself in lavish costumes he knelt before glittering altars inlaid with gold and precious stones in a vain overture to a "pretentious god."

8. All these things had he done, and more, in accord with the god of his own invention: the god equal to his own lusts, customs, and practices. Thus, through man's own selfish conventions, has he recognized God.

9. For many centuries man's freedom of choice had been tolerated by the true God but too far had he strayed from the purity of his divine creation; too well had he clothed truth with falseness. Too long had the prophets cried out in vain. Too rudely had the Scribes and the mouthings of Priests made the laws of God of none effect.

10. "Our fathers have inherited naught but lies," cried Jeremiah; "worthless things in which there is no profit. Can man make for himself gods? Such are no gods: therefore, shall I make them know that I am the true God." *

11. And so it came to pass that upon a certain night and in a certain place, the spirit of the Most High came into the world.

12. He came not in the searing fire of retribution nor in the blinding light of fearful splendor surrounded by hosts of conquering angels; but, in the dim light of a single candle, among the humble and innocent creatures of His creation, came He.

CHAPTER III

God's Chosen Ones to Make Straight the Highway in the Desert

1. "When these men exist in Israel, these are the provisions whereby they are to be kept apart from any consort with froward men, to the end that they may indeed go into the wilderness to prepare the way; make straight in the desert a highway for our Lord." [1]

2. "Now the members of this community will be in all justice the witnesses of God's truth, and the 'elect' of His favor, effecting atonement for the earth." [2]

* Jer. 16: 19-21.
[1] From the Manual of Discipline, Dead Sea Scrolls.
[2] From Dead Sea Scrolls.

3. "Thou hast acted for thyself and for Thy glory and hast sent among mankind those to be schooled in Thy council.

4. "The seeds which these men sow shall yield a flower unfading. The twig shall put forth leaves, becoming an evergreen to give shade to all things. Its branches shall tower to heaven and the rivers of Eden shall water its boughs, and it shall thrive beyond all bounds, that all nations may know the truth and all peoples Thy glory." [3]

5. For many years these faithful souls had kept watch here in the desert for the coming of the Messiah, as Isaiah had foretold. They built in the wilderness a watch tower from which they scanned the heavens for a sign. They built assembly rooms to meet together and pray; they collected books and took from them knowledge that was of most benefit to their souls.

6. Now it came to pass that there should be among these "Chosen Ones" certain writers who were destined to select and to record a most subtle but particular code of learning.

7. Little did these men realize that the appointments of the "Anointed One" himself were being woven into the very words of their scripture.

8. Thus the hand of Providence wrote again, not on tab-lets of stone, but upon parchment scrolls, a message for the eyes of the only One who would understand their meaning: One who verily would read himself into the fulfillment of his own destiny.

9. "And Thou O God of mercy has in Thy bounty given me place among those to whom Thou art pledged. Thou hast chosen me and sent me unto them whom Thou hast made exemplars of men." [4]

10. Now it came to pass that the wicked king, Herod the great, had built his winter pleasure palace not far away, towards Jericho.

11. The intrusion of this alien spirit upon the sanctity of their holy ground caused them no little concern.

12. Oft-times the wind from the north carried boisterous sounds of riotous living to contaminate the serenity of their night watch, and they were sorely troubled.

13. Then it was so ordered that the "Chosen Ones" meet together in solemn assembly.

14. They pondered long and thoughtfully. "Why," they asked among themselves, "had God permitted this thing to be done? Why had Satan moved into this holy place in the wilderness? Had their fathers before them been mistaken? Was this not the area that God had appointed for His coming,

[3] Book of Hymns, Dead Sea Scrolls.
[4] Book of Hymns, Dead Sea Scrolls.

or was the time still not yet for his appearance?"

15. While these questions were still on their lips an earthquake came upon the world. The "Chosen Ones" fell upon the floor in fear. Great cracks appeared in the ground and darkness overcame the light of day. Then just as suddenly as the tumult had begun, all again became calm and the darkness moved on.

16. Surely this was God's answer to their questions, and they knelt down and praised His name.

17. Thereafter t h e y prepared to vacate their holy place. Some of the brethren returned to their people in Jericho and other towns of Judaea, some to Galilee, and others to a community called "Nazareth," after their own sect.

18. Now, there were a few among these "Chosen Ones" who saw in their exile from this holy place the will of God and his prophets. "I will cause you to go into exile beyond Damascus, out of Judea shall go forth a remnant."

19. Thou wilt raise a reviving for thy people and grant to Thine inheritance a remnant and refine them, and purge them of guilt. 5

CHAPTER IV

"And . . . they shall return to their desolate country and shall renew the house of the Lord." *

1. The better part of thirty-five years had passed and the little remnant that went into exile near Damascus had become burdened with years.

2. But it came to pass in their watch at night that the planets Jupiter and Saturn formed a fiery conjunction in the Zodiacal sign of Pisces.

3. And they glowed in full regal splendor and their position of alignment appeared to point south towards Jerusalem and Bethlehem.

4. The little group of pious souls fell to their knees and raised their hands to the heavens.

5. And then a voice spoke to the wisest among them, "you and your brethren are my Chosen Ones." Return in due time to the desert where the River Jordan spills its waters into the lifeless sea. There prepare you a place of learning, for one shall come among you in whom I am well pleased, but you shall know him not until his time is full well. Go ye in due time; make straight in the desert a highway for His coming.

6. And the little band of Holy Ones questioned these words a m o n g themselves:

5 Book of Hymns, Dead Sea Scrolls.
* Testament of Levi (Essene).

"What is the meaning of 'due time?'" "Surely," they reasoned, "not while the evil King Herod casts a sinful pall over the land."

7. Then the wisest among them said: "In due time is the Lord's time: We must maintain our trust in Him and keep our watch, for from the heaven we shall in due time receive our appointment."

8. And it came to pass that on a clear night in the month of March the moon in the heavens slowly began to disappear and its light faded and was no more. Then again it came forth even as it had faded and shone again with even greater brilliance.

9. This was indeed the awaited sign, for even as the light of the moon had faded, so had the life of the great King Herod. His passing had at last removed the pall of evil from the holy area of Qumran.

10. And the little band of Holy Ones set out on their long journey south, towards where the bright zodiac constellation of pisces (the fish)* had previously alerted them.

11. And the word went out to the brethren as they passed through Galilee and into Judea; and they came eager to be among those preparing the way in the desert.

12. And it came to pass that the building with the watch tower, on the shore of the sea where the River Jordan spills its water, was again inhabited.

13. The Holy Scriptures were again brought from the secret caves. A library, reading and study rooms were established, for it had been foretold that one, whose time was not yet, would find learning therein.

14. "For in the time of Thy good pleasure Thou wilt choose unto Thyself a people; and Thou wilt make them to be set apart unto Thee as an holy thing distinct from all the peoples; and Thou wilt renew Thy Covenant unto them with a show of glory, and with words of Thy holy spirit, with works of Thy hand, and with a script of Thy right hand, revealing unto them both the basic roots, of glory and the heights of eternity . . . and Thou wilt appoint for them a faithful shepherd, one who will (have mercy on) the lowly and (bring peace) to the (Kingdom of God)." *

CHAPTER V

The Conception and The Union of Mary and Joseph

1. God is Spirit, therefore does He create in spirit. The flesh is of nature, therefore does it generate in nature.

2. God creates life, for life is not a thing. A body without life is a thing, for things are generated from the earth and

* This later became the sign of the early Christians.
* From the New Covenant of the Dead Sea Scrolls.

so return to the earth. Life is created in God and so, unlike a thing, life returns to God.

3. God creates life and life organizes matter. Through this means does nature operate. The Spirit of God is in the co-operation of these interacting systems.

4. Wherever the flesh of nature is in harmony with the Spirit of God, there, also, is peace and well-being. But, wherever the flesh of nature is not harmonious with the Spirit of God, then fear and pain are the consequence.

5. The Spirit of God is at times more fully evident in man than in other creatures, even as His Spirit is more fully evident in some men than in other men.

6. In accord therewith, it came to pass that in a particular man the fullest measure of God's nature was to be revealed, and the Spirit of God and the flesh of nature fused, and a child was conceived in the womb of one blessed among women.

7. Soon, thereafter, was all mankind to know of the God of mercy, love and understanding; of the God of hope instead of despair; of forgiveness instead of vengeance; of life instead of death.

"Thou alone it is
That hath created the righteous One
Preparing Him from the womb
For the time of Thy good pleasure
To heed Thy covenant
And walk in Thy ways.
Thou hast lavished upon Him
The abundance of Thy mercies
And opened all of His soul
To everlasting salvation
Thou hast raised His inner glory out of the flesh." [1]

8. Now when the family of Mary learned that she was burdened with child they were filled with fear, for the law of the priests was strict to the utmost.

9. They sought the advice of Joseph of the forty-first generation of Abraham. In him they had complete faith and trust.

10. Upon witnessing the extreme radiance of the girl, Mary, Joseph was overcome with warmth of heart and spirit. Surely, he mused, a girl such as this must not fall victim of the laws of the Scribes and the Pharisees.

11. Joseph and the family talked long among themselves till darkness was great upon them. Joseph was tired out, even from his journey, so the parents of Mary showed him to his bed.

12. That night he had a dream. A voice said to him, "Hearken to the rod of the stem of Jesse, a branch of its roots is even now before your house: a child shall be born

[1] Book of Hymns, Dead Sea Scrolls.

even as Isaiah has prophesied. Through him God shall declare himself, and the spirit of the all-good shall be brought to witness in the flesh of man. Take Mary to wife and give praise to God for you are favored among men."

13. The next morning Mary and Joseph were in solemn agreement, and he went his way with joy in his heart.

CHAPTER VI

The Sheltering of Mary
Joseph Carries Her Away

1. Then Mary went off to the hill country to visit with her cousin, Elizabeth, the wife of Zacharias; and there was great confidence between Mary and Elizabeth, for she also was burdened with child.

2. Mary was in the house of Zacharias until the delivery of Elizabeth; then she, being quite burdened with child, returned to her own home.

3. Being foretold of Mary's condition, Joseph hurried to her side and prepared to take her away.

4. Even before the first cock crowed, Joseph entrusted his most precious burden to the back of a gentle ass, and they went on their way "unbeknownst."

CHAPTER VII

God's Lesson to Mankind
The Holy Spirit's First
Appearance Upon Earth
is Among Creatures Suffered
by the Hurts of Man.

1. The glorious rays of a setting sun bathed the little town of Bethlehem in a warm glow, and the blessings of God were upon two lonely travelers.

2. The town this day was full of people, and it was said that there was no room at the inn. Even so, Joseph was in the home country of his fathers before him, and he was possessed of means which bring ready favor.

3. But even as he and the innkeeper b a r t e r e d, Mary walked quietly towards the rear of the place.

4. Hurriedly Joseph sought to restrain her, not knowing that the hand of God was leading her on towards a place where bedded the lamb, the ox, and the ass.

5. And Joseph was amazed that Mary sought this place, but he bowed his head as Mary whispered softly, "God wills it so."

6. And it came to pass that, in a stable among the innocent creatures of God's creation, a child was born.

7. And they wrapped him in soft cloths and laid him in a bed of hay: in a manger warmed by the gentle breath of the ass and the ox they laid him.

8. Now a caravan bearing three holy men from the east arrived as the conjunction of Mercury and Jupiter cast shafts of light upon the holy place.

9. They were poor in things, but rich in the wealth of God. Thus were they wise.

10. And they saw in the child the grace of God, for the whole of nature round about was at peace.

11. The ass, the ox, the she goat with her kid, the ewe with her little one, stood silently by. An old mother hen clucked softly as she nestled her chicks neath her wing: Creatures all, in trusting communion with the Spirit of pure love and mercy, for this night the highest recognized the lowest and all nature rejoiced.

12. "The wolf also shall dwell with the lamb and the leopard shall lie down with the kid, and the calf and the young lion and the fatling together, and a little child shall lead them." [1]

13. Thus God brought to the witness of man that His love was for *all* His creation, for on this momentous occasion he selected a place that sheltered the lowly—the innocent creatures of His kingdom — to bring forth His spirit in the flesh of man.

14. And the three wise men bowed down, for a great reverence for all life was upon them, and they understood.

"And the pangs of travail set in

New life is coming to birth as at last there enters the world the man-child long conceived." [2]

CHAPTER VIII
The Boy Jesus

1. There were three sects residing in all Judea: the Sadducees, the Pharisees, and the Essenes—or "Holy Ones."

2. Now these "Holy Ones" differed from the other sects. Unlike the Sadducees, they worshipped God, and unlike the Pharisees, they denounced animal sacrifice as the Prophets had done before them.

3. They were known as "the Saints," the "Pious Ones," the "Poor," the "Chosen Ones," the "Elect," and the "Messianists" — from which comes the ordinary oriental word, "Nasara."

4. Now a short distance west of the mountain known as Tabor, there came to be a settlement of Messianists, and their community was called "Nasarath." Thus was Jesus to become known as a Nazarene, as the prophets had foretold.

[1] Isaiah 2:6.
[2] From Essene Scriptures.

5. Here in "Nasarath," the boy Jesus grew strong and beautiful in body even as he was in spirit. He was eager to learn about the world and had a keen interest in nature.

6. Many times he walked alone to the brow of the hill that looked out across the valley towards the distant mountains, and there He would meditate.

7. He loved nature, and all creatures were His friends. The little wild animals and the doves ate crumbs from His hand, for He was at peace with all life even as He was at peace with the Father of it all.

8. The boy Jesus was an apt student, studying the available literature of the world as well as memorizing the teachings of Moses and the Prophets. In the little village synagogue, he sat attentively listening to the reading of scripture, and he looked forward to the time when he too might stand before his brethren and expound the law and the prophets.

9. Now "Nasarath" (or Nazareth) was on the trade routes from the South and the East. Caravans carrying rich wares and travelers from Egypt, Persia, and India paused there to rest.

10. Young Jesus w a l k e d among the travelers and talked with those who had knowledge. He learned of the great healing powers of the Therapeutae in Egypt, of the ethics of Confucius, Buddha, and other profound mystics of the East, and he felt at peace with the words of these great teachers.

11. He mingled with the caravans arriving from Ptolemais, carrying travelers from Achaia and Macedonia, and learned of the Greek philosophers. He was deeply impressed by the sublimely ethical teachings of Pythagoras, and he compared them with the words of the prophets and the customs of his own sect.

12. The boy Jesus longed to see some of the outside world, and so it came about that his parents took him on the long five-day journey to Jerusalem, for Joseph had business of his father's to attend to in Bethlehem, just south of the walled city.

13. Being of the sect of the "Holy Ones," they were excluded from the temple worship but celebrated the feast of the unleavened bread in a neighborhood synagogue.

14. It was here that the boy Jesus astounded the learned doctors with his knowledge of the scriptures.

15. And when Joseph admonished him for causing such delay, for he had business to attend to in Bethlehem Jesus answered, "But I am about my Father's business who is in Heaven."

16. Whereupon Joseph and Mary looked understandingly at each other and Mary put

her arm around the boy; and they went on their way.

CHAPTER IX

The Conception of John the Baptist

His Childhood Tormentors and His Parents' Extreme Act of Devotion

1. It happened during the reign of Herod, King of Judea, that a certain priest named Zacharias was away from his wife Elizabeth, doing priestly duty, as was his custom at the temple.

2. During his time of prayer, he would often feel deep within his own heart the longings of his wife Elizabeth, for they were growing in years and were still without child.

3. And it came to pass while Zacharias was away about his duties that word came whispered in his ear that Elizabeth had conceived, that even now her womb was blessed with child.

4. Now Zacharias was a man of wisdom and spoke not when questioned of this thing, but straight away did he go to the side of his wife.

5. Upon seeing the light of motherhood in her eyes, a deep understanding came upon him, for was this not the fulfillment of their prayers?

6. And Zacharias spoke not a word lest he might speak an offense to God.

7. Then did Elizabeth hide herself five months to avoid re-proach among men, but still Zacharias did not speak out to those who questioned.

8. Now the time was at hand for delivery and Elizabeth brought forth a son.

9. On the eighth day they came to circumcize the boy and to name him after the name of Zacharias. But Elizabeth said, not so; he shall be named John.

10. And they said there is none of the family named John. Turning to Zacharias they said, "Is this so?"

11. Then did Zacharias speak out in answer to their questions.

"Let it be known among you that I speak in faith and trust and without reproach, for God has answered our prayers and brought unto us a son. In His name do we rejoice and of His will do we call the boy John."

12. Now they were all confounded and spoke in question even though they feared to doubt. And all their sayings were noised abroad and there was much loose talk even as there was much wonder and reverence round about.

13. At the time of his birth, the infant John was pledged by his parents to the ways of the Nazarenes, for strict were they in virtue.

14. The years, about ten, had passed and the child John was even now highly sensitive to the waywardness of human conduct.

15. The neighborhood chil-

dren reproached him and called him unkind names, and he began to draw away and wander alone on the hillside.

16. With deep concern the watchful eye of Elizabeth observed these things, and she took her son aside and spoke earnestly to him.

17. "Your father and your mother are they that love you even as your Father in Heaven loves you. Love needs not the ties of blood nor the bonds of flesh. Through your spirit only does love find witness, for both your spirit, and the love it affords, are of God. But vain mouthings and corrupt practices are of the flesh and know not of God; therefore they know not of love. He who lives in love, lives with God, but he who lives for the flesh, perishes with the flesh."

18. Greatly disturbed, Elizabeth that night counseled with her husband, Zacharias. Kneeling in prayer, they saw through the eyes of their mind the finger of the Lord pointing towards the desert.

CHAPTER X
The Holy Ones

1. Now in those days when one spoke of being in the desert he meant he had visited at the "Holy of Holies," in the desert by the shores of the Dead Sea.

2. Here, surrounded on three sides by desert wilderness, was a monastery where lived those chosen from among the most learned of Judea's Sons of Peace.

3. Here they worked, prayed, studied the sacred writings, and kept constant watch for the appearance of the Messiah, as Isaiah had foretold.

4. Here also, came those of the sect to be prepared to expound the scriptures in the synagogues.

5. They knew that the Law of Moses had been falsely interpreted by the Scribes, and that the priestly code was made to do service for the Temple authorities.

6. Having had knowledge of the true God of love, they, unlike the Pharisees, practiced not the merciless ritual of animal sacrifice. Neither did they spill the blood of innocent creatures to feast upon their flesh. Their food, therefore, was pure, innocent, and strictly in accord with the "Divine Formula" of Genesis.

7. Thus did they grow strong and pure in mind and body, even as Daniel and his brethren. Thus did they average over a hundred in years, and were blessed with wisdom.

8. Now it was the practice of these humble souls to receive at the monastry exceptional children of the brethren and raise them in full knowledge of God.

9. It was here, in sincere devotion to God and the welfare of their son, that Elizabeth and Zacharias entered into

agreement that their son might be among those preparing the way in the desert for the coming of the Lord.

10. It was here that the boy grew and waxed strong in spirit. It was here that "he was in the deserts till the day of his shewing into Israel." (Luke 1:80)

CHAPTER XI
The Baptist Admonishes the Multitude
The Baptism of Jesus

1. As it is written in the book of Isaiah, the voice of one crying in the wilderness, Prepare ye the way for the Lord. The crooked shall be made straight, and the rough ways, the selfish merciless ways, shall be made smooth and all flesh (all creatures)* shall see the salvation and shall know the love and mercy of God. [1]

"So am I come to know
that in Thy loving kindness
lies hope for them that repent:
And for them that abandon sin
Thou bestowest freely Thy love
Therefore though people roar
though kingdoms rage
I shall not be dismayed
knowing that in a space

Thou will grant Thine inheritance
and all the sons of evil will be no more." **

2. The blue of the heavens rolled forth in undraped splendor as a God-inspired teacher stood waist-deep in the waters of the Jordan, exhorting all man to repent of their sins and to come forth and cleanse the temple of their soul.

3. And it so happened that as the people gathered on the river bank, a taunting voice called out, "Rabbi, why not first baptize yourself?" Whereupon a ripple of laughter was heard in the crowd.

4. John stood quietly as his eyes sought out the reviling one. Recalling for a brief moment the tormentors of his youth, he looked upon them with mingled pity and contempt.

5. And then in a clear ringing voice he tore asunder their false veil of vanity and laid bare their abominations.

6. Oh ye generation of vipers* who hath given warning of the day of your retribution. Dare you to come in jest to lay your sins at the feet of your God? What fruit have you brought forth? None but of the seeds of lust. The living tree have you hacked to the ground. Its roots laid you

---

* All flesh, all creatures that are of flesh.
[1] Paraphrased from Luke 3: 4-5-6.
** Selected from the Book of Hymns, Dead Sea Scrolls.
* See Commentary p. 201.

bare to the suffering winds.

7. From your fingertips drips the blood of innocents. Now come you to cleanse your conscience of greed and shame, but I say to you, cleanse first the temple of your soul that God might see fit to dwell therein. Cease more to make the sanctuary of your God a tomb for corpses.

8. Hearken not to the temple priests for 'twas they who slew the prophets. Look you instead to the voice of God through his servant who says, "I am full of your burnt offerings of rams, and the fat of fed beasts; and I delight not in the blood of bullocks, or of lambs, or of he goats.

9. When you come to appear before me, who hath required this at your hand? Your new moons and your appointed feasts, my soul hateth: they are a trouble unto me; I am weary to bear them:

10. When ye spread forth your hands, I will hide mine eyes from you: Yea, when you make many prayers, I will hear not: *Your hands are full of blood.*" * 1

11. It profits you little to baptize the body from without as long as it houses the stench of dead things within.

12. Go ye therefore and fast ten days. Make not a sacrifice in the temple but "make" thanksgiving your sacrifice to God." 2

13. There were loud protestings among the multitude. Some turned and went their way, while others lingered to be further instructed.

14. Some who had strayed from the ways of the brethren came forward and were baptized. Others, asking questions, said, "but the Law of Moses gives to us the flesh of creatures to eat; does it not?" And John answered them saying:

15. "Moses said of your fathers, 'I am unable to bear all these people alone for they lusteth for flesh.' And God gave them flesh till it stank in their nostrils, and he sent a wasting disease among them and they fell by the thousands." 3

16. Nowhere is it written that God gave his blessing to the eating of flesh unless His word was falsified.

17. "Our fathers have inherited nought but lies, worthless things in which there is no profit. How can we say we are wise and the law of the Lord is with us, for behold, the false pen of the Scribes have made it into a lie." 4

18. God commanded, "Thou shalt not kill." "He that kills an ox is as if he slew a man." 5

1 Isaiah 1: 11-16.
2 Psalms 50: 13, 14.
3 Num. 11: 13-14-33 P. 106: 13-15.
4 Jer. 818, 16: 19.
5 Isaiah 66: 3.

19. Kill is to an animal as murder is to a man, therefore to kill is to murder, and to murder is to kill; so says the Lord God through the voice of His prophet.

20. Cease more to do evil. Love thy neighbor. Lust not for anything that God has not commanded. Take pleasure in nothing but the will of God. Keep His commandments, not through the lusts of your appetites, but through the righteousness of your heart.

21. Then spoke one dressed in the garb of the military. "Rabbi, what you say may be well for priests and holy men, but what of me? I am a soldier."

22. And he said to him: "The voice of God would speak within you, but you hear him not through the thickness of your breastplate. Your armor and sword are not the means to proclaim His glory. Seek first His Kingdom, and your bonds and shackles shall fall away. For to know His love is to extend His mercy and loving kindness in all the earth. Peace can never come by the sword: peace to your brother or peace in your own heart. Therefore, "do violence to no man." Heed your conscience for it should you obey over the commands of men.

23. But r e m e m b e r this thing: You cannot serve two masters. If your allegiance be to Caesar, then your honor among men is sustained by the faithfulness of your service to him:

24. But if your allegiance be to God and His everlasting glory, then your honor transcends the institutions of men and becomes worthy of His Kingdom, which is even now close at hand.

25. Therefore I say to you: Repent, and renew in truth God's everlasting covenant.

26. And the soldier went off a little way and sat down alone by the waters, and deep was his meditation.

27. And John turned again to those before him, saying: Sink to your knees and hide your face in your hands, for even now, One is at hand who shall speak with far greater authority than I.

28. Listen, for I bring to you the voice of the Prophet Isaiah, saying: "The Lord Himself shall bear you a sign: Behold, a virgin has conceived, and borne a son, who shall be called Emanuel. Curds and honey shall *he eat*, that he should know to refuse the evil and choose the good." *

29. Then forth came One whose white linen garment and long hair to his shoulders were like those of the Holy Ones who dwelt in the desert by the lifeless sea.

30. Slowly he walked into the water waist deep beside

* Isaiah 7: 11-15 R.S.V.

John. Then spoke John: "Why do you come to me for baptism? It is *I*, by your hand, should be made clean.

31. Are you the One who comes before, or are you the "anointed one"?

32. Then the voice of him who was born in a stable where bedded the lamb, the calfling, and the ox, spoke softly.

33. "John, you know me for whom I am even as you know yourself for whom you are. To the people you have already spoken, but I have yet to speak. But who are those to believe our report, and to whom shall the arm of the Lord be revealed?

34. "You proclaim the New Covenant of the 'Elect,' but by your hand henceforth am I the evidence of that Covenant."

35. And a dove flew low over His head, and a voice seemed to say: "My covenant is your covenant: Blessed shall be those who heed your calling."

36. Then Jesus was baptized and straight away to the wilderness did He go.

CHAPTER XII
The Temptation

1. For forty days and forty nights did he remain in solitude, with only the companionship of a few lesser creatures of the ground and of the air. By day he wandered over the barren hills, and by night the silent splendor of heaven com-forted him with its soft light, and he felt not alone.

2. Through the long nights he prayed, and at times he sat by a fire kindled out of dried things, pondering the words of the Baptist which were still full in his ears.

3. It was one of these nights as he sat in deep meditation, staring into the glowing embers, that a familiar sound came upon his ears. He stood up and called softly in the direction of the sound.

4. Thereupon the form of a lamb appeared out of the darkness. Slowly it came to him, and he gathered it—hungry and cold — into his arms. Gently, he comforted it, and the wanderer was at peace.

5. Jesus sat and gazed into the dancing flames. For forty days had he fasted, and great was his hunger. And now the flames seemed to take the form of a fiend, holding out before him those things for which men lust.

6. The taunting odor of roasted flesh came to his nostrils. On the fire he could see the tempting morsel.

7. A low cunning voice seemed to say, "You have the lamb and the fire is hot; why do you hesitate? Kill and eat that you may rejoice with me, for tomorrow is another day and fullness thereof shall be of thy choosing.

8. "For even the prophet sayeth, 'Behold, joy and gladness, slaying oxen and killing sheep, eating flesh and drink-

ing wine, let us eat, drink and be merry for tomorrow we shall die.' " [1]

9. Then spoke Jesus: "Satan, you would trick me, for of this did the prophet also declare: 'Surely this iniquity shall not be purged from you till ye die.' " [1]

10. Therefore such a tomorrow is of your choosing and not of mine.

The iniquity of the day is by your hand and by your death is its purge.

11. But the hand of God purges not. In Him there is no iniquity. In Him there is no death.

12. And the spirit of evil was set back by the words of Jesus, but he c u n n i n g l y awaited his time in silence.

13. Again spoke Jesus: "Oh Fiend, what say you of God's commandment as confirmed by the voice of His prophet Isaiah? 'He who kills one of God's creatures is the same as if he murders a man.' " [2]

14. Now here was Satan's chance to confound Jesus, saying: "The lusts are of the flesh, appetites and strong drinks are rewards of the day.

15. "Is man not to have his just desires? Does not one kill for the rights of his law, and for the glory of his conquest?

16. "How be it 'tis written that your God gave unto the sword, the enemies of Israel?

Did not David kill Goliath for the honor of his people?

17. "Is it less righteous to murder for honor's sake than to kill for the meat of your table?

18. "Does the temple priest do worse when he prays on the life of the lamb he sacrifices, or the master of the feast when he asks the grace over its charred remains?

19. "Is it not custom that even God's emissaries be clothed in the uniforms of soldiers?

20. "Do not the religious among men pray for the victory that requires of their sons to kill the sons of others?

21. "If all these are condoned by your God, why should you not rejoice with me?"

22. Then said Jesus, "Get thee hence, Satan, for you confess things not of God, but things that are of men.

23. They worship falsely and know not the sorrow of my Father."

24. Holding the lamb close to His breast, He arose and turned His face t o w a r d Heaven, saying: "Deliver me from blood guiltiness, Oh God, Thou God of my salvation; and my tongue shall sing forth thy praise." [3]

25. And Satan turned his back: In desperation he cunningly garbed his next appeal in the cloak of prophesy.

[1] Isaiah 22: 13-14.
[2] Isaiah 66: 3.
[3] Psalm 51:14.

26. Said he, "Are you not of the branch of the stem of David? Is it not prophesied that you shall restore Israel to the Jews and be their king?

27. "Therefore, as the voice of prophesy has so singled you out, your destiny cannot be denied.

Take my sword forged of the finest steel and claim your Estate. All the enemies of Israel shall fall before you.

28. "Even Rome shall be your slave and you shall sit upon a throne of gold and silken cloth, and all men shall scrape their foreheads in the dust before your feet."

29. For a moment Jesus turned away in silence as He weighed the crafty words of the Prince of Darkness. Then he faced His tormentor saying: "Satan, you speak with forked tongue, but of this one thing do you speak the truth: The sword is indeed your creation; it exemplifies your curse in the affairs of men. It wins men's obedience, but not men's hearts.

30. "Men's hearts are won not by violence but only through love, mercy, and understanding.

31. "My kingdom shall not be gained through violence; nor will I sit on a throne fashioned by the lusts of conquest,

32. "But upon a footstool fashioned by the pure in heart will I sit."

33. Then Satan threw his cloak over his shoulder and slipped off into the night.

34. The fire flickered and burned out, and the glorious light of a star-filled sky focused its glow upon the Son of Man.

35. And a voice grew loud within Him, saying: "You are truly of Me, go forth and bring the evidence of My Being to all mankind.

36. "Tell them that they interpret me falsely: that I seek not revenge, but am merciful, just, honorable, and trustworthy: that my character is one of love, compassion, and understanding: that I am truth personified, therefore I can not be compromised by the inconsistencies of men.

37. "Tell them that 'all of the fowls of the mountains, and all of the creatures of the fields are mine: that I will not eat the flesh or drink the blood of any of my creatures.' [4]

38. "As thou art of Me, tell them to be like Me also, for I desire mercy and loving kindness for all the innocents of my creation.

39. "Do these things in my name 'and thy glory shall be made known, and thy wonders told forth in all thine unerring works, that thy righteousness may be proclaimed and thy name be praised in the *mouths of all things*, and that *all crea-*

---

[4] Psalm 50: 10-13.

tures may know Thee each to the (meed of his insight)* and bless Thee always.' " [5]

40. "And you, My Son, shall be even as I, and all life shall know you as the Prince of Peace."

CHAPTER XIII
Jesus Becomes Aware of His Mission

1. Thereafter Jesus went on towards Galilee, making note of the ways of the people as He went.

2. He well knew by now His appointed mission, for in Him was entrusted the pure and unblighted spirit of Love.

3. Well he knew that only through extending mercy and compassion towards all of God's creatures could the full realization of love be enjoyed by man; that only then could the God of love replace the false gods of human invention. Thus did Jesus set about to save man from himself.

4. And Jesus went into Jericho and took the road through Salim, and Scythopolis to 'Nasara,' or Nazareth.

5. Here he was at home among His Nazarene brethren for they knew Him as the son of Joseph and Mary.

6. Having attained his thirtieth year, according to the laws of the "holy of holies," He was well qualified to lead the Sabbath services in the village synagogue.

7. It was here upon the Sabbath day that Jesus took up the book of Isaiah and read:

8. "The Spirit of the Lord is upon me, because He hath anointed me to preach the gospel to the 'poor';* He hath sent me to heal the brokenhearted, to preach deliverance to the captives, . . . and set at liberty them that are abused: To preach the acceptable year of the Lord." [1]

9. "And the eyes of all them that were in the synagogue were fastened on Him. And he began to say unto them, "This day is this scripture fulfilled in your ears.'

10. "And all bare him witness and wondered at the gracious words which proceeded out of His mouth," for they alone were the sect of the "poor" who were expecting the coming of the Messiah.

11. But little did even these chosen ones know that Jesus, the son of Joseph the village carpenter, was the one in whom God was well pleased. Jesus had always been a faultless young man, they said, but now he has taken it on to himself to speak in error.

12. So t h e y admonished Him and led Him from the synagogue. Whereupon He

---

* A creature's worth of discerning through its inner nature.
[5] From the Book of Hymns, Dead Sea Scrolls.
* The Essenes were known as the "poor" Heb. *ebionim*.
[1] Luke 4: 18-21.

turned to them and said: "Verily I say to you no prophet is accepted in his own country."

13. You look for one to come in glory with a host of angels from Heaven, but the son of man was born in a stable; therefore, you know him not.

14. Then turning His face towards the Heavens he continued, "Behold for mine own part I have reached the inner vision; I have heard Thy wondrous secret through Thy mystic insight. Thou hast caused a spring of knowledge to well up within me: a fountain of strength pouring forth waters unstinted in loving kindness.

15. "Through me thou has kept Thy pledge. All them that challenge me Thou makest to stand rebuked, distinguishing *through me* the right from the wrong." [2]

16. And then He passed through the midst of them and went on His way.

17. Leaving Nazareth, He came to dwell in Capernaum, which is upon the sea coast in the borders of Zabulon and Nephthalim: even as the prophet Isaiah had written.

18. From that time, Jesus **began to preach and to say,** "Repent of your sins, cleanse the blood from your hands, for the Kingdom of Heaven is at hand."

CHAPTER XIV

The Parable as a Lesson to the Fishermen—

Jesus Admonishes Them and Bids Them "Follow Me"

1. "Thou didst put Me in a dwelling with many fishermen, spreaders of nets on the face of the water, as hunters for the sons of error; and there for judgment thou didst make strong in my heart." [*]

2. And Jesus went down by the shore of the lake and He saw the ships standing by.

3. He went into the ship where sat Simon Peter, looking downcast; and Jesus asked him why he was so.

4. "Simon answered Him saying, 'We have toiled all night and have nothing.'" [1]

5. Jesus stood for a while looking deep into the soul of Simon, saying: listen to the parable of the fisherman.

6. There was a man who had traveled far and wide seeking for a sign from God, but not finding it he returned to his former endeavors as a fisherman. All through the long nights he toiled but his luck was poor and he was sorely tried.

7. Then a voice spoke to him. "Cast out into deeper water and again let down your nets for a draught.

8. "And when he did this, his nets enclosed a great

[2] Book of Hymns, Dead Sea Scrolls.
[*] Essene Scriptures.
[1] Luke 5: 5-8.

multitude of fishes: and they broke." [2]

9. And the man wondered why this should be, for his nets were strong enough to hold twice the weight.

10. "And he beckoned to his partners which were on other ships to come and help them.

11. "And they came and filled both ships so full they began to sink." [3] Frantically they labored to throw the fish back into the water, but still the ships continued to sink.

12. In panic the man fell to his knees saying, "Forgive me O Lord I am a sinful man." [4] Long have I denied Thee but henceforth will I do thy will and follow thee.

13. Meanwhile James, John and Andrew had gathered around to listen to the parable but they understood not.

14. Then Jesus reproached them by saying: Must ye also look for a sign. Know you not it is contrary to the pleasure of God for one to take the all out of life while putting nothing back into it again?

15. Man should not live at the expense of the harm and hurt of the other creatures of the kingdom. He was not made out of the sperm of a parasite but out of the spirit of God was he made. "Follow me and I will make you fishers of men."

16. And they forsook all and followed Him, for even though they had been delinquent as Essenes, they, unlike the Sad-

2 3 4 Luke 5:5-8.

ducees and Pharisees, were actually expecting the appearance of the "Anointed One."

CHAPTER XV
Jesus Preaches the Love of God in All Things He Sits at the Table With Sinners

1. And Jesus went about Galilee, speaking to the people; and many came to Him who were sick and sorely troubled, and He ministered unto them.

2. And they were amazed and took on new hope as they began to realize that life and love were of God Himself: that to love all life was to love God and to share in the fruits thereof.

3. The truth of His Words and deeds spread from Galilee to Judea and beyond the Jordan, and many people sought Him out.

4. "As Jesus passed on from there He saw a man called Matthew sitting at the tax office; and he said to him, 'Follow me.'

5. And as they sat at a table in the house, behold, many tax collectors and sinners came and sat down with Jesus and His disciples.

6. And when the Pharisees saw this they said to His disciples, "Why does your teacher eat with tax collectors and sinners?"

7. But when Jesus heard it He said, 'Those who are well have no need of a physician,

but only those who are sick.'

8. Go and learn what this means: 'I desire mercy and not sacrifice," (Matt. 9:9-13) "the knowledge of God more than burnt offerings." *

9. If you have no knowledge of this, then you too should sit down beside us, for I came not to call the righteous, but sinners.

CHAPTER XVI
The Sermon on the Mount

"In the mouth of Thy Servant Thou didst open as it were a fount as a wellspring of truth, as a herald of Thy good tidings bringing cheer to the humble, blessings to the wounded in spirit, and joy everlasting to those that mourn." [1]

> But the meek shall inherit the earth and shall delight themselves in the abundance of peace.[2]

1. Jesus retired from the multitude with His disciples up into a mountain, and He sat down and spoke to His disciples and taught them the full meaning of love, for of such is our Father in Heaven.

2. "The Spirit of the Lord God is upon me to bring good tidings to the afflicted. He has sent me to bind up the brokenhearted, to proclaim liberty to the captives, and to release all who are in bond, to proclaim God's favor and to comfort all who mourn." [3]

3. Despair not if men shall revile you for speaking the words I teach you, for this the prophets were persecuted before me.

4. Blessed are the peacemakers (pacifists), for they shall be called the children of God.

5. Blessed are they that are persecuted for righteousness sake for theirs is the Kingdom of Heaven.

6. Blessed are they which do *hunger and thirst* for righteousness sake, for they shall be filled.

7. Blessed are the merciful: for they shall receive mercy.

8. Blessed are the pure in heart, for they shall know God.

9. Blessed are the humble, for they shall inherit all knowledge.

Blessed are the "poor" in spirit: for theirs is the Kingdom of Heaven.

Blessed are they that mourn: for they shall be comforted.

10. You are the salt of the earth: Your savor is your good works; lose it not lest it be trodden under the foot of men.

11. You are the light of the world. A city that is set on an hill cannot be hid.

12. Put not your candle under a basket and hide not your good works which glorify

---

* Hosea 6:6 Micah 6:6, Prov. 21:3-15-8, Jer: 7-21.
[1] The Book of Hymns, Dead Sea Scrolls.
[2] Psalms 37: 11, Dead Sea Scrolls.
[3] Isaiah 61: 1-2.

your Father which is in Heaven.

13. Think not that I am come to destroy the law, and the Prophets, I come not to destroy but to fulfill the Prophets, for through Me shall Heaven and earth be joined in a New Covenant.

14. Whosoever shall break one of these Commandments and shall teach men otherwise, he shall be called the least in the Kingdom of Heaven.

15. For I say unto you that except your righteousness shall exceed the teachings and customs of the Pharisees and the Sadducees, you shall in no case enter into the Kingdom of Heaven.

16. For you have heard it said by them of old time, "Thou shalt not kill," but I say to you: He who kills by choice, or he that is forced to kill and repents not, is in danger of the judgment.

17. Lest you be opinioned otherwise, to kill is to take a life whether it be of man or creature, so sayeth the Father through the mouth of His prophet Isaiah. [4]

18. Therefore I say to you: Strike down not a living creature lest you strike the hand of Him who created it.

19. "The righteous man regards the life of his fellow creature, but the mercies of the wicked are cruel." [5]

20. You have heard it said by them of old times: "Thou shalt not forswear thyself." But I say unto you, Swear not at all; neither by Heaven, nor by the earth, nor by the province of the King. Say you yea, or nay; whatsoever is more than these intimates your integrity, for no honorable man stoops to falsehood.

21. You have heard that it has been said, "An eye for an eye and a tooth for a tooth." But I say to you, Evil begets evil: one harm cannot be righted by another hurt.

22. The bitterness of remorse lingers long after the sweetness of revenge, for the rusty blade of retribution contains no oil to heal the wound.

23. Therefore I say to you, Love your enemies, bless them that curse you; do good to them that hate you and to those who persecute you.

24. Love is not only for those that love you, for if you salute only your brethren, then you love not as God but as a publican.

25. God makes the sun to rise and the rain to fall on both the just and the unjust, but where love abides, barren fields blossom, and the bitter becomes sweet to the taste.

26. Love your servant and he shall be worthy of his hire.

27. Let no man set forth his brother, his son, or his daughter in bond with another

[4] Isaiah 66:3.
[5] Prov. 12-10, beast instead of fellow creature.

for the payment of a debt. If the debt be just, so should also be the conscience of the debtor.

28. Let no man take unto himself a hireling and pay him not the worth of his day: neither shall a man, by force or guile, require his brother to serve him against his own good fortune or his own free will.

29. Verily, I say unto you: The peace and contentment of one creature reflects the love and compassion of another.

30. Dwell ye all therefore within the bounds of God's love; bring cheer to the careworn and the helpless; give to the needy; pity the wayward; succor the sick; give counsel to those who seek it; sympathize with those who sorrow; seek understanding with all men, and extend loving kindness to the innocents of God's creation.

31. Take heed that you do not give alms before men. Sound not a trumpet before you that you may have the glory of men, for in this your reward is on earth.

32. Let not your left hand know what your right hand does, that your alms might be in secret; then only your Father in Heaven shall know your secret and reward you openly.

33. And finally; Give your alms with the same wisdom that you would your counsel.

34. Isaiah sayeth, "He who sacrifices a lamb is as if he slays his dog." * Therefore, make not the blood of a lamb a sacrifice to God. This the Pharisees do. By the sweat of your brow, lay your offering before the altar. Inasmuch as the forfeit be your own and not the lamb's, so shall the reward be yours also.

35. It was written in the law by those of old time: If a bird nests its young in a tree or on the ground in the way of your work, thou shalt scare away the mother and take her young unto your own care. [6]

36. But I say to you: If a bird nests its young in a tree or on the ground in the way of your work, disturb it not. Do your work elsewhere till the young have flown and the nest is left vacant.

37. All creatures are of my Father, even the birds, for it was from the breast of a dove that He revealed His Spirit to me.

38. All flesh shall see the salvation of God, said Isaiah: all have equal rights to His green earth even as you have likewise.

39. There is nothing beneath the Father more sacred than the delivery into this world of a new life, whether it be your own or one of God's lesser creatures.

40. Second only to this is the loving and devoted care of

[6] Deut. 22: 6-7.
* Isaiah 66:3.

a mother for her young.

41. Regard you therefore these things: Revere all life and your own ways shall be made more beautiful.

42. Verily, I say to you: It is folly to expect consideration from the highest of the High if you extend it not to the lowest of the low.

"What ye sow so shall ye also reap," was not spoken in jest.

43. And when you pray, pray not in the temple where others may see you pray; for then your reward is only in your show before men.

44. But when you pray enter into the silence of your chamber, close the door, and in the solitude of your own heart, commune with the Father, and He shall hear you in secret and reward you with His blessing.

45. And when you pray, use not vain repetitions: for true meaning is lost in familiar recitation. Pray from your heart, and not from your mouth. Through your voice do men hear you, but through your heart does your Father hear you.

46. Do these things when you pray to Our Father which art in Heaven. Beseech Him that He shall bring His Kingdom to earth as it is in Heaven.

47. Thank Him for the bread He gives to you daily.

48. Pray that He will forgive the debts we are without

means to pay, and assure Him that you will forgive others who are in debt to you and are unable to pay.

49. Pray that He guide you along the path of virtue and make strong your spirit to resist temptation.

50. Beseech Him to deliver your soul from the forces of evil and to help you to know mercy and to live righteously.

51. Pray for your fellow man that he may be spared misfortune and pain, and pray that all creatures may tread His good earth in peace forevermore, Amen.

52. For if you forgive the faults of others, so also will your faults be forgiven.

53. And if you pray that your brother be free from sickness and pain, so shall you be also, for all men yea, all creatures, are one with the Father.

54. Moreover, when you abstain from gross food, do not wear your good intentions upon your sleeve that he who sits beside you shall be made uncomfortable.

55. If your host asks you, "Why do you abstain?" tell him in secret, for your Father sees in secret and shall reward you openly.

56. Lay not up for yourselves treasures upon earth: these things do you leave behind for men to quarrel over.

57. But lay up for yourselves treasures fitting for the Kingdom of Heaven; these

you take with you, leaving no scruples behind.

58. For where your treasure is, there will your heart be also.

59. The light of your spirit shows in your face. If your thoughts be evil, your character shows this evil in your countenance.

60. No man can serve two masters and be wholly faithful to either: costly raiment and glittering things do men covet. The greed for gold and its power over men bow to mammon. Have a care lest your service be less to God.

61. Take no thought for your life, for the fullness of your stomach, or the draught of your taste, nor yet for the apparel of your body.

62. Is not a life more to God than meat, and the body more to His use than raiment?

63. Behold the fowls of the air; does not nature provide them with food? Is nature more bountiful to them than to you?

64. Which of you by taking thought for raiment can add one cubit to his stature?

65. Consider the lilies of the field, how they thrive through their knowledge of God's law and are clothed in heavenly raiment. Even Solomon in all his glory was not arrayed as one of these.

66. If God so clothed those in the sheen of His own spirit, shall He not even more clothe you, "O ye of little faith?"

67. Therefore take no thought of things that tempt the palate or the draught that whets the taste; neither for the glitter of raiment or extravagent apparel.

68. For after all these things do the vain glorious seek: Your Heavenly Father knows the things you have need of.

69. Seek you first the Kingdom of God and His righteousness, and all good things shall be for your pleasure.

70. Take therefore no thought for tomorrow, but give care to what you plant today, and tomorrow shall you reap the fullness thereof.

71. Judge not that you be not judged. Who among you is so true to the law that he can judge his brother. Cast out the mote first from your own eye and your brother shall see the clearness of your sight and cast out his also.

72. Give not that which is good to be destroyed, nor afford the best of your products for evil use, lest it return to rend you for your folly.

73. Ask that which pleases your Father and it shall be given you: Seek and you shall find wisdom; knock and the door of knowledge shall be opened to you.

74. Every man that so asks, receives; and he that seeks shall find, and to him that knocks it shall be opened.

75. What man among you whose son asks for bread, will

give him a stone? Or if he asks for water to drink, point him to the gutter?

76. If you, being evil, know how to give good things unto your children, why should you not also receive good things from your Heavenly Father?

77. But mark you; the son that brings happiness to his father receives his father's love, and his estate shall not be cut off.

78. And he that pleases our Father in Heaven with his good works shall share even more in the bounties of Providence.

79. Each man earns according to his worth, but even the lesser among you shall not be without the Father's concern.

80. All things whatsoever you would that men do to you, do you even better things to them.

81. Enter not into the gate that swings wide before you, for the easy way leads to destruction.

82. Enter instead through the gate that requires you to knock, for that leads into the fullness of life and the reverence thereof: but few there be that find it.

83. Beware of false prophets, which take on the ways of the meek and the pious, for they are both full of conceit and barren of mercy.

84. Not every one that says to me, "Lord, Lord, I accept you," shall enter into the Kingdom of Heaven; but only he that does the will of My Father, which is in Heaven.

85. Many may say to me in that day: "Lord, Lord, have we not partitioned in your name? And in your name, healed the sick and done many wonderful works?"

86. And then will I say to them: "I never knew you," for only to appease your vanity and to favor your purse did you appear to do these things in my name.

87. Therefore whosoever hears these sayings of mine, and profits thereby, I will liken him to the wise man who built his house on a firm foundation.

88. And anyone who hears these sayings and profits not thereby, I will liken him to a foolish man who built his house upon the sand.

89. And the rains came and the flood poured out and the winds blew and the house fell; and great was its fall.

90. And when Jesus had finished His sermon the people were astonished and reasoned among themselves the simple logic of His teachings.

Thou foundest thy house on a rock
that its rafters are truly poised
and its stones well laid
that all that repair unto it shall never be moved.
No armed band can storm it,
Neither all the hosts of wickedness together,

For I have stayed myself by Thy truth, O my God. [7]

CHAPTER XVII

The Things That Defile a Man

Making My Word of None Effect

1. Then there appeared before Him the Pharisees and certain Scribes who came from Jerusalem.

2. And when they saw some of His disciples eat bread that was defiled, that is to say, with unclean or unwashed hands, they found fault.

3. For the Pharisees and all the Jews eat not unless they wash their hands, for this is the tradition of the elders.

4. And when they come from the market they eat not unless they wash their hands, for tradition says that this defiles a man.

5. Then the Pharisees and Scribes asked Jesus, "Why do your disciples not behave according to the tradition of the elders?"

6. And Jesus answered saying, "There is naught such as this that enters into a man that can defile him, but the things which come out of him; those are they that defile the man."

7. If any man have ears to hear, let him hear, for thus does he learn what defiles a man.

8. And when he had entered into the house from the people, his disciples asked Him concerning the Parable.

9. And he said, "Are you so without understanding also? Do you not perceive that only through the heart is a man defiled: that the bread taken into the belly by unwashed hands goes out through the draught." [1]

10. "It is that which comes out of the man that defiles the man. For from within, out of the heart of men, proceed evil thoughts, adulteries, fornications, killings, thefts, covetousness, wickedness, deceit, lasciviousness, an evil eye, blasphemy, pride, selfishness, foolishness and self righteousness. All of these evil things come from within and defile a man." [2]

11. Well as Isaiah prophesied of the hypocrites, as it is written: "This people honoreth me with their lips, but their heart is far from me.

12. "Howbeit in vain do they worship me, teaching for doctrines the commandments of men.

13. "Full well they reject the commandment of God that they may keep their own tradition.

14. "For Moses said Honor thy father and thy mother, and who so curseth father or mother, does not keep the com-

---

[7] From the Essenes book of Hymns.
[1] Mark 7:18 See Commentary page 226.
[2] Mark 7:20 St. James version Vs. R.S.V. 7:14-7:20

mandment of God.

15. "But they say, If a man shall say to his father or mother, it is corban, that is to say, a gift, by whatsoever thou mightest be profited by me; he shall be free.

16. "And they suffer him no more to do aught for his father or his mother, making the word of God of none effect." [3] They a r r a n g e their own rituals and practices to suit their own convenience, their own indulgence and the aspirations of their own social and political order.

17. Yes, even as Isaiah saith: They make the word of God of none effect; so likewise shall tradition make my word of none effect.

18. But I say to you, those who passively resist violence, who love their enemies and take not up the sword against their brother, but do in all things as I do, them shall I appoint as my true disciples.

CHAPTER XVIII
He That Knoweth Love Shall Better Serve Me
The Prophecy of Blood
Let the Dead Bury Their Own Dead
The Swine and the Casting Out of Devils

1. I am come to bring peace to the world: to dignify My Father in Heaven whose coun-

tenance the Scribes have vainly misrepresented.

2. Their blood letting vengeful God is not of my Father: It is for this that I came that you might witness the love which is His Being.

3. Behold, the prophets and Elijah 'And he shall turn the heart of the fathers to their children and the heart of the children to their fathers." [*1]

4. Through me shall this come to pass: for I came not to destroy but to fulfill the prophets. [*2]

5. Therefore those among you who love and honor father and mother; who love sister, brother and their neighbors; him shall I appoint for my disciple for he already knows of love therefore shall he better serve me.

6. But alas! it shall come to pass that because of me swords shall drip with blood; sons shall be set at variance with their fathers and a man's foes shall be even in his own household.

7. But he who falsely thinks he has found his life shall lose it but he that loses his life for love's sake shall find it.

8. He that loves vain demonstrations more than he loves me is not worthy of me but he that takes up mercy and compassion and follows me is worthy of me.

[3] Mark 7: 6-14.
[*1] Malachi 4:5, 6.
[*2] Matthew 5:17.

9. "He that receiveth a righteous man in the name of a righteous man shall receive a righteous man's reward." *

10. Now when Jesus saw great crowds around Him He gave orders to get into the boat and go over to the other side. And a scribe came up and said to Him "Teacher I will follow you wherever you go." Another of the disciples said to him "Lord let me first go and bury my father." (Matt. 8:18-19-21)

11. And Jesus said to him: It is well that you do this. Tarry not for wherever your heart is, *there* also shall be your salvation.

12. And when he had gone Jesus turned to His disciples and said: "I know of this man, his father has been dead these many months: "Let the dead bury their own dead," for this man is himself dead, already buried in his own deceitfulness.

13. Therefore, I say to you, "Despair not but follow the way I lead you and you will find life more abundant."

14. And when they came to the other side of the country of the Gadarenes two demoniacs met him. And behold they cried out: "What have you to do with us, O Son of Man? Have you come here to torment us before the time?"

15. Now a herd of many swine were feeding at some distance from them.

16. And the sick men begged him, "Cast out our demons and send them away into the herd of swine." (Matt. 8:28-31)

17. But Jesus said, "God gives of His green earth, even to swine, that they might feed in peace.

18. Would you have me curse these creatures with the torments of hell? In due time they shall be sacrificed upon heathen altars, but not of my choice will they perish.

19. The love of God is in all of His creation, but the devil is the evil thereof.

20. I deal not in evil, but only in love; therefore I cannot cause pain to those things which are of God's creation.

21. Seek you therefore the Kingdom of Heaven and that which is evil shall be cast into the sea.

22. "Show mercy that you may be shown mercy. Forgive that you may be forgiven. As you do, so it will be done to you; as you give, so it will be given to you; as you judge, so will you be judged; as you are kind, so kindness will be shown to you. The same measure you use will be used in measuring you." [3]

23. You may expect consideration to be extended to you from the highest in proportion to that which you extend to the lowest.

[3] Saving of Jesus, according to the first letter of Clement to the Corinthians (88 A.D.).

* Matt. 10:41.

24. And they fell to their knees before Him, for they understood; and even at that moment was the evil cast from them.

CHAPTER XIX
The Enemies of Jesus Revile Him

So for mine own part
because I have clung unto thee
I shall yet arise and stand upright
against them that revile me
and my hand shall yet be upon all
that hold me in contempt.
Though Thou show Thy power **through me**
They regard me not.
Howbeit Thou In Thy might hast shed upon **me the perfect Light.**
They that walked in the way Thou desirest
have harkened unto me
and rallied to Thy cause
in the legion of the saints.[1]

1. And Jesus began to say to the multitude, about John the Baptist and of Himself,

2. What did you go into the wilderness to see? A man clothed in soft raiment? Behold! They that wear extravagant clothing take pride in raiment of the flesh but the simple in heart glorify the raiment of their soul.

3. Verily I say unto you, Among them that are born of woman there has not risen a greater than John the Baptist.

4. For all the prophets and the law prophesied of John, Behold, I send my messenger before me.

5. And if you consider it, this is Elias which was for to come.

6. He that has ears let him hear. For from the days of John the Baptist till the days of the Son of Man, the Kingdom of Heaven suffers violence and the violent take it by force.

7. They pipe to the people and the people dance.

8. They slur their fellows like children competing in the market place.

9. They say John is sustained by demons for he comes neither drinking nor eating the temple fare.

10. They defile the dignity of the One coming after him.

11. *They say* the Son of Man came eating and drinking. "Behold, a glutton and a drunkard, a friend of tax collectors and sinners."

12. But wisdom is justified by deeds and not by slurs.

Thou hast made me a reproach and a derision
To them that live by deceit
But a symbol of truth and understanding
To all whose way is straight.[2]

---

[1] Book of Hymns, Dead Sea Scrolls.
[2] Book of Hymns, Dead Sea Scrolls.

CHAPTER XX

The Meaning of the Words, "I Desire Mercy and Not Sacrifice"

Who Are My Mother and My Brethren?

1. "And Jesus went on the Sabbath day through the corn and His disciples were hungry and began to pluck the ears of corn to eat.

2. "But when the Pharisees saw it they said unto them, 'Behold your disciples do that which is unlawful upon the Sabbath day.'

3. "And Jesus answered them reproachfully. 'You blind guides which strain at a gnat and swallow a camel,

4. 'Have you not read what David did when he was hungry: How he entered the house of God and ate the bread of the presence, which was not lawful for him to do?

5. 'Have you not read in the law how that on the Sabbath the priests in the temple profane the Sabbath and are blameless. I tell you something that is greater than the temple.' " [1]

6. "You are they which justify yourselves before men, but God knows your hearts: for that which is highly esteemed among men is abomination in the sight of God." [2]

7. "You make clean the outside of the platter but within you are full of excess." [3]

8. You are like whited sepulchres; you make your bodies tombs for the corpses of dead things and all uncleanness.

9. But if you know what this means; "I desire mercy and not sacrifice; the knowledge of God more than burnt offerings," you would not condemn the guiltless. [4]

10. It was said by those of old time: "Show mercy to your neighbors and have compassion towards all, not towards men only, but also towards the creatures." [*]

11. Then the Pharisees went out and held a council against him, how they might silence him.

12. But when Jesus knew it, He withdrew Himself and went on to minister to those in need of His love.

13. "Now when Jesus talked to the people His mother and His brethren came about to see Him.

14. "And when He was told that His mother and brother were present He answered to them, 'Who is my mother? and who are my brethren? Are they not of my heart and my love?'

[1] From Matthew.
[2] Luke 16:15.
[3] Matt. 23: 25.
[4] Matt. 12:7 - Hosea 6:6.
[*] From Essene Scriptures.

15. "And He stretched forth His hands towards His disciples and said, 'Behold, inasmuch you also are my mother and my brethren,

16. 'For whosoever shall love one another as ye love my Father in Heaven, the same are my brother, and sister, and mother.' "⁵

CHAPTER XXI
The Parable of the Sower
The Secrets Are for the Twelve

"Through me has Thou illumined
The faces of full many,
And countless be the times
Thou hast shown Thy
power through me.
For Thou hast made known unto me
Thy deep, mysterious things,
Has shared Thy secret with me
And so shown forth Thy power;
And before the eyes of full many
This wonder stands revealed,
And Thy glory may be shown forth,
And all living know of Thy power." ¹

1. The next day Jesus went out of the house and sat by the sea side; and when the people gathered around, He spoke.

2. But He spoke to them in Parables, saying: Behold, a sower went forth to sow. Some seeds fell by the wayside and were eaten by fowls.

3. Some fell upon stony places where there was no depth of soil and forthwith sprung up.

And when the sun came up it scorched them because they were in shallow soil.

4. And some fell among weeds which grew up and choked them.

5. But others fell into good ground and brought forth fruit, some of small amount, some of medium amount, and some large and full to the utmost.

6. Who hath ears to hear let him think upon this.

7. And the disciples came and said unto him, Why do you speak in parables to these peoples?

8. Jesus answered them and said: Because it is given to you to know the secrets. They need much learning and are not yet ready to know the whole truth.

9. I teach you that you may follow me and instruct them also.

10. For w h o s o e v e r has knowledge, to him shall be given, and to whosoever has not, he shall be sore in need.

11. Hear you therefore to the parable of the sower:

12. When any one hears the

⁵ Paraphrased from Matt. 12: 46-50.
¹ Book of Hymns IV, 5-40 Dead Sea Scrolls.

word of the Kingdom and understands it not, then comes the wicked one and snatches away that which was sown in his heart.

13. And he that received the seed into stony places, the same is he that hears the word with yes, yes, — but when inconveniences arise because of the word, he is offended.

14. And he that hears the word as the seed among the thorns, hears but deceitfulness, for lusts, prejudices and lewdness choke the word and he becomes unfruitful.

15. But he that received the seed into the fullness of his heart, as into the good ground, hears the word and understands it.

16. Thus the fruits of joy, mercy, love, and thanksgiving are brought forth, and great is their goodness.

17. And it came to pass when Jesus had finished these parables he departed towards the great Sea. [2]

CHAPTER XXII
The Woman of Canaan

1. "Then Jesus came into the coasts of Tyre and Sidon. And, behold, a woman of Canaan came out and cried unto him, saying, Have mercy on me, O Lord, thou son of David; my daughter is grievously ill.

2. *But Jesus answered her*

not a word." [1]

3. But his disciples besought him, saying, Send her away; for she crieth after us. Thou hast been sent, only unto the lost sheep of the house of Israel: It is not fair to take the children's bread and cast it to the dogs.

4. And Jesus answered saying: But even the dogs eat the crumbs that fall from their Master's table: Does not this woman, even though she is a Canaanite, feel the same pain, suffering, heartache and despair as would a daughter of Israel?

5. Would she not feel the same love and devotion to the offspring of her womb as would a mother of an Israelite?

6. Have you forgotten so soon where I told you that mercy, pity and understanding are the three blessings through which love triumphs? Verily I say to you all creatures have an inalienable right before God to expect and to receive these blessings.

7. Turning to the woman he said: Let your concern be stilled for even now I go and minister to your daughter.

CHAPTER XXIII
The Cursing of the Fig Tree

1. "Now in the morning as Jesus returned to the city He hungered.

[2] Paraphrased from Matt. 13.
[1] Matt. 15: 21-23.

2. And when he saw a fig tree in the way He came to it but found nothing but leaves, for the tree had since given up its fruit." [1]

3. Then one of His disciples who was quick to anger said, Lord will you that no fruit grow upon these limbs henceforth and forever and that its leaves wither and die.

4. But Jesus turned to him, saying: For shame! why would you curse the tree so that its leaves wither away and die?

5. Has it not provided food for our brothers before us, and will it not also provide food for those who come after us?

6. If you would know your works as faithfully as does this tree, your appointment would be well deserved.

7. Verily I say to you if your faith was as true to the love of God you would not render spite upon His creation but would instead give to it your blessing that others might in due time feast upon its bounties.

8. Standing beneath the cooling shade of the tree's broad leaves he said, May your branches which give for us shelter from the noon day sun be blessed with blossom, and may your seed endure as long as the earth shall stand.

9. "I give thanks unto Thee, O Lord
For Thou has placed me

Where waters gush in thirsty soil;
Where an oasis blooms in the desert,
Where all trees live on Thy water,
Stand planted, for Thy glory alone,
And never die." [2]

10. Later, as they again passed by the same fig tree, Peter, calling to remembrance, said to Jesus:

11. Master, behold the fig tree which you blessed is fresh with blossom.

12. And Jesus answered, saying: Have faith in God, for by His hand does the tree bear fruit and make its seed.

13. Only that which is evil blights a tree so that it withers away.

14. "In my Father my soul exults and brings my tongue to full blossom, that it bears not blighted fruit which withers ere it come to flower." [3]

CHAPTER XXIV
The Greatest of All Sins

1. Then Jesus went into the city and a group of Pharisees, seeing Him, gathered around.

2. And one of the Pharisees which was a lawyer asked Him a question, tempting Him, saying: "Master, which is the great commandment in the law?"

3. Jesus said unto him:

[1] Mark 11: 12 Matt. 21: 18.
[2-3] Book of Hymns, Dead Sea Scrolls.

"Thou shalt love the Lord thy God with all thy heart, and with all thy soul, and with all thy mind."

4. "And the second is like unto it: Thou shalt love thy neighbor as thyself. On these two commandments hang all the law and the prophets," for they dissolve the greatest of all sins.

5. And what is the greatest of all sins? said the lawyer.

6. Jesus answered him, saying: The greatest sin man can commit is to needlessly, selfishly, and ruthlessly cause pain and suffering to any of God's creatures.

7. Oh!, exclaimed the lawyer, with a gleam of triumph in his eye, but the law says that to curse, or to revile the Lord thy God is the greatest of sins. What say you now?

8. And Jesus answered him, saying: Is your heart so hardened into stone that you cannot understand that love and compassion are the living countenance of the Father in Heaven?

9. The Lord thy God is life: the lives of all creatures therefore are of Him.

10. If you take into your hand one of these and ignore God's pleasure in its creation do you not in a manner disparage Him?

11. You have not the power to create life therefore you have not the right to destroy it.

12. God gives and God takes away.

13. Again, as God's countenance is love and mercy, should not the deed that is contrary thereto be of sorrow to Him?

14. Your Heavenly Father is indeed deeply grieved by the waywardness of man, for he brings upon all flesh a contradiction of His love and mercy. Herein does man revile God.

15. Thus do I say unto you that which is the greatest of all sins.

16. "The wise man departs from evil but the fool rages and is confident." [1]

17. "The heart of Him that has understanding seeks knowledge: but the mouths of fools feed on extravagance." [2]

18. "Learn not the way of nations for the customs of the people are false." [3]

19. Thereafter many of the Pharisees departed in haste, but there were those among them who were impressed by the logic of His words, for they too were searching for truth and love beyond the staidness of secular custom.

20. How can man say aught,
How argue in excuse of his misdeeds?
How can he enter reply

---

[1] Proverbs 14:16.
[2] Proverbs 15:14.
[3] Jer. 10: 2-3 R.S.V.

To any just sentence
upon him?
Thine O God of all
knowledge
Are works of righteous-
ness
And the secret of truth. [4]

CHAPTER XXV
Jesus Heals Through Prayer and Fasting
The Divine Formula

1. And Jesus went about among the sick and the troubled and He helped them to cleanse the temple of their soul.

2. He demonstrated to them how prayer and fasting [1] would cast out all manner of ill health.

3. He prescribed to them the Divine Formula [2] that enabled man his long life before the fall: the Formula that gave Samson his great strength, and Daniel his remarkable wisdom and understanding in all things.

4. "Thou has created plants
For the service of man
And all things that spring
from the earth,
That he may be fed in
abundance,
And to them that acknowl-
edge Thy truth

Thou hast also given in-
sight
To divine Thy wondrous
works." [3]

5. "I will sing to him at the common board as ever I raise my hand to enjoy the rich fruits of the earth with that which flows from my lips. I will bless Him as with an obla-tion." [4]

6. "Thou dost cause the grass to grow for the cattle; and plants for man to cultivate, that he may bring forth food from the earth." [5] "Mercy and truth are met together: righte-ousness and peace have kissed each other.

7. "Truth shall spring from the earth and righteousness shall look down from the sky.

"Yea, the Lord will give what is good and the land will yield abundantly." [6]

8. And saith the Lord Jesus: "A grain of wheat will produce ten thousand heads, and every head will have ten thousand grains, and every grain will produce ten pounds of fine clean flour. And other fruits, seeds, and grass will produce in corresponding proportions, and all the animals will use those foods that are the products of the soil, and become in turn

---

[4] From Hymns, Dead Sea Scrolls.
[1] See Commentary—Page 260.
[2] See Genesis 1:29-30; Daniel 1: 12-13.
[3] Book of Hymns, Dead Sea Scrolls.
[4] Book of Hymns, Dead Sea Scrolls.
[5] Psalms 104:14.
[6] Psalms 85:10-12.

peaceable and in harmony with one another and in complete tranquility to man." [7]

9. "Verily I say to you, 'If ye do not fast to the world, ye shall not find the Kingdom of God; and except you make the sabbath a real Sabbath, ye shall not see the Father.'" [8]

CHAPTER XXVI

Blessed Are the Little Ones
Jesus Advises the Rich Man

1. "And He took a child and set him in the midst of them: and when he had taken him in his arms He said to them.

2. Whatsoever receives the least one of these receives my Father in Heaven, for whosoever abideth in the Lord thy God, in Him do I abide also."

3. Whosoever leads one of these little ones astray, and causes it to indulge in wickedness, is of the lowest among men.

4. But whosoever give freely of themselves that these little ones might avoid tribulation and be led in the paths of virtue are of the greatest among men, and by their deeds shall they be known.

5. And then when Jesus had gone forth into the way, there came a certain rich man to Him and asked: "Good Master,

what shall I do that I may inherit eternal life?"

6. "And Jesus said to him: 'Why call me good? There is none good but one, and that is God.'

7. "You know the commandments: 'Do not commit adultery, Do not kill, Do not steal, Do not bear false witness, Defraud not, Honor thy Father and Mother, Love thy Neighbor.'

8. "And he answered and said, 'Master, all these have I observed from my youth.'"*

9. Then Jesus said, This I can promise you: See to it that your wealth is put to wise use that it might find favor with God. Not that you must become poor at the moment, for every man deserves that for which he labored or came by through honest effort and careful saving; for these you are entitled to all comforts short of excess.

10. Leave not your wealth behind for your kin to fight over and squander uselessly, for he who has come by wealth without effort is given to extravagance.

11. Instead, will your belongings to a forthright and honorable cause so that all men may enjoy the fruits of your labors. Thus is your treasure made secure in Heaven.

---

[7] Papias, a pupil of the Apostle John, quoting Jesus (See Comment—Page 346).

[8] From a Logia cited by Clement of Alexandria; probably from the Gospel of the Hebrews, also the Gospel of Thomas.

* Luke 18:18-21.

CHAPTER XXVII

The Wedding at Cana
The Wine of God

1. "And the third day there was a wedding in a place called Cana of Galilee." Among the guests were some of the Disciples and the kin of Jesus.

2. Now it was a custom to celebrate these occasions with merrymaking and feasting. It was considered proper for the host to offer generously of his wine store, and it was indeed embarrassing to him if his supply be depleted before all had drunk their fill.

3. It was at such a time as this that Jesus appeared unnoticed to the revelers. Standing aside, he surveyed the scene before him, and was deeply concerned.

4. For he saw there those for whom he had regard, who had already drunk too much.

5. Now at this time, the Governor of the feast begged the indulgence of his guests, for he had no more wine.

6. And a voice among the crowd was heard to say: Where is Jesus? Surely if this "Man of Miracles" were here, He could turn yon earthen jars of water into wine.

7. Then in the doorway appeared Jesus the Nazarene, who for forty days and forty nights of fast in the wilderness had resisted the temptations that weaken the spirit.

8. He, like Daniel and the Prophets before Him, knew the evils of feasting and drinking.

9. A hush fell upon the revelers as Jesus stood before them.

10. A great glow of light seemed to surround Him, but His face expressed deep concern mingled with understanding, for He realized that upon occasions such as these, the flesh is weak.

11. Then he spoke. You tempt me to turn the water of yonder vases into wine. Even if I desired so to do, I could not, for it is not I that do wondrous works; it is my Father within me that does these things.

12. Think you that my Father would give His blessing to the making of wine?

13. Wine is made by the presses of man. It provides him with both the pleasure of indulgence and the pain of consequence. It therefore contains inconsistencies equal to the flesh.

14. Then He turned to the Governor of the feast and said: Pour from the jars and fill every cup.

15. And they all brought forth their cups and they were filled.

16. Then Jesus took a goblet in His hand and gazed intently upon it as he raised it up, bidding the others do likewise.

17. This is the wine I give to you. It is the living water, the nectar of the spirit of God. Through His blessing shall your soul be cleansed. Drink

you, therefore, of the living spirit; of the wine that heals all woes: of the draught that anoints your soul with everlasting life.

18. And they drank of the living water and were filled with new life, and great was their joy; And the Governor of the feast said: Thou hast kept the good wine until now, for truly this is the wine of God.

19. Then Jesus blessed the bride and groom and her parents and 'went out of the house.

20. Several of His Disciples followed Him out, saying: Lord, why did you not also admonish them for drinking the wine made by the presses of men?

21. And Jesus answered them: Every one within the sound of My voice knew that the Prophets condemn it. The consequences are their own to bear.

22. I came not here to condemn but to teach. It would be unkind and unjust to suffer this household with criticism upon this memorable occasion.

23. Love does not condemn; it mitigates.

24. The Spirit of Righteousness transcends sin and the good finds agreement in understanding.

25. Do unto others as you would have them do unto you is the ethics thereof.

26. Beware of the self righteous, who condemn others but who are blind to their own faults, for, like the drunkard and the glutton, they shall come to poverty.

CHAPTER XXVIII
The Adulteress
Condemnation and Acquittal

1. "Early one morning Jesus 'went to the temple and the people came about Him and He sat down and taught them.

2. "And the Scribes and the Pharisees brought to Him a woman taken in adultery in the very act.

3. "Now the law of the Elders commanded that she be s t o n e d to death, so they brought her before Jesus and said: 'Rabbi, this woman was caught in the very act of adultery, what say you should be done.'

4. "Jesus paused while the Pharisees taunted Him for an answer.

5. "Then arising to His feet He said to them. 'Let him who is without sin among you cast the first stone at her.'

6. "And as they heard His words, they themselves felt convicted in their own conscience.

7. "And they 'went out one by one and left Jesus standing alone with the woman.

8. "And Jesus, seeing that all her accusers had left, said, 'There is no man left but me to judge you, and I condemn you not. Go and sin no more." *

* Paraphrased from John 8: 1-11.

CHAPTER XXIX

The Light of the World Jesus Explains What He Means When He Says: "Follow Thou Me." God Is the Word and I am the Example Thereof

1. Then Jesus spoke again to the people, saying, "I am the light of the world: He that follows me shall not walk in darkness but shall shine his light before Him."

2. He that has ears let him listen: When I say follow Me I mean not that you should merely store My words in your memory where you can bring them forth to instruct others.

3. Words are like seeds fallen from a pod; they have no worth unless they find fertile soil, where they can bring forth blossom and fruit.

4. My word is the seed, My way of life is the blossom and the fruit. Therefore when I say, "Follow Me" I mean that you do as I do. Take upon your own way of life the way of life I exemplify.

5. Love others as I love you. *Have mercy and kindness for all living things, for the lower a man carries his love, the loftier he lifts his life.*

6. Keep the temple of thy soul clean that My Father may dwell within you in the same fullness that He dwells within me.

* Psalm 82:6.
** John 10:34,35.

7. God is the word and I am the example thereof.

8. I, therefore, teach you not through word alone, but by example do I teach you.

9. Be you like me; live the life that is of me, and all things will be made known to you.

CHAPTER XXX

Jesus Explains That All Men Are in God

1. And it was at Jerusalem, the feast of the dedication, and it was winter.

2. And Jesus walked into the temple and was surrounded by the Pharisees.

3. "And they said to Him: You being a man, how can you make yourself to be God? Is not this blasphemy?

4. "Jesus answered, Is it not written 'I said Ye are gods: and all of you are children of the most High!' * If he called them Gods, the word of the Scriptures cannot be broken. **

5. The sons of men, even as the Scriptures affirm, are therefore gods.

6. The Kingdom of Heaven is within. It is not I that speaks; it is the Father within me who speaks.

7. If I do works of my Father, believe me that God is with the Son of Man, and I in Him.

8. He would dwell within

you also if you would but allow him to enter.

9. But they understood not, and sought to seize Him, but He escaped out of their hands and went away towards Galilee.

CHAPTER XXXI
Five Thousand Fed

1. And Jesus went into Galilee and to Tiberias by the Sea.

2. And He went up from the shore and the people began to gather and it was evening.

3. And one of the disciples, whose name was Andrew, Simon Peter's brother, said; Where shall we buy bread that these may eat?

4. Philip answered him: Two hundred pennyworth of bread is not sufficient for them, that everyone of them may not hunger.

5. And Andrew, pointing his finger to the side, said: There is a lad who has five barley loaves, but what are they among so many?

6. And Jesus, Who had heard these remarks, said: Have them all sit down. Then He took up one of the loaves in His hand and stood before them, saying: It has been said that you hunger. Here is bread fashioned out of the leaven of man. Of it you eat your fill, but it satisfies only the stomach and soon you hunger again.

7. Bread such as this you shall all have in good time.

8. But I came not to feed your stomachs: I came to give you food for your soul.

9. Food that, when taken into your heart, shall provide never ending satisfaction: food that you shall take up and carry with you so that you shall hunger no more of life.

10. "Labor not for the bread that perishes, but for the bread that endures unto everlasting life, which the Son of Man gives unto you. For the bread is the spirit which comes down from Heaven and gives life unto the world.

"I am the bread of life: he that walks with Me shall never hunger: and he that goes my way shall never thirst.

"Yea, whosoever drinks of the water that I give you shall tap a well of water springing up into everlasting life." [1]

For an hour did He talk to them and they marveled at His teachings, and when they got up to go they carried bread of the Spirit gathered from Heaven: more than would fill twelve baskets, and they hungered not.

CHAPTER XXXII
The Twelve Sent Out
The Seventy Sent Out
Luke 10:1-10 Explained

1. And Jesus sent out His twelve, charging them to go nowhere among the Gentiles, and to no town among the Samaritans, for He realized that those

[1] John 6: 27-32-35.
John 4:14.

who would take them in abided within every town of Judea. Only in these houses would their salute be recognized.

2. "And preach as you go, saying, 'The Kingdom of Heaven is at hand.' Heal the sick, cleanse the lepers and cast out demons. You received this power without pay; give it also without pay.

3. "Take no gold, or silver, nor copper in your belts. No bag for your journey nor extra clothes and sandals, but the laborer deserves his food.

4. "And whatever town or village you enter, find out who is worthy of it and stay with him until you depart.

5. "As you enter the house salute * it: And if the house is worthy, if the sons of peace dwell there, therein your peace will be also." (Matt. 10:5-13)

6. "After this the Lord appointed seventy and sent them on ahead of Him into every town and place where He Himself was about to come.

7. "And He said to them: 'The harvest is plentiful, but the laborers are few; pray therefore the Lord of the harvest to send out laborers into the harvest.'

8. " 'Go your way: Behold, I send you out as lambs in the midst of wolves.

9. " 'Carry no purse, no bag, no sandals, and *confide*** *in* no one on the road.

10. " 'Whatsoever house you enter, first say, *Peace be to this house* (a salute of the brethren).

11. " 'And if a *Son of Peace* is there (an Essene or Nazarene), your peace shall rest upon him: but if not, it shall return to you' (for your salutation has fallen upon unfamiliar ears). 'And in the house of the *Son of Peace* (an Essene's), remain eating and drinking *such things as they give* (simple or innocent food, pulse). And into whatsoever city you enter and *they* receive you (*they* meaning the Sons of Peace), eat such things that are set before you," Luke 10:1-8 (for in these things will your faith be made strong even as was Daniel's before you).

CHAPTER XXXIII
Gathering the Lost Sheep
The Prodigal Son

1. "Then drew near Him all the Publicans and sinners to hear Him. And the Pharisees and the Scribes murmured saying, 'This man receives sinners and sits at the table with them.' " (See Luke 15:1)

2. And Jesus said to them,

* This salute as told in Luke combines a raised hand with the words, 'Peace be with you' and is Essenic.

** The words *confide in* substituted for the word salute as suggesting more the intent of this saying. The other words and phrases in italics and parentheses suggest what appears to be an explanation of the charges given to the Disciples. See Commentary pp. 290-1.

"What man among you having a hundred sheep does not leave the ninety and nine to go after the one which is lost in the wilderness?

3. "And when you have found it you rejoice, do you not?

4. "I say to you likewise shall my Father rejoice if I bring to Him a sheep that is lost to the fold.

5. "And a certain man had two sons:

"And the younger of them said to his father, 'Give me now the inheritance that shall fall to me for I want to make out for my own way.'

6. "And his father divided for them his living.

7. "Thereafter the younger son gathered up his things and journeyed to a far country and there wasted his substance with riotous living.

8. "And when he had spent all, there came a famine and he was in want.

9. "He went to the fields to feed swine and he ate the husks that they did eat and no man gave to him.

10. "And when he came to himself he said, 'How many hired servants of my fathers have bread and to spare but I am about to perish with hunger.

11. " 'I will arise and go to my father and say, Father, I have sinned against heaven and before you. I am no more worthy to be called your son; make me one of your servants.'

12. "And he came home to his father, but his father saw him coming and had compassion, and came to him and embraced him.

13. "And the son said to him, 'Father, I have sinned before heaven and in your sight and am no more worthy to be called your son.'

14. "But the father said to his servants, 'Bring forth the best robe, put shoes on his feet and a ring on his hand;

15. 'And bring the (best ripe fruits, the pulse, the honey of the comb, the bread, the cakes and the wine) ; * let us eat and be merry, for he who was lost is found,' and they began to be merry.

16. "Now the elder brother was in the field, and he came by and asked the servants by what reason is all the merriment in the house.

17. "And they said, 'Your brother is come home and your father rejoices to receive him safe and sound.'

18. "And he was angry and would not go in; thereafter his father came out and entreated him.

19. "And he answered his father, 'These many years have I served you. I have always

* Scholars and Humanitarians have pointed out that this phrase in parentheses was later corrupted by copyists to read, "Bring hither the fatted calf and kill it." Certainly the "Son of loving kindness" would not have said this. See Commentary Book 3, Ch. 33, p. 294.

obeyed your wishes, but you have never given me a feast with wine to make merry with my friends.

20. " 'But as soon as he who has devoured your substance with harlots returns, you give for him a feast.'

21. "And he said, 'My son, you are ever with me and all I have shall be yours, but my heart is glad, for your brother that was lost is found.' " (From Luke 15)

22. Thus does God receive with open arms he who repents and returns to Him.

CHAPTER XXXIV
The Costly Ointment
I Am the Healing Lotion

1. Then Jesus, six days before the Passover, came to Bethany, where Lazarus, who was thought dead, had been returned to good health.

2. There they made a supper, and Martha served, and Lazarus sat at the table also.

3. Then Mary took a pound of very costly ointment of spikenard and was about to anoint and kiss the feet of Jesus.

4. But He protested, saying, Hold do not humble yourself as a slave to his master, for I do not desire the attentions sought by vain men.

5. Spare your good intent, for I came not to be served, but to serve.

6. Devotion is an honorable virtue. Rise up that I may press the warmth of your hand

to my breast and let the light of your eyes shine into mine.

7. My Father within me loves humility of thought and deed. Except that a man kiss the hand of his lady, it is not for any one to kiss the hand of another; and for no person to kiss the foot of another, for all men are equal in the eyes of God.

8. Vanity or self-glorification cannot be demonstrated by him who kisses the hand of another. Neither can mortification or servility be exemplified by him who is so kissed.

9. Verily I say to you that even the reserve of this order can not justify the dignity of conscience and the honor of spirit that God expects of man.

10. I did not come that you should worship my person. I came that you might instead worship with the Spirit within My person, for of this is my Father in Heaven.

11. In Me have faith, for I am the healing lotion the balm that soothes the weary and gives peace to the soul.

12. Then spoke one of His disciples, Judas Iscariot, Simon's son: "Lord, you have given me thought. Would it not be wise for to sell this costly ointment and give the money to the poor?"

13. And Jesus answered him, saying, Inasmuch that Mary offered to give of the costly balm, it is in the same sense hers to do with as she pleases.

14. And as He spoke those

around Him recognized the dignity of God in His manner, and the whole place round about seemed to glow with the humble warmth and simple truth of His words.

* * *

Thou it is did determine my being according to Thy will

Thou hast left me not to depend upon worldly wealth

Nor made me rely upon luxuries of wine and oil. *

CHAPTER XXXV

The Parable of the Faithful Servant

The Destruction of the Cities Foretold

The Coming of the Kingdom of God

(From Matt. and Luke)

1. And Jesus went out upon the Mount of Olives. His Disciples came to Him and He spoke to them.

2. "Take heed that no man deceive you. The time shall come about when the Son of Man shall come in all His glory. Watch, therefore, that thou be not a hypocrite."

3. Then He spoke to them this parable: "Who, then, is a faithful and wise servant whom his lord hath made ruler over his household, to give them 'meat' in due season? *

4. "Blessed is that servant whom his lord, when he comes home, shall find so doing.

5. "Verily I say to you that this servant can be trusted with the welfare of the house.

6. "But if the servant be evil and say to himself, 'My Lord is delayed and will not come soon,

7. "And in his absence he does smite his household with unclean food and give them to drink until drunken,

8. "Then the lord of that servant shall come in a day he is not looked for, and appoint him in his portion with the hypocrites."

9. "Take heed therefore lest the cares of this life overcharge your heart with gluttony and drunkenness and the Kingdom of Heaven catch you also unawares.

10. "Watch ye therefore that ye may be accounted worthy to stand before the Son of Man." (Luke 21:34-36)

11. And some spoke of the place where people come to worship and sacrifice burnt offerings to the nourishment of their bodies.

12. Then said Jesus, "The

---

* From the Dead Sea Scriptures by Gaster.

* In Bible days the word *meat* described foods such as cereals, fruits, vegetables, etc. (See Lev. 2:1-14) K.J.V. In the R.S.V. the word *meat* is changed to *cereal*. "Sitting at meat" may therefore be interpreted as eating foods other than flesh. The words *in due season* (Matt. 24:45) also suggest fruits, vegetables, etc. in season.

days will come in which there shall not be left one stone upon another nor one rafter that is not put to the fire."

13. "Take heed that you be not deceived, for many shall speak in my name, saying: 'Follow me for the time of judgment is at hand,' but go you not after them."

14. "But when you hear of wars, be not terrified, for these things do come to pass."

15. "Nation shall rise against nation and he that speaks in My name shall lead them."

16. The banners of their false Christ shall betray all: parent, brethren, kinfolk, and friends; and their hands shall drip with blood.

17. They pray to My Father for victory, enamored of the sword, but He shall hear them not, for not a government will stand that raises its sword in My name.

18. "The earth will shake and there shall be famines and pestilences and fearful sights, and great shall be fires in the heavens.

19. "And let them which are in cities flee to the country and to the mountains.

20. "Men's hearts shall fail them for looking after those things which shall shake both heaven and earth.

21. "And when these do begin to come to pass, lift up your heads, for your time draws near."

22. But there shall be left among you those who shall realize the futility of shedding blood, for a great reverence for all life shall come upon them and there shall be no more harm or hurt upon all my holy mountain, for the earth shall have full knowledge of the Lord as the waters cover the sea.

CHAPTER XXXVI

Jesus Enters Into Jerusalem
The Purging of the Temple
The Roman Authorities
Take Note

1. "Behold the King cometh unto thee: He is just and having salvation: lowly and riding upon an ass." (Zech. 9:9)

2. "The next day, the people heard that He was coming to Jerusalem and, when He approached them an ass was provided to carry Jesus into the city. *

3. "And as He entered through the gates, the people laid palm leaves in His path and went on before Him shouting: "Hosanna!"

4. "Blessed be the Kingdom of our father David.

"Blessed be the King of Israel who comes in the name of the Lord." All hail! the King of the Jews has come to release us from bondage in the name of the Lord.

5. The multitude that acclaimed Jesus was impressive.

* Riding an ass to exemplify humility.

6. By what authority, said the Romans to one another, does this man pretend to be King? Surely he bears watching, for he has many followers.

7. And Jesus went straight towards the temple, and the crowds followed Him in.

8. He paused in the Court to stoop down and caress a lamb brought in to be sacrificed. He looked into the frightened eyes of a faithful ox. The gentle kid and the calfling cried out for their mothers, and His heart went out to them. Like little babes torn ruthlesly from their mothers' breasts: they stood on tottery legs, awaiting the pain of the merciless knife.

9. There, too, were crates filled with doves, the very symbol of God's spirit. And Jesus remembered the Father's voice the day of His baptism.

10. Slowly His great heart swelled with righteous indignation; the love and compassion of the Spirit of God cried out within Him for mercy instead of sacrifice; for moral justice and humane dignity instead of vain pretenses.

11. Deliberately, but with merciful hand, he opened all the crates and let a thousand doves fly free;

12. And they circled overhead to form a great living crown, for indeed it was a head dress worthy of the Prince of eternal life.

13. The lambs, the calves and the oxen He liberated from their stalls.

14. Sensing their freedom the frightened creatures stampeded through the courts, upsetting the trays of the money changers, scattering t h e i r wares over the floor.

15. Away! away! all of you He cried out. You blaspheme the name of God and make His house a shambles, * a den of thieves and devils.

16. And as the priests came forward to restrain Him, He denounced them, saying:

17. You desecrate the temple with the iniquitous rites of a barbaric people.

18. You killed the Prophets for opposing your heinous acts. Like them whom you murdered before Me, I censor you in the name of My Father.

19. "I will take no bullock out of thy house nor he goats out of thy folds. For every creature of the forest is mine and the cattle upon a thousand hills. I know all the fowls of the mountains; and the wild creatures of the woods. If I were hungry, would I ask you for food? Will I eat the flesh or drink the blood of my own creatures?" [1]

20. "When you come to appear before me who hath required this at your hand to tread my courts? Your new moons and your appointed feasts my soul hateth. They are a trouble unto me; I am weary to bear them.

"And when ye spread forth

---

[1] Psalms 50:8-13.

* A slaughterhouse.

your hands, I will hide mine eyes from you: yea, when ye make many prayers I will not hear; your hands are full of blood." [2]

21. "Woe to ye who lie upon beds of ivory, and eat lambs out of the flock, and the calves out of the midst of the stall;

"Who sing idle songs to the sound of the viol, and drink wine in bowls." [3]

22. "Ye have no faithfulness or kindness and no knowledge of God. Ye swear falsely. Ye lie, steal, ye kill and kill and pour blood where ye have poured other blood. And the land mourns and all creatures that dwell therein resign themselves, for they know not whether they live or die: the lamb, the ox, the she-goat with her kid, the doves of the air; Yea! even the fish of the sea languish. Yet has no one contended, no one accused; but with you, O Priests, I contend." [4]

23. "Ye love sacrifice because ye love to eat flesh, but the Lord has no delight in you." [5]

24. My Father sayeth: "Cursed be the man that does not heed the words of My Covenant which I commanded your fathers when I brought them out of the land of Egypt." [6]

25. "Add ye burnt offerings to your sacrifices and eat flesh but I commanded ye not to do these things." [7]

26. As for you, O Sons of Men, I shall speak to the birds of every sort and to all the creatures of the field to assemble, to come gather around from all sides to (scorn) the great sacrificial feast which I am preparing for you, for you shall eat flesh and drink blood till ye are drunk, for I deal with you according to your uncleanness and your transgressions and I hide my face from you. [8]

27. Through the Prophet Ezekiel you were shown the design of the temple by a man of "brass," * which was Ezekiel's manner of interperting the "false one," the "brazen one," And he laid down his measuring rod beside your profane designs, to gloat over the length and breadth of your abominations. And he showed you the cruel knives with which you slay the sacrifice, the stone slabs upon which you slaughter your victims, the gate posts where you wash the burnt offering, and the kitchen where you boil the bodies of your innocent victims and eat them.

[2] Isaiah 1:11-15.

[3] Amos 6:4-6.

[4] Hosea 4: 1-4 R.S.V. & K.J.V.

[5] Hosea 8:13 - R.S.V.

[6] Jer. 11: 3-8.

[7] Jer. 7:21.

[8] Ez. 39:17-24.

* See Commentary p. 312.

On the walls of every room and on every door, Satan placed the two-faced symbol of your deceitfulness, for Ezekiel said one face was that of a man and the other the face of a lion. [9] So be it, for on one side you nurture, protect, and love the lamb, and on the other you treacherously take its gentle life and feast upon its flesh. [9]

28. But even as Jeremiah has said, "You make the law of your fathers into a lie;" [10] so have you made the book of Ezekiel to deny itself.

29. You garble and confuse the words of the Prophets who would cleanse you of your abominations.

30. Take no more the life of God from the throats of His gentle creatures, but instead, let your hearts become aware of loving kindness.

31. "For I desire mercy and not sacrifice, the knowledge of God more than burnt offerings," [11] said the Lord.

32. "Wash your hands in innocence," as it is written, "and go about your altars singing aloud a song of thanksgiving." [12]

33. When Jesus had finished speaking, "all the people were astonished at His doctrine." (Mark 11:18) The Priests and the temple Scribes stood speechless before the power of His words, for to deny His authority would be to deny the word of God in the Scriptures.

34. Great was their concern, for they reasoned that this man might bring about a change in the temple customs, for he spoke as did the prophets before him. He must not be allowed to enter the temple again for he challenged their authority over the people.

35. And while they were talking among themselves, a solicitor of Roman law came before them, saying:

36. Who is this man — by whose authority does he cause unrest among the people? Caesar does not approve of disorder.

37. And they answered him, saying, He presumes to be sent by our God to free the Jews. The people claim Him as their king. He would destroy our temple rituals, and we would have Him barred from the temple and sent back to Galilee from where He came.

38. And the solicitor replied: Neither Caesar nor the gods will tolerate insubordination. They alone are the judges of mercy; not this man. When he speaks against the sacrifice, he disparges the pleasure of Jupiter. No man is king over Caesar, and no God is superior to the gods of Rome.

---

[9] Ezek. 40:3-38-41-42-43 41:18-19 K.J.V.

[10] Jer. 16:19-21, 8:8.

[11] Hosea 6:6.

[12] Psalms 26:6. R.S.V.

CHAPTER XXXVII

Ye Are the City
The Feast and the Plague
The Proof of the Nature
of Jesus

1. And Jesus sat among His disciples while they asked many questions.

2. "Ye ask who are those that drew us to the Kingdom in Heaven? . . . the fowls of the air, and all beasts that are upon the earth and the fishes of the sea: these are they which draw you.* The Kingdom of Heaven is within you and whosoever shall know himself shall find it. Strive, therefore, to know yourselves and ye shall be aware that ye are the sons of the Father: And ye shall know that ye are in the city of God and ye are the city." [1]

3. But his disciples understood not, and said: Lord, what does this mean?

4. And Jesus answered them: Do you not know that God is life, your life, my life, and the life of every creature upon the earth?

5. The Scriptures say "In wisdom hast Thou made all the earth full of Thy creatures, even the sea to teem with life. When Thou sendest forth Thy Spirit, they are created."[2]

6. Thus when God gives life, He lends forth of Himself to inhabit the world. In consequence, the fowls of the air, the beasts of the earth, and the fish of the sea are of the living essence, which is of the nature of God.

7. They are part of the Kingdom. Mercy towards them is reverence for their Creator.

8. To know yourself as the life of God is to know also other creatures as of the life of God;

9. It is to be aware of their joys, their sorrows, and their pains and sufferings.

10. Through this awareness you find within you the city of the Kingdom: the Kingdom of all life, for you are the city thereof.

11. You have heard it said that God gave you dominion over all the earth. The earth is a city of the Kingdom and you are Lord thereof.

12. Suffer your s u b j e c t s therefore beneath your wing, and not beneath your heel.

13. It has been said by those of old time that the first murder was when Cain killed Abel.

14. But I say to you that the first murder was when Abel killed the firstling of his flock.

15. Its blood cried out from the ground and still cries out, for atonement.

16. Thus did the hand of man corrupt the whole of living things, for thereafter did the fear of him and the dread of him fall upon every beast

*See Job 12:7-10, 5:23
[1] From a First Century Papyri found in 1903 at Oxyrhynchus.
[2] Psalms 104:24-30.

of the earth and upon every fowl of the air; upon everything that moves upon the earth and in the waters of the sea.

17. And His disciples wondered and said, Is it not written that the Lord had respect unto Abel and to his offering? And Jesus said, Has God not spoken through the prophets about "vain Scribes and false witnesses?" *

19. Was the sacrifice of a lamb or an ox any more the pleasure of God in that day than it was in the days of Daniel, Hosea, Isaiah, Jeremiah, or them that wrote in the Proverbs and the Psalms?

20. Do you think God to be as fickle as man?

21. Have I purged the temple in vain that you should put this question to me?

22. And they said, Forgive us, Lord; we do not doubt you.

23. And then said Jesus: "When Elijah lay down in the wilderness, an angel came and said, 'Arise and eat.' And he looked, and behold, there was a cake baked on hot stones, and a jar of water. And he arose and ate and drank, and went in the strength of that food forty days and nights." 3

24. And when the children of Israel cried out for food in the wilderness, God sent them manna to eat. This was food equal in kind to that which He prescribed in the beginning: the kind that the angel gave to Elijah in the wilderness.

25. But the people cried unto Moses and fell to lusting and said, "Give us flesh to eat."

26. Moses was also displeased, and he said: "If your souls lusteth for flesh, ye shall have flesh."

27. And God was angry and sent them flesh in His wrath, and they ate of corruption till it stank in their nostrils and they fell by the thousands in the wilderness by reason of the plague.

28. "And He called the name of that place Kibrothhattaavah (graves of lust) because there they buried the people that lusted." 4

29. It was said by those of old time: "Hear thou, my son, be wise and guide thine heart in the way (of love and mercy); be not among wine bibbers, among riotous eaters of flesh." 5

30. "If thou refrain to deliver them that are ready for slaughter; if you say, 'I don't know about this,' does not he that has a conscience feel it?

---

* Jeremiah 8:8. R.S.V.
3 I Kings 19:6-8.
4 Num. 11:33—also see (1. Cor. 10:6) "Now these things were our examples to the intent we should not lust after evil things as they also lusted."
5 Prov. 23:19-20.

and he that keeps your soul—does he not know it? And does he not render to every man according to his works? Therefore, my Son, eat honey and that which is good: So shall the knowledge and the wisdom be of your soul; when you have found it, there shall be a reward and your expectations shall not be cut off." [6]

31. This secret I give to you that you might know the way that is of my being. But there will be one to come after me who will say: "Does God care for oxen?"

32. But I say to you, "Not one sparrow shall fall to the earth without my Father."

33. Lest you also may be tempted by the lusts of men to interpret me falsely, look you for all time to come to the prophecy of which I am the living evidence.

34. "And there shall come forth a rod out of the stem of Jesse and a Branch shall grow out of its roots." [7] In Me is this prophecy fulfilled.

35. "Even the sparrow finds a home, and the swallow, a nest for herself where she may lay her young on my altars. Blessed are those who dwell in My house, for they shall sing of loving kindness." [8]

36. Through Me all creatures will find peace, for I come to lead them back to the Kingdom of God. Through My ways man shall rise again; through the justice, mercy, and love that are of my Being there shall be no more harm or hurt upon all my holy mountain.

37. No man shall harm his brother, neither shall he kill his fellow creature, and neither shall a creature harm his fellow creature, "for the wolf shall dwell with the lamb and the leopard shall lie down with the kid; and the cow and the bear shall lie down together, and the lion shall eat straw with the ox." [9]

38. Follow me, for I am the fruit of the Branch of the stem of Jesse: the way, the law, and the peace without end.

CHAPTER XXXVIII
Jesus Prophesies
The Sacrifice of His Life

1. Meanwhile Jesus had left with His disciples and gone into a secluded place.

2. "Wherever there are two, they are not without God, and wherever there is one alone, I say I am with him. Raise the stone and there thou shalt find Me; cleave the wood and there I am." *

3. For there is nothing covered that shall not be revealed: neither hid that shall not be known.

4. The time is not far off when I shall be leaving you, for even as the lamb will be

[6] Prov. 24:10-14.

[8] Ps. 84:3-4.

[7], [9] Isa. 11:1-10.

* From the Logia of Oxyrhynchus.

sacrificed to satisfy their lusts at Passover, so will I be also.

5. And they looked at one another in astonishment, and they e x c l a i m e d excitedly, "How can this be, Lord, for Thou art the lamb of God?" Surely no evil can befall You.

6. You witnessed My final act of mercy at the temple. For this I stand condemned by My enemies.

7. Already the Governor's agents seek me out.

8. But I say to you, My friends, be not afraid of them that kill the body, for after that they have no more that they can do.

9. But I have forewarned you of the one to fear: not for the life of your body, but for your soul.

10. Are not five sparrows sold for a farthing, and are not a thousand lambs sacrificed at Passover?

11. But I say to you, not one of them is forgotten before God.

12. Even the very hairs of your head are all numbered. Fear not, therefore. Are sparrows more valuable than you?

13. "The knowledge of Thy Lord is a fountain of life to save you from the snares of death." [1]

14. After that Jesus went out on the mountain side and stood, with heavy heart, looking down upon the city.

15. "O Jerusalem, Jerusalem, thou that killest the prophets and stonest them which are sent unto thee, how often would I have gathered thy children together, even as a hen gathereth her chicks under her wings, and ye would not." [2]

CHAPTER XXXIX
The Love Supper
The Night Before Passover

1. "Now *before* the feast of the Passover, when Jesus *contemplated the hour* that He should depart out of this world," He called His Disciples together in a secret place.

2. Then Jesus spoke: Truthfully I say that one of you shall I *choose* to reveal me to my enemies.

3. I speak not of you all for I know whom *I have chosen:* but that the scriptures may be fulfilled.

4. Now I tell you this beforehand, that when it comes to pass, you may believe not evil of whom I send.

5. Verily, verily, I say to you whomsoever I send has received me, and he that has received me has received him that sent me.

6. "Then the D i s c i p l e s looked one on another, questioning of whom He spoke."

7. Quietly Jesus broke a portion of the bread and as

---

[1] Proverbs 14:27.
[2] Matthew 23:37.

Judas Iscariot, the son of Simon, came close to receive it, He whispered softly to him: "Make haste do it quickly."

8. "Now, *no man at the table knew* for what intent He spoke this unto him." (John 13:28)

9. "Some of them thought because Judas had a bag that Jesus had said for him to buy for the feast or to give to the poor."

10. But Jesus knew the anguish in the face of Judas as he took the morsel and hurried away on his mission.

11. Then Jesus turned to His disciples and said: "Now shall the Son of Man be glorified and God glorified in Him."

12. This is the last night I shall be with you in the flesh, for tomorrow they spill the blood of the paschal lamb upon the altar.

13. Yea, the lamb that is sacrificed to pacify the lusts of men and the one that is sacrificed to glorify the conscience of men.

14. To the former I give my body and with it all the pity that has dwelled therein.

15. To the latter I give my humble Spirit that it may live again within the heart and soul of every man.

16. Yea, the flesh of the lamb shall be defiled, but the life thereof,* which is the blood thereof, shall be sacrificed and returned to God.

17. Thus shall the lamb of God be sacrificed to end all sacrifice.

18. Thus will I die that the conscience of man be awakened to know mercy, compassion, and brotherly love:

19. Thus shall man be saved from himself, and the prophecy be fulfilled: the wolf shall lie down with the lamb; the deer and the bear feed their young ones together, and all living things rejoice, for there shall be no more harm or hurt within My Holy Kingdom. The earth shall have full knowledge of My love as the waters cover the sea. [1]

20. Love you one another and teach all men to love one another and to have mercy upon all creatures. I give My life that all the life under God may be revered by mankind.

21. Life, My life, or any life, glorifies not the life of him whose hands are stained with its blood.

22. God is life, and I am the Spirit thereof. "Reverence for life is, therefore, the truth and the way to eternal life." [2]

23. And He picked up a loaf of bread and brake it and gave a piece to each to His Disciples.

24. And He filled a cup with the prepared wine and held it

---

* Leviticus 17:14.
[1] Criticism of this doctrine will be that this will come to pass when Christ returns; a pretext to put off discipline needed today.
[2] Schweitzer.

above in solemn benediction. [3]

25. The bread I give to you is blameless of sin even as is the Lamb of God, mutilated by the pitiless and redeemed through compassion. Eat it in rememberance of me.

26. The cup I give to you is the wine of eternal life: even as is the life of the blood[4] I shed that man in his remorse may find life more abundantly.

27. May you now and forevermore revere that which only My Father in Heaven can give; and may your love for all men, and for all creatures, be equal to My love for you.

28. Do these things in remembrance of Me.

29. Go forth hereafter and teach all men to love one another. For I am of My Father, which is love in all things.

30. In Me there is no line to separate one man from another. All men are one in Me even as they are one in My Father.

31. Does God love a bird because of the manner of its flight, or a horse because of its color?

32. For twelve years, remain teaching among the Jews, and then go forth into every nation. For the Jews shall inhabit the world, and as you teach them, the world shall be taught also.

33. Verily I say to you: The God of Israel is the same God of the Gentiles.

34. There is only one Lord, and He is in Me even as He is in thee.

35. May He speak through the Spirit within you even as He speaks within Me.

36. Therefore I say to you: Make of your temple a fitting place that He may dwell as fully within you as within Me.

37. This I tell to you that you may know mercy and love, and obtain understanding and wisdom in all things, even as Daniel did before you.

38. When I am gone from you, and after your time among the Jews, spread to the four corners of the earth the joyous news that God has revealed His love for all His creation.

39. Through my sacrifice may the world be full of knowledge of the Lord as the waters cover the sea and the hearts of men be softened and learn of mercy, love and understanding.

40. Thus shall the prophetic vision * be brought to pass within the souls of men even as it is fulfilled in me,

41. But I charge you again: When you go forth among men, teach not alone through words, but equally through the way of life I exemplify.

---

[3] Prepared (or mixed) wine; water, colored or flavored with wine. The Essenes used prepared wine in their rituals.

[4] The blood thereof, which is the life thereof (Lev. 17:14).

* See Isaiah 11:1-10.

42. Wherever you go make of yourself the environment of which you preach, for then will people not only hear you, but follow the way of your conduct.

43. Thus can you truthfully and sincerely say, even as I say to you: "Follow thou me."

CHAPTER XL

The Agony in the Garden
Judas Concludes His Mission
The Disciples Desert Jesus

1. Then He came out and His disciples folowed Him to the Mount of Olives.

2. He withdrew from them a little way and kneeled down to pray.

3. As He meditated, the **words of the prophet Isaiah** fell heavily upon Him: "The wolf shall lie down with the lamb and there shall be no more harm or hurt upon all my holy mountain, for all creatures will have full knowledge of the Lord as the waters cover the sea."

4. Was not all this to have come to pass through Him? Had He failed to fulfill the prophecy?

5. The more He pondered these thoughts, the greater became His agony, for bitter indeed were His disappointment and sorrow.

6. And He prayed to the Father to remove this bitter cup of reproach, for He was now ready to suffer Himself as a soul-purifying example of all the harm, hurt, and sorrow in the world: to atone for His own failings and the failings of men to make all creatures to lie down s a f e l y through knowledge of Him.

7. As He prayed, His great heart swelled with compassion and pity, and it reached out towards a thousand fields and forests: towards a million homes and firesides, to gather in to itself all the pain, suffering, and sorrows upon the earth.

8. These He would, in final expiation, pour out through His own tortured flesh upon the cross in acme of protest against the sins of men. *

9. And when He arose from prayer and came to His disciples, He found them sleeping.

10. He was disappointed in them and said, Is your love no greater; for all of you sleep when you should keep watch even at my last hour with you.

11. And they all said, "Lord, forgive us. Our flesh is weak but our faith is strong."

12. J e s u s answered and said, Have you forgotten so soon what I spoke to you about words alone?

13. Verily I say that not one of you shall bear me out to the end.

14. You shall all deny Me and leave Me alone and without your comfort.

15. Even as He spoke, a company of soldiers came upon

* See Comentary p. 327.

them, with drawn swords, saying, Which among you is the one that is called "King of the Jews?"

16. At that moment His Disciples fled and left Jesus standing alone.

17. And Jesus spoke saying, It is I whom you seek.

18. "Put up your weapons, for verily I say to you: He who lives by the sword shall die by the sword."

19. Then Judas, who was with them, came forward and put His arms about Jesus and kissed Him.

20. And Jesus saw the remorse in his soul and said, Friend, you have done it well and my heart sorrows with you.

21. Then they took Jesus away and confined Him.

"All that ate of my bread,
lifted their heels against me
and they with whom I consorted
turned their backs upon me
and deny me up and down. *

CHAPTER XLI
The Trial Before Pilate
The Crucifixion

1. Soon it was morning and they brought Him before Pilate.

2. And Pilate asked Him: "Are you the King of the Jews?"

3. Jesus answered and said, You have said it.

4. Then His enemies cried out: He has been stirring up the people, teaching throughout all Jewry, from Galilee to Jerusalem!

5. Turning to Jesus, Pilate said: Do you seek to rule over the Jews in defiance of Caesar?

6. And Jesus answered: That which is Caesar's, I covet not. My Kingdom is the Kingdom of Heaven;

7. Those who follow me carry no weapons. My love goes out to all men, even to Caesar and to you.

Then said Pilate, You condemn the Jews for their temple sacrifice. Do you in like manner condemn the Romans?

And Jesus answered, I condemn no one. My heart overflows with pity and concern for all creation; I would that all life be liberated from pain and suffering.

8. Then Pilate turned to the people before him and said, I see no harm in this good man. He shall be punished for the disturbances he has caused and set free.

9. Then one of his advisers cautioned him, saying, Forget not that you also have enemies. What would you when Caesar hears that one has gone throughout the countryside conspiring with the people, and you have set him free— even though great multitudes have proclaimed Him King of the Jews? Is this not treason punishable only by death?

10. Has not Caesar shown

* Book of Hymns, Dead Sea Scrolls.

displeasure to those who extended mercy instead of loyalty to the laws of the empire?

11. I feel even as you that this man is harmless, but the circumstances as they may be presented to Caesar could be most condemning. Have a care, my friend.

12. For whosoever makes of himself a king, speaks against Caesar. And whosoever proclaims mercy instead of sacrifice disparages the pleasure of the gods.

13. When Pilate heard this saying, he brought Jesus forth and sat down in the judgment seat in a place called the Gabbatha.

14. "And it was the preparation of the Passover and about the sixth hour.[1] And he saith unto the Jews, 'Behold your King.'"

15. Then he turned to the priests who were there to witness and said, Is this man your King?

16. And they answered: We have no King but Caesar, but it is unlawful for us to put any man to death.

17. Then said Pilate: What would you then?

And they answered him, saying: The decision is in your hands, not ours.

18. Then Pilate gave the orders and the soldiers took Jesus and led Him away amidst loud protests from the people.

19. They scourged Him and put a crown of thorns upon His head and led Him to His execution.

20. Thus upon a cross designed by the evils of human nature was nailed the living symbol of all that is kind, merciful, and just.

21. Thus was perpetrated the blackest deed in all history: a glaring example of the merciless practice of sacrificing the living blood of God's creation to appease the selfish brutality of humanity.

22. And as the spirit of God had so chosen to come into this world among creatures suffered by the hurts of men, so likewise did He choose to leave the world along with creatures suffered by the slaughter of sacrifice.

23. Both His coming into and His going out of the world were therefore intimately timed to reveal and to demonstrate a great truth.

24. For even as the spirit of God first became flesh among the lives of His gentle creatures in a stable at Bethlehem, so also did His spirit again leave the flesh on the day of preparation along with the lives of a hundred thousand of His innocent creatures. The first choice was that of the Father, the last choice that of the Son, and the Holy Ghost was the witness thereof.

25. Thus the Lamb of God

---

[1] John 19:14—Here John contradicts the apparent editing of the other gospels which make Jesus appear as eating the paschal lamb.

gave Himself in sacrifice that man might, in his shame and remorse, seek atonement for his sins.

26. Thus the crucifixion became the means through which man might realize the immensity of his guilt, and make restitution through becoming aware of the pure divinity of LOVE and MERCY uncompromised by the inconsistencies of his own selfish nature.

27. Thus Jesus died as he had been born, among and along with those innocent creatures who, unlike the carnivores, were guiltless of the fall in Eden. As at His birth, they alone among the living provided the necessary environment and the pure innocence of spirit compatible with His advent into the world, so, likewise, in guiltless communion, He went out of it, companioned by the sufferings of a hundred thousand lambs. Even as the Scriptures cry: "The Spirit of God had gone forth to create them." * so had His Spirit returned with theirs to the Father. By the bloodstained hands of men did they suffer, both man and creature, as One.

28. Where, then, should one look for the devil but within the evil propensities of man.

29. O vain man, where is the proof of your superiority? Are you not peer to the wolf and the tiger; for have not they, too, fallen by token of the first blood spilt in Eden?

But the lamb, the calf, the ox, and the ass, and all of their kind — over whom you claim dominion—are far purer, being merciful; for in them is revealed the same innocence that existed before the Fall.

30. Is y o u r superiority, then, in your greater means to tyrannize and to kill? Not only the innocents of God's creation, whose consciences are as pure as the swirling snow, do you torture, maim, and slaughter, but also to your own kind do you do these things.

31. Do you vie in your superiority for posession of the three-pronged fork of fiends whose monstrous talents and diabolical designs you even now surpass? Or will you, in your spiritual heritage, choose the staff of justice, mercy, and loving-kindness as it is held out to you by the Prince of Peace?

32. "He has showed you, O man, what is good; and what does the Lord require of you, but to do justice, and to love mercy, and to walk humbly with your God."

33. The paths divide
        The choice is yours
        Where goest thou,
            O man?

* Psalms 104.

SOURCE REFERENCES

BOOK TWO

The Gospel of the Covenant of Love

Chapter III

1 Selected, in part from the translation by Theodore Gaster *The Dead Sea Scriptures*. (Doubleday & Company Inc., N. Y.)
2 *Ibid.*
3 *Ibid.*
4 *Ibid.*
5 *Ibid.*

Chapter IV

* Taken from Gaster's translation, *Dead Sea Scrolls*.

Chapter V

1 From Gaster's translation, *Dead Sea Scrolls*.

CHAPTER VII

2 From Gasters Translation of the *Dead Sea Scriptures*.

Chapter XI

** From Gaster's translation, *The Dead Sea Scriptures*. (Doubleday & Co., N. Y.)

Chapter XII

5 From Gaster's translation, *The Dead Sea Scriptures*.

Chapter XIII

2 Translation by Gaster, *Dead Sea Scriptures*.

Chapter XVI

1 Translation by Gaster, *Dead Sea Scriptures*.
2 *Ibid.*
7 *Ibid.*

Chapter XIX

1 Taken from Gaster's translation of *Dead Sea Scriptures*. (Doubleday & Company Inc., N. Y.)
2 *Ibid.*

CHAPTER XX

* Zebulun 2:1 *Twelve Patriarchs Lost Books of the Bible*. World Pub. Co. N. Y., Cleveland.

Chapter XXI

2 Gaster translation, *Dead Sea Scriptures*.
3 *Ibid.*

Chapter XXIII

* Gaster translation, *Dead Sea Scriptures*.

Chapter XXIV

4 Gaster translation from *The Dead Sea Scriptures*.

Chapter XXV

3 Gaster translation.
4 *Ibid.*

Chapter XL

1 Gaster translation book of Hymns. *The Dead Sea Scriptures*.

BOOK THREE

Commentary on the

GOSPEL OF

THE COVENANT OF LOVE

COMMENTARY

1 — The Creation and the Fall

"The Book of Genesis* (of the beginning) consists of the Pentateuch (five books) and the Hexateuch (six books).

The first eleven chapters represent the antecedents of Hebrew history. However, during the Persian period Jewish Scribes proclaimed the Mosaic authorship of Genesis and the Pentateuch.

In either case, bible students generally agree that the composite documentary theory is the best explanation of the formation of the book.

"In this theory Genesis is the result of the blending of accounts that express varied points of view, emphases, and characteristics which make it the product of not one but of many minds." [1]

Thus it seems necessary for anyone of sound mind, which of course includes a high degree of moral sensitivity, to recognize the natural inconsistencies of human nature that apparently dominate throughout Genesis.

In other words, before the word of God could be authored by man, it first had to be edited by all the varied complexes of the human mind. Thus one must recognize in the construction of these narratives the influences of all the sordid, vengeful, and merciless complexes of the human emotions, as well as all the good, sincere and truly ethical nature of man.

Human reason will tell us that only that which harmonizes with the latter can seriously be considered as rep-

---

* It is indeed doubtful, whether our present Genesis conforms in any way with the intent of its original author, or authors. (See Ency. Britt. 11th Ed. VXI p. 586.)

[1] Harpers Bible Dictionary — Genesis p. 219.

resenting the word, personality, or the pleasure of God.

Here, even the devout conformer must admit that a man truly inspired by God would expose to this fellowman only those things that are best for his welfare, and that these must be consistent with all that is true, merciful, considerate, equitable and just.

If Genesis is to be interpreted as a religious explanation of the origin of things, then it should be equal, theologically, to the integrity of the religion it serves.

Today religion is being rebuilt in ever increasing conformity with the concept that LOVE is the actual evidence of God. Mercy, justice, peace, kindliness, righteousness, etc., are all subordinates of LOVE, which is the nature of God.

The metaphorical interpretation of the fall of man as it now appears in Genesis is in dire need of revision or reconstruction to conform it, consistently and equitably, to both God and man.

For example, how could a loving, honorable, understanding and all-knowing God have created man in His own image, then placed him in a beautiful garden in which He had prearranged a decoy, a trap, so that he could toy with His creation as a cat does a mouse, knowing in advance that in due time man would accept the lure, thereby humiliating not only himself but causing frustration, discord, pain, suffering and death to all of his future descendants.

How could a merciful God have encouraged Abel to slay an innocent lamb, knowing in advance (as only God can) that when He smiled upon him for his burnt offering that his brother would become jealous and slay him.

It seems here that one must either strip God of His capacity of all-knowing or characterize Him as both Devil and Deity.

The alternative is preposterous, and completely out of harmony with theological concepts. One might say that God gave man the freedom of making his own decisions, Even so, this does not in the least compromise the lure of the red apple as entirely unbecoming the sublime dignity, the love, the elevating and ever helpful understanding of the God of all creation.

Furthermore, one must maintain that the character, the countenance, and the word of God is as consistent as it is dependable.

It cannot be unreliable, changeable, or willy nilly like that of man. God could not have had one type of character yesterday and a different one today. His nature necessarily is constant. He could not approve of a certain act in the Book of Genesis and then change His mind and condemn the same act in His word to the Prophets.

For example, in Genesis Abel offered the firstling of his flock and the fat thereof in sacrifice to God and God had respect for and was pleased with his offering.

However, again and again, through the voice of the Prophets, He vehemently denounced the slaying of animals and the blood offering as an affront to His nature.

Now Chapter Four of Genesis begins with Eve saying that she had conceived and had gotten a man from the Lord.

Thus a "man to be" was recognized: a man sent by the Lord, therefore a man of God.

In fact, this man seems to have been sent for a special purpose, for he represented the very means of producing the ingredients of God's Formula for feeding both man and beast.

> "For I give you every herb
> bearing seed and the fruit of
> the tree yielding seed, to you
> it shall be for meat." (Gen. 1:29-30)

Thus one might say that the firstborn of Eve was also the first gardener sent to earth purposely to bring forth from the soil food as prescribed by God.

It is quite obvious, therefore, that this firstborn, this gardener, who in Genesis is called "Cain," was the one actually favored by God. From this probably came the belief that developed into the sacrificing of the firstborn as the one most pleasing to God.

As to the second son of Eve, he came merely as a tender of sheep. As God's word through His prophets denounces the practice of blood sacrifice, He likewise would look upon the tending of sheep FOR THIS PURPOSE with equal disfavor.

It seems, therefore, that along with the certainty that justice, mercy, love, and understanding are the criteria of God's nature, one can have little doubt as to who killed whom.

It seems quite obvious, since the Prophet Jeremiah had said, "Our fathers inherit nought but lies" (16: 19-21), and again the "false pen of the Scribes make it into a lie," (8: 8) and since the Essenic Scripture also denounces the garbling of the laws of Moses, that the original construction of the symbolic narrations of Cain and Abel had been purposely reversed to make them conform to the sacrificial rites as set up by the Priests.

"With blasphemous mystic lore they convert the works of God into that which they guiltily imagined."*

Let us again remember, what the evidence clearly indicates, that when God, through the voice of His prophets, denounced the sacrificial system as abominable, He automatically declared it to be a lie that He had respect and was pleased with the blood offering of the herdsman.

It is evident, therefore, that the original symbolism, before it was altered to satisfy the priestly code, described God as respecting the fruit of the ground as offered by the gardener, and as not having respect for the animal sacrifice offered by the herdsman. Whereupon the herdsman, in a jealous rage, killed the gardener. As to which one of the brothers, the gardener or the herdsman, the name Abel or Cain should apply seems to be irrelevant, for it is characters, and not names, which perpetrate either good or evil.

But to be consistent with the Prophets, as well as with

* Book of Hymns, Dead Sea Scrolls.

the evidence of evil in man, he who first spilled the blood of one of God's creatures, he whose hand caused the first death in Eden and therefore the "original sin," was indeed equal to the crime of killing his own brother.

> For death its own avenger breeds
> The fury passions from that blood began
> And turned on man a fiercer savage, "man." [2]

Ellen G. White, the God inspired prophet of the Seventh Day Adventists, writing on this subject says: "God gave our first parents the food He designed that the race should eat. It was contrary to His plan to have the life of any creature taken. There was to be no death in Eden. The fruit of the tree in the garden was the food man's wants required." [3]

Joseph Krutch, in his book, "The Great Chain of Life," remarks: "No animal can be innocent as a plant may be. The latter can turn mere inorganic chemicals into living tissue; the animals cannot. All of them must live off of something else. And that, perhaps, is the deepest meaning of Original Sin." [4]

However, according to Genesis, if God intended plants to be the sole and complete food for man, then original sin is not in the eating of plants, but in the act of one animal taking the life of another for food.

God, in His wisdom, separated what might be termed "voluntary contribution" on the part of plants in supplying food, from what we recognize as determined opposition on the part of animals in their efforts to avoid being taken for food. A simple illustration of this is the tree's free and open contribution of its ripened fruit in contrast with an animal's fear, flight, and its otherwise violent fight against being slaughtered.

Plants alone supply the means of qualifying the term "Gifts of Bountiful Providence." Perfect health and peace of mind result only through man's recognition of the sufficiency of these gifts. The "Gifts of Bountiful Providence" means the gratuities of a living God. These gifts contain within themselves the very essence of the living God. We use the common expression "Germ of Life" in endeavoring to describe this living essence. It is prevalent in all fruits, nuts, berries, grains, melons, vegetables, and herbs.

Only in the carcasses of animals is it absent. One is a food relevant to life and the other a food relevant to death. One, a "Divine Formula," and the other a "Belial Recipe."* The former omits the evils of pain, suffering, and the horrors of the kill, for as food it represents merely the transference of the living essence of the plant to the mind and body of man. The latter represents as food all the cruel devices producing suffering and pain, without the mind- and soul-stimulating properties of the life essence contained in the former.*

Many of the great minds of the past have lamented the fall of man as retarding the full development of his intuition. They feel that the intuition, being a spiritual expedient, is hampered by a lack of harmless or innocent food taken into the body; that where the living essence is opposed by dead flesh, with its EVIDENCE OF CRIME against God and nature, the potential of the human mind is effectively restricted.

All the great poets, mystics, philosophers, and teachers of the ancient world, from the Orient to the Mediterranean, have recounted in song or story the way of life of early man upon this earth. Invariably they described him as living in an earthly paradise free from fear, want, or disease. Bountiful providence provided him with innocent food free from the blood curse of pain and death. Man lived completely free, even to the extent that his departure from this world was a matter of his own peaceful and happy choice. There was no harm or hurt among the beasts of the field or those of the forest, and all life dwelt in peace and feasted upon common fare even as that set forth in the First Chapter of Genesis. According to scholarly opinion, the cradle of man upon this earth proximated the

* See Appendix p. 419.

Isle of Java.[5] Here in the paradise, the Galean age of bounteous nature, were born the Themes of the Elysian plain of Homer, the Orphic characters of Hesiod, and the fruitful orchard-garden of Alcinous which lent Milton an image of Eden, and Rousseau his ideal in the Odyssey.

Both Plato and Empedokles refer to an age of innocence as having actually existed in past times before the sin of flesh-eating was known among men.

Virgil also associates the golden age with the abstinence from flesh eating.[6]

That this was actually the way of life of early man may be realized wherever human reason is allowed full freedom of expression unsoiled by the brainwashing of authorized custom.

However, as of this writing, one need no longer doubt the basic truth which has been for ages past preserved only in song and legend. Dr. D. S. B. Leakey, noted British archeologist, and his wife, working under the sponsorship of the National Geographic Society, have uncovered while digging in a fossil deposit in the Olduvai Gorge of Tanganyika a human skull over a half million years old. Here at long last has been unearthed actual proof that early man was a vegetarian. Upon examination the teeth verify this, for reports Dr. Leakey, "the big molars, small canines and incisors show he was by nature a plant eater." [7]

Tanganyika is in the exact same latitude with the Isle of Java across the Indian Ocean which approximates the area of the world where man is first supposed to have been cradled.

Considering again the many songs, poems, and legends of this golden age of mankind, one can readily suppose that the Garden of Eden was but an ancient Hebraic interpretation of the same. In the Garden scene, the plucking of the forbidden fruit parallels the slaying of the lamb as contrary to the interdiction, "Thou Shalt Not Kill".

The tasting of its flesh which was forbidden by the divine formula, Gen. 1:29,30 brought upon man all the many diseases of the flesh while the sacrifice of the life of the first animal, contrary to the laws of God, brought in its train the moral degradation of the human race. Thus did man fall.

No one can in justice to the dignity that is his birthright, do other than lament the consequences of such a fall, for, in truth, man has not only become the only animal who collectively kills its own kind, but he has also fallen to the feeding levels of the hyena and the carrion-eating vultures in their consumption of dead, moldy and putrid flesh.

How great was the fall of man! In creatures such as the innocent beings he slaughters for food are the only evidence we have to illustrate the way of all life "before the fall." In their eyes we see not the yellow fire of the carnivores, but only the serene depth of a wistful soul, pleading for mercy and understanding.

According to the Gospel of Luke, it was among creatures such as these that the Christ child came into this world. Thus the story which places the birth of Jesus in a stable has a far greater spiritual significance than has been supposed for it reveals the Christ spirit as extending special favor and concern to the meek and lowly of God's creatures.

Certainly a sincere believer cannot evade the intent herein exposed if he ever expects to attain the spiritual accord he seeks with his God.

The Divine Formula

To those Christians and Jews who pay little heed to the importance of Genesis 1: 29-30 or to those who consider these passages to be merely legendary and without any relation to the nature of living creatures, it might be pointed out that they do appear to be quite authentic. Indeed, they might well be described as actual prerogatives which seem to have a a priori place in the scheme of things, even primordial to the firstborn creature in nature.

If one were to read through every passage in the entire

Bible with the deliberate intent of discovering a valid and factual proof of the existence of a great "cosmic intelligence," he would find nothing that would reveal more clearly an answer to his quest than the message in Genesis 1: 29-30.

The truth which these passages hold forth seems to precede even the actual habits of living creatures which we, in our customary way of thinking, call "natural."

For example, first: It has been recognized that man, even when compared with the system we call "nature," is not a carnivorous creature. The closest animals to man are the great apes, orangutangs, gorillas, monkeys, etc. They are vegetarians: their physiological makeup is almost identical to that of us humans. But please don't be offended, dear reader, if you are an anti-evolutionist, for here we are merely comparing anatomical, and not genetic, intellectual or spiritual relationships. However, it might be pointed out here that even though our anatomical first cousins do not have access to the written word, as we do, they actually transcend, as far as diet is concerned, our human obedience to these divine precedents.

Space here will not permit an extensive discussion of the great physical, moral, and spiritual remunerations obtainable through obedience to the "divine formula." (Gen. 1: 29-30) However, in what we call "nature" is found overwhelming proof that all the beasts of burden, those creatures who both obey and abide are comparatively stronger, have greater endurance, and are longer lived than those who do not observe the "humane formula" as set forth in the First Chapter of Genesis. Also, as another proof of divine authorship of these precedents, the creatures that conform are more gentle and peaceful, while, on the other hand, those who disobey are vicious and bloodthirsty.

Now to verify the existence of a super authority behind this (Gen. 1:29-30) suppose we pass over Gen. 1:29 which applies to man, and discuss Gen. 1: 30 which applies to animals.

Here we discover through experiment that the basic validity of this formula transcends even the so-called natural habits and customs of animal life.

It has been illustrated that creatures whose ancestors have for thousands of years been vicious carnivores, have not only shown physical improvement but have become gentle and peaceful when fed on a diet equal to the divine formula of Genesis 1:30.

Recently a woman in the state of Washington raised a lion on a strictly vegetarian diet. After it was full grown they tried to tempt it with a chunk of beef. The lion took one sniff and turned away in disgust. This creature was so gentle that his owners would take him to the children's hospital, where the youngsters showered him with caresses. (See footnote*) It is well known that domestic cats thrive well and are much less prone to hunt birds when raised on a meatless diet.

The author obtained a German shepherd dog from a newly weaned litter of pups. As an experiment, we fed him in accord with the "humane formula" without the use of meat of any kind. He never had to be wormed as is customary with other puppies. We compared him with others from the same litter after about six months, and he was found to be much larger, had a longer and more beautiful coat, and was more alert than any of his brothers or sisters.

These, as well as many other experiments of a similar order, seem to actually prove that the dietary precedents of Gen. 1.29-30 transcend in truth not only human but also animal habits and customs: i.e., their source seems to antecede the so-called "natural" way of life as it is practiced by flesh eating creatures.

Man may not realize it but he also is subject to the same determining factors which mold and shape the physical and psychic nature of other creatures.

* Read *Little Tyke* by Westbeau, Pac. Press Pub. Assn. Mountain View California.

He can no longer afford to ignore the evidence which so clearly points out that wherever the seeds of harm, hurt, pain and discord are sown, gnarled and bitter fruit shall be of their reaping. Where one creature in nature makes necessary the pain, suffering and death of another creature in order to maintain its own life both its physical and psychic characteristics reflect the inevitable consequences.

For example, compare the eyes of the flesh eating beasts with those of the herb feeders. *Separate the vicious and the loathsome creatures from those which are timid and harmless and you also separate the flesh eaters from the vegetarians.* Here we find also that the truly beautiful has a spiritual quality that distinguishes it from the gaudy or the grotesque.

It is probably due to our years of familiarity with the nature of the many flesh eating or carnivorous creatures that we have grown to overlook the particular leaning they have towards the evil side of the psychic state, as opposing the peaceful, the merciful, the good, and the wholesome which characterizes the "God head."

It is to be noted here that even though experiments have shown a carnivorous beast to become more docile when raised on a meatless diet that it would still require many generations of the same feeding before its physical characteristics would respond in a like manner. An animal's physical characteristics generally conform to the nature of its feeding habits. The question, therefore, is were its physical characteristics such as claws, fangs, intestines, formed merely as a means of devouring and digesting its food or, did they develop through the desire of the creature to pursue a certain method of obtaining food.

The latter seem to be most likely. In fact today scientists are becoming increasingly more cognizant of developmental effects through "psychic" causes, rather than holding fast to the past century idea that organic change is brought about entirely through accidental means.

Coincidently, the idea of "Psychic Causes" also conforms to the events as suggested in Genesïs, wherein the desire of the creature to pursue a method, represents its destructive way of life after the "fall."

But as further proof that the physical nature of an animal is in a large degree brought about by its inward or "psychic" impulses suppose we examine the probability that the psychological, or, psychic nature of a creature is actually a prototype of its spiritual nature.

If one could set aside his traditional and superficially conditioned way of looking upon a carnivorous beast he would view it through an entirely different pair of eyes. He would see written upon the countenance of the creature a reflection of its distorted soul: as the psychic consequence of its cruel, blood letting diet. In order to illustrate this more effectively suppose we, who are not specialists in the field, look upon a strikingly strange but revealing illustration of a comparative assortment of winged mammals or bats.[8]

Seeing these for the first time one immediately recognizes the astounding psychic comparison exhibited by these creatures. Here the doubting one is brought face to face with the evils of flesh eating. (See Plate 4) He can no longer deny the inevitable consequences of a blood feast. Here, out and away from the viewpoint of the familiar, is illustrated the true and the good. Note the innocent purity of the spirit or "soul life" of the species who fed upon the "Divine formula" as set down in Genesis 1:29, 30: observe their "deer like" heads which, in bible lore, symbolizes the unblemished life and the tireless battle against sin. Then note the demonaic "Spirit life" of the species who feed according to the "Belial recipe."

It is also most interesting to note the sort of "half way between" appearance of the tube nosed or *nyctymene* bat. This creature has neither the innocent countenance of the total fruit feeders nor the demoniac countenance of the strictly carnivores. While it is classed as a fruit feeder insect remains have been found in its digestive tract, which may indicate that it is an omnivorous feeder. One might say that this creature of the bat world has, even as man, suffered the physical and psychic consequences of adding flesh to its diet.

This brings to mind a reference from an ancient scripture "Through participation in the unnatural eating of flesh-meats man becomes a fellow-eater with devils." (Clem. Hom. XIX., 22)

Here in the full force of these enlightening comparisons of the bat families, both the saintly and the satanic may be revealed in the "soul life" of living creatures. One can but meditate, where we as human beings, are in this manner capable of perceiving or evaluating the "soul life" of creatures below us, that some higher spirit may also be evaluating our "soul life" in a similar manner.

Here again in this illustration of the comparative psychic nature of bats one might recognize the existence of a "supernatural" or, rather the truly natural over the pseudo-natural * as actually being in accord with Genesis 1:29-30.

The fact that this formula holds true over contrary habits and practices in nature as providing for better health, and longer life together with a personality that reflects the glory of a pure untarnished soul makes it stand out against all criticism and doubt as transcending the authority of man.

The revelation that comes through the realistic application of this formula is in itself proof of a higher intelligence to which the pseudo-natural is much like a disobedient and wayward child. Where it can be demonstrated that both the physical life and the social attitude of an habitually carnivorous animal is changed for the better and where the personal character and spirit of a creature is developed in proportion to its obedience to the thirtieth verse in Genesis, Theologians can at long last, apply logic to the belief that a higher nature does exist as superior to the ordinary. In other words where habitually vicious

* See Conclusion.

beasts can be raised to be docile and affectionate in their relationships with other creatures by following these same dietary authorizations verifies the higher, or, the truly natural to be both the source, the means, and the way to loving kindness and to the peaceful relationships of all creatures. (see Papias quoting John on Jesus p. 86)

And yet, despite these divinely ordered compensations resulting from obedience to this "humane formula," both the orthodox Jew and Christian alike have for centuries not only ignored the evidence of truth contained therein, but have actually upheld what the prophets denounced as the work of "false scribes," in order to discredit it. This undoubtedly represents one of the most irreverently stupid acts that religion could be guilty of, and it is high time, if they ever expect to reach a turning point towards the bettering of humanity, that they listen more attentively to the spiritual prerogatives of Holy writ, than to the corporeal compromises which contradict them.

The Sixth Commandment made all inclusive of sentient life by Isaiah 66:3 is actually a restatement of the intent contained in the command to use for food only those things which spring from the earth. This is the first law of God. All other dietary rules and regulations are completely without precedent and are therefore not laws of God but laws made by men.

To put it in another way, Genesis 1:29,30 is the first word on the subject of food recorded in the Scriptures. As a precedent it therefore, cannot be set aside or overruled by subsequent references: for such references would in effect represent a direct affront to the integrity of "Absolute Truth" which is unchangeable and not willy-nilly as is the word of man.

COMMENTARY

2 — The True God of Creation
Succeeded by False Gods

It is interesting to note that the moral development of man has paralleled through the centuries the moral nature of his god, or gods.

In other words, the many types of religious customs and practices have illustrated the progress of man's spiritual development in direct relation to the form and character of the God he worshipped.

Pliny declared that "the weakness of humanity had embodied the Being of God in many human forms endowed with human faults and vices."

Beginning from the earliest of historical records we find man endeavoring to characterize in his god, or gods every extravagance the human senses and emotions are capable of. The gods of the Greeks, the Romans, the Egyptians; the gods of the early Europeans, Asians; those of primitive Americans, and those of the Islands and the jungles of Africa; all represent gods *by, for,* and *of* man. That is to say, *by* his own invention, *for* his own security, and *of* his own character.

It does not require a great deal of imagination or reason to recognize a similar tendency to invent, when one reviews the many sided character of the God of the ancient Hebrews.

In only a casual reading of the Old Testament one is amazed to find characterized therein a God whose word is as changeable and "willy nilly" as is that of man: a God who having set forth a list of moral and ethical rules for men to abide by, discredits his own word by either giving silent approval of, or by voicing encouragement to those who proceeded to disobey them.

If one can consider disposition, temperament and behavior as means of identity, then it is quite obvious that the Old Testament sets forth and describes two totally different characters which, in effect, portray either two separate individuals, or two conflicting ideas or concepts of God. For example, check and consider the following contrasts and their text references:

(1) A God of Peace and (10) A God of war
(Mic. 4:3) (Jos. 10:40,6:21,)
(Ps. 145:8,9) (II Sam. 23:10)

(2) A God of forgiveness and (11) A God of vengeance
(Ps. 78:38) (Deut. 32-43)
(I Kings 8:36) (II Kings 9:7)

(3) A God opposed to sex and (12) A God who encourages
offenses (Ex. 20:14) fornication and rape
(Gen. 19:29-36)
(Num. 31:18)
(II Sam. 11:14)

(4) A God opposed to the and (13) A God who approves
eating of flesh eating of flesh
(Gen. 1:29,30) (Gen. 9:3)

(5) A God opposed to the and (14) A God who is pleased
sacrifice of animals by a burnt offering
(Is. 1:11-16) (Gen. 4:4)
(Hos. 6:6)

(6) A God who blesses man and (15) A God who encourages
with one wife bigamy
(Mal. 2:14-16) (Deut. 17:17) (I Sam. 25:42,43)

(7) A God who desires all and (16) A God who approves
men to be free the keeping of slaves
(Jer. 34:8,9) (Lev. 25:44)

(8) A just God and (17) A terrible God
(Ps. 89:14) (Ex. 20:5)
(Neh. 9:32)

(9) A God of mercy and and (18) A merciless God
loving kindness (II Kings 10:1-30)
(Ps. 103:3,4)
(Hos. 6:6)

These are only a few of the many scriptural references which expose the conflict in human ideas and human emotions which in effect characterized the Gods of the early

Hebrews.* Is it any wonder therefore that the prophets cried out: "Can man make for himself gods? Such are no gods."

Now there were among certain peoples of the past those who recognized that the god exemplified through false doctrines and vain ceremonial practices was not the true God. They were aware of His pure nature and condemned the cloak of falseness put upon His character by both the temple priests and the people who adhered to their doctrines.

These were the early prophets, or religious reformers, who appeared among all nations and peoples long before the First Century.

Even though these great souls lived and died a life of protest against the falseness of man's knowledge of God, they succeeded only in making the people conscious of their guilt which resulted in their devising a variety of defense mechanisms, set up to justify their behavior.

In other words, peoples of the world had begun to realize that there was a true light even though they persisted in shutting it out. In accord with Essenic prophesy, the time had now arrived in the evolution of human consciousness for a more decisive influence to be brought to bear.

This, from a theological or metaphysical point of view, suggests that God found it necessary to use exceptional means to alert mankind of His true nature.

Thus it might be said that God brought forth the evidence of His own Being through the incarnation of the '.Teacher of Righteousness," the "Son of His handmaid" as He is referred to in the Dead Sea Scriptures.

Here is suggested to Christians the basic purpose behind the coming into the world of Jesus the "Essene Christ": i.e., to demonstrate first hand the true character and Spirit of God.

---

* The Jews today however consider the character of God as being in accord with categorical references of column one rather than of column two.

In him God projected evidence of His own Being: His own truth, dignity and integrity: His own love, mercy, compassion and infinite kindness, that it might be brought to witness before all mankind.

As we have illustrated before, man's moral and spiritual nature has always paralleled his religious characterization of God. Therefore, if his emotional nature and his sensual desires formed the character of the god he worshipped, why should not a reverse of this order favor a spiritual rebirth? i.e., why should not an uncompromised and unprejudiced awareness of a true God of love and mercy, in effect, bring about a similar parallel in man's emotional and sensual nature?

The answer is obvious, for in reversing the order, man no longer is guilty of making his God conform to his own sensual nature but makes his sensual nature conform to God. Therefore if God is the criterion of the ALL GOOD, then a conscious awareness of this fact must bring about a change in the individual's own way of life. In harmony herewith it might be said that in Jesus Christ, the personification of a "divine plan" was brought to witness before man.

Here, now, the full freedom of human choice is brought face to face with spiritual alternatives. The turning point is at hand. Man can now know God in proportion to his willingness to subordinate his emotional and sensual nature to all that is kind, merciful, loveable, compassionate, just, and good. In other words, through becoming of himself the life which Jesus exemplified, man attains the means of bringing to pass the "Kingdom of Heaven" upon the earth.

The person of Jesus, as described in "The Covenant of Love" exemplifies the Spirit of God incarnate. To the Christian, this is a necessary truth. But to the non-Christian, he is free to recognize herein an allegorical characterization of the human potential at its highest moral and spiritual level: an example, or a symbol of Perfect Being: an Ideal well worth the attention of any man seeking the highest good.

Only through the realization that man, any man—Christian or non-Christian—can achieve, within his own consciousness, a parallel of the highest ideals of God, will love triumph and bring about the redemption of all flesh: "and all creatures themselves shall be delivered from bondage and corruption into the glorious liberty of the children of God." (Rom. 8:21)

In all due respect to the great religions of today, it seems necessary to place an emphasis on their not too apparent awareness of the relationship of a God of love to His creation. In other words, they put limitations on humane teachings which in turn inhibit a fuller expression of the doctrine of mercy and loving kindness. This discrepancy in the ethical system of the Christian church is not excusable in view of the fact that Christians freely admit they alone have been blessed with the living example of the pure and sublimely ethical nature of God in the person of Jesus Christ. Therefore, in accord with Christian thought, no other religion has had the privilege of knowing God first-hand through his own incarnated spirit. This advantage seems to stand out as a challenge to the Christian who seeks the fullness of God's mercy and loving-kindness while failing to extend to other creatures the very blessings he himself seeks.

"The heart is the center of the body and the fountain of life, but a heart without love is a sick heart and the whole body is affected. So a religion without a warm and feeling heart becomes spiritually a sick religion for no religion, in fact, no civilization is complete which does not include in its sphere of charity and mercy, the dumb and defenseless of God's creatures." [1]

The flow of love between man and God is metered in direct proportion to the respect and concern man extends towards all created beings.

COMMENTARY

3-4 God's Chosen Ones

This Chapter, from a theological point of view, suggests that in the discovery of the Dead Sea Scrolls might be found the long lost preface to the coming into being of the Son of Man.

In the gospel of John we find that "He was in the beginning with God." Then in Matthew, "He is born in the flesh at Bethlehem." In Mark and Luke the spirit in the flesh again appears a quarter of a century later, to be recognized by John the Baptist, who is preaching on the banks of the Jordan. This gap in the continuity of the story of Jesus has for centuries led to much speculation as well as to a certain amount of uncertainty and insecurity on the part of the Christian student.

Certainly such an unprecedented happening as the appearance of the Son of man among the people of Israel must have been anticipated. The event certainly seems to warrant considerable planning and forethought on the part of someone selected to prepare the way. But the gospel records seem to rest the total of this momentous responsibility upon a wandering evangelist who was merely a messenger: one who acted out but did not himself prepare the script. We now know that he received his gospel of repentance from the "Chosen Ones," the Essenes.

Through the finding of the Dead Sea Scrolls we are now able to link together not only the birth of Jesus and the time he began his ministry, but we also seem to discover in the preparations of the Essenes an astounding fore-knowledge of the great event. They alone were expecting the Messiah and were busy preparing for His coming in the desert. Their monastery was only about five miles from where John appeared on the banks of the Jordan to baptize the Son of man.

The question among scholars involving the historical placing of the Teacher of Righteousness might actually be answered in the subsequent appearance of Jesus. That is to say the writers of the Scrolls envisioned in their characterization of the Teacher of Righteousness a sort of messianic prototype of the suffering servant of Isaiah. He appears at first to be a mythical figure who later came to life in the historical character of Jesus Christ.

It now seems most obvious as our Covenant of Love suggests, that these Holy Ones actually prepared the way in no uncertain terms through the particular manner of their writings. In these writings, whether intentionally designed by the hand of Providence or otherwise, can be found the educational means of preparing the way wherein Jesus learned of His destiny and John the Baptist received the inspiration for his preaching.

> For out of the seeds which these men sow
> shall yield a flower unfading, (Jesus)
> the twig shall put forth leaves becoming
> an evergreen to give shade to all things.
> Its branches shall tower to heaven and it
> shall thrive beyond all bounds that all
> nations may know the truth and all peoples
> Thy glory.* [1]

This verse might very well symbolize Christianity on its way towards eventual blossoming and fruit.

And now, as to the known evidence which supports this theological concept, we recognize, first of all, the unusual conditions pertaining to the discovery of the Dead Sea Scrolls. For instance, the incidental throwing of a stone, the coincidental striking of a clay jar by the stone, the clatter of broken pieces, the later exploration of the cave where the sound came from, and the discovery of a treasury of musty old documents. Now to those who believe in pre-

* From the Dead Sea Scrolls.

destination, the hand of Providence is here beginning to show itself.

There were many other unusual incidents leading up to the safe-keeping of the scrolls and their translation, but space herein restricts further discussion at this time.

Next therefore, we shall discuss the startling compatibility of the "time element" associated first, with the finding of the scrolls and next, with reference to a particular period during the First Century B.C.

For two thousand years, a portion of the Essene Scriptures had remained hidden from the prejudiced mind and destructive hand of man. But now, after nineteen centuries had passed, they have been either accidentally, coincidentally or purposely revealed to man.

It goes without saying that if these old documents had been discovered during the past century or before, they would never have been made available to open examination and discussion. It is questionable whether they would have even survived translation. Was this again the hand of Providence at work?

According to historical records, Herod the great built his winter pleasure palace not far from the Essene monastery toward Jericho.

The intrusion of this alien spirit upon the sanctuary of their holy ground must have indeed caused them no little concern.

Thereafter, as it is historically recorded, in 37 B.C., an earthquake shook the area. It caused much loss of life in Judea as well as inflicting some damage to the Essene monastery.

Archeological evidence seems to indicate that at this time the inhabitants of the Qumran sanctuary abandoned the place. Some scholars seem to think that a remnant went to Damascus while others suppose they returned to their home communities in various parts of Judea and Galilee.

Again archeologists point out that, according to their findings, the Essenes again returned to Qumran some time between 4 B.C. and 6 A.D. These dates were established by the discovery of coins and other archeological debris. Time, here again, seems to favor a connection between the Essenes and the birth of Jesus.

The torrid reign of Herod the great ended with his death in the year 4 B.C. This does not necessarily mean that the Essenes returned in 4 B.C. because of the passing of their son of darkness. They may have returned a year or two before this event, having probably foreseen his death, even as they may have foreseen the birth of Jesus. Josephus says, "There were those among them who foretold things to come by reading the holy books, and using several sorts of purifications and being perpetually conversant in the discourses of the prophets; and it is but seldom that they miss in their predictions."

According to Matthew, Jesus was born in the "days of Herod the King," (2:1) The flight into Egypt and the massacre of the infants (Matt. 2:13) apparently happened the year Jesus was born. Herod could very well have died later the same year. He was, no doubt, a sick man both in mind and body, when he ordered the murder of the infants. Certainly this atrocious act was not at all favorable to his well being.

According to Christian tradition* the date of the crucifixion was Friday the 14th of Nisan A.D. 29. Hippolytus A.D. 200 writes that Christ suffered in his 33rd year.** This places the birth of Jesus in the later part of the year 5 B.C. or the early part of 4 B.C. the same year Herod died, and according to archeologists the same year the Holy Ones returned to rehabilitate the monastery on the shores of the Dead Sea.

It has been pointed out that somewhere between the year 6 B.C. and 4 B.C. there was a conjunction of the planets Jupiter and Saturn in the zodiacal sign of Pisces. Also this same time a comet appeared in the heavens, and

* See appendix, p. 416.
** Bible, Encyp. Britt. 11th Ed. p. 891.

again in this same period there was an eclipse of the moon. The extraordinary thing is that all of these phenomena of the heavens approximated in time both the birth of Jesus, the passing of Herod, and the return of the "Chosen Ones" to their desert sanctuary: there to "prepare the way" (to make available the means) for the coming forth of the Lord.

COMMENTARY

5 — The Conception and the Union of
Mary and Joseph

The actual conditions leading up to the birth of Jesus will always remain a mystery. Matthew and Luke report Him as having been conceived by a virgin while Mark and John are silent on this point. The claim that Jesus was the offspring of a virgin has always been subject to much controversy.

There are those who hold that the present recordings of this event grew out of a later invention, probably championed by Paul. They recognized in Paul a great organizer, a powerful personality whose outspoken nature all but overwhelmed any opposition he might have had from the more timid natures of the disciples. They point out that Paul was ambitious and clearly foresaw the possibility of his organizational efforts being limited to an obscure Jewish minority. In other words, they assume Paul realized that if he was to found a world religion, he would necessarily have to make a dramatic appeal to the Gentiles.

It is said that this was done through emphasizing the virgin birth, thereby confusing the Jewish heritage of Jesus. Thus was made possible a more extensive appeal to the Gentile world. Proponents of this argument point out that even today the person of Jesus is at times illustrated as a non-semitic, blond-haired, blue-eyed Anglo-Saxon.

However, aside from this rather biased viewpoint of the methods of Paul, it can hardly be doubted that his forceful personality did compromise the ascetic practices of Peter, James, Matthew, and others in order to appeal to the free-living desires of the masses.

Again, aside from this, it is also the opinion of many

that the idea originated within the family of Mary in order to appease the suit of the much older Joseph, thereby gaining the protection of a husband to avoid the customary death by stoning.

However, even this notion is not without ameliorating factors, for if Jesus was born out of wedlock, of an unknown flesh and blood parent, as may have been the case of the Baptist, the child would be subject only to a stigma processed in the little minds of men. In this case the transcending of such an obstacle merely emphasizes the greatness of Jesus. Certainly the extreme act of kindness, justice, mercy and forgiveness demonstrated in that memorable admonition, "Let him who is without sin among you cast the first stone" indicates an understanding far superior to the mere tolerance of a self-righteous society.

Could it not have been that God purposely introduced in the birth of Jesus a lesson to mankind such as this: that the son is of the sins of the flesh, but the life thereof, which is the Spirit thereof, is of God?

Thus, would a son be responsible not for the sins of the father bearing witness in his flesh, but only to the Father bearing witness to his spirit? This might be said to have been "God's way" of denouncing not only the lack of kindness but also the extreme lack of understanding present in our social system.

To many people the very mention of the phrase, "born of a Virgin," is intolerable. Such a stand is indeed based more upon reason than speculation, or, more upon fact than fiction.

However, when one seeks beyond the commonplace, he often becomes less critical of what appears to be fiction and more doubtful of what appears to be fact. Truth is, at times, even more strange than fiction.

Natural processes have strange ways of behaving, and the seeking minds of the greatest thinkers are invariably more mystified than satisfied with their conclusions.

Throughout all our studies of natural phenomena, we

seem to open door after door only to find more doors that our carefully worked pass-key will not unlock. Oftentimes we retrace our steps through doors that would better have remained closed, but still we seek even though we are far from understanding the impact of our present discoveries. Nature has many means of operation, all of which are realized through certain formulas of design and certain principles basic to available ingredients.

Thus in nature is found the principle of generation through which all organic development is made possible. In other words, in the construction of an organized living body the principle of generation presupposes a design formula which in turn results in organized development.

This principle of generation is in nature the coming into existence of a material system as creation is of God the coming into existence of a psychic system. It seems quite evident that of the two systems the psychic alone contains the "know how," the enabling facilities to arrange the perfectly balanced designs that constitute a mature organism. The fact that the organism in its generation and development is always indigenously attended by the psychic "know how" suggests that somehow this same property may have anteceded in time the union of life and matter in the generation of a living thing.

Returning to nature's principle of generation, one finds several processes at work.

First, in the theory of "genes" the principle is manifest in their duplication. Again the same principle is witnessed in the process of mitosis and cell division. Both of these phenomena might be described as creation subordinated by generation.

It is the usual case in nature that sexual association enters into the inception of the process; however, this is not without exception. Certain single celled organisms parallel creation with generation without the needs of copulation. Also, in nature, many plants reproduce themselves without the necessity of contact through association.

It has been suggested that man himself might have been a bi-sexual creature at one time; that the rib of Adam is associated with Eve as underlying the breast where suckled the newborn. This notion presupposes a creature more woman than man and contradicts the scripture writers who stressed the superiority of the male animal.

One may find support of this notion by the fact that many humans today appear as men but are extremely feminine in their nature even to the extent of sexual motivation. The superiority of male hormones may have been developed through evolutionary processes which paved the way to sexual differences. How else can one explain the almost perfectly formed, but otherwise insufficient, breasts of the male animal? Body parts such as breasts, appendages, etc., become useless in conformity with the Lamarckian hypothesis of "use and disuse." In time the female breast may also become inefficient through its use being replaced by bottle feeding.

Extending this sort of speculation still further, one finds that the Hebrew words for God are ELOHIM and ELOAH. The first describes a bi-unal principle involving the term "God-mother" or "Father-Mother-God." The second is a singular form, or feminine. Thus God is both masculine and feminine in being One. In which case it seems that if man was made in the image of God he was necessarily a bi-sexual creature. One might suppose that he was also immortal in the flesh, even as were certain unicelled organisms before they adopted the mortal processes of sexual generation.

Considering the notion of a probable bi-sexual age in the development of man, one might suggest that a throwback in evolution could, in a remote case, alter the usual trends of generation with extraordinary results.

It is well known in medical circles that a woman may be even three months pregnant and then, for some unexplained reason, the embryo gradually shrinks in what might be termed a reversed form of generation and creation, until it is completely absorbed into the body of the mother.

Does it seem one bit more remarkable for a living thing to appear contrary to customary process of generation than for one to disappear contrary to customary processes of growth and development?

Not so long ago, a leading scientific paper carried an article describing the possibility of a female in remote instances being able to conceive without the necessary fertilization of the male creature.

Be that as it may, it seems that the mechanics have always existed in nature wherein living things have been created and generated without the need of copulation.

Thus the Christians' argument supporting the idea of the virgin birth might resolve in the supposition that God is provided with a device in nature which He might choose to use in an extraordinary manner, while at the same time remain within the laws which are of His Being.

Notwithstanding, however, there are still several scriptural irrelevancies which the Christian must compromise before his belief in the virgin birth can be sustained. For example it was foretold by the prophets that out of the stem of Jesse shall a son of David come, to bring the love of God to the world. The writer of Matthew records the lineage of Jesus from Abraham through forty-two generations up to Joseph, the husband of Mary of whom was born Jesus, called the Christ.

Thus he affirms in context that a seed of the seed and the blood of the blood shall witness the fulfillment of prophecy in the birth of Jesus.

However, in almost the very next verse he refutes completely the whole idea of genetic lineage and substitutes in its place not a descendant of David through Joseph but, instead, a descendant of heaven through a conception completely unrelated to the stem of Jesse.

Many claim that the conception of Mary before her coming together with Joseph all but invalidates the prophecy because of its particular cleavage to genetic succession. While this was an obstacle to Jewish conversions, it did, however, provide for, along with other concessions, the wide acclaim of the otherwise unsympathetic Gentiles.

On the other hand, one might consider the flesh and blood lineage as merely subordinate to a psychic or spiritual succession. Thus one might say that through the bonds of holy matrimony a spiritual union took place between Joseph and Mary which made of Joseph not only the legal, but the spiritual father of the flesh-and-blood Jesus.

"We observe also that the doctrine of the Virgin birth, without which no prophet or saviour-god could be a divine incarnation, was so common among ancient cults that it was impossible for any religious founder to achieve acceptance without it. In the mystery-cults . . . all saviours, past, present and future, were incarnate gods, born of virgins; this was an idea which came so easily and so naturally to primitive priests in order to establish their own authority that it sprang up independently in many places; Jesus was simply accorded the same honor by universal demand after His cult began making converts in the pagan world." [1]

However, considering the Essene Scriptures as pre-Christian documents and giving the historical Jesus His rightful identity as the incarnated "Teacher of Righteousness," one discovers that the Son born of a virgin, according to the gospels, and the "Son of God's handmaid," * as referred to in Essene Scriptures, are one and the same. (See pp. 59, 60)

Thus it might be said that the doctrine of the Virgin birth is traditionally Christian and was not borrowed directly from the mystery religions, as most scholars and theologians have heretofore assumed.

According to Epiphanius the texts used by the Ebionites which have been previously described as of the original Aramaic Matthew read "Thou art my beloved Son: this day

* (Also see Luke 1:38).

have I begotten thee." * This indicates that it was upon the day of his baptism that Jesus was mystically transformed into the Son of God.

"Justin Martyr quotes Matthew 3:17 using the same wording as Epiphanius attributes to the Ebionite gospel." [2] Thus we know that the canonized Matthew was altered in order to strengthen the doctrine of the virgin birth. One must suppose that similar alterations in Mark and Luke took place at the same time.

A passage from the Testament of Levi seems to support the Ebionite texts as follows:

"And the voice of the Most High shall be uttered over him and the spirit of understanding and sanctification shall rest upon him in the water."

However a supporter of church doctrine might point out that in spite of alleged alterations God even in the Ebionite gospel did say "Thou art my beloved Son," and that the phrase "This day have I begotten thee" was to affirm that on this day has my new covenant been declared in the person of Jesus. This would be in accord with Essenian scriptures and the purpose of the Teacher of Righteousness.

In concluding this chapter on the little known circumstances pertaining to the conception of Jesus called "The Christ," it might well be said that what He means to the world does not depend upon the manner of His birth, but rather upon the way of life He practiced and the doctrine of Love He brought to all men of good will. On this every Christian should agree.

* Also quoted in 1 Clement, *Epistle to the Carinthians* (17:20) A. D. 95,6.

COMMENTARY

6-7 — The Birth of Jesus

One cannot help but wonder why Christians of almost every denomination have failed to grasp the significance of the "place" or the "environment" into which the babe Jesus was born.

They repeat the story of his birth and reconstruct at Christmas time traditional replicas of the nativity, but somehow fail to recognize the fullness of the sublime message disclosed in the very scene they strive to reproduce.

The report that there was "no room at the inn" could not have in itself decided the place where Mary was to deliver into this world the Son of Man. Joseph, as well as the parents of Mary, was of comfortable means, and Joseph was in a position to bargain either at the inn or elsewhere for shelter. Certainly, someone would have provided a bed for a woman in travail.

If, as seems to be the case the Christian accepts the conditions surrounding the crucifixion of Jesus as being part of a Divine Plan, then he must also consider the conditions surrounding his birth to be of momentous significance. Every incident, every occasion involving every place wherein Jesus made his appearance upon the earth, must be construed by the Church as providing a means of instructing mankind of the pleasure of God.

As we have previously discussed, the evidence seems to indicate that the parents of Jesus inhabited the Nazarene community in Galilee which was a sect of the Essenic tradition.

Josephus tells us that the "Holy Ones" lived in all the towns of Judea and that they were always ready to give food and shelter to the needy or deserving.

No doubt Mary would have been most tenderly cared for by these Sons of Peace. But even with all these possible means of obtaining shelter among humans, the birth of Jesus, according to the records in Luke, was in a stable.

It appears, therefore, that a force greater than the affairs of men was at work, for indeed the time, the place, and the occasion of the birth of the Son of Man all seem to be part of a Divine expedient to instruct man in both the word and the truth of the way.

Whether or not Jesus was actually born into the environment reported in Luke is of little importance historically. The important thing is that the story indicates a great spiritual truth to all those who are prepared to receive it.

No doubt the gentle St. Francis both knew and felt its sublime significance when he said, "All creatures are created from the same paternal heartbeat of God. Not to hurt our humble brethren is our first duty to them; but to stop here is a complete misapprehension of the intentions of Providence. We have a higher mission. God wishes that we should succor them whenever they require it." [1]

"Christ is both human and divine. The revelation which comes through Him shows that the highest can be in every sense united with the lowest and be revealed through it . . ." [2]

Let us recall again the allegorical significance of the original sin, i.e., the causing of the first death, the taking of the life of the lamb, and eating the "forbidden" flesh thereof, *contrary* to the Divine Formula as set down in Genesis 1:29,30.

Down through the centuries the horrible crime of taking life has illustrated in blood the immensity of "the fall." Still retaining the purity of Eden, however, were the innocent creatures of God's creation. They alone abstained from the blood feast and abode by the Divine Formula provided for them in the beginning.

It would seem, therefore, not only fitting but proper that the Spirit of God should seek out the environment of the faithful and gentle of His creation to reveal His presence on earth.

Not in the plush luxury of kings and princes came He, not in the simple comfort of the merchant or tradesman, nor even among the cares and wants of the poverty stricken among men; but, instead, among the innocent creatures of His creation: among those suffered and sacrificed by the lusts of men did He come. And they laid the babe Jesus, not on a bed of silks and downs, nor in any sort of crib customed in the manner of men, but upon a bed of hay, even as the newborn of the she goat, the ass and the ewe.

Thus, do the gospels suggest that Jesus was endowed at birth with a deep understanding for even the least of God's creatures. Thus do they illustrate that along with his body and spirit was born the tender love and humble compassion which so beautifully and courageously found expression in His teachings and in His demonstrations before the minds of men.

And the lowly creatures upon a thousand hills stood still at that moment as the prophesy of Isaiah was about to be fulfilled: "For the earnest expectation of the creature waiteth for the manifestation of the sons of God:" * that "There shall be no more harm or hurt upon all my holy mountain for the earth shall be full of the knowledge of the Lord as the waters cover the sea."**

> "Hush! little colt," said the mare,
> "And a story I will tell
> Of a barn like this one of ours
> And the things that there befell.
> It was weather much like this
> And the beasts stood as we stand now
> In the warm, good dark of the barn
> A horse and an ass and a cow."
>
> "And sheep?" asked the colt. "Yes, sheep,
> And a pig and a goat and a hen.

* Rom. 8:19.
** Isa. 11:9.

All of the beasts of the barnyard,
The usual servants of men.
And into their midst came a Lady,
And she was as cold as death,
But the animals leaned above her
And made her warm with their breath.

There was her Baby born
And laid to sleep in the hay,
While music flooded the rafters
And the barn was as light as day,
And angels and kings and shepherds
Came to worship the Babe from afar,
But *we looked at Him first of all ceatures*
By the bright, strange light of a star!"

Elizabeth Coatsworth

O great mystery and wonderous sacrament, that animals should see the Lord born and lying in a manger.*** 3

*** Response to the second nocturnè before midnight mass on Christmas Eve. (Roman liturgy).

COMMENTARY

8 — The Early Life of Jesus

It seems strange that the writers of the Four Gospels were silent on the early life of Jesus. The only mention of Him following His birth is at the age of twelve, when He visited the temple with His parents.

Certainly, there would have been many unusual happenings during the developing stages of His life worthy of reporting other than the lone incident given in Luke. The biography of every great man invariably unfolds an interesting childhood. The greatness of Jesus must certainly have shown itself in no uncertain terms during his twenties. It is difficult to believe that a character of His stature could have remained practically unnoticed for almost twenty years.

It has been suggested that the eighteen years left blank in the reported life of Jesus were due either to careless copying or to prejudiced editing of the original manuscripts, which unfortunately no longer exist. In either case, it might be said that if somewhere in the Four Gospels Jesus had been clearly described as a member of the Essene brotherhood, instead of being only vaguely reported as associated with them, the ascetic practices of the primitive Christians could not have been so conveniently replaced by the more liberal doctrine of Paul.

One thing is certain: Jesus was neither a Pharisee nor a Sadducee. According to Josephus, the third and remaining of the sects were the Essenes. In the time of Jesus they were the most talked about of all peoples, not only in their own country, but in foreign countries as well, because of the purity of their way of life.

Here again it is strange that while both the other sects

were freely spoken of in the Four Gospels, the Essenes seem to retain their importance in the life and times of Jesus only through their not being mentioned. The obvious, therefore, is that the Essenes and the early Christians were one and the same sect. This assumption seems to provide a reasonable explanation of how Jesus obtained at an early age His great knowledge of the Scriptures and where He spent many of the years that are unaccounted for in the Four Gospels.

On the other hand, there has been for centuries the opinion that Jesus spent some time among the Buddhist priests in India. This idea is indeed evidenced by the fact that "the ethical system of Buddhism reappears substantially unaltered in the Gospel Jesus: We must never be proud, nor harbor anger or resentment against anyone. Whosoever exalts himself shall be degraded; harsh language must never be used to anyone. 'Let a man overcome anger by love . . . evil by good . . . the greedy by liberty, the liar by truth!' Let us live happily, then, not hating those who hate us . . . among men who are greedy, let us dwell free from greed!' We must not scrutinize the mote in another's eye, and fail to see the beam in our own. No matter how unjustly one is attacked or abused, one must never strike back at an aggressor,' i.e., instead — 'turn the other cheek.' If we possess two garments, we must give one to a less fortunate. If the whole world and all of its treasures were yours, you would still not be satisfied nor would all this be able to save you." [1]

These all parallel the message of Jesus. Furthermore, the doctrine of love and mercy towards all the creatures was a basic teaching of Buddha. However, as we have seen before, this ethic was also observed by Jesus' own sect, the Essenes, also known in part as Nazarenes.

One might suppose that Jesus may have departed the Essene monastery some time during His middle twenties, taking the caravan route East to the land of the Buddha. In any case, whether Jesus did or did not go to India, it appears quite evident that He was influenced in no small degree by Buddhist teachings, and that these, when combined with Essenic doctrine and saturated with Hebrew tradition, created a new and comprehensive system of teaching so profound that it astonished and fascinated all who heard Him preach. This, in effect, is corroborated by Scripture.

COMMENTARY

9 — The Conception of John the Baptist
10 — His Childhood and The Holy Ones

The conditions involving the birth of John the Baptist as recorded in the Gospel of Luke represent a rather strained course of events which were climaxed by his mother's insisting that he be known as "John" contrary to the tradition of naming him after his father's house.

No doubt the neighbors were shocked and probably many wondered who had influenced Elizabeth to choose the name John? The long intervals of time Zacharias spent away from home, coupled with his old age, provided additional incentive for neighborhood gossip.

As reported in Luke, "Fear came on all that dwelt round about them and all the sayings were noised around throughout all the hill country:" Probably anxiety and doubt would be more to the point than the word "fear"; anxiety and concern for the peace of the house of Zacharias, and doubt as to the manner of Elizabeth's conception.

It might be said that the neighborhood children of many of these who doubted the mystic interpretation of Elizabeth's conception later played with the boy John. No doubt many childish disputes ended with the boy tearfully telling his mother the slanderous names he had been called.

Fearful that their son's personality would become warped, his parents overruled their own devotion to him and took him to the desert community of the Essenes.*

This explains the final words of the First Chapter of Luke: "And he was in the deserts until the day of his shewing into Israel."

---

* According to Josephus, these "Chosen Ones" of the Essene sect that dwelt in the desert near the Dead Sea adopted children and raised them "to walk blamelessly before God."

196

On the other hand, the bringing of the boy John to the desert monastery might not have been a grievous self-sacrificing undertaking. It might well have been the fulfillment of a plan long cherished in the heart of Elizabeth.

As we noted before, the Essenes lived in communities everywhere in Judea, but they also maintained an academy or monastery in the desert wilderness near the dead sea.

It appears that those who dwelt here were purposely selected for their spiritual leanings that they might be qualified to maintain a constant "watch out" for the coming of the "anointed One": who was imminently expected by all good Essenes.

It was no doubt considered a great honor to be appointed to serve God and the law as a member of this inner circle, and many a mother dedicated her unborn child to be one of those selected to prepare the way in the wilderness.

Thus one might suppose that Elizabeth dedicated her unborn child to the Nazarenes instead of the Nazarites which some scholars have assumed.

The early church fathers also point out that James the Lord's brother, was holy from his mother's womb, ate no flesh and drank no wine. This also confuses James with the Nazarites but we now know that he was instead a Nazarene, who had probably received his early religious training with the desert "Holy of Holies."

According to Num. 6:1-21, the Nazarite vows do not require abstinence from flesh eating; on the contrary they advocate the sacrifice of animals. Neither James the Lord's brother nor John the Baptist ate the flesh of animals or indulged in the evils of the sacrifice.

In accord with our new evidence John the Baptist appears to have been accepted as an apprentice by the brethren of the inner circle to learn the hidden teachings of the scriptures.

This again coincided with Luke 1:80, that, "he was in the deserts till the day of his shewing into Israel," as well as his pre-natal dedication to an ascetic way of life.

The reference to James, the Lord's brother, also points to Jesus as being in the same manner dedicated to Essenic priesthood. Certainly Mary would not have done other with Jesus than she had done with his brother James.

COMMENTARY

11 — The Baptist Admonishes the People
The Baptism of Jesus

It might be said that occasionally one of the more zealous of the brethren would go forth into the wilderness, hoping to be the first to meet the Messiah in the desert.

"Behold I will send my messenger before me: the messenger of the Covenant whom he delights in." (Malachi 3-1)

John the Baptist was one of these for he was indeed inspired with the feeling that he himself was the messenger sent by the Lord to announce His coming.

With this idea in mind, he set forth toward the river Jordan wearing a single garment and carrying in his pouch a few corn cakes made with oil and honey.

The original Aramaic gospel which according to Jerome, appeared to be the "logos" of the gospel of Matthew, described the food of John the Baptist as wild honey and cakes made with oil and honey instead of wild honey and locusts as set forth in our traditional copy.

Some scholars have suggested that the word "locust" refers to the locust pods or seeds of the carob trees which are called St. John's bread.

However, either one of these explanations is evidence enough that John the Baptist was a vegetarian and therefore an Essene, or vice versa.

It is quite obvious that the original Greek translator of the Aramaic Gospel used by the Jewish Christians set down the word "enkris," which is Greek for oil cake. Later copyists either misunderstood or misspelled this same word, thus making it read "akris" or locust, instead of oil cake.

This is only one of the probable thousands of variants in New Testament literature.

The Catholic scholar Daniel-Rops says, "Of the Vulgate of St. Jerome, dating from the Fourth Century, we have nearly 8,000 copies. A comparison of these copies is extremely instructive. It goes without saying that being made by so many different hands a number of faults have crept in, sometimes even intentional ones. Frequently a copyist has modified the spelling, misplaced a word or added an explanation of his own or forgotten a phrase." [1] Errors such as the misspelling of the word "enkris" were not uncommon in the copying of the scriptures, even as was the forgetting of a phrase, which often was no doubt intentional.

Returning to the going forth of John the Baptist from among the 'Chosen Ones,' we next find him on the banks of the River Jordan, preaching salvation to the people of Israel.

On this the prophet Ellen White writes:

"John the Baptist went forth in the spirit and power of Elijah to prepare the way of the Lord, and to turn the people to wisdom of the just. John was a reformer. The angel Gabriel, direct from heaven, gave a discourse upon health reform to the father and mother of John. He said that he should not drink wine or strong drink and that he should be filled with the Holy Ghost from his birth. His diet, purely vegetable, was a rebuke to the indulgence of appetite and the gluttony that everywhere prevailed. John came in the spirit of Elijah to prepare the way for Christ's first advent. The great subject of reform is to be agitated, and the public mind is to be stirred. Temperance in all things is to be connected with the message to turn the people of God from their idolatry, their gluttony and their extravagance." [2]

Becoming known as the voice of one crying in the wilderness, or the Prophet of the wilderness, the fame of the Baptist spread and crowds of both eager and curious people came to hear him speak.

It was at one of these gatherings beside the River Jordan that there appeared several people from his own home neighborhood who knew him as a boy.

John recognized them in the crowd before he began to speak. They already had aroused his ire by their loud and ludicrous talk. The deep-seated torments of his boyhood were slowly brought back to mind and his usual timid personality suddenly gave way to anger. "Oh ye generation of vipers," cried he, "In whose name do you say these things?" This stinging introduction was probably followed by torrid condemnations of their indulgent ways of life: condemnations which most likely pertained to their addiction to wine, strong drink, and the fleshpots of Kibroth-hattaavah:* for it is well known that John was himself conscientiously opposed to such practices.

This might explain why an otherwise Minister of Peace might have addressed those whom he sought to convert with such scathing words as "Ye generation of Vipers."

When John challenged his listeners to fast, he followed the Essene custom wherein baptism is preceded by fasting to make clean the flesh.

According to the Manual of Discipline: "Only by a spirit of uprightness and humility can one's sin be atoned. Only by the submission of his soul to all the *ordinances* of God* can his flesh be made clean. Only thus can it really be sanctified by waters of purification."

In "accordance herewith except that you repent and follow the ordinances of God your sin cannot be atoned." To repent is to cleanse both the mind of evil thoughts as well as the body of abominations. A body that is a tomb for corpses is not a fit temple wherein God may dwell in his fullness, for through the voice of Isaiah and the Psalms, God abhorred the flesh of slaughtered beasts.

Theologians have endeavored for centuries to find in the gospels some suggestion whereby a Christian might feel justified in becoming a soldier. Augustine cites, as

* (Graves of Lust) Num. 11: 34.
* In re: to the dietary ordinance of Gen. 1:29,30.

proof of this, the answer to the soldier's question by the Baptist: "Do violence to no man, neither exact anything wrongfully and be content with your wages."

Here it is pointed out that John did not admonish the man as a soldier but spoke to him the same words he might say to anyone else. The phrase "be content with your wages" may be interpreted as, "be in accord with your hire." However, the words "do violence to no man" completely disallows the use of weapons, either for defense or offense. Therefore, if the soldier accepted John's baptismal provision, of non-violence, he necessarily was obliged to give up his profession.

It might be pointed out that at the time the Gospels were written there was no conflict between the military and religion.

No one was forced against his will to take up arms. The Roman army was small in comparison with the population, and recruiting was on a voluntary basis. It was not before nearly the end of the Second Century that the question of military service became a problem to the Christians.

In the foregoing Fifth Gospel John is suggested as having answered the question of the soldier in a far more voluminous manner than is reported in Luke.

The Essenes were most adamant in their views on war. According to Josephus they made no weapons of any kind. Their entire way of life was centered around the anticipation of the coming of the Kingdom of God. Harm, hurt, pain, or suffering were not part of the coming Kingdom. Realizing this, they prepared themselves in advance for ready acceptance into the new state to come. They separated themselves from any pain of sacrifice and the slaughter of warm-blooded creatures for food.

"Let not a man make himself abominable with any living creature or creeping thing by eating of them." [3]

Thus one might see the justification of John in exhorting his tormentors to cease more to make their bodies an abomination as suggested in the foreging Gospel.

It is quite probable that if both Jesus and John were for a while together at the desert community, they may have speculated silently upon their particular position thus bringing about a sort of benign understanding between them which was to grow later into a realization of a definite commitment in both of their lives.

It has been considered that if Jesus was, or had been, an Essene, he would have previously been baptized by them and would not now have required it at the hand of John.

However, as various scholars have pointed out, the Essenes had established for themselves a new covenant, using secret meanings from the "Law" which they claimed had been successively garbled by the Scribes.

John, in crying to the multitudes, "repent for the Kingdom of Heaven is at hand," was careful not to reveal the secret of this new covenant, but he did denounce the people in its terms.

On the other hand, Jesus, realizing that John was speaking in terms of this new covenant, decided to appear before him and proclaim his own amended version.

Thus it became necessary for Jesus to again be baptized in order to be reborn as *Himself*, the new covenant between God and the hearts of men.

COMMENTARY

12 — The Temptation

In Matthew and Luke Jesus is reported as being in the wilderness forty days and nights and after that time he hungered.

Then the tempter came to Him and said, "If thou be the Son of God command that these stones be made bread."

Of course if Jesus did go forth into the wilderness and fast for forty days, no one knows what actually took place there for there were no reporters shadowing His every move. Certainly Jesus would have been reluctant to discuss with anyone His inward struggles between the spirit and the flesh.

However, to be realistic in describing the temptations of a hungry man, mere bread would be far less alluring than the savor of roasted flesh. Besides, Satan would have no point to make in tempting Jesus with bread, but he would have gained quite a victory if he could have succeeded in luring Jesus to eat flesh.

Milton, in his Paradise Regained, describes this attempt of Satan to disparage the sublimely ethical nature of the Son of man and reduce him to the level of those buried in Kibroth-hattaavah* (graves of lust).

> Full forty days He passed — whether on hill
> Sometimes, anon in shady vale, each night
> Under the cover of some ancient oak
> Or cedar to defend him from the dew,
> Or harboured in one cave, is not revealed;
> Nor tasted human food, nor hunger felt,
> Till those days ended; hungered then at last.

* Num. 11: 33-34.

204

Among wild beasts, they at sight grew mild,
Nor sleeping him nor waking harmed; his walk
The fiery serpent fled and noxious worm;
The lion and fierce tiger glared aloof.

Satan muses how he might ensnare Jesus.

"By that which only seems to satisfy
Lawful desires of nature not beyond.
And now I know he hungers, where no food
Is found, in the wide wilderness:
The rest commit to me; I shall let pass
No advantage, and his strength as oft assay.
He ceased, and heard their grant in loud acclaim."

Satan approaches Jesus.

"Tell me, if food were now before thee set,
Would'st thou not eat?" "Therefore as I like
The giver," answered Jesus. "Why should that
Cause thy refusal?" said the subtle fiend.
"Hast thou not right to all created things?
Owe not all creatures, by just right, to thee
Duty and service, nor to stay till bid,
But tender all their power? Nor mention I
Meats by the Law unclean, or offered to Idols
Nor proffered by an enemy — though who
Would scruple that, with what oppressed? Behold,
Nature ashamed, or, better to express
Troubled, that thou shouldst hunger hath purveyed
From all the elements her choicest store,
To treat thee as beseems, and as her Lord
With honor. Only deign to sit and eat."

He spoke no dream: for, as his words had end,
Our Savior, lifted up his eyes, beheld,
In ample space under the broadest shade,
A table richly spread in regal mode,

With dishes piled and meats of noblest sort
And savour — beasts of chase, or fowl of game,
In pastry built, or from the spit, or boiled,
Crisamber-steamed; all fish, from sea or shore,
Freshet or purling brook, of shell or fin,
And exquisitest name, for which was drained
Pontus, and Lucrine bay, and Africa coast
Alas! how simple, to these cates compared,
Was that crude apple that diverted Eve.

The Tempter now earnestly renews his invitation to
Jesus to fall to:

"What doubts the Son of God to sit and eat?
These are not fruits forbidden; no interdict
Defends the touching of these viands pure:
Their taste no knowledge, works, at least of evil.
But life preserves, destroys life's enemy,
Hunger, with sweet restorative delight."

Christ answers that he might command all:

"Why shouldst thou then, obtrude this diligence
In vain, where no acceptance it can find?
And with my hunger what hast thou to do?
Thy pompous delicacies I condemn,
And count thy specious gifts, but guiles."

Satan complains:

"What I can do or offer is suspect,
Of these things others quickly will dispose,
Whose pains have earned the far-fet spoil."
With that
Both table and provisions vanished quite,
With sounds of vultures wings and talons heard."

Satan reluctantly admits,

"By hunger that each other creature tames,
Thou art not to be harmed, therefore not moved;
Thy temperance, invincible besides,
For no allurement yields to appetite;
And all thy heart is set on high designs,
High actions."

Thus Satan is defeated and Christ's victory is celebrated
by the true feast:

"So, struck with dread and anguish, fell the Fiend,
And to his crew, that sat consulting, brought
Joyless triumphals of his hoped success,
Ruin, and desperation and dismay,
Who durst so proudly tempt the Son of God.
So Satan fell; and straight a fiery globe
Of angels on full roil of wing flew high,
Who on their plumy vans received him soft
From his uneasy station, and upbore,
As on a floating couch, through the blithe air,
Then, in a flowery valley set him down
On a green bank, and set before him spread
A table of celestial food, divine
Ambrosial fruits fetched from the Tree of Life,
And from the Fount of life ambrosial drink,
That soon refreshed him wearied, and repaired
What hunger, if aught hunger, had impared,
Or thirst; and, as he fed angelic choirs
Sang heavenly anthems of his victory
Over temptation and the Tempter proud." [1]

Here the sublimely spiritual insight of Milton sets forth
in his Paradise Regained, the spirit of Jesus as victorious
over evil: as representing the way to the restoration of
man to the grace he enjoyed before the Fall.

Thus did Jesus validate his rebirth, thereby symboliz-
ing his person as representing the New Covenant between
God and the hearts of men.

Returning to the scene of the temptation, we find Satan (on page 113 of the Gospel of the Covenant) again endeavoring to tempt Jesus. He cleverly reminds the Son of Man of the voice of prophecy which had selected Him to be the King of the Jews.

No doubt this was one of the greatest problems Jesus had to face. He realized if He accepted the Messiahship as the legal heir to the throne of David that He must inevitably force his claim through taking up arms against Rome.

As violence leading to bloodshed was completely distant from His nature, he again frustrated the Son of Darkness in favor of a campaign for the glory of God and the brotherhood of man. Thus he fulfilled the Essene scriptures which say "Thou didst open the ear of one that he might heed Thy teachings and deliver Thy chosen people from the *uncleanness* which surrounds them."

The fast of Jesus in the wilderness represented, allegorically, the denouncing of fleshy lusts and carnal ambitions as hindering spiritual growth.

His discourse with Satan suggests a dramatization of an inward struggle between the sons of light and the sons of darkness.

It was through the intensity of this struggle in the mind and heart of Jesus, over the many disagreements between his own views and the Law as interpreted by the Scribes on one hand, and the tremendous inconsistencies in the interpretation of "God's law of Love" on the other, that His future plans became crystallized.

COMMENTARY

13 — Jesus Becomes Aware of
His Mission and Begins to Preach.

In stating that Jesus became aware of his mission, an explanation seems in order of the writer's viewpoint on this subject.

First, I trust that the Christian who feels that the Lord Jesus's full purpose upon earth was to insure His own personal hopes and aspirations, will not feel offended if I point out that this assumption must be contingent upon the carrying out of the major issues that Jesus represented.

First and foremost, as was suggested in a former Chapter of this Commentary, Jesus came to earth, or if you will, the Spirit of God appeared in the flesh of man to exhibit His true nature to all mankind.

Thus one must discard all previous concepts of God wherein He is presented as exhibiting all the emotional characteristics and all the sensual attributes of men.

The true nature of God has been suggested by the prophets. It had been partially demonstrated in the characters of Confucius, Buddha, Socrates, Pythagoras and others, but never before had it been brought face to face to man in its full light. This was the prime purpose of the character of Jesus.

Second in purpose was to exemplify in His being a new covenant: a clarification of the Law, reconstructed by the Chosen Ones as it was first given to Moses on the stone tablets and interpreted through the humble and compassionate nature of the Son of Man.

Thus was Jesus prepared to go forth and reveal to the world the pure and uncompromising will of God, born of His grace through baptism by John and resolved in His resistance to the temptations of the Angel of Darkness.

In the name of the Father of all creation was He to set forth upon His ministry to preach the New Covenant of Love, mercy and understanding that "all the earth might be full of the knowledge of the Lord as the waters cover the sea." (Isaiah) "And in that day I will make a covenant for them with the beasts of the field, and with the creeping things of the ground: and I will break the bow and the sword and the battle out of the earth, and will make them to lie down safely." (Hosea)

Thus the third purpose of the ministry of Jesus becomes immediately evident. It was to bring this realization of the nature of God to all men of good will; to plead with them to repent of their evil ways; to deliver them from the sufferings of false teachings written by vain Scribes; to exemplify to them through the evidence of His own nature the ethical criterion by and through which all men may regain their rightful dignity of spirit as brothers together and as true Sons of the Heavenly Father.

And again out of this threefold purpose was man to be saved from the fear of death — from the pains, sorrows and abuses of an untimely and unnatural* death — for in natural death there is no sting, no forcing of the issue, no outside influence or damaging nemesis, no destroyer to interfere with the will of God in the will to live of the flesh and the will of God in the will to live beyond the usefulness of the flesh.

"Follow thou Me for I am the life and the way." "Do these things even as I do and ye shall be one with the Father for in Me is the way of life everlasting."

* See Chapter: Jesus Preaches and Heals, p. 260.

COMMENTARY

14 — The Parable of the Fishermen

The Lucan story of the fisherman has all the earmarks of a parable that later acquired the authority of a miracle.

As a parable it might illustrate that all those who played a game of chance with nature flouted the indulgence of fate. The breaking of the nets parallels the consequences of greed. It reminds one of the monkey that put his hand into the cookie jar grasping such a fist full he could not get his hand out.

Then again, according to Luke, they filled the ships so full of fish that they began to sink. This is apparently a lesson on the futility of unearned rewards.

The Covenant of Love version of this parable suggests that man should not live by taking the all out of nature without giving a share equal to that which he takes. This seems to be a requirement of man in his dealings with nature. All peoples who have lived entirely "off of the land" so to speak, have never prospered economically, morally or spiritually. Consider for example all the tribal peoples who down through history have made hunting and killing for food their only means of sustenance.

COMMENTARY

15 — Jesus Preaches the Love of God.

Along with his healing practices Jesus preached the love of God. He stressed the oneness of God and life, for God is life, therefore all life is sacred.

One of our day, who is as close to the Christ Jesus as were His immediate disciples — for time is no barrier to the communion of great spirits — sat by the dim light of an oil lamp in the sweltering heat of Equatorial Africa and extolled in pages of love, marked by the sweat from his noble brow, the ethics of Jesus, Reverence for Life. He did this, not to commercialize his God-given talents but to plead prayerfully with the souls of men through the heart of Jesus Christ to give honor to the "will to live" in all creatures and to seek the Kingdom of God through reverence for the life of His creation.

Certainly if Albert Schweitzer is worthy to be called an apostle of Jesus, then his gospel of "Reverence for Life" is well worth the highest ethical response of all peoples.

"The ethics of "Reverence for Life" is the ethics of Jesus brought into spiritual significance, extended into cosmical form, and conceived of as absolutely necessary." (Albert Schweitzer)

He Sits at the Table With Sinners.

"And when the Pharisees saw this they said to His disciples: "Why does your teacher eat with tax collectors and sinners?" (Matt. 9:11)

Thus "the Master was accused of dining with publicans and sinners, but this does not imply that He shared their dishes anymore than vegetarians do today when they sit down with meat eaters. It is strange that in the passages

212

in question (Matt. 11: 18-19: Luke 7, 33-5) the Master's way of life is contrasted with John's asceticism. However this contrast is proved a false one by the fact that some of the people thought of the Master as John the Baptist (Matt. 16: 14, Mark 8; 28: Luke 9; 19) The identification of two such supposedly opposite characters would be ludicrous." [1]

But when Jesus heard the Pharisees accuse him he said: "Those who are well have no need for a physician, but only those who are sick.

"Go and learn what this means: 'I desire mercy and not sacrifice.' For I came not to call the righteous, but sinners." (Matt. 9: 11-13)

Here Jesus again condemned the custom of animal sacrifice as the prophets had done before Him. Like Hosea He asked for mercy and the knowledge of God rather than burnt offerings.

There were few cases of human sacrifice reported during the early periods of Hebrew worship; this practice had been abolished long before the time of Jesus.

The Pharisees were deeply religious and were considered by Josephus to be an honorable people. Their major offense, as far as Jesus was concerned, was the practice of animal sacrifice.

Jesus took up the crusade against this merciless custom where the prophets had left off.

Barnabas the companion of St. Paul and teacher of Mark, said "God has manifested to us by all the prophets, that He opposes *our* sacrifices saying: 'I am full of the burnt offerings . . . . I delight not in the blood of the lamb or the ox, . . . etc.' " [2] Here Barnabas quotes Isaiah who concludes with the words, "When ye hold forth your hands I will hide mine eyes from you. Yea, when ye make many prayers I will hear not: *your hands are full of blood*. Wash you, make you clean, do away with your evil doings from before mine eyes." (Is. 1: 11-16) Here God protests the slaying of his creatures; "cease to do evil," "guard your steps when you go to the house of God; to draw near to listen is better than to offer the sacrifice of fools; for they do not know they are doing evil." (Eccl. 5:1) Here the writer of Ecclesiastes supports Isaiah that the sacrifice of animals is doing evil, i.e., stain your hands no more with the blood of my innocent creatures.

Barnabas* continues: "For as much then, as we are not without understanding, we should apprehend the design of our merciful Father . . . . . that the adversary may not have entrance into us, and deprive us of our spiritual life." [3]

It is pitiful how few Christians know what Jesus meant when he said: "I desire *mercy* instead of sacrifice." Is it any wonder that when men make many prayers God hears them not? "I will hide mine eyes from you. I will hear not! Your hands are full of blood!" (Is. 1:11-16)

---

* The Epistle of Barnabas was pronounced genuine by Origen, and other of the early Church Fathers. According to scholars it was written before Jude and the two Johns.

COMMENTARY

16 — The Sermon on the Mount

The writer's version of the Sermon on the Mount is plainly the result of an extended adaptation of the Gospel of Matthew. This chapter refers to teachings the author intuitively believes were similarly contained in the "logos," or the Aramaic original, from which our Greek adaptation of Matthew came.

Jesus said many things that were not includued in the reports we have with us today. (See John 21:25) Assuming His nature to be all inclusive — embracing everything good, merciful and just — the writer sees it as his obligation to set down here some of the principles, which he feels Jesus surely must have discussed.

The Sermon on the Mount might be called the platform of the ministry of Jesus, or the "Manual of God" given to man through Jesus even as were the Decalogues given to man through Moses.

It includes a variety of instructions to His disciples as to how and what they should believe, teach and practice.

"Blessed are the peacemakers (pacifists) for they shall be called the children of God.

"Blessed are they that are persecuted for righteousness' sake for theirs is the Kingdom of Heaven." (Matt. 5:9-10)

Note the continuity of these two verses. It seems that when Jesus spoke of the peacemakers, those who allied themselves with sons of peace (pacifists) rather than the sons of war, he was immediately mindful of their inevitable persecution, under the laws of the militaristic state.

The early Christians were pacifists. They would have nothing whatsoever to do with war.

215

Up to the time of the union of church and state, Christians did not become soldiers.

It was after this unholy union that a sword was put in the hand of the prince of peace who said, "Love thy enemies, resist not, but instead turn the other cheek." "Let no man serve two masters." "Render unto Caesar those things that are Caesar's and unto God those things that are God's" "Do violence to no man."

Thereafter were men persecuted for righteousness' sake as prophesied by the Lord Jesus.*

Jesus said, according to Matthew, "Think not that I am come to destroy the law, or the prophets: I am not come to destroy but to fulfill."

The following verse emphasized this by the words, "not one tittle".

Here Jesus recognized how loosely the law had been observed; how the Scribes and Priests had interpreted it falsely; how they had changed many important things proportionate in size to a camel but had strained at other things unimportant as a gnat.

Jesus said, "I am come not to destroy the prophets but to fulfill that which they stood for." Evidence of this is presented in the foregoing "Gospel of the Covenant of Love." Herein Jesus repeats various admonitions of Isaiah, Hosea, Jeremiah and others.

The Law as interpreted by Jesus conformed in many ways to the interpretations of both the prophets and the Essenes. Adding His own revelations to their interpretations, one is aware of a new law and a new covenant: A COVENANT OF LOVE.

"Except that your righteousness exceed that of the Scribes and the Pharisees ye shall in no case enter the Kingdom of Heaven."

The most reliable testimony we have about the Pharisees

---

* Thus in so called Christian America (1959) Marvin Irving Tamarkin, a vegetarian and a peace maker is sentenced to prison for refusing to bear arms and kill people. (Miami, Florida).

may be found in Josephus (Book XVIII Chap. 1.) :

"Now the Pharisees, they live meanly and despise delicacies in diet: and they follow the conduct of reason, and what prescribes to them as good, they do. They believe the will of God and that souls are immortal. Whatsoever they do about divine worship, prayers and *sacrifices,* they perform them according to their direction; insomuch that the cities give great attestations to them on account of their entire virtuous conduct, both in the actions of their lives and their discourses also."

According to the Encyclopedia Britannica, "The writers of the gospel had Jesus denouncing the Pharisees for things on which they were in agreement with Jesus."

Accordingly, one may assume that the basic issue between Jesus and the Pharisees was the *sacrifice* eschewed by the Essenes.

Jesus did not protest the oblation of fruits, corn, etc. laid upon the altar, but he did protest the slaughter of animals. This to Him was a sin of almost unforgivable magnitude, for He saw that it reviled both God and nature.

Only the practice of sacrifice as denounced by the prophets could have prompted Jesus to say, "Except that your righteousness exceed that of the Pharisees ye shall in no case enter the Kingdom of Heaven." Here, "in no case" presented a definite and final obstacle set up by the "greatest of all sins." (See Chapter XXIV of the Covenant of Love.)

"For ye have heard it said ye shall not kill."

The temple priests ignored the stringency of this commandment and followed the interpretation of the Scribes even against the protests of the prophets. (See interpretation of Isaiah 66:3)

Inasmuch as the other differences were minor, this seems to have been the one outstanding evil practice that could have prompted Jesus to close the door of Heaven to the Pharisees.

"Ye have heard it said thou shalt not forswear thyself but shall perform unto the Lord thine oaths."

"But I say to you swear not at all, neither by heaven nor by earth nor by the province of the King."

In commenting on this directive of Jesus, as worded by the writer of Matthew, it might be well to discuss here what several scholars have previously referred to as a lack of agreement between the doctrine of Jesus and the Manual of Discipline of the Dead Sea Scrolls. They point out that this document requires all volunteers to commit themselves by a binding oath to abide by the commandments of the Law, and to adhere to the truth of God.

However, it should be considered that in the interpretation of this provision of the Manual the word 'oath' involves a ceremonial commitment to God. In other words, through ritualistic ceremony one enters into solemn agreement with others similarly pledged to keep faith with God. The very act of joining together before witnesses necessarily involves phrases such as "Do you?" and "I do." There is no more binding oath to God and man than the customary pledge of marriage. Thus two people are united through a solemn promise before God. Herein Jesus' reporters contradict him by saying, "Swear not at all," for Jesus actually gave his blessing to ceremonial swearing before Heaven when he said, "Those whom God has joined together let no man put asunder."

The Manual of Discipline proposes a ritualistic ceremony wherein not just two people are joined together in solemn trust and confidence through a pledge before God, but instead many men are in effect bound together in mutual accord that they should behave honorably and truthfully to one another and to walk according to the pleasure of God. It might be said that Jesus actually found no fault with ceremonial swearing wherein the pleasure of God was the object involved; that is, in the manner of vowing allegiance, wherein one swears to be bound to God. This is considerably different from swearing "by God" or "by heaven," as Matthew puts it, for "by God" one involves God as the responsible party of the covenant, where, in ceremonial swearing the responsibility is upon the one seeking allegiance. To swear *by heaven* is to commandeer the power of God, not to seek harmony with it.

The prior First Century followers of Jesus, according to Pliny, came together and, "obliged themselves with an oath not to do anything that is ill." This involves a similar ceremony practiced by the Essenes, and described elsewhere herein.

According to First Century historians and the Encyclopedia Americana, the Essenes "forbade oaths and held that a man whose word needed to be confirmed by oath was not to be believed at all."

According to Matthew, "to swear by Jerusalem" actually represented the point Jesus endeavored to make: that it was unbecoming the dignity of the Spirit of God in man to swear to tell the truth before any political, religious or other institution. This, according to evidence just presented, describes the same standpoint held to by the Essenes.

Thus, instead of disagreement, one may suppose that Jesus actually taught the Essene law which denounced swearing.

"Let no man set forth his brother or his son in bond with another to insure the paying of a debt."

"Let no man by force or guile require his brother to serve him against his own good fortune or his own free will."

These, or words similar to them, must surely have been said by the Son of man.

We, as ordinary people, long ago recognized the injustice of slavery. In fact, many Christians have sacrificed their lives so that others might be free to choose their own way of life.

If we, in our small understanding of justice and mercy, abhor slavery, did not He who fully understood these virtues still more oppose the system that robs men of their freedom? One feels that he was wont to weep for those so oppressed.

Indeed when he opened the book in the synagogue and

read from the sixty-first chapter of Isaiah, He said, "The spirit of the Lord is upon me. He hath sent me to bind up the broken hearted, to proclaim liberty to the captives and the opening of the prison to them that are bound."

Here Jesus by proclaiming liberty qualified himself as opposing any system or custom that captivates, binds, or in any way restricts the freedom of man. Whether the translation from the Hebrew reads "to," "for," or "of" the captives, it is the same thing; proclaiming freedom for the slaves or those bound or in bond.

It is strange how the Christian church has avoided the subject on down through the centuries.

No mention of the injustice of the horrible traffic in human bodies and frustrated lives is made anywhere in the New Testament.

In fairness to the kind, considerate and freedom-loving heart and soul of Jesus, one has no choice but to conclude that such references have been purposely omitted from the records.

Even if it were possible that for some reason they were overlooked in the original manuscripts (which are now lost), the church cannot be excused for neglecting to write in a just stand on this issue. Indeed, the correctors of the Nicene Council edited, rearranged, retranslated—and probably omitted much of the original writings to make them conform to church doctrine. But even at this time, the question of slavery was still considered outside the responsibility of Christian teachings.

Surely Jesus must have protested many times the slaughter of animals and the thoughtless attitude of people towards their rights and privileges as his words, "I desire mercy instead of sacrifice" reveal. Yet the purging of the temple is the only indication in the Four Gospels wherein one might consider Jesus as actively opposing the custom. If it were not so obvious one would wonder why this is so, for certainly the least of God's creatures would be the concern of any one who rightly claimed a compassionate and all-loving way of life.

To say or even think that the heart of the "Son of God" was not big enough to contain within it enough mercy, compassion and understanding to include the lesser creatures is to blaspheme God.

Today there are many ordinary people among us who recognize the injustices done to other creatures. They are described by the word "humane." According to Funk and Wagnalls College Dictionary, the word "humane" denotes what may rightly be expected of mankind *at its best* in the treatment of sentient beings. "The humane man will not needlessly inflict pain upon the meanest thing that lives."

Does any Christian doubt that the Lord Jesus would qualify under this definition of "humane?"

Would not a lamb or even a fish be considered better to him than the "meanest thing that lives?" If so, would Jesus be in any way a party to the inevitable pain they suffer in the hands of the butcher or the fisherman?

Certainly if many kindhearted people today are aware of the violence to which the creatures are subjected and openly protest the horrors of the slaughter houses, would not the Lord Jesus, the very essence of mercy and compassion, have been even more devotedly concerned and grieved at similar treatment to creatures in His time?

The answer to these questions is in itself witness to the underlying truth of the attitude of Jesus as put into words in the foregoing gospel.

In the Sermon on the Mount of the "Covenant of Love," are the words: "There is nothing beneath the Father more sacred than the delivery into this world of a new life, whether it be your own or one of God's lesser creatures."

As part of the sordid system which operates exclusively to satisfy the lusts of appetite, some 39,000 calves born in transit are trampled to death annually in overcrowded stock cars. It is pitiful to imagine the speechless suffering endured by these helpless mothers. Here at the hand of man is systematically committed the "unforgivable crime" against nature and God.

But please don't cease to continue on, gentle reader, for the guilt you may feel is not all yours. Besides, this condition is only a small part of the system you support and have so innocently been made part of. Listen now to what happens when these suffering creatures reach their final destination.

The following is reported by an observer of the Humane Society and published in a leaflet entitled, "Facts about your meat."

"Suppose you saw a man kill a dog in the following manner:

"He slips a chain noose around one of the dog's hind legs. With an overhead hoist he jerks the dog aloft, the whole weight of the struggling animal suspended by the one leg. This may dislocate or break the leg or pelvis.

"Then the man sticks a knife into the dog's throat—carefully avoiding any spot that would cause quick death.

"And then the man steps back and waits for the dog to bleed to death. It takes several minutes for the dog even to lose consciousness.

"If you saw such a sight you probably would call the police—if you did not faint first.

"You would certainly feel that such a deed was cruel—intolerably, impermissibly cruel.

"Last year nearly 90,000,000 animals were killed in the United States by precisely the method described above. They were hogs, not dogs. But the hogs suffered just as much as would the animals that so many of us keep as pets.

"The 'shackling and sticking' technique of killing hogs is used in almost every slaughter house in America.

"Lambs and calves are killed by much the same method.

"In some slaughter houses lambs and calves are jerked off the floor and hung by one leg, like hogs, before being 'stuck.' In other plants these infant animals are violently thrown to the floor, the head is pulled back almost to the shoulders, and the throat cut. The lamb or calf lies on the floor until it bleeds slowly into unconsciousness and dies.

"Last year our slaughter houses did this to about 10,000,000 calves and 90,000,000 lambs.

"Cattle are more trouble to the slaughter house than are hogs, lambs and calves. And the cattle pay the penalty.

"A half-ton steer or a 1,500-pound bull cannot be easily hoisted by a hind leg or thrown on its side. In most slaughter houses, therefore, the animal is first driven into a "knocking" pen—a pen narrow enough to hold the animal under close control.

"Alongside the pen, on a slightly raised platform, stands a man who is called a "knocker." The knocker uses a long-handled sledge hammer, or axe, to knock the animal to the floor.

"If the knocker is expert and lands his blow squarely at the proper spot on the head, he knocks the animal down with one blow. Knockers, however, are by no means always expert. And even experts are far from perfect. The hammer sometimes knocks out an eye, or smashes the nose to bloody pulp, or splinters a horn.

"After a faulty blow the agonized animal lunges and jerks madly and the knocker may need five, six, or even ten blows to fall the animal.

"When the big animal is finally "immobilized," as the slaughter men say (the animals are not always unconscious), it is dragged out of the knocking pen. Then its throat is cut.

"Last year about 20,000,000 cattle went through this process in American slaughter houses.

"The procedures described above are the ordinary routine of our billion-dollar meat packing industry. But the animals going to their death often are not given the "benefit" of the routine.

"Many plants often dispense with the knocker for cattle. At such times the huge beef animals are merely shackled around one hind ankle, then the struggling animal is lifted aloft by a power hoist, and its throat is cut while it hangs, head down, fully conscious. Small imagination is needed to tell what happens to leg and hip joints and to tendons and flesh, when a thousand-pound animal, struggling in agony, is jerked off the floor by a chain around one ankle.

"A U.S. Department of Agriculture inspector who has worked in many packing plants in the last 25 years wrote to The Humane Society of the United States:

"When calves are slaughtered . . . they are shackled and pulled up to an overhead rail and bled. Sometimes the hind feet are skinned out and cut off while the animal is still alive and they come out on the floor by a moving chain still kicking."

"This same man — not an emotional layman but a man who has worked in slaughter houses for a quarter of a century — wrote:

"I have seen cattle which were knocked with the hammer and rolled out on the floor and hung up for bleeding after sticking, and the header started to skin out the head while the animal was still alive and was trying to bellow." *[1]

Would the Lord Jesus approve such a system? Again the answer to this question must be admitted as evidence to support the true attitude of Jesus as it is represented in the Covenant of Love.

* * *

The next item of this Commentary on the Sermon on the Mount as it is set forth herein pertains to prayer. It seems that on this subject Jesus was quite explicit. One can hardly compromise His instructions to go "privately into thy chamber and close the door" with the custom of open assembly verbal praying.

___

* A so-called "humane slaughter" bill was recently signed by the President. However, the bill applies only to meat packed for government purchase. Local markets will continue to provide your family with the questionable flesh of these terrorized creatures, every pound of which may in fact pass along to those you love the inevitable consequences of its horrible processing.

Jesus also said, "when ye pray, use not vain repetitions that ye may be heard by your much speaking."

Jesus, in instructions to His disciples on how to pray, merely suggested a variety of things to ask of God. He did not intend for them to be set up in exacting form, for ritual is precisely what he wanted to avoid when he said, "use not vain repetitions." Jesus, no doubt, knew that a ready made prayer is comparable to the paper a student reads before his class after someone else has prepared his lesson for him. It is not the thought of the student but the thought of the one who wrote it. Such a prayer satisfies the vanity of its composer more than it seeks the attention of God. Thus it becomes a vain repetition.

One might conclude therefore that the Lord's Prayer as it is known to us was not directly composed by Jesus but rather by the evangelists who wrote the Gospels. Jesus as interpreted in the foregoing Gospel of Love must have given various suggestions to His disciples upon which they could build their own prayers.

However, like many other of the sayings of Jesus, the customs of the times have made them of little avail.

COMMENTARY

17 — The Things That Defile a Man
Making My Word of None Effect

This chapter contains a most vivid example of the constant efforts that have persisted down through the ages to conform the Gospel of Jesus to doctrinal custom.

One can have little doubt in reviewing the several changes made in the scriptures of our own day in reference to diet that the same thing has been going on for centuries. The fact that the original gospels are no longer available indicates that they contained rigorous protestations on the custom of flesh eating as denounced ethically by the Jesus of "The Covenant of Love" and historically by the early Christians of the Old Apostles.

Referring to the subject of this Commentary, namely, "The Things That Defile a Man," we are told, according to Mark, that the disciples of Jesus were seen by the Pharisees eating bread without washing their hands. This was contrary to the customs of the Jews.

"When they come from the market they eat not unless they wash their hands, for tradition says that this defiles a man."

Then the Pharisees and the Scribes asked Jesus, "Why behave thy disciples not according to the tradition of the elders?"

And Jesus answered, saying: (according to Mark) "There is nothing from without a man that entering into him can defile him: but the things that come out of him, those are they that defile the man."

Then when He had entered into the house the disciples asked him concerning the parable.

And he said, "Are ye so without understanding also?

Do ye not perceive that whatever things from without enter into a man cannot defile him since it enters not into his heart but into his belly?"

At this point the R.S.V. has inserted in parenthesis (Thus he declared all foods clean). The point here is that *all foods* were not the basis of the argument with the Pharisees.

Jesus made His answer in response to the Pharisees' criticism of eating bread with unclean hands. This they pointed out defiles a man.

It was perfectly natural for Jesus to say, "It is not what goes into the body but what goes out of it that defiles a man," for He was merely emphasizing the moral and spiritual responsibilities of the heart and soul and their expression as being more important than traditional rules of sanitation. "From out of the heart proceed evil thoughts," etc. This was the point Jesus endeavored to make in his discourse.

If one were to corrupt this saying of Jesus still further, i.e., "There is nothing from without a man that goes into him that can defile him," one could add alcohol, opium, morphine, nicotine and other such things that men put into their bodies.

Jesus was just as much aware of the moral and physical consequences from the consumption of wine and strong drink as He was of those from the eating of flesh. He would surely at no time have erased all restrictions upon what man could put into his body, for that would have given His approval to both overeating and over-drinking: to both gluttony and drunkenness.

With the evidence clearly before us, we cannot doubt that the texts as presented, even before their modern bit of editing, were purposely arranged to confuse the question of flesh eating. Certainly Jesus, speaking for Himself, would not have given His blessing to anything and everything that man might choose to put into his body.

However, the whole truth of the immediate incident rests

entirely upon the question of eating bread — eating bread with unwashed, unclean hands.

In the foregoing Gospel Jesus is saying, "There is naught such as this (meaning dirt from unwashed hands) that enters into a man can defile him." Here He neither gives His blessing to the consumption of alcohol, narcotics, nor the eating of flesh. Our modern day correctors seem to follow the same pattern as their predecessors. They have stricken out the word *fast* from the sayings of Jesus even though the word also describes a restricted diet. (See dictionary definition of *fast*.)

They also make a change in Proverbs in the verse:

"Be not among wine bibbers, among riotous eaters of flesh."

Here the word *flesh* is changed to meat. This also confuses the issue for the use of the word *meat* in the Old Testament and even in the New refers to grains, fruits, vegetables — anything *other* than flesh. (See Leviticus 2, Matt. 24: 45 K.J.V.)

Evidently the correctors thought the word *flesh* aroused a feeling of guilt for it applies to the life and death of an animal while the word *meat* merely refers to a commodity put up in cellophane packages and bought by the pound.

In Mark 7: 6-12 Jesus is again in contention with the false scribes and adherents to the priestly code. Here He admonishes his listeners by saying: "Well hath Isaiah prophesied of the hypocrites, as it is written: This people honoreth Me with their lips but their heart is far from me.

"Howbeit in vain do they worship me, teaching for doctrines the commandments of men.

"Full well they reject the commandments of God that they may keep their own tradition.

"They make the word of God of none effect through their own traditions which they pass on and many other things like this they do." Through their own rituals and practices they arranged to suit their own conveniences, their own indulgences and aspirations, their own social, political, and doctrinal order.

Here Jesus stands out as a true witness to the falsity in the teachings of the scribes and priests who were both the auditors of oral tradition as well as the editors of the written traditions. He quotes Isaiah, who along with the other prophets, has continually protested the corruption of the holy records by the scribes. Among these Jeremiah appears to be the most contentious. "Is this my house which is called by my name become a den of robbers? Behold, even I have seen it, saith the Lord. Trust ye not in lying words, saying 'the temple of the Lord,' 'the temple of the Lord are these.' Behold, ye trust in lying words that cannot profit. The Prophets prophesy falsely and the priests bear rule by their means and my people love to have it so." [1]

"How can you say, 'We are wise,' and the law of the Lord is with us? But, behold, the false pen of the scribes has made it into a lie. Our fathers have inherited nought but lies, worthless things in which there is no profit. But I commanded them not, the day I brought them out of the land of Egypt, to make sacrifices and to eat flesh." [2]

"I hate, I despise, your feasts and I take no delight in your solemn assemblies. Did you bring to me sacrifices and offerings the forty years in the wilderness, O house of Israel?" [3]

In the translations of the Dead Sea Scrolls we find further evidence to support the protestations of Jesus and the prophets before him.

"The Torah — that is, the Divine Teachings (or guidance) as revealed to Moses — had, it was held, been successively garbled and perverted by 'false expositors.' The community's purpose was to exemplify and promulgate the true interpretation." [4]

"When the formal seasons come on the days
of the new moon,
When they reach their turning-points,
And when they yield place to one another
And each comes around anew,

When the natural seasons come at
whatever time may be;
When too, the months begin;
On their feasts and on holy days,
As they come in order due,
Each as a memorial in its season
I shall hold it as one of the laws
Engraven of old on the tablets
To render to God as my tribute
The blessing of my lips." [5]

It is quite obvious here that the Essenes took up the
protestations where the prophets left off in regards to
animal sacrifice. They affirmed that the laws engraved on
the tablets of Moses provided only for the praises of the
tongue as an offering.

"The oblation of the lips will be in all justice like the
erstwhile 'pleasant savor' on the altar: righteousness and
integrity like that free will offering which God deigns to
accept." [6]

In other words, for peace, sin, guilt, and for all feast
and holy days, offerings, according to the laws engraved on
the tablets of old, were to be a 'broken and contrite heart'
the giving of one's own self to God in penitent restitution.
Thus, in effect, the human will sacrifices its carnal nature
and receives the benediction of the Father.

In complete accord with the protests of the prophets who
had firsthand knowledge of the falsifications of both the
oral and the written records, the writer adds his small
voice against the continued reverence for these false and
ungodly records. Even the strict fundamentalist cannot
help but feel the moral injustice of the priestly code as it
is exposed in the pages of Leviticus, Deuteronomy, Nehemiah, and in other parts of the Old Testament.

But as for thy people
lying priests flatter them

And deceitful scribes lead
them astray
They have plotted wickedness
seeking to exchange Thy
Holy engraven word
For the smooth things they
address to thy people
Making them turn their gaze
into the errors they teach
Revel in their feasts
Ensnaring themselves with lusts.[7]

For over two thousand years the pleading voice of the prophets has fallen upon deaf ears. The priestly code which claimed the lives of all the prophets who opposed it still maintains, without a sign of apology, a prominent place of honor as part of the Holy Bible. How can a religion retain within its "holiest of Holies" the baneful lore of a merciless and selfish God along with the divine eloquence of a God of love and compassion without it also becoming divided against itself? To revere under one cover both a God of peace, mercy, justice, and loving kindness and a jealous, vengeful, capricious, and lustful God is to becloud the spiritual awareness of man and to heap upon him both the blessings of Heaven and the abominations of Hell.

Still with us is the shameful evidence which involved the condemnations of the prophets and the Holy Ones of the Dead Sea Scrolls.

The Bible seems to be divided into a number of moral and spiritual planes of thought. In consequence, anyone can find within its covers his own particular level of understanding: that is, the frame of reference which best conforms to his own sense of values.

The religious conformer who follows a strictly literal interpretation of the God of Leviticus, Deuteronomy, Numbers, etc., as actually representing the nature of divine

[7] From the Dead Sea Scrolls.

Providence, is apparently not far enough advanced on the road to spiritual unfoldment to clearly understand the wisdom of a God of mercy, justice, sympathy, humane dignity, or loving kindness. One who still insists upon revering the bloodletting, God of the false scribes and lying priests is not yet ready to receive Jesus: for and according to the most illuminating of all metaphysical criteria concerning the purpose of Jesus it was primarily to implant in the hearts of men the knowledge that the true God is a God of uncompromised mercy and loving kindness that, in the words of John, "He was sent."

In the character of Jesus is to be found the evidence that the ALL GOOD is also the ALL MERCIFUL, the ALL HUMANE, the ALL KIND, the ALL JUST, the ALL COMPASSIONATE and the ALL UNDERSTANDING.

It is difficult to conceive why a Christian of our day would prefer to interpret literally all of the Old Testament literature. Even in the time of St. Paul, Philo of Alexandria allegorized it. In fact, Paul himself sympathized with this method of interpretation, as evidenced in Galatians 4: 24. "Before the end of the First Century allegory had been adopted as a Christian approach to the Old Testament." [8] "In the earliest form of the Letter of Barnabas,* the evangelist wrote that the food laws of Leviticus only mean that we are not to be like swine or birds of prey. He further claims that the Jews' literal understanding of the law (probably regarding the sacrifice) was the work of a wicked angel." [9] In the Clementine Homilies 11-XXXVIII, Peter makes "the rather startling admission that quite a number of the chapters in the Old Testament have been interpolated by the devil." [10] These early Christian records parallel the denunciation of the "vain scribes" by Jeremiah and the repudiation of the "false expositors" by the Essenes.

---

* "The letter of Barnabas was accepted by Clement of Alexandria toward the end of the Second Century. Origen, too accepted it as Scripture. In 850 A.D. it was classed among the disputed but not among the rejected books."

Therefore one may justly declare with a forthright sense of spiritual dignity that wherever God is involved in a passage of scripture, that particular phrase is from the pen of a false expositor unless it can stand the test of purity, that is, conform in every way with the concept of St. Paul when he said: "Whatsoever things are true, honest, just, pure, lovely, and of good report, if there be any virtue, if there be any praise, consider these things."

These words actually put on trial the capricious God of Genesis, the lustful God of Leviticus, the vengeful God of Numbers, the jealous God of Deuteronomy and the war God of Joshua.

Conclusively, truth, honesty, justice, purity, loveliness, everything good and virtuous are those things worthy of praise.

These are the truths the Essenes realized had been prostituted by the scribes in order to make doctrinal custom conform with the ambitions of the priests and the appetites of the temple worshipers.

These are the truths that Jesus stood for when He admonished the scribes for "making the word of God of none effect" by "teaching for doctrines the commandments of men."

Truly, even a casual review of the first few chapters of Leviticus will reveal to the sensitive reader what Jesus meant by the "doctrines and commandments of men."

For what purpose do we still preserve these false* doctrines? Why must religious tradition insist upon contaminating the Holy Scriptures with these sickening pages? Is it because mankind is still traditionally bound by its own sensual nature to the shameful practices of animal sacrifice?

* ... "there is absolutely no guarantee that the present Pentateuch is in any way identical with the five books which tradition ascribes to Moses, and, the necessity for a comprehensive critical investigation of the *present contents* makes itself felt." (Ency. Britt. 11th Ed. VXI, p. 586).

"But let him that glorieth, glory in this, that he understandeth and knoweth me, that I am the LORD which ever is loving kindness, judgement, and righteousness in the earth: for *in these things I delight saith the Lord.*" (Jer. 9:24)

COMMENTARY

18 — He That Knoweth Love
Shall Better Serve Me.
The Prophecy of Blood.
Let The Dead Bury Their Dead.
The Demons and the Swine.

In this chapter of the "Gospel of the Covenant of Love," the writer presents a reconstruction of what seems to be a rather ambiguous narration in Luke: "If any man come to me and hate not his father and mother, and wife, and children, and brethren, and sisters, yea, and his own life also, he cannot be my disciple." (Luke 14: 26)

"How strange such words sound in the mouth of a teacher who had made 'love' the cardinal virtue, who regarded the sanctity of marriage so highly that He rejected all possibility of separation, who had ranked filial duties above ceremonial works in divine service, who had frequently evinced his own warm love of children." [1]

It is quite obvious that Luke fashioned this saying out of a passage in the Old Testament (See Micah 7:6). If Jesus did refer to the words of Micah, He certainly must have used them in a much kinder sense than they were presented in Luke.

In a former discourse with the Pharisees, Jesus is reported as rebuking them for attempting to compromise the commandment "Honor thy father and thy mother." Notwithstanding, however, in Luke Jesus is represented as even opposing His own teachings of "Love thy neighbor," "Do no evil," "Blessed are the pure in heart," "Whosoever is angry with his brother is in danger of the judgment," which are all contrary to hate.

How can a man who hates his own life do other than

hate God for God *is* the life. In fact, the very word "hate" is opposed to any condition of love. Therefore, if a man hates all mankind, including himself, he is better timber for a disciple of the devil than for the Lord.

Again Jesus says in Matthew, "He that loveth father, mother, son or daughter more than Me is not worthy of Me."

Surely Jesus did not say this in that manner. This is not the humble, sympathetic, unselfish Jesus speaking, for He would have had far greater sense of discrimination than this. Jesus knew that any man who loved his father mother, son and daughter—also his neighbor and his sons and daughters—loved all mankind as well. Such a man being opposed to hate would necessarily be in harmony with love which is God himself. Therefore, no man's love can be greater than when he loves God through the loving of His creatures.

Again in Matthew: "For I come to set a man at variance against his father and the daughter against her mother, etc." (also influenced by Micah 7:6). A declaration of this kind might qualify the behavior of the self-righteous fanatic but it is not shaped for the mouth of Jesus.

However, the gospel, according to Thomas, throws a new light upon these sayings. Here Jesus says: "Whoever does not hate his father and his mother *in My way* will not be able to be a disciple to Me." viz., "in My way" is to mean, as I hate which is not at all, for again He says, "And whoever does not *love* his father and his mother in My way (which is with all My heart and with all My soul) will not be able to be a disciple to Me." * 2

"Think not that I am come to send peace upon the earth: I come not to send peace but a sword." (Matt. 10:34)

If Jesus actually did use words similar to these, his references surely must have been more prophetic than they were personal. Here it might be said that the Evangelists, or, more likely the transcribers who later edited the gospels, have made not only much of the Sermon on the Mount of "none effect" but they have abrogated the divine intent of God in the appearance of Jesus in the first place for, if it was not God's intent to reveal His true nature in the Son of man, then the whole idea of a God of peace, justice and loving kindness as opposed to harm, hurt, discord and conflict seems to be completely remote to Christian thought. "He that receiveth Me receiveth Him who sent Me" does not refer to the Roman God Mars, or any other god of the sword.

It has been suggested that much of the aforementioned character of the words attributed to Jesus were purposely arranged to demand the strictest of allegiance, or, if necessary, a fanatical blindness to everything but the authority of the church. One must disregard, if needs be, his devotion or love for family, neighbors, or for any institution other than the one symbolized by the cross.

This sort of what the Essenes referred to as "garbling of the scriptures" might be verified by the self-evident "write in" of the words, "He that taketh not up his cross and followeth Me is not worthy of Me." Simple reason tells one that this saying originated some time after the cross became a symbol of the church.

The cross was an instrument of execution used by the Assyrians, Persians, Phoenicians, Egyptians, Greeks and Romans. It was to them what the guillotine is to the French, the two-handed sword and the block to the Chinese, and the scaffold and the electric chair is to our modern culture. One needs merely to replace the word "cross" with any one of these other means of execution to observe how ridiculous would be the attributing of this saying to Jesus. It required 'time' along with the growth of tradition, to bring forth the cross as a symbol of Christian faith.

A reconstruction of the prophecy (Matt. 10:34-37) in which history has so clearly been witness to, is set forth in the preceding "Gospel of Love" as follows: "But alas! it shall come to pass that because of Me swords shall drip

with blood. But he that knows mercy and love and enters
not into violence is worthy of me."

The writer here humbly repeats that his interpretations
are not to be considered as a critique of the canonized
Jesus, but rather to verify the sublimely ethical nature of
the living Christ as transcending all doubtful disputations.

In re: to "Matt. 8:19-21-22:" And a scribe came up and
said to Him: "Teacher I will follow you wherever you go."

"Another of the disciples said to him: 'Lord let me first
go bury my father.'

But Jesus said to him, 'Follow me, and leave the dead
to bury their own dead."

Apparently Jesus sensed that this man was not willing
to face the disciplines of a true disciple; but, instead, had
resorted to deceit.

In the gospel of the Covenant, the words "leave the
dead to bury their own dead' are interpreted to read:
"There are those who live that are already dead, for they
are buried in their own deceit."

In Matthew 8:28-33 one finds the following words:

"And when they came to the other side of the country
of the Gadarenes two demoniacs met him.

"And behold they cried out: 'What have you to do with
us, O Son of God? Have you come here to torment us before the time?'

"Now a herd of many swine was feeding at some distance from them, and the demons begged him: 'If you cast
us out, send us away into the herd of swine.'

"And He said to them: 'Go'. So they came out and went
into the swine; and behold, the whole herd rushed down
the steep bank into the sea and perished in the waters."

It is quite obvious why the swine were used to illustrate
his narrative.

In the first place, the tradition of the Elders was prominent in the mind of the scribe who arranged the words
of Matthew. The Israelites had a particular aversion to
swine, probably because they were sacred to neighboring

peoples from whose sacrifices and gods the Hebrews wished to keep their people separate. Swine were supposed to carry disease and to live in tombs. They were unclean and were associated with idol worshippers and demons. Therefore, to liquidate a herd of many swine was, to the Hebrew mind, a triumph over the forces of evil. What a far cry this attitude was from that of St. Francis, Gandhi, the author of "Reverence for Life," Dr. Albert Schweitzer, and our own definition of humane manhood as found in our modern dictionary, quote: "The humane man will not needlessly inflict pain upon the meanest thing that lives."

Jesus must have used similar words as these to illustrate the necessity for human compassion and mercy towards the creatures.

The swine, the lamb, and the ox were to Jesus creatures given life through the eternal spirit and will of God. He had not room in His heart for carnal desires for He ate neither of swine meat nor of the flesh of any other creature. "Mercy intead of sacrifice" was His constant rebuke to the Pharisees: *Mercy* for the life of the victim; kindness instead of the ritual of blood. Nothing else connected with the sacrifice deserved the word mercy but the creature that was made to suffer at the hands of the temple priests.

If Jesus was so insistent on the subject of mercy for the lamb, surely He would not have been less considerate of a herd of swine grazing peaceably on God's green hills.

Ordinary common reasoning does not therefore permit one to accept the construction in Matthew of the swine incident as worthy of the character and dignity of the Son of Man.

COMMENTARY

19 — The Enemies of Jesus Revile Him.

In the gospel that now bears the name of Matthew may be found the following words, "The Son of Man came eating and drinking." Most assuredly the disciple who lived upon seeds and nuts, fruits and vegetables, without the use of flesh or wine, would not have been guilty of vulgarizing the humble dignity of his Lord and Master in this manner.

To what extremes will man suffer his very soul to justify his own lack of discipline, his own selfish regard for the pleasures of the taste — even to the slandering of One whom they worship as their God! Of these men well has the scripture said, "Their God is their belly."

"If a man walking in the spirit but in falsehood do lie saying, I will prophesy unto thee of wine and strong drink; he shall even be the prophet of this people" (Mic: 2:11). Thus he who prophesied of the "wine bibber" is even now the prophet of those who believe his words, for they choose to invest the authority of the Lord in their own abominations.

To refer to Jesus as one divided between the appetites of men and the glories of Heaven is to seek salvation through alternating prayer with fleshly lusts.

While this sort of scriptural interpolation cleared the way for Christians in general to adopt what is referred to today as "gracious living," it still sounded a false note to many of the more temperance-minded among them. While these might not openly dispute the word as written, they have evidenced disfavor by abstaining from alcohol and from gross foods as well. In the gospel as written herein, parts of the Eleventh chapter of Matthew are recon-

240

structed, to return to Jesus the dignity that is rightfully his.

In the first place, Jesus apparently was in the act of reprimanding his enemies, as well as those opposed to John the Baptist, through addressing himself to the people.

He said in reference to the Baptist, "What did you expect to see, one dressed in fine clothes?" Evidently some had criticized the apparel of John, for he wore only a simple coarsely woven garment.

"But you did see a prophet; one whom, among them that are born of woman, there has been no greater. But from John the Baptist till the time I stand before you, the Kingdom of Heaven suffers violence and our enemies take it by force. They are like children competing with one another in the market place, slandering each other's goods before men by saying. We warned you but you would not listen. We are sorry for you but you would have this shoddy fare."

And Jesus is represented as saying: "John the Baptist came neither eating nor drinking but they say he has a devil," that is: John must surely be of the devil for he does not eat of the food the priests of the temple make holy unto God. And again, the gospel has Jesus saying, "The Son of Man came eating and drinking and they say behold a man gluttonous and a wine bibber, a friend of publicans and sinners." Now it is quite obvious that this verse has either suffered from careless copying or from a deliberate misplacement of the words *And they say* in order to justify in the behavior of Jesus a criterion of Christian indulgence. However, if we place the words *and they say where* they probably were in the Greek original, we find that after Jesus laments the criticism of John by the enemies of Heaven, he turns to Himself as also being a target of criticism and says, "and they say the Son of Man came eating and drinking: Behold a man gluttonous and a wine bibber, a friend of publicans and sinners."

Thus one may find that in arranging the words *and they say* at the beginning of the sentence, the continuity of Jesus's complaint before the people, as well as his own dignity, is preserved. He therefore does not speak of Himself as "come eating and drinking" but complains that His enemies *say* this to slander Him. He ends this talks of the enemies of heaven as doing violence to the persons of John the Baptist and to Himself by saying the words, "But wisdom is justified by her children." The R.S.V. uses the word "deeds" instead of "children." However the metaphysical aspects of the phrase seem to "personify" *wisdom* as a property of mind whose responsibility is justified, or witnessed through various attitudes, opinions and behaviors of the self. Hence these complexes of the self are the "children" which when applied to Jesus's accusers justified or qualified the extent of their wisdom. It is apparent that Jesus used this metaphor as an evaluation of the moral and ethical responsibility of his accusers.

Remember that Jesus had sat at the table with sinners who were drinking wine and eating flesh.

The Pharisees criticized him for associating with sinners, whereupon Jesus told the parable of the lost sheep. His purpose of sitting with wine bibbers and gluttons was admittedly to persuade them to mend their way of life, for, as he answered to the Pharisees, "I say to you likewise shall my Father rejoice if I bring Him a sheep that is lost to the fold." (Luke 15:10-10)

Today if a man is caught with gamblers and drinkers in a place raided by police, even though his purpose there was merely to care for a wayward friend and to help him home, he would have a hard time convincing the Judge or even the people of his own neighborhood that he was not also drinking and gambling.

In a like manner then, would Jesus have been identified by His enemies as a wine bibber and a glutton?

"But wisdom is justified by her children."

COMMENTARY

20 — The Meaning of the Words
"I Desire Mercy and Not Sacrifice."
Who Are My Mother and My Brethren?

According to gospel writings, Jesus and His disciples were admonished by the Pharisees for picking corn to eat on the Sabbath.

They said, "Behold, your disciples do that which is unlawful on the Sabbath Day."

And Jesus answered them, "You blind guides which strain at a gnat and swallow a camel." How well this admonition might be applied to the gnat like laws which Christian authorities have been guilty of. It has not been so long ago that it was unlawful even to smile on Sunday. It is still unlawful to do many things on this day. The old Blue Laws, fostered along with the Salem witch hunts of the past century, are still being enforced by Christian authorizations.

The Pharisees had a legitimate right to censure the disciples for doing what was unlawful on the Sabbath, because that day, according to Old Testament authority, was the Lord's day, a day that Jesus Himself observed in the quiet dignity of His spirit. But the Christian does not possess this authority. His day of worship is the day not set aside by the Judaeo-Christian God, but a day that had been set aside by the pagan worshipers of the god of the Sun; the god Mithra. Here it appears that the Christian tradition in its insistence upon Blue Law enforcement is in truth straining at a gnat created by human commands and not by the command of God.

It is of course unfair to suggest that Christian attitudes are basically "gnat-like."

Even though the Church as a mighty tree grew from a sapling transplanted in alien soil, it still retains beneath the calloused growth of its bark a somewhat impassive or restricted awareness of the simple purity of its seed. A full and complete awakening would, in effect, send its roots back into the "rivers of Eden" and its branches ever more closer to the "portals of Heaven."

Again, referring to the incident of the cornfield, Jesus admonishes the Pharisees, this time on a major issue. The many disagreements which Jesus had with the Pharisees at various times were in proportion comparable with the size of a gnat. According to scholarly opinion and as described elsewhere herein, the gospels report Jesus as admonishing the Pharisees on subjects on which they were more or less in agreement with Him. On one point alone, it is evident that He and the Pharisees were completely irreconcilable — on the question of sacrifice. His warm compassionate heart rebelled against any act of cruelty. Doing violence to any of God's creatures was to Him a major sin.

In reference thereto, Jesus concluded by admonishing the Pharisees with the words, "But if you know what this means, 'I will have mercy and not sacrifice,' you would not have condemned the guiltless." Hence, His disciples were guiltless in contrast with the Pharisees' brutal custom of animal sacrifice.

Here Jesus referred to the prophet Hosea when He said, "If you know what this means" — "for I desired mercy, and not sacrifice: and the knowledge of God more than burnt offerings." (Hosea 6:6)

"For the Son of Man is Lord even of the Sabbath day." Here Jesus in his unswerving allegiance to the "will to live" in all creatures becomes Himself the "will of God." As God is life, all life, then "reverence for life" is reverence for God. Therefore, He who lives in God loves all life, and *every day to him is the Lord's day*. Thus was Jesus Lord even of the Sabbath.

"Then Jesus withdrew and went out to minister unto the people (Matt 12:46-50). While He was still speaking to the people, behold His mother and His brother outside asking to speak to Him." And Jesus answered, according to Matthew, "Who is my mother and who are my brothers?" And, stretching out His hand toward His disciples, He said: "Here are my mother and my brothers. For whosoever does the will of My Father in Heaven is My brother and sister and mother."

The manner of this reported incident is such that one can hardly fail to recognize the obvious. Surely there must have been some error in the arrangement of this text. Here Jesus is made to appear rather cold and aloof, if not downright insulting, to His mother and brothers. That is to say, He appears to both ignore their presence, as well as imply that His mother and brothers were not as sensitive to the will of God as were His disciples.

This has been corrected in the reconstructed "Covenant of Love" to conform in principle to the well meaning nature of the comparison made by Jesus before His disciples: "Who are My mother? and who are My brethren? Are they not of My heart and My love?" Stretching forth His hands towards His disciples, He said, "Behold! inasmuch you also are My mother and My brethren."

COMMENTARY

21 — The Parable of the Sower
The Secrets Are For the Twelve

It seems strange that when Jesus spoke to the people, He usually formed His lessons into parables. If His purpose was to teach them, surely He would have spoken simply so they could understand.

The only explanation for this method of teaching seems to be that if He spoke to them plainly about things not in accord with their traditional customs, they would resent His frankness. On the other hand, if He gave to them food for thought clothed in simple parables, they might think things out for themselves, thereby arriving at the truth through their own deductions. In this way their egos would feel more pacified than condemned.

However, Jesus usually clarified the parables to His disciples, who were sometimes no better than the others at understanding Him. No doubt there were many other parables of the highest order spoken by Jesus that were lost to our time through His reporters' inability to reconstruct them.

It is evident, however, that He took particular care to pass on to the Twelve certain truths about the great sublime system we call "life."

When Jesus said, "It is given to you to know the secrets," he realized the people were not ready to receive the fullness of the truth. He therefore confided in The Twelve in the hope that they would understand the sacredness of God's creation and pass this knowledge on to those who were ready to receive it.

"The Essenes believed they possessed, through the revelations symbolized by the Teacher of Righteousness and through other mystic lore of their sect, a special knowledge of the hidden meanings. Jesus, too, appears to have believed that He and the disciples possessed a special understanding of the meanings of Scripture. 'To you it has been given to know the secrets of the Kingdom of Heaven,' He told His disciples, "but to them it has not been given." [1]

In lieu of any written evidence as to what either the Essenes and Jesus meant by "secrets of the Kingdom of Heaven," it must be supposed that these inner teachings were transmitted orally — by word of mouth only.

There are many planes, phases, or stations of spiritual evolvement upon this earth, all of which vary in degree of moral aptitudes in proportion to the individual's awareness of the GOOD.

According to Dr. Ferrier, the great English compassionist, the Holy Bible is in itself a composite of several moral and spiritual planes representing various steps or phases of man's approach to God. In this great book one can find passages or sayings that satisfy his own particular plane of spiritual development. He can read himself into his own desired phase and custom of living, varying all the way from the authorization of human sacrifice and the bloody reign of the God of ancient Israel on into our modern day, with its still prevalent ceremonial of animal sacrifice, and finally to the high plane of peace with a God of love, through becoming at peace with His creation.

The highest earthly plane of awareness of the good that a human being is capable of, approaches the prophesied Kingdom of Heaven upon this earth. Here the secrets entrusted to the 'Twelve' become known to the individual, and a great understanding of all things comes upon him. He is at peace with his creation. No man can ever find complete happiness, peace of mind and soul until he first seeks peace with God. This cannot be done by prayer alone, for prayer, — sincere prayer — expresses only a willingness to co-operate with God.

All the resting on the knees or the murmuring in the

throat, all the deepness of concentration and all the meditative moods of solitude will not alone bring the suppliant into tune with his God.

"Seek ye first the Kingdom of Heaven and all things will be made known to you."

To seek the Kingdom of Heaven is to discover first the "will" of God. When one finally arrives at an understanding of God's will, then the human spirit becomes one with all life, and, in consequence one with God. (See page 146.)

One need not ask God for a sign as evidence of His will as did the Pharisees of old. The will of God is most obvious in the "will to live" of all creatures. The Twentieth Century apostle of Jesus Christ, our beloved Albert Schweitzer, pointed this out in his own revelation, "Reverence for life:"

"The deeper we look into nature, the more we recognize that it is full of life and the more profoundly we know that all *life is a secret and that we are united with all life that is in nature.* From this knowledge comes our spiritual relationship to the universe." [2]

The "will to live" is an indigenous sense of permanence; a sense of maintaining itself forever if possible. This is the creature's unconscious awareness of the immortality of that which both causes life, and is life. The *striving of one creature to protect itself is actually an innate demonstration of the eternal life's opposition to death. It is the will of God revealing, in the defensive activity of the creature, a counter evidence of death — not death of the physical body but of the 'will' which is the spirit or life of the creature.*

Therefore both the will and the life are one and the same in God. For out of God come these things.

However, the *will* in the *will to live* should not be confused with desire. Desire is of the flesh, and the flesh yields to lust. God creates life; and wills it to seek perfection.

Pain is of the body but the awareness of it is in the "will to live."

Thus, violence of any sort to man or beast causes pain

and suffering of the body of which the higher senses are aware. Immediately the "will to live" goes into action by bringing encouragement to the mind-like properties of the damaged cells in their efforts to again return the natural body to a state of equilibrium.

Here an understanding of the will of God may be approached. Every cell is an individual psychic system, each contributing to the awareness of a combined conscious system, or body. Harm or hurt is opposed to the "will to live" whether in man or beast; therefore it is opposed to the will of God.

All creatures through their "will to live" seek freedom from pain. Where there is no pain, there is no anxiety and where there is no anxiety there is well being, and with well being come happiness and peace.

Thus, when man lives in peace with the "will to live" of God's creation, he necessarily becomes at peace with God.

By no longer supporting the "shambles"* or any other institution of pain and death common to our so called civilized way of life, a person removes from his shackled spirit all its opposition to life beyond the intimidation of body or physical death. Eternal life becomes more clearly assured, for, in complying with the will of God, man no longer by the very act of being himself an instrument of death opposes the eternal thing he seeks.

Here one realizes the sacredness of life, and finds in his heart a reverence for everything spiritual. Thus does he come into an understanding of the fullness of God's love, for he has removed from the very word LOVE all the human inconsistencies of its definition. He can now say without the least doubt or guilt that he loves animals, birds, etc., for he has learned of mercy, compassion, dignity of spirit, cleanness of body and soul, hence the peace of God.

This appears intuitively to the writer as being the essence of the secret Jesus passed on to the Twelve.

In accord with this discussion of the secret of the Twelve,

* Archaic for Slaughter House.

it might be well to mention the gnostics of early century Christianity. The word GNOSIS equals UNDERSTAND-ING, knowledge or revelation.

The Gnostics were in many respects Essenic in custom, following a humane way of life. According to the Encyclopedia Britannica: "Of the actual writings of the Gnostics very little has survived; they were sacrificed to the destructive zeal of their ecclesiastical opponents.

"These little Gnostic sects and groups all lived in the conviction that they possessed a secret and mysterious knowledge in no way accessible to those outside, which was not to be proved or propagated but believed in by the initiated and anxiously guarded as a secret. This knowledge was derived directly from the times of primitive Christianity; from the Savior Himself and His disciples and friends, with whom they claimed to be connected by a secret tradition." [3] One can hardly discount the possibility that the common bond between these early Christians and Jesus was in their knowledge of the secret as proposed herein.

Finally and without equivocation the primary evidence of Life is God, or, conversely, the primary evidence of God is life. Thus the "will of my Father" is of necessity the "will to live" in all creatures.

To transgress the sacredness of this declaration is to deny the very will of God in the will-to-live. "But he that doeth the will of my Father shall enter into the Kingdom of Heaven." (Matt. 7:21)

COMMENTARY

22 — The Woman of Canaan

"Then Jesus went thence, and departed into the Coasts of Tyre and Sidon and, behold, a woman of Canaan came out of the same coasts and cried unto him, saying Have mercy on me, O Lord, thou son of David; my daughter is grievously vexed with a devil.

But He answered her not a word." (Matt. 15:21-28)

Here the phrase *"He answered her not a word,"* infers that someone, other than Jesus, made a direct answer to her request.

Remindful of the many mistakes that have been made especially in the arrangement of scriptural passages one might suppose, according to the above, that here again careless reconstruction put words in the mouth of Jesus which were, in the original texts, said by his apostles.

Surely if "He answered her not a word" then one may assume that when Jesus did finally speak He addressed himself first to the Apostle who had spoken so rudely and thereafter to the woman who sought his condolence.

It has been pointed out that the original Aramaic Matthew was translated into Greek by Hebrew writers. In fact they had a hand in the rendition of the very copy, much of which has come down to us in the New Testament.

Remindful of the rivalry which existed in the First Century between the Jewish Christians and the followers of Paul, one may assume that the story concerning the woman of Canaan was purposely interpolated by the Hebrew translators and copyists, to imply that Jesus was sent especially to receive and to comfort the Jews.

In effect the Canaanite woman was to represent the Heathen Christians who could at best perceive only "the

251

crumbs which fall from their master's table." (Matt. 15:27)

Again the inferiority of the Gentile Christians was further emphasized by making Jesus to say: *I was sent only to the lost sheep of the house of Israel.*" (Matt. 15:24)

If this statement was actually made by Jesus then the Gentiles have for 2000 years been worshipping a Savior whose blessings were obviously not intended for them.

It does not require much persuasion to convince the Christian that this saying is somewhat in error, but can he look with equal disfavor upon other similar ambiguities which the writer has pointed out herein? "I wonder."

On the other hand the story as it now appears in Matthew might indeed be quite meaningful allegorically. From a metaphysical point of view the story quite obviously refers to the unworthiness of the Christian who due to either his ignorance or his thoughtlessness is not a true follower of the Master: that only Jesus' immediate followers, those of the house of Israel are described as obedient to his teachings: that to actually be one of the recovered of the lost sheep was to receive the bread: but those who were not of the flock were to receive only the crumbs that fall from the table. However in the crumbs might be found the incentive for a return to the doctrine of the Master as it was practiced by the Apostles and by the early Palestinian Christians. In so doing one becomes a lost sheep of the house of Israel to whom the Lord was sent: i.e., one who equals in thought and practice the ethics of the Palestinian Christians. Thus in consequence the Lord Jesus recognizes his own even as He recognized the sincerity of the woman of Canaan. (Matt. 15:22-28)

The Christian, in fact all men, have a deep longing in their Being to recognize and look up to an example, an ideal, worthy of the highest, most ethical, and consistent degree of love and understanding. Toward such an ideal all men of good will tend to reach. Even though the sublime purity of such an ideal may transcend the customs of our social and religious institutions, it still can stand out before all men as a challenge to the spiritual life of which he is capable. For when man ties his wagon to a star, it must be the brightest star in all the heavens.

In the reconstructed gospel, or the "Covenant of Love," Jesus is this brightest star, He is the Ideal, the one true spirit of a God of love, mercy, consideration, and understanding. He rises from out of the deep spiritual underlay of early Christian literature to stand before all men as the criterion of ethical supremacy. He severs by one stroke the rusty chains of inconsistency which dominate human interpretation of the word LOVE.

COMMENTARY

23 — The Cursing of the Fig Tree

"Now in the morning as He returned into the city He hungered. And when He saw a fig tree in the way He came to it, and found nothing thereon but leaves, and said unto it, "Let no fruit grow on thee henceforward forever." And presently the fig tree withered away.

And when the Disciples saw it, they marveled, saying, "How soon is the fig tree withered away!"

Jesus answered and said, "Verily I say to you, if you have faith and doubt not, you shall not only do this which is done to the fig tree but also you shall say to this mountain, be removed and it shall be cast into the sea." (Matt. 21:18-21)

In examining this construction of Matthew, one finds first that there is quite a variance of both interpretation and reporting between the synoptists.

Matthew and Mark treat the subject as a narrative, while Luke presents it as a parable.

In the narration of Matthew, the fig tree withers immediately, before the eyes of the disciples, while in Mark it is the next day before the withering is recognized.

The motive behind the construction of both of these reports is quite evident. The sensational aspects of Mark's treatment of the subject were somewhat exaggerated in the narration of Matthew in order to re-emphasize the extraordinary powers of Jesus.

It has been well said that "truth shrinks as exaggeration expands." In other words, an overstatement is always at the expense of truth.

The whole tenor and tone of this narrative exploits the sensational at the expense of the ethical.

254

Here Jesus is made to appear both ill-tempered and spiteful as He reproaches the fig tree. "Let no fruit grow on thee henceforth and forever." So be it that its branches die and its leaves wither and fall to the ground.

O where in this is the sympathetic, patient, and understanding Jesus of the Sermon on the Mount? Surely, it is not He who spitefully exhibits such extraordinary power at the expense of a beautiful tree whose life's work is dedicated to the giving in due season of delicious and healthful food. Even if Jesus desired to produce a sign to prove His divine inheritance, He would not have contemptuously and ruthlessly defiled one of the purest evidences of a gracious God — a fruit-giving tree.

He could, in truth, have used many other examples to demonstrate the power of faith, any one of which would have been just as sensational without jeopardizing the wholesomeness of ethical practice.

In the foregoing "Covenant of Love," the narrative has been reconstructed. In so doing, however, the text reads less sensationally but with a more ethical vibrancy. It is now much less extraordinary, but a great deal more considerate and understanding. This way, it illustrates the spiritual truth of the fig tree narrative without intimidating the honor of the Master.

COMMENTARY

24 — Love as a Universal Ethic
The Greatest of all Sins

The first law of God as demonstrated by Jesus Christ is the Law of Love. The spirit of this law is not to be confused with the fervid mating instinct of the sexes. It is rather in the drawing together of two hearts and two souls in mutual consideration and trust. It is a patient and protective concern which endures unquelled, throughout the many trials and tribulations of husband and wife, parents and offspring. It is a deep seated pity for the inevitable sufferings of others, and a hopeful longing for the fulfillment of the brotherhood of man and the Fatherhood of God. It is not the shallow emotionalism that dramatizes the misfortunes of others, pretending to be concerned; nor is it the frothy sentimentality which laments the death of a beautiful songbird at the hand of a neighborhood delinquent, but changes face over the roasted remains of a beautiful pheasant.

It is rather, a compassionate understanding uncompromised by the inconsistencies of human indulgence.

This is LOVE unrestrained, unlimited and unalloyed. It is the law which identifies the Cosmic Christ in the way of life of the Historical Christ. It is a basic Universal Love uncontaminated by human customs and practices. It is a Love that transcends the subjective and becomes aware that the criteria of ethics are the objective concerns for the whole of life, beyond, as well as inclusive of, the Self. Thus in an objective sense, the Spirit of God within the Self, reaches out to join with the Spirit of God in other life, to effect an unbroken chain of universal harmony. Again, in a subjective sense, it is the Love of God within endeavoring to shape and form a self-environment in which other life might find peace and happiness.

This, therefore, is the Love of the Cosmic, or Humane, Christ. It is a deep understanding and concern for the rights and privileges of all of God's creatures. It is associated with a desire to cooperate with nature; to refrain from harming, hurting, or destroying either through unconcern or through self-indulgent habits, any of God's creatures.

"God gives the lesser idea of Himself for a link to the greater, and in return, the high always protects the lower . . ." [1]

"God is the life, or intelligence which forms and preserves the individuality and identity of animals as well as of men." [2]

In the re-discovery of the Humane Christ as set forth in the "Covenant of Love," one can, if he chooses, arrange his life so that it will harmonize with the practices of the Master and His apostles. It might here be of interest to the spiritual healer to consider well the ameliorating possibilities involved. It is quite obvious that, when the consciousness of the practitioner is freed from any connection or association with customs or habits contrary to the forces of harmony in the universe, his efforts towards bringing about equilibrium in the mind or body of a sick patient, would in consequence be more rewarding. That is, when a person actually "lives the life," he becomes in full harmony with the Spirit of the Master, and all things may in due time be made possible to him.

The greatest commandment is: Thou shalt love the Lord thy God with all thy heart, and with all thy soul, and with all thy mind." (Matt. 22:37) If this is the greatest commandment, then anyone who disobeys it commits the greatest sin.

But what do these words really mean: With *all* thy heart, *all* thy mind, and *all* thy soul?

The word "all" leaves no room for the encroachment of

any thoughts of behavior contrary to the full and uncompromised meaning of the word love.

The heart, mind, and soul refer to the whole man; the means of directing the emotional, the sensual and the spiritual life of man.

It is through these mediums that the awareness of God is realized.

It is also through these mediums that the commandment to love must be acknowledged.

Love is actually the criterion of life itself. For example, unless a newborn kitten or a lamb is licked and nuzzled by its mother, it will die. All animals need love to thrive. There have been many cases reported where babies have died for the want of fondling and love.

According to Jo. 1:4.1, Jo. 4:8, God is life and God is love. Therefore, life and love are inseparable. Where love does not support life, life ceases to be, and where life does not support love, God ceases to be.

This is both a natural and a spiritual axiom. To love God with all thy heart, mind and soul is to love the life of all His creatures, for God IS life. If we support life with love then we support God; therefore God is with us. But if we do not support life with love, God, Who *is love,* ceases to be or is not with us.

To love God with all thy heart is to make it overflow with the milk of mercy, pity, compassion, and loving kindness. To love thy God with all thy mind is to reason out ways and means to spare every creature pain and suffering, and to retrieve those that are drawn into death: and to love God with all thy soul is to become one in Him, through protecting and revering the life that is of His creation.

When one kills one of God's creatures he breaks both the Sixth Commandment and the great commandment, "Love thy God."

The "will to live" *is* the will of God affirming itself in the life of every creature.

To ignore the "will of God" by coldly, thoughtlessly, or

lustfully indulging in practices contrary to His nature is in effect deliberately castigating the Great Commandment, for here the heart scorns God in its coldness; the mind slights God in its thoughtlessness, and the soul spurns God in its lustfulness.

Thus does one abuse the greatest commandment and commit a threefold sin against God.

COMMENTARY

25 — Jesus Heals Through Prayer and Fasting:
The Divine Formula

"The New Testament did not condemn fasting though the act was considered inconsistent with the imminent approach of the Messiah (Matt. 9:14). Jesus ever simple in His own habits, probably fasted frequently." [1]

However, Jesus many times criticized the insincerity of those of His day who made a public show of their fasting. Like an act of prayer, He urged that these things be done in the privacy of one's own thoughts and person.

Fasting had many different meanings. In general, it was to ward off evil spirits or to cast out sickness or the demons which infected the body and to evoke the favor of God. Much of that spoken of as fasting in those days we, today, describe as dieting or abstaining from particualr foods.

Funk and Wagnalls interprets the word "fast" as abstaining from food, partially or totally, or abstaining from particular kinds of food.

When Jesus said "this kind can be cured only by prayer and fasting," (Mark 9:29) He shed additional light on the methods He employed to bring about His miraculous cures. He suggests to us that prayer and faith coupled with the eating of, or the abstinence of certain foods is the only positive way of effecting a permanent cure of human ills.

In the R.S.V. of the scriptures many changes have been made which alter in some cases the entire meaning of the text. In Mark 9:29 the word "fast" is omitted while in Matthew 17:29 the entire twenty-ninth verse relating to prayer and fasting is omitted.

With this firsthand evidence before us, one wonders if

260

other and more pertinent references of this kind have not
in the past either been rephrased, or omitted completely
from the texts. However, the one tiny reminding reference
of Jesus to fasts (or diets) as a necessary contingent to
prayer in the casting out of body and mental ills reveals
the unquestionable honesty of Jesus.

"Diet and after-treatment played a great part, though
the evangelists say little about this because directions on
these points would not be given publicly. Thus the saying,
'This kind goeth not out save by prayer and fasting,' is interpreted as an instruction to the Father as to the way in
which He could make the sudden cure of the epileptic (or
diabetic) into a permanent one, viz. by keeping him to a
strict diet and strengthening his character through devo-
tional exercises.

"The disciples too, (as appears from Mark 6: 7, 13) were
not sent out without medicaments, for the oil with which
they were to anoint the sick was, of course, of a medicinal
character." [2]

It is well known today that up to 90% of all body and
mental ills can be traced to unnatural habits of various
kinds, the greatest offender being the habit of consuming
food and drink unfavorable to a state of well being.

In complete violation of the protests of God and the
prophets, man not only pollutes his body with the corpses
of dead things, but he also overfeeds or overworks his
digestive system which hastens its breakdown contrary to
natural consequences.

Human nature has not changed much from Bible times.
The Scriptures are full of references pertaining to the
evils of overeating and overdrinking.

Jesus, no doubt, had to contend with the same violation of
health and well being in His time that are our bane today.
It is mere (illusion) to suggest that a cure of any kind can
be brought about without first removing its cause. Can
prayer heal a stab wound as long as the blade remains in
the flesh? Can an alcoholic be cured by mixing prayer with

alcohol, or a diabetic by diluting his sugar intake with a petition to God? Can lung cancer be avoided by praying the curse off cigarettes, or a coronary by petitioning the Lord to purify the fats of animals? Can Bright's disease and gout be cured by eating roast beef seasoned with prayer, and can a fat person be made thin by overindulging in both food and prayer? The answer, of course, is NO, for one cannot deny the existence of harmful things. But he can avoid them. In fact, not to do so is to prostitute the wisdom of God in His giving of intelligence to man in the first place.

Jesus, the great reformer, well knew the laws of cause and effect, and He applied them to the healing of suffering humanity. He also knew that the lack of spiritual security contributing to emotional frustration could be cured by confidence in the love of God. This He demonstrated in the extraordinary healing of many troubled minds and spirits.

In the time of Jesus there lived in Egypt a Hebrew sect known as the "Therapeutae." It is the opinion of many scholars that they were closely related to the Essenes in their manners and customs, for they had many things in common. One of these was their knowledge of the psychophysical or the physico-spiritual art of healing. "They were called 'healers.' "*

They were known for their study of the natural processes in regard to health. They evidently knew that what we call "nature" is constantly working towards a state of equilibrium. Specifically, God in nature is the incentive in the healing processes in every cell of every living thing. The will to live is the will of God. Therefore, the mind of all creatures is necessarily synchronized with the will of God in providing for a true state of nature which is a state of health.

Again, the minds of creatures seem to be synchronized with the mind-like properties of the cells making up the body structure.

The Essenes probably recognized that the basis for the

* Hastings Ency. on Religion and Ethics Vol. 5 p. 400.

continuation of a state of cellular equilibrium must be in the food and drink that nature — or rather God — provided.

If, according to Genesis, God made the body of man and gave it a mind with which to think, he also, according to Genesis, prescribed the proper food which only the creator of such an intricate mechanism would know to be necessary for its natural operation.

Any type of food which the choice of man might select other than that prescribed would be unnatural. Hence, it is unnatural to be anything but healthy.

The mind of man, through its awareness of the laws of God, responds to the mind-like properties of the body cells and satisfies them by leading the way to their return (in case of illness) to a state of equilibrium. Pain is a psychic reaction of the cell. It is a protest against being disturbed by outside irregularities.

The entire universe may be referred to as a "psychic system": as a living system. God is life and His is the will to live in all creatures.

The incentive in all nature, from the cosmic bodies to the atom, is to seek harmony and a state of equilibrium. Without this incentive, all would be chaos. Cause and effect, stimulation and response, are the factors in time and space which are in constant operation. Thus the whole of space and matter is continually alert to psychic activities.

In consequence, psychic reactions to good or bad operate both within the individual's own system as well as between his system and other individuals, or systems outside it. This is fundamental to the existence of a unified whole.

The psychic system of one person, especially when it is upset through irregularities centered in the consciousness, may be set aright through the therapeutic influence of another, especially if that person is himself in a reasonable degree of harmony with the laws of God. In consequence, the purer and more sensitive the practioner's own state of moral equilibrium, the more effective will be his ministry.

Thus it becomes difficult for one to doubt what seem to be the miraculous healings performed by Jesus.

However, Jesus recognized the necessity of treating ills of the body through the patient's mind by influencing him to return to natural practices, of eating, sleeping, relaxation, and the like.

No doubt after his first buildup of the patient's feeling of wellness, he admonished him to cleanse his system by fasting, which evidently meant a rigidity of diet.

Well he knew that almost all ills of man come about through unnatural habits of food and drink. He also knew that a permanent cure could not be effected as long as the cause of it remained unaltered. To expect such a cure would be to invalidate the laws of cause and effect, or the existence of God Himself.

Jesus, ever simple in His own habits, probably fasted frequently, for He realized the therapeutic benefits to both body and spirit. To Jesus the practice of fasting was not the same as it was to the Scribes and Pharisees. They fasted to evoke the favor of God, but Jesus already had such favor.

According to what we know today of the many illnesses brought about through unnatural habits such as smoking, drinking alcohol, coffee and other stimulants, along with the unnatural habit of flesh eating, to say nothing of the effects of overeating and drinking, one would be rather naive to argue that Jesus was not faced with similar conditions: conditions wherein all the means as described herein were used by Him to effect His many cures.

Ellen G. White, a Nineteenth Century Prophet of God, inspired by the light of the Master, wrote: "Christ knew that in order to successfully carry forward the plan of salvation He must commence the work of redeeming man just where the ruin began. Adam fell by the indulgence of appetite.

"In order to impress upon man his obligations to obey the law of God, Christ began His work of redemption by reforming the physical habits of man. The decline in virtue and the degeneracy of the race are chiefly attributable to the indulgence of perverted appetite.

"God has bountifully provided for the sustenance and happiness of His creatures; if His laws were never violated, if all acted in harmony with the divine will, health, peace, and happiness, instead of misery and continued evil, would be the result.

"God will not work in a miraculous manner to preserve the health of persons who are taking a sure course to make themselves sick by their careless inattention to the laws of health.

"God does not see fit to answer prayers offered in behalf of such for He knows that if they should be restored to health they would again sacrifice it upon the altar of unhealthy appetite.

"The true fasting which should be recommended to all is abstinence from every stimulating kind of food and the proper use of wholesome simple food which God has provided in abundance. The Lord intends to bring His people back to live upon fruits, vegetables, and grains . . . God provided fruit in its natural state for our first parents.

"Is it not time that all should aim to dispense with flesh foods? How can those who are seeking to become pure, refined, and holy, that they may have the companionship of heaven, continue to use as food anything that has so harmful an effect on soul and body? How can they take the life of God's creatures that they may consume the flesh as a luxury? Let them, rather, return to the wholesome and delicious food given to man in the beginning, and themselves practice, and teach their children to practice, mercy towards the dumb creatures that God has made and placed under our dominion.

"Human beings are suffering the result of their own course of action in departing from the commandments of God. The beasts also suffer under the curse.

"Animals are often transported long distances and subjected to great suffering in reaching a market. Taken from the green pastures and traveling for weary miles over the hot dusty roads, or crowded into filthy cars, feverish and exhausted, often for many hours deprived of food and water, the poor creatures are driven to their death that human beings may feast on their carcasses.

"God gave our first parents the food He designed that the race should eat. It was contrary to His plan to have the life of any creature taken. There was to be no death in Eden. The fruit of the tree in the garden was the food man's wants required." [8]

The truth of this inspired prophet's teachings are rather amazingly verified by the discovery and translation of a manuscript attributed to the Gospel of John.

In a work published a few years ago bearing a similar title, Dr. Edmond Szekely writes, "The contents of this little book is only a fragment — about an eighth — of the complete manuscripts which exist in Aramaic in the library of the Vatican and in Old Slavonic in the Royal Library of the Hapsburgs (now the property of the Austrian state). The texts date from the First Century. The part now given deals chiefly with the healing works of Jesus and His teachings upon the right relation between man's body and nature to which he gives the name Earthly Mother.

"And Jesus Himself sat down in their midst and said: 'I tell you truly, none can be happy, except he do the law.'

"And the others answered: 'We all do the laws of Moses, our lawgiver, even as they are written in the Holy Scriptures.'

"And Jesus answered: 'Seek not the law in your scriptures, for the law is life, whereas scripture is dead. I tell you truly, Moses received not his laws from God in writing, but through the living word.* The law is the living word of a living God, to living prophets for living men. In everything that has life is it written.

"And from all temptations of your body and your spirit

---

* This saying is supported by both the protests of the prophets and the writings of the Dead Sea Scrolls.

coming from Satan, withdraw beneath the shadow of God's heaven.

"Renew yourselves and fast. For I tell you truly, that Satan and his plagues may only be cast out by fasting and by prayer.

"For I tell you truly from one mother proceeds all that lives upon the earth. Therefore he who kills, kills his brother. And from him will the Earthly Mother turn away, and will pluck from him her quickening breasts. And he will be shunned by her angels, and Satan will have his dwelling in his body . . . For only in the service of your Heavenly Father are your debts of seven years forgiven in seven days. But Satan forgives you nothing and you must pay him for all. Eye for eye, tooth for tooth, hand for hand, wound for wound, life for life, death for death. For the wages of sin is death.

"Kill not, neither eat the flesh of your innocent prey, lest you become the slaves of Satan. For that is the path of suffering and it leads to death. But do the will of God that His angels may serve you on the way of life. Obey, therefore, the words of God. Behold! I have given you every herb bearing seed in which is the fruit of a tree yielding seed; to you it shall be for meat!" [4]

Here Jesus, in Dr. Szekely's translation, refers to the food man shall eat as set down in the first chapter of Genesis. The writer refers to this in his "Covenant of Love" as the "Divine Formula."

Here it seems necessary to point out that the gospel writings represent Jesus, as using fish along with bread in the feeding of the five thousand. Also that Mark and Luke present him as being interested in eating the Passover lamb.

Now as to the feeding of the five thousand this, as most unprejudiced authorities agree, should be interpreted as describing the giving of "food for the spirit," or, the "bread of eternal life." Thus, the spiritual hunger of the five thousand was fully satisfied and they carried away with them food of the soul, which compared with ordinary food would have filled many baskets.

Now as to Jesus partaking of the Passover feast we find, according to John, that Jesus was crucified on the 14th of Nisan the day of preparation: that in accord therewith the body of Jesus lay in his tomb during the ritualistic feast of the Passover which makes His eating of the paschal lamb not only impossible but which also reveals the references to His having done so, as being little short of blasphemy.

Certainly the ethics of Jesus could not have been less righteous than were those of his fellow Essenes who opposed the "Paschal Sacrifice," by declaring "according to the law written upon the tablets of old that all holy days and the beginning of the natural year should be observed by offering to God as my firstling the praise of my tongue or the fruits that flow from my lips." (See page 230.)

The fact that the historical evidence supports in perfect chronological order the Johnean reports of the crucifixion is verification enough that either the synoptic writers erred in their reports or their writings were later corrupted by other hands.

Of the two alternatives however, the latter is the more satisfying, for it removes the otherwise blot on the consistency of the four gospel references pertaining to the chronology of the crucifixion and the paschal feast. It is interesting to note that these interpolators cleverly placed their propaganda so as to merely suggest preparations for the eating of the paschal lamb, and that they did not dare to be so bold as to place the lamb upon the table before Jesus, or, to describe Him as actually eating of it. Furthermore, if the lamb had actually been on the table would it not have provided a more positive demonstration for Jesus to have picked up a shank of the flesh of the lamb and say, "this is my flesh," rather than using, such an otherwise unrelated symbol as a loaf of bread? Common sense therefore tells us, even without the fourth gospel's verification, that Jesus and His disciples did not eat the flesh of the paschal lamb on that memorable night in the upper room.

This leaves one more reference to flesh eating that needs to be explained.

The only place in the four gospels where Jesus is represented as eating flesh is when His disciples report the appearance of His spiritual body after the crucifixion. Here Jesus is four times described as eating fish. There can hardly be any doubt that these references were later added to the gospels in order to substantiate the doctrine that the resurrection involves the material body even in contradiction to Paul's definition, for he says, "It is sown a natural body; it is raised a spiritual body. There is a natural body, and there is a spiritual body." (Cor. 1, 15:44) "Flesh and blood cannot inherit the Kingdom of God; neither doth corruption inherit incorruption." (15:50).

If Christ appeared to His disciples in the flesh after His crucifixion, which according to Paul would be in a "natural body" or a "corruptible body," then the eating of fish would be both a "natural" and a "corruptible" act. In this case the resurrection forfeits its reliability as a phenomenon in fact, and needs to be explained as a natural consequence. In other words, Jesus was taken down from the cross while he was still alive.

However a more rational "religious" explanation would be that Jesus appeared to His disciples not in the flesh and blood which, according to Paul, cannot inherit the Kingdom of Heaven, but in an incorruptible 'spiritual body.' Such a body being of the plane of the incorruptible would not and could not partake of those things sufficient only to the natural or corruptible. Therefore, in support of the more rational religious viewpoint, as well as to comply with the overwhelming evidence that the doctrine of the humane Jesus forbade the eating of flesh, the contrary references in the gospels, would be in fact no more than irresponsible interpolations.

The doctrine of the "fall" presupposes an age wherein all creatures dwelt in peace; there was to be no blood spilt in Eden. It was only after man became heavy with sin that he became a flesh eater: and the fear of him and the dread of him was upon every living thing, even the fish in the sea.

The purpose of Jesus was to teach man how to recover his lost manhood: how to return to that golden age when "there shall be no more harm or hurt on all my holy mountain": to bring to pass the kingdom of heaven upon the earth i.e., "Thy will be done on earth as it is in heaven."

When Papias the pupil of John quoted the elders as how Jesus spoke of a creation renewed and liberated, how that all animals will use the products of the soil for food and become in turn peaceable with one another he may also have recalled to mind the Master's words: "I have come to proclaim the acceptable year of the Lord." Surely a return to a condition of life before the first blood was let in Eden, when men lived in peace upon the fruits of the soil, would truly be proclaiming an acceptable year of the Lord.

When the gospel "correctors" made Jesus to eat fish they thoughtlessly profaned his pure unblemished spirit. In consequence they made him to be also one fallen from grace; one of the sinful, one among those feared and dreaded by every living thing including the fish of the sea.

It is obvious therefore that the Church in its zeal to conform the scriptures to its doctrine again created a situation which is not only contradictory, but theologically preposterous.

COMMENTARY

26 — Blessed Are the Little Ones.
Jesus Advises the Rich Man.

Jesus made special note of children in His various talks before the people. He referred to their helplessness and their dependence upon the good graces of their parents to illustrate the people's need of dependence upon the Heavenly Father for guidance. He used childhood to define entrance requirements for the Kingdom of God (Mark 10: 14,15). He thanked God for revealing to babes what He had hidden from "the wise and prudent" (Matt. 11:25) (Luke 6:20-38).

In the time of Jesus the Hebrews as a whole were considerate of the welfare of their offspring.

"Train up a child in the way he should go: and when he is old, he will not depart from it." (Prov. 22:6)

However, the children of the Gentiles were not always as well treated as those of the Hebrews. Before laws were passed in Rome to afford some protection for the unwanted child it was entirely the parents' privilege to deal with it as they saw fit. It was a common practice to drown newly born children even as some people today still drown newborn kittens or puppies. It was also a prevalent custom to sell one's own children into slavery. Even today this is still the practice in some sections of our world.

"Whosoever leads one of these little ones astray and causes it to indulge in wickedness is of the lowest among men."

Jesus recognized the plight of the unwanted child, the orphan, and the children of unfortunate or shiftless parents: "Suffer little children and forbid them not to come unto me," was his reproach to those who neglected to lead

271

their little ones in the paths of virtue.

"Love children for they too are sinless like the angels; they live to soften and purify our hearts, and, as it were, to guide us. Woe to him who offends a child.

"Every day and every hour, every minute, walk round yourself and watch yourself, and see that your image is a seemly one. You pass by a child, you pass by, spiteful, with ugly words, with wrathful heart: you may not have noticed the child, but he has seen you, and your image, unseemly and ignoble, may remain in his defenseless heart. You don't know it, but you have sown an evil seed in him, and it may grow — and all because you were not careful before the child; because you did not foster in yourself a careful, actively benevolent love." [1]

"Parents and teachers have the all important responsibility of training children to be loving human beings.

"It is in the development of the capacity for love that the future of humanity lies.

"Love is the leavening of relationships of one to another. Particularly important are the relationships of parent (or teacher) to child, because this is the model, or the pattern of the human relationship of parent (or teacher) loving child: this pattern will be carried over by the child, when an adult, into the next generation, he loving his child, and so on: the flow of love not only continuing in this progressive process but increasing and growing toward the goal to ultimate fulfillment and completeness.

"Love is the medium through which love itself expands and grows. It is the *Supreme Value*. The warmth of love stimulates love and so sets the tenor of the environment which will nurture the child into a loving human being.

"Training children in the ways of love opens up more avenues of love experiences thus stimulating its growth from within and increasing the capacity of love for child and parent or teacher alike.

"This process of increasing love from one to another is the 'Coming of the Kingdom of Heaven Within', and thus we enter 'Heaven' by way of little children." [3]

* * *

In the case of the "rich young ruler," the gospels report the following:

"It is easier for a camel to go through the eye of a needle than for a rich man to enter into the Kingdom of God."

According to the Evangelists, Jesus told the rich young man to give away all of his wealth to the "poor."

This was a rigid rule of the Essenes. They were known as "the poor" for they renounced all wordly goods. Even as it was later recorded in Acts 4:35, "distribution was made unto every man according as he had need." It was required that every Essene or Messianist, (later known in the Greek tongue as Christian) must, upon receiving the faith, give up all of his holdings to the "poor;" that is to say, turn all of his natural possessions over to the general fund, for it was the custom that everything be held in common.

It must be remembered that Jesus, in his day, was adhering to a particular custom practiced only by those "holy ones" who were expecting their present world order to soon be replaced by the Kingdom of Heaven. They, therefore, would have no further need of earthly possessions.

However, in view of the fact that the "kingdom come" did take place during the time anticipated, the position of the rich man who had acquired a comfortable estate through extended effort and fair dealings was not to be condemned to hell.

It is evident, therefore, that the text was later supplemented by the words "for with God all things are possible," meaning that the final judgment of the rich man rested in God. Thus was extended to him an opportunity to find favor with God through the Church. It goes without saying that many abuses resulted through the administration of this doctrine.

Today the rich man is looked up to with envy by those

who have acquired only a small portion of the world's goods, but he is also respected by those who recognize the many commendable contributions he has made to improve the welfare of mankind. In the "Covenant of Love" Jesus does not completely bar the gates of Heaven to the rich man, (a misunderstanding no doubt of the gospel writer) but, instead, He presents a fair and equitable alternative whereby a man of wealth has the opportunity of either relinquishing or gaining a spiritual victory.

COMMENTARY

27 — The Wedding at Cana
The Wine of God

Several of the larger Christian denominations have for many years been opposed to the drinking of alcoholic beverages. They consider such practice to be immoral because it so often leads to shameful consequences.

Whereas these same Christians have been brought to realize the evils of wine and strong drink, it seems that they must also doubt the evangelists' reports that Jesus was a wine bibber; that He actually invoked divine measures to supply the revelers at Cana with several barrels of wine.

On the other hand, they cannot doubt that Jesus did, according to Matthew 11:19, drink wine, and that in mutual sympathy did perform a miracle at Cana (John 2:7-10) without also questioning the authority of the Gospel.

The idea of substituting grape juice for wine only confuses the issue, for here one must also doubt the authority of the texts since they clearly describe what is traditionally known as an alcoholic drink. Whatever one may attempt to make out of the word *wine* in its translation from the Hebrew, Greek, Latin, or Aramaic, it still describes a ferment that is as different from grape juice as apple juice is from hard cider. In fact, this Gospel narrative is itself testimony as to the quality of the miracle beverage.

In John 2:10 one may find the description of a familiar ruse which for centuries has been optional to the server of intoxicating drinks. For example, if a host either wishes to conserve his liquor supply, or observes that his guests have already drunk too much, or — as John 2:10 puts it— "when men have well drunk" — he takes advantage of their now dulled judgment and dilutes his later offerings.

But not so according to the texts of John, for now the miracle wine was even better than the wine served at the beginning of the feast. Therefore, according to the host's own judgment, the miracle drink appears to be what any connoisseur might describe as "good wine." This could hardly be recognizable as describing the quality of simple grape juice.

It is generally conceded that the Gospel of John stresses a more spiritual characterization of Jesus than the works of other evangelists. Somehow the narrative describing Jesus as a "brewer of wine" does not seem in keeping with the otherwise deep spirituality of the Gospel of John. Could it be that, through the adoption of some doctrinal expedient, the texts of the original manuscripts were altered to reinterpret the wine incident? It certainly would be more fitting with the full Gospel of John to suppose that Jesus requested all the guests to fill their goblets from the jars containing water, whereupon He blessed the contents of their cups as living water which, as they drank of it, became the wine of God. Here one may observe a demonstration of the spiritual John: "If any man thirst, let him come unto Me and drink;" "He that believeth on Me shall be filled with living water." (7:37-38)

Thus one might recognize a similar miracle as in the feeding of the five thousand (See Commentary Chapter 31.) "I am the bread of life; he that cometh to Me shall never hunger; and he that believeth on Me shall never thirst." (John 6:35)

"Wine is made by the presses of men. It provides them with both the pleasure of indulgence and the pain of consequences." (Covenant of Love 27:13)

Certainly Jesus Himself would not have given His blessing to a form of indulgence which His personal prophet Isaiah, had condemned fully eight times in as many chapters of his holy work.

What *is* one to believe: the character of Jesus as one intuitively interprets it in his own heart, or as it is less than ethically presented in certain gospel narratives?

It was a Hebrew custom to prepare days ahead for such a wedding feast as the affair at Cana. Food was collected and prepared, and wine was carefully accounted for in sufficient quantity to supply the full capacity of every guest.

Many of the revelers reclined on couches, eating and drinking themselves into a stupor from which they would in time arouse themselves and begin all over again.

The feasting and drinking often lasted for three days, and sometimes the calculated wine supply became exhausted. This was somewhat embarrassing to the governor of the feast, for on occasions such as this the pleasure of his guests was of paramount concern since, to him, no man should be denied the overtaxing of his capacity to indulge.

It was at such a time as this that Jesus is represented—through what must obviously have been a misinterpretation by the evangelist who wrote the Gospel of John — as invoking divine intervention in the interest of a Bacchanalian custom.

This brings up another point of discussion. It has been pointed out by various scholars that in order to combat the early century threat of Mithraism, the church in many instances arranged Christian observances so that they coincided with pagan customs. Thus the traditional Sabbath day was changed to Sunday, the day of the Sun god; the birthday of Jesus was placed on December 25th, the birthday of the pagan Sun god, and many other Christian feast and holy days were placed on similar feast days of their pagan contemporaries.

Compatible with these many efforts of the church to console, or compromise, the mind of the heathen candidate, it seems quite probable that this same attitude was also carried over to include a partial rearrangement of the evangelistic literature. Thus, as previously suggested, Jesus was made to do many extraordinary works — works that astounded the followers of the pagan gods. Unfortunately, however in so doing, they emphasized the sensational at the expense of the ethical.

Of all the traditional pagan gods none was closer to the Greek and Roman heart than Dionysus or Bacchus. He was the first Greek god to hold out the hope of personal salvation. He was the god of the grape, the giver of wine, purveyor of the law, and lover of peace.

It is unthinkable that this first love of the Greco-Roman people could ever have been replaced in the heathen heart by the virtue loving Messiah of an abstentious Hebrew Sect without some drastic compromises being made in their favor. Here it must be assumed that the hands of certain "correctors," rearranged or reinterpreted that which was formerly described merely as a sacramental offering or blessing wherein the contents of the vases represented the "living water," "the heavenly vintage," or the "wine of God," (see John 4:14). Thus a miracle in spirit was made into a miracle in fact wherein the devotedly moral, and sublimely ethical Nazarene became the Master brewer of Cana, or, in effect, the Christian God of the vintage. Here also they emphasized the superiority of the Christian God, for where Dionysus or Bacchus merely blessed the fermenting of the juice the Christian God was the creator in fact of the Elysian vintage: where the juice of the grape was a necessary "prop" to the magic of the heathen god, the Christian God used only water to perform his magic. Also as an added compromise the "correctors" made the personal behavior of Jesus to conform in part to the bacchic indulgences of the heathen candidates through arranging the texts to interpret him as being a heavy eater and a heavy drinker, i.e., one who was called a glutton and a winebibber. They did this even though the scriptures many times condemn such behavior as ungodly.

"How unworthily", wrote the first century Christian Father Tertullian, "do you present Christ as have 'come eating and drinking' into the service of your lusts". "The Kingdom of God is not meat and drink, but righteousness". (Rom. 14:17)

It might be pointed out here to those of weak faith who fear to question the propriety of the written word, that it is indeed far more elevating to one's spiritual security to preserve the honor, dignity, and integrity of the very symbol of all that is pure, wholesome and good than it is to hold fast to the authority of the "letter."

COMMENTARY

28 — The Adulteress's
Condemnation and Acquittal

"He that is without sin among you, let him first cast a stone at her." (John 8:7)

These words contain one of the greatest of all lessons to mankind. Herein every prejudice, every ill will, and every accusing finger that one man might point at another falls unconditionally before the great swelling power of love, mercy, and forgiveness.

What powerful words these are, and how well they fit into a companionship with the sublime Rule: "Do unto others as you would have them do unto you." The soul-stirring affinity of these profound utterances stand out as the greatest moral and spiritual teaching of all time. Together they provide for the only positive means through which the brotherhood of man might be realized upon this earth.

"Judge not lest ye be judged" and "Love thy neighbor as thyself" are the ethics thereof.

COMMENTARY

29 — The Light of the World
The Meaning of "Follow Me"

"He that follows me shall not walk in darkness but shall shine his light before him." (John 8:12)

When Jesus said, "Follow Me," He must have realized that many would be those who would confess before men their emotional acceptance of Him while failing to discipline their moral capacities to follow Him. He evidenced this realization when He said, "In that day many will say, 'Lord, Lord, have we not professed unto you?' but I shall know them not."

There is a marked difference between a public ceremonial acceptance of Jesus Christ as one's Saviour, and a sincere unemotional resolve within the privacy of one's own soul to live the life Jesus exemplified. For example, in the customary practices of "conversion," one finds a means of escaping the fears of "a day of reckoning." Here one's troubled conscience finds temporary security among others, where mass feeling motivates, and numbers stimulate confidence.

But alas, solitude is inevitable, and the time comes when one is alone with his fears. It is here, then, that ceremonial acceptance must prove itself. If it becomes necessary at this time to re-enact in one's imagination the acceptance ceremony, or to constantly repeat prayers in order to continue pacifying the deep seated fears of a troubled conscience, then the customary acceptance service has failed to impart the hoped-for peace and security which makes man one with his God.

The church is a means through which many people find peace, but it should not be considered as a house of mira-

cles. It cannot purify a sinner as long as he lives in sin.
One cannot put on clean clothes over a dirty body and say,
"I am clean." To other men he may appear to be so, but
somehow within, he will be reminded that his well laun-
dered front is only a sham.

"Rites and ceremonies in themselves are nothing apart
from their signification. That which is true, is true without
authority; and that which is false, authority cannot make
true." [1]

"God, who is pure spirit and pervades all, does not regard the forms and rites, but the hearts that offer them." [2]

Many religious devotees are more interested in their own
cloistered ceremonials and the growth of their particular
denomination than they are in the welfare of their fellow
man, or in the moral improvement of the world as a whole.
They live with the self-centered notion that they will some
day find peace in a spiritual world, and that this, our natural world, will soon be destroyed. The danger of this sort
of thinking is to lose sight of the fact that in our natural
world is to be found the only means through which any
man can even hope to transcend its estates and gain eternal
peace.

All the facilities are at hand through which each one of
us must earn his right to aspire to a higher plane of life.
The idea of suddenly becoming "saved" may be deceptive,
for it presupposes a gift unearned, a gift in return for a
mere belief.

"But wilt thou know, O vain man, that faith without
works is dead." (James 2:20)

Faith alone, without the dignity of simple reason, is
blind. It is the spawn of mingled fear and wishful thinking. But faith within the light of a clear vision has no fear
of consequences. It does not depend upon a symbol to avoid
the evils dotting the pathway to spiritual security.

A verbal acceptance alone, of Jesus Christ as one's "personal Saviour," is to walk in the darkness of blind hope,
but to actually follow the living Christ is to transcend the

ceremonial devices of men by truly living the life His teachings demonstrated.

This is what Jesus means in His words: "Follow Me." He means FOLLOW HIS EXAMPLE.

Only when one becomes aware of LOVE in its pure state, free from all compromise, will he, too, exemplify the Spirit of God in the flesh and be qualified to walk with Jesus in the spirit. The Master Himself said, "Ye too are gods:" You too can be like the Father even as Me.

The faith that saves is the faith that exemplifies in act and deed the true nature of the Lord Jesus as a way of life. "What doth it profit, my brethren, though a man say he hath faith, and have not works; can faith save him?" (James 2:14) Faith with works is to adopt the character of the Lord Jesus, for to be like Him the question of "saving" has no meaning whatever. But, on the other hand, to look for salvation through faith alone is to espouse inevitable disillusion.

"Blessed is the man that endureth temptation: for when he is tried he shall receive the crown of life, which the Lord hath promised to them that love him." (James 1:12)

It seems that one's future life — if, when, or where it may be realized—is contingent upon one's spiritual growth. Love, honor, mercy, and humble dignity are the developing media of the soul. Jesus demonstrated this in His every act and deed. In fact, if these were not the necessary criteria of spiritual security, Jesus would never have walked hundreds of wearisome miles over primitive trails and rough roads, teaching these truths to men. If He did not intend that man should follow Him — to live the life of love and mercy that He lived — in order to attain spiritual security, or salvation," why would He have made such a sincere effort to qualify man for a life to come?

All His strivings to help mankind to help themselves would have been unnecessary if the sacrifice of His life alone provided the means for man's achieving eternal life. Let the Christian not delude himself with false hopes. Let him realize that to accept Jesus Christ as his Saviour is to accept *for himself* the very nature and character of Jesus Christ.

The acceptance of Jesus Christ is not an "act"; it is a dedication to a progressive way of life. The teachings of Jesus are the means. The only act of acceptance is in the activating of these means firsthand, in an unfolding endeavor to live the life which He exemplified. Thus one accepts the Christ by becoming wedded in a spiritual unity with Him; by the remaking of one's self into a fitting companion; by letting "this mind be in you which was also in Christ Jesus." (Phil. 2:5)

This is what Jesus meant when He said, "Follow Me, for I am the way and the means."

"He that hath My commandments and keepeth them, he it is that loveth Me: and he that loveth Me shall be loved of My Father and I will love him, and will manifest myself to him." (John 14:21)

"Truth, knowledge, and spirituality flow from individual discovery. Every man, in a very real sense, is 'on his own,' and that being on one's own is precisely what it means to be a man." [3]

COMMENTARY

30 — Jesus Explains That All Men Are in God.

"Is it not written in your law, 'I said ye are Gods; and all of you are children of the most High?'

Here Jesus (in Jo. 10:34, 35) quoted from Ps. 82:6, the latter portions of which have been deleted from the records for obvious reasons.

"Say you therefore that I blasphemeth because I said I am the Son of God?" (John 10:36) "Behold, the Kingdom of God is within you." (Luke 17:21).

In studying these sayings one finds that all men are declared to be sons of God; that God is within all men, and that the Kingdom of Heaven is the birthright of every creature. "God sends forth of His spirit to create life," (Ps. 104:30) therefore the spirit of God is in *all* creatures.

Jesus said, "If you love God, you love Me; and if you love Me, you love God." Then the spirit of God is of him who loves, whether it be Jesus, Moses, Buddha, Confucius, Gandhi, Pythagoras, St. Francis, Schweitzer, or any other sons of God who have brought to man a code of ethics overflowing with love, mercy, and understanding.

If one recognizes the one God in Jesus Christ, he is indeed justified in his judgment; but on the other hand, he is equally as shortsighted as he is observant if he does not also see God in other great souls. They are all sons of the Most High. Every great religion has its Chosen One, its prophets, and its God. If God were not in all creatures, this could not be so. Not always, however, does He shine forth in His true glory. Only when men exemplify love and mercy uncompromised do they cast their light down through the dark centuries, bringing to humanity an awareness of the one God of all space and time.

Our God must be our one Ideal. He must transcend all human frailties and stand forth as the supreme example of all that is kind, merciful, and good.

Whosoever joins in the rediscovery of the divinely ethical Jesus of the "Covenant of Love," it shall profit him to follow — yes, to walk *with* Him, that he too will know love, honor, mercy, and spiritual dignity undiluted by carnal inconsistencies.

> Great God what splendid temples
> Our souls may build again
> When self is slain by pity
> And pride is killed by pain!
> Lord Christ renew the vision
> That brought our hearts release,
> Till the cries of all Thy creatures,
> Shall turn to sons of peace.[1]
>
> (*Frida Harley*)

COMMENTARY

31 — The Five Thousand Fed

It is generally recognized today among progressive clergy and Christian laymen, that the miracle of the loaves and fishes was a solemn ceremonial affair in which the breaking of bread held a spiritual meaning.

According to Schweitzer, *"The occasion was a solemn cultus meal."* After the loaves which He had broken were consecrated by a prayer of thanksgiving, Jesus had them distributed to the multitude by His disciples. Except for the addition of the two parables, (My body — My blood), we have exactly the same solemn ceremony as at the Last Supper. There, He personally distributed the food to his table companions. The descriptions of the distribution of the bread in both cases coincide perfectly. (Mark: 6:41) He took the loaves and, looking up to heaven, He blessed them and He gave to the disciples to set before them. (Mark 14:22)

"Hence the solemn act of distribution constitutes the essence of that meal by the seashore, as well as of the last meal with His disciples. 'Lord's Supper' is a name appropriate to both, for that meal by the sea also took place at an evening hour. (Mark 6:35)[1]

At the Last Supper Jesus referred to bread as His body, while in the "cultus meal" in the desert near Bethsaida, He also referred to Himself as the bread of life, or, as we find in John 6:33, "The bread of God is He which cometh down from heaven, and giveth life unto the world."

"Verily, verily, ye seek Me, not because ye saw miracles, but because ye did eat of the loaves and were filled. Labor not for the bread that perisheth, but for the bread that endureth unto everlasting life, which the Son of man giveth unto you." (John 6:26-27)

"I am the bread of life; he that cometh to me shall never hunger." (John 6:35)

In John 6:26, Jesus makes it clear that the miracle wherein the hunger of the multitude was satisfied was not by the bread that perishes but by the bread that endures. The miracle, therefore, was in the conversion of the physical hunger of the multitude into a spiritual hunger, which Jesus in turn satisfied.

According to Schweitzer, "The story of this event has been distorted into a miracle: the 'cultus meal' which Jesus improvised by the seashore has been represented as a hearty and filling supper. A scanty provision was at hand, but through a supernatural process the multitude was filled by it; that belongs to the miraculous character which the later age ascribed to the celebration because its significance could be apprehended." [2]

In harmony with the Jesus of the "Covenant of Love," it is the writer's opinion that the "later age" distortion of the "miracle" into a filling supper was done purposely, to involve the blessing of Jesus in the eating of flesh, which, in this case, was fish. This same motive was carried out by the writers or the copyists of the synoptic gospels in regards to the Paschal lamb. In the interest of truth, however, the same narration in the gospel of John has fortunately been spared distortion. (See Chapter 39, p. 320 of this Commentary)

The same thing was done wherein the risen Jesus is described as eating fish. (See pp. 269, 270)

It is the purpose of this writer to uncover the truth wherever the evidences make it discernible. It has many times before been brought to his mind during the construction of this work that most of the reported miracles are permeated by a rather undignified sensationalism; also that many of these "miracles" existed in their original form as parables spoken by Jesus, which in later years were reconstructed as "narratives in fact" in order to emphasize the extraordinary powers of Jesus. A sensational approach may have been felt necessary during Christianity's early century competition with pagan cults, but in our less superstitious age it has outlived its need.

Sensationalism can no longer take precedence over the ethical. The rediscovered Jesus of today is the Lord of love, mercy, humility, dignity, and humane kindness. The Bible miracles, with few exceptions, are completely out of character with Him. Thus, the equitable Christian is faced with the following alternatives: He can either continue to compromise the true nature of Jesus in order to make Him adhere to the very letter of the Scriptures, or he can discover His divinely ethical spirit in the historical Jesus of the "Covenant of Love."

COMMENTARY

32 — The Twelve Sent Out
The Price of Healing
The Seventy Sent Out

"These twelve Jesus sent out, charging them, 'Go no where among the Gentiles and enter no town of the Samaritans, but go rather to the lost sheep of the House of Israel.' " (Matt. 10:5)

As these words read, they exclude everyone but the Jews from the ministry of Jesus. This is contrary to the teachings of the church which claim Jesus to be the Savior of all mankind.

The only way this apparent slight can be satisfactorily explained is by comparing the Gospel narrative with Josephus' description of the Sons of Peace.

Jesus realized that few, if any of the disciples had ever ventured far from their immediate countryside. He was concerned for their welfare and spoke of them as being sent out as lambs among wolves.

He knew also that only in the many towns and villages of Judea could be found the homes of the worthy — "the holy ones," "the saints," "the sons of peace:" those who by such various names were known as "Essenes."

According to Josephus, there were groups of Essenes in all the towns of Judea and their doors were always open to deserving strangers: "They have no one certain city, but many of them dwell in every city: and if any of their sect come from other places, what they have lies open for them just as if it were their own, and they go into such as they never knew before as if they had been ever so long acquainted with them. For which reason they carry nothing at all with them when they travel to remote parts. Accordingly, there is in every city where they live, one appointed particularly to take care of strangers and provide garments and other necessities for them." [1]

Here Josephus points specifically to the certain house or houses referred to in Matthew and Luke.

The instructions given by Jesus in Matthew to "the twelve" were the same as those given to the seventy sent out in Luke.

In Matthew He instructs them to seek out the houses of the worthy and salute them. In Luke the raised hand of salute is accompanied by the words, "Peace be upon this house." Here He says, "If the 'Son of Peace' answers," and again, according to Matthew, "You are among the worthy."

The salutation, "Peace be with you," or "Peace be upon this house," was an Essene manner of greeting. They were known as "the sons of peace." The latter name they acquired through their passive denunciation of violence in any form, either to man or beast. According to Josephus, they prohibited their people from manufacturing any type of weapon. They were truly the "sons of peace."

In Luke, the seventy sent out were mere novices. They were not as familiar with Essenic customs as were "the twelve," for as some scholars suggest, quite a few of "the twelve" were former disciples of the Baptist, who, as the evidence indicates, was an Essene.

To the seventy, therefore, He added these words of instruction: "Eat such things as are set before you," that is to say, don't complain if the food is meager. Here Jesus anticipated the probable results of a poor growing season whereby the table of the worthy might not be overburdened with the bounties of Providence, for the Essenes abstained from the use of animals for food.

According to Matthew and Luke Jesus charged his disciples: "Take nothing with you for your journey, neither money, bread, nor extra clothes, for there will be those in every city ye enter into whom ye shall find worthy."

Accordingly Josephus says of the Essenes: "They carry

nothing at all with them when they travel to remote parts, for there is in every city where they live one appointed particularly to care of strangers and provide garments and other necessities for them."

It is quite obvious therefore, that the houses of the worthy spoken of by Jesus and those referred to by Josephus are one and the same.

It seems most important also to note the significance of another charge Jesus gave to his disciples: "Go, heal the sick, cleanse the lepers, and cast out demons. You received this power without pay, give it also without pay. Take no money in your purse, or extra clothes, but the laborer deserves his food." (Matt. 10: 8-9)

In the next verse He points out that there will be those who will supply this food. He charges His disciples to accept no money or gifts of any kind for the healing they are privileged to bring about. Here He definitely points out that "pay" (Meaning "Caesar's silver") shall not be the price of their healing services: that the worthiness of their hire can only be compensated through natural consequences, that is, as bread cast upon the waters.

When Jesus said, *"You received this power without pay, give it also without pay,"* He meant that to do otherwise would be to violate the benevolent dignity of the very source through which divine healing may be realized.

In accord with this statement of the Master, one must in consequence assume that any person accepting money or gifts, either for himself or for the pleasure, convenience, or comfort of any organization in which he is financially interested, as compensation for invoking the power of Divine Authority, is guilty of an offense against the Author of this power, in which case his pretenses are of "none effect" and his practices fraudulent.

Jesus Himself anticipated this when He said (Matt. 7:22), "On that day many will say to Me, 'Lord, Lord, did we not prophesy in Your name, and cast out demons in Your name, and do mighty works in Your name? And then will

I declare to them, 'I never knew you; depart from me, you evildoers.' "

This does not mean that a minister or priest should not invoke the healing power of Christ or God to benefit any member of his congregation, but it does restrict him from accepting any material compensation directly or indirectly for so doing.

Healing represents an act of mercy, love, and compassion beyond the call of common practice. It is, therefore, according to Matthew, "divinely authorized."

On the other hand, the evangelist who publicizes himself and his organization as coming to town to save souls and to minister to the sick, with special emphasis put upon healing services, is, if he asks or accepts an offering of any kind from those who respond to his advertising, unfaithful to the prerogatives of Jesus, and therefore, a fraud. His works can only bring unhappiness to those who are unfortunate enough to come under his influence. God cannot be made a partner in the commercializing of His blessings. His love and mercy cannot be bought or sold on the whims of men.

COMMENTARY

33 — The Parable of the Prodigal Son
(Luke 15:11-32)

The parable of the Prodigal Son as interpreted in the Covenant of Love is truly a parable of love and mercy. Herein Jesus presents the perfect analogy. He illustrates how, through the consequential rewards of folly, the human spirit may find itself and return to a station of honor and dignity. Here the return of the wayward son to the father parallels the return of a contrite spirit to the love and mercy of God.

Differing, however, from the traditional story as told in Luke, the Covenant of Love version exemplifies the merciful kindness of the Heavenly Father without compromising the boundless scope of His love for all His creation. In other words, Jesus would not have contradicted the supremely ethical nature of the Father of all creation in order to construct a parable wherein contrition is rewarded by the slaying of a calf.

Fortunately, however, the humanely ethical character of the Lord Jesus Christ has endured down through the centuries, above the continuous efforts of self-indulgent men to write, or read Him down to their own level.

A person with even an elementary knowledge of psychology combined with a little imagination can clearly recognize that the reference, "the fatted calf," is irrelevant to the lesson intended by the parable in the first place, and that it has all the earmarks of a deliberate interpolation.

The words, "Bring hither the fatted calf and kill it and let us eat of it," are again emphasized near the end of the parable by the words, "Thou has killed for him the fatted calf." The intent here is rather tactlessly exposed. The attempt to conform the ethics of Jesus to doctrinal authority by crudely emphasizing the selection of food for the feast, in the words, "kill it and eat it," is self incriminating. It appears that all the other dishes for the feast were purposely omitted to make the killing and the eating of the fatted calf a "standout."

Again, in the same parable, flesh meat is represented as the sole means of celebrating: "Thou never gavest me a kid that I might make merry with my friends." Here it is quite obvious that the original parable contained the word *wine* and that the word *kid* is the result of a later rather awkward substitution. Wine has always been the traditional means of "making merry" with one's friends.

It has long been recognized by scholars that the original text of the parable — before it was somewhat clumsily made to sanction the self-indulgent customs of the heathen Christians — presented only harmless or innocent food such as described by Pliny in discussing the habits of the early Christians of Bithynia under Peter.

The parable of the Prodigal Son as presented in the Covenant of Love parallels quite closely the items of food and drink as they were probably first described by the Master Himself.

COMMENTARY

34 — Mary and Martha
The Costly Ointment

The narrative of Mary and Martha concerning the costly ointment appears, even as many of the other reported incidents in the life of Jesus, to have been garbled or grossly exaggerated through the passage of time.

The story as told in Luke seems to be more in keeping with the character of Jesus, the great teacher who stressed the importance of food for the soul.

As the story goes, Martha received Jesus into her home for dinner, and her sister Mary sat at His feet, listening to His teachings. But Martha was "cumbered with much serving," and she complained, feeling that Mary should be helping her. Whereupon Jesus said, "Martha, you are concerned about many things; but one thing is needful, and Mary has chosen the good part."

Here Jesus reminded Martha, as he probably taught the five thousand, that the spiritual food which soothes the heart and gives strength to the soul is the "good part." It has been pointed out, however, that the Greek rendition of this story seems to present Jesus as reminding Martha that only one sort of food is required: "a single course will be sufficient for the meal."

Vegetarians hold this to mean one course of "blood guiltless" food such as Pliny wrote about in describing the Christians of Bithynia, under Peter: "one sort of innocent food." Now, however, as of this writing, vegetarians need no longer grasp at straws to prove their point, for we can know beyond all question of doubt that the historical Jesus and His followers were strictly humane in their eating habits.

Let us, then, interpret the story as it appears in Luke as meaning food that enters into the heart rather than into the stomach. Still, this beautiful portrait by Luke of the dignified relationship between Martha, Mary, and Jesus suffers considerable change as it is again depicted in the fourth gospel.

In Mark 14:3 and Matthew 26:6-11, "a woman came with an alabaster jar of costly ointment and poured it on His head as he sat at the table." But when the disciples saw it they had indignation, saying: "This ointment might have been sold for more than three hundred pence and given to the poor." And Jesus answered, "Ye have the poor with you always; but Me ye will not have always."

In Luke 7: 37-39, the woman with the alabaster box again appears as Jesus sits at the dinner table. This time the action takes place in the house of a Pharisee in a city called Nain instead of at the house of Simon the leper in Bethany, as told in Mark and Matthew.

Now then, when the Lucan story of Mary and Martha is retold by the evangelist who wrote the fourth gospel— or as it may have been exaggerated by later copyists—parts of the framework of these other stories were added. In consequence, the beautiful informal relationship between Mary, Martha, and their dear Friend Who many times sat at their table, was replaced by an emotional display of hero worship.

Where Luke had Mary merely sitting at the feet of the Master, listening eagerly to His teachings, John brings the costly ointment of Mark and Matthew into the scene and portrays Mary as anointing the feet of Jesus, followed by her wiping His feet with her hair.

All of these stories are somewhat in conflict with the humble self-immolating nature of the Son of man.

In the first place, as the story is told, the ointment could have been sold for a large sum to benefit the poor and the needy. Certainly Jesus would not have desired the extravagance of a perfumed body at the expense of providing bread for the hungry.

Again, the saying, "You will always have the poor with you, but you will not always have Me," (John 12:8 and Matt. 26:11) does not ring true to the gracious self-giving Christ. Surely, One Who sacrificed the very life of His body in the cause of the poor and the lowly of God's creatures would not have belabored them to emphasize His own importance. This cannot be the same Jesus Who said: "If I honor Myself, My honor is nothing," and "Take My yoke upon you, for I am meek and lowly in heart." (Matt. 11:29)

However, the most distasteful part of the story as told in the fourth gospel is the description of Mary's wiping the feet of Jesus with her hair. This idea was probably taken from the gospel of Luke wherein Jesus is made to say: "Seest thou this woman? She has washed My feet with tears and wiped them with the hairs of her head. Thou gavest Me no kiss, but this woman since the time I came in hath not ceased to kiss my feet."

Imagine, if you will, the very criterion of modesty and reserved dignity submitting to such a distastefully sentimental demonstration. Picture the One Who denounced the self-glorification of the temple priests and the vain pretenses of the Pharisees, allowing a confused woman to humiliate her person by wiping the sticky ointment from His feet with her own hair.

It is in opposition to these and other even more shameful misinterpretations of the Son of man that the Covenant of Love was written. Certainly, one who believes in the supreme dignity of the divine kinship cannot help but question the objective significance of the motivation behind these apparent interpolations.

There is a vast difference between the modest dignity of true spiritual humility and a patronizing exhibition of self-mortification as the means of attaining the rewards of divine providence. While the latter may conform to the expediencies of authoritarian practices, it fails to emphasize that spiritual remunerations are earned, not through disparaging, but by improving upon the self.

"According to Hegesippus the Second Century historian of the Jews, 'James the Lord's brother habitually *eschewed* the use of oil and wore linen garments only' — two of the characteristic traits which Josephus attributes to the Essenes."

Thus again, knowledge gained through the discovery of the Dead Sea Scrolls has pointed out the necessity of reconstructing another gospel rendition of an obscure incident in the life of Jesus: i.e., to overrule another case of garbled facts and fancies which have through centuries of interpretation, copying and editing, inadvertently underrated the sublime integrity, honor and humble dignity of the true historical Jesus.

COMMENTARY

35 — The Parable of the Faithful Servant
The Destruction of the Cities Foretold
The Coming of the Kingdom

The parable about the servant whom his lord made ruler over his household, as reconstructed from Matthew and Luke, seems to refer to the responsibilities of certain dietary reforms. It likens the servant who cannot be trusted to feed the household its customary vegetable diet while the master is away, to those who fail to follow a responsible way of life — who become "over charged with gluttony and drunkenness" (Luke 21:34), and are consequently to be counted as unworthy when the Son of Man returns.

Blessed is that servant whom his lord shall find to have been faithful to his household while he is away: who has continued to serve them "meat in due season" (Matt. 24:45), and has not smitten (stricken) them "to eat and drink with the drunken." (Matt. 24:49)

In Bible times, the word "meat" had an entirely opposite meaning from what it has today. "Meat," as translated from the Hebrew, refers to cereals, fruits, vegetables, etc., *exclusive* of flesh. (See Lev. 2: 1-14 K.J.V.) Here and in many other places, the R.S.V. changes the word "meat" to read "cereals," and in some cases, simply "food." But, as noted before, these R.S.V. interpretations seem to be more sympathetic to the flesh-eating public than to the dietary reforms of the conscientious abstainers.

In the original Aramaic Matthew, the phrase, "meat in due season," obviously must have been the purpose of the parable in the first place; otherwise, why was it made the object of the servant's trust? However, the condition of the trust is clearly stated even in our present day translations.

300

It is fully obvious that the word "meat" refers to fruits, cereals, and other foods set down in the "divine formula" (Gen. 1:29-30), as evidenced by the words, "in due season."

In reference to the words, "eat and drink with the drunken," (Matt. 24:49) it has been recognized for centuries that heavy drinkers are invariably heavy flesh eaters. Wine is always associated with either white or red meat. To "eat and drink with the drunken" means to eat flesh and to drink wine.

Here in Matthew and Luke, Jesus plainly referred to the Proverb: "Be not among wine-bibbers among riotous eaters of flesh: for the drunkard and the glutton shall come to poverty." (Prov. 23:20-21) — "Take heed therefore lest the cares of this life overcharge your heart with gluttony and drunkenness and the Kingdom of Heaven catch you also unawares. Watch ye therefore that ye may be accounted worthy to stand before the Son of Man." (Luke 21:34-36)

"But in that day there shall arise false Christs and false prophets, and shall shew great signs and wonders: take heed that ye be not deceived and go ye not therefore after them. For wheresoever the carcass is, there will the vultures be gathered also." (Matt. 24:23,24,28)

It must be evident to those who believe in the divine integrity of Jesus that the phrase, "Verily I say unto you, this generation shall not pass till all these things be fulfilled," is either the result of an error in translation or was intentionally written in to command the attention of the people living during the generation of Paul, Mark, and Luke. One could not believe Jesus preached that all things would be fulfilled within His generation without also doubting the trustworthiness of His other promises.

To the writer, this is only one of many inconsistencies found in the four gospels, which tend to depreciate the integrity of the Son of Man. Like one crying in the wilderness, however, the humble voice of the "Covenant of Love" speaks out in His defense. When Jesus said, "The Kingdom of Heaven is at hand," He was not referring to a particular point in time. He was speaking in the ever-present NOW. It was the heathen-converting evangelists who saw in these words a means of promoting their immediate ambitions.

The Kingdom of Heaven is still as much at hand as it was the day Jesus proclaimed it. The door is as close to mankind as the width and breadth of their will to receive it. All man needs to do is reach out and lift up the latch.

Those today who contemplate the "end of the world" as promised by the voice of scripture have a far stronger claim to its actually coming to pass in our time than in any other period of history.

For example, consider the following words of Jesus as recorded in the gospels: "Let them flee to the mountains, out of the cities. The earth shall quake in many places and fearful sights shall there be in the heavens. Men's hearts failing them for fear and for looking after those things which are coming on the earth for the power of heaven shall be broken." (Luke 21)

Although we may not care to admit it, these words seem to actually describe the destruction of the world in an atomic age.

The horrors attending such an event suggest more vividly an entry through the doors of Hell than into the Heavenly Kingdom. But fortunately these words may only suggest an alternative, wherein the power of choice is the guiding contingency capable of achieving the promised Kingdom of Heaven upon this earth. Let us strive, therefore, to vindicate by equitable decisions the wisdom of God for giving us this power in the first place.

COMMENTARY

36 — On the Custom of Sacrifice
Jesus Enters Into Jerusalem.
The Purging of the Temple

No one knows just how the practice of sacrifice began, but one might suppose that the first offerings were made to a sun god, probably by some primitive creature who lived in a tree house. To such a man the sun would be the most impressive of all things in nature. Indeed, he probably welcomed it as his best friend, for it not only banished the demons which lurked in the darkness of the jungle paths, but it also provided him with warmth and heat to drive away the cold and the damps of the jungle night.

It is probable that this primitive man, as a gesture of gratitude, tossed choice morsels of food towards his benefactor from his leafy retreat high above the jungle floor. These, however, either lodged somewhere among the branches of the trees or fell to the ground where they were eaten by birds or rodents.

Later, along with the discovery of fire, came the observation that food laid upon it was eaten by the flames and transformed into smoke and vapor which in turn arose toward the habitation of the sun.

Thus fire, being of the same character as the sun, also came to be worshipped as a minor god; as the earthly son of the Father God, or as His officient who effectively transferred the gifts of man to Heaven. One might even see suggested here a relationship that later became recognized as angels, or agents, of the Lord.

The Iroquois Indians practiced a system of sacrifice that had much in common with the first century mystery religions. "They decorated a white dog with wampum and strangled it. Then before they burned the carcass, they transferred to it the sins of the people and later sprinkled its ashes before every abode." [1] Thus, in effect, the dog was made to be sacrificed to take away the sins of the people.

In ancient Greece, "the Attic sacrifice of the Pipalid: cakes were laid on the altar of Zeus and oxen driven around; the one which touched the cakes was the victim. An officient at once struck it with his ax and another cut its throat; then all save the one who struck the first blow partook of its flesh. Then the hide was stuffed with grass and yoked to a plow; the participants were charged with 'ox murder' and each laid the blame on the other; finally the ax was thrown into the sea." [2]

The moral of this ceremony appears to be the natural concern that is more or less active in all men; i.e., the feeling of guilt or the awareness of committing or being party to a deed contrary to the powers of creation, or to the pleasure of God. It is the feeling that expanded in the prophets to induce them to denounce the sacrifice. It was a feeling that in the heart of Jesus demanded "mercy instead of sacrifice" even as Hosea had done before Him.

"Sacrifice first began as a gift to a supernatural being for securing favor or to minimize hostility. From the gift theory it transformed into the homage theory, from which it made an easy transition to the renunciation theory," [*] or rather, the theory of Redemption through Compassion.

The definition of the word "sacrifice" is "to make sacred." The sacrifice involves a burnt offering of a living creature. An altar offering of other things, such as cereals, is called an "oblation." Therefore the sacrifice is not in the making of something sacred. It is in the offering of that which is in itself sacred: i.e., God is of life and life is of God. The essence of the word, "sacred," is in consequence, "Life." Thus the term "sacrifice" is to make sacred through the forfeiting of a life.

* Encyc. Brit.

"When God sends forth His spirit, life is created." (Ps. 104:30). God creates life; the flesh is generated in nature. Therefore, life alone is actually the only value that can be sacred.

The spiritual essence of the sacrifice, aside from the selfish motive, is, that life having been sent forth out of God, returns again to Him through the altar ceremony. Thus, the returning of a life to God carries with it the appeal of the suppliant: i.e., the life of the lamb, which is the blood thereof, poured upon the altar, becomes a means of transmitting to God the entreaties of the worshiper.

This is probably one reason why doves were so much in popular use. No doubt the spirit or life of the dove was considered to be a better messenger because of its earthly use as a carrier of messages, and because of its ability to soar in the heavens.

This is the spiritual or metaphysical aspect of the practice as it was probably conceived of by the more sensitive of the worshipers. The other aspect was purely material or sensual because it represented to the offerer the giving of a thing of material value. Thus he felt entitled to compensation for his act of giving.

It is quite obvious that all the references in Leviticus and other portions of the Bible in regard to the requirements of sacrifice are merely prerogatives of the priestly code and have nothing to do with the law of Moses.

As this reference has been discussed before herein, it is only because of a particular narration that it is again mentioned. Jeremiah was barred from the temple even as later were the Essenes, for eschewing the sacrificial system. "With Jeremiah it was only a matter of time before the temple worship would cease to be. But he could do without them because he had discovered God in his own heart." (26:9) (Harpers Bible Dict.)

Jeremiah ordered Baruch, saying, "I am debarred from going to the house of the Lord: so you are to go, and on a *fast day* in the hearing of all people in the Lord's house, you shall read the words of the Lord from the scrolls which you have written at my dictation."

The selecting of a "fast day" for the reading of the scrolls is quite obvious in view of Jeremiah's attitude toward the drinking of wine and the sacrificial excuse to eat flesh. This scroll was burned by the king and Jeremiah was obliged to remain under cover. (36:26)

Later Baruch rewrote the scroll, but it goes without saying that the second edition was made more in keeping with his priestly calling. Baruch was no doubt an author in his own right, which indicates that much of the wording attributed to Jeremiah came out of the mind of Baruch.

Evidence that his opinions favored the priestly code rather than the prophet's is in the fact that he was one of the signers of the covenant of Nehemiah, supposing to reclaim the commandments and statutes of Moses but which was actually no more than a covenant between the king, princes, priests, and Levites: set forth by them to confound the people into submission to their lusts and powers.*

This covenant holds forth with a god that is both mighty and terrible. (Neh. 9:32) It is written therein to bring offerings to the house of God, to the priests who minister in the house of our God, the first born of our sons and of our cattle as it is written in the law, and the firstlings of our herd and of our flocks. (Neh. 10:36)

It was this, as well as many other false reconstructions of scripture that were similarly denounced in the Psalms, by the prophets, and by the Essenes, as the garbled writings of false scribes. "They make the law into a lie," said Jeremiah.

According to the evidence, then, the true law of Moses opposed rather than ordered the custom of sacrifice.

It appears that the Essenes may have admonished the Pharisees by implying that the sacrifice of animals was a heathen custom which did not belong to the worship service

---

* The same can be truthfully said of the garbled texts of Deuteronomy.

of the Hebrew people. For example:—
> "I shall hold it as one of the laws
> engraved on the tablets
> to offer to God as my fruits (sacrifice)
> the praises of my tongue*
> that *no heathen filth shall be found thereon.***

A striking parallel of these Essene lines are found in our book of Psalms. (141:2,3,4)
> "Let my prayer be counted as incense before Thee
> and the lifting up of my hands, as an evening sacrifice
> Incline not my heart to those who work iniquity
> and *let me not eat of their dainties"*

A letter in the name of Barnabas, the companion of St. Paul reads in part: "For He made it plain to us through all the prophets that He desires neither sacrifice nor burnt offerings. A heart that glorifies its maker is a fragrant odor to the Lord. So brethren, we ought to inquire closely about salvation, so the evil One may not smuggle some *error* in among us and *dislodge us from life.*" [3]

There was a saying attributed to Christ, probably from the original "Aramaic Matthew" used by the Nazarenes and preserved by Epiphanius, (XXX16) "I am come to abolish the sacrifices; and if you do not cease from sacrificing, the wrath of God will not cease from you."

This saying coincides with the New Testament version of Matthew, "I desire mercy instead of sacrifice." (Matt. 12:7) (Hosea 6:6)

As was pointed out on a preceding page, to sacrifice is to take a life. The word "mercy" — or its other Biblical equivalent, "loving kindness" — as the alternative of sacrifice, directly concerns the welfare of the animal in question. Nowhere in the Scriptures is it written, "I desire mercy instead of an oblation" — the giving upon the altar of fruits, grains, etc. In fact, here the reference to mercy would have no meaning whatsoever.

* See (Heb. 13:15) i.e., "Sacrifice as the fruits of my lips".
** Selected from The Book of hymns, Dead Sea Scrolls.

But mercy instead of sacrifice is the pleading for consideration, for kindness, for compassion, and for love—instead of harm, hurt, or the lust for flesh.

The altar in the sanctuary of many Christian churches today is merely a carryover of the ancient stone upon which the lamb was sacrificed as an offering to God. Instead of spilling the blood of one of God's creatures upon the altar, today the collection plates containing the worshipers' offerings are laid thereon while the congregation sings praises to God.

However, it might be pointed out here that as far as Christ's plea for "mercy instead of sacrifice" is concerned, the modern Christian Church is still without understanding.

Instead of sacrificing the life of the creature, beast, or fowl upon the altar with the saying of prayers over its charred remains, the shameful deed is now transferred to the basement kitchen of the church and the charred remains are thereafter removed to a dining table where the ritual of the sacrifice is said in reverse: Instead of blessing the sacrifice to the heavenly Being, as did the Pharisees, God is asked to bless the sacrificed carcass to the use of human beings. Here also, the words "through Jesus Christ, our Lord" are innocently but paradoxically added thereto.

To take the life of one of God's creatures is to sacrifice its life, whether it be for the supposed service of God as practiced by the Pharisees, or for the supposed service of man as practiced by Christians.

When the Pharisees, whose principal religious practices involved the sacrifice, admonished the disciples of Jesus for picking corn on the Sabbath, He returned the rebuke a thousand fold by saying, "If you knew what this means, 'I desire mercy instead of sacrifice,' you would not condemn the innocent." (Matt. 12:7)

If Jesus desired mercy for the creatures from the Pharisees, would He not expect the same from Christians?

* * *

The entry into Jerusalem has been the subject of much discussion by various writers. First, it is held by some that the story originated in the mind of the evangelist, who then made it part of the record; next, that it did happen according to the gospel records but that it was all part of a plan acted out by Jesus as the main character—part of a pre-arranged plot engineered by Joseph of Arimathea, which was climaxed by His apparent death and reappearance in the flesh, thereby proving the Messianic claims of a certain Hebrew sect. While this idea may have a few points in its favor, it must be rejected as contrary to both Essenic principles and the character of Jesus Himself.

The gospel narrative of the entry into Jerusalem has also been criticized as a public display of self gratulation which, it has been pointed out, is completely out of character with the otherwise modest nature of the Son of Man.

However, if one takes into consideration the approaching crisis in the life and teaching of Jesus, the entry into Jerusalem actually represents the preface to the greatest humane demonstration in all history. It brought to a climax many months of toil and effort to bring to mankind the knowledge that God loves all of His creation.

When Jesus entered Jerusalem through the portal that later became known as "the Essene gate,"* He was intent upon the final carrying through of a cherished responsibility He shared with the Father.

There was probably more than one purpose in His mind when he chose to ride upon an ass. The ass was mentioned in the prophesy of Zechariah: "That One Who is just and considerate of the lowly shall come riding upon an ass." The ass was a symbol of gentleness and peace, while the horse was always represented as a mechanism of war: "Thus ye shall be filled with horses and chariots and with all men of war." (Ezek. 39:20)

It was an humble but determined Jesus Who that day straddled an ass for the express purpose of attracting as

* Mentioned by Josephus (Wars, B.,V.,IV.2).

many persons as possible to bear with Him: to follow Him to the temple and to hear His final plea for "mercy instead of sacrifice."* Straight through the gate He rode, straight toward the temple, amid tumultuous shouts of, "All Hail to the King of the Jews! He has come to release us from bondage." But the Son of Man heard them not. He had not the least desire to be the Messianic king that some of His supporters expected of Him. He came this day into Jerusalem for only one purpose: to purge the temple of its traffic in the flesh and blood of God's innocent creatures.

"When He saw the busy activity of the dealers in sacrificial animals and Jewish coins over-running the outer court he drove them out with their wares. This business was connected with the sacrifice service and therefore Jesus' reformatory action seemed to be an attack on the sacrificial service itself and indirectly on the Hierarchs who derived their income from and based their social position of power on the sacrificial service" 4

Jesus probably knew before He entered through the gates of the city that this last effort on his part to cleanse the temple of God of the evils which all the prophets before him had failed to accomplish, would lead him to a fate not unlike theirs. He knew that the Roman authorities meted out severe punishment to all those who were found guilty of inciting any sort of demonstration contrary to political or religious ordinances

It must be remembered too that the Romans also practiced animal sacrifice: that the sacrifice of an ox to Jupiter

---

* I desire *mercy* instead of sacrifice had been His constant rebuke to the Pharisees. (Matt. 9:13, 12:7) The prophets had used the same term many times in denouncing sacrifice: "I desire mercy instead of sacrifice. (Hos. 6:6) The word *mercy* as translated from the Hebrew also means "loving kindness." He has showed you, O man, what is good; and what He doth require of you but to do justice and to love kindness" (Mic. 6:8) instead of sacrifice. The stressing of mercy instead of sacrifice as written in Matthew conforms to the evidence that this gospel came out of the original Aramaic Matthew used by the Nazarenes, who themselves denounced the slaughter of animals as a crime against God.

was just as important to them as the sacrifice of an ox to Yahweh was to the Pharisees.

To call for "mercy instead of sacrifice" was to denounce the slaying of victims for this purpose. It was, therefore, equally as blasphemous to heathen practices as it was to those of the Jews. Jesus must have realized this in contemplating the inevitable consequences of His plan, for He had hinted several times to His disciples that His time upon earth was nearing an end.

He thought of Himself as the suffering servant of a New Covenant: a Covenant of Love and Mercy "In that day I will make a covenant for them with the beasts of the field and with the fowls of the air and I will abolish all means to kill upon the earth, and will make them to lie down safely." (Hos. 2:8) "Sacrifice and offerings thou didst not desire: mine ears hast thou opened. Lo, I come: in the volume of the book it is written of me. I delight to do the will of my Father, yea, His law is within my heart." (Ps. 140)

In the gospel used by the Ebionites, or Nazarenes, those primitive Christians close to Jesus and His twelve apostles, Jesus is reported as saying, "Think not that I came to destroy the law; I came to destroy sacrifices." In other words, "to deliver those that are stumbling to the slaughter." (Prov. 24:11)

The fact that Jesus waited till within a few days of the Passover before He denounced the practice of animal sacrifice indicates that He planned His own fate to parallel that of the Paschal lamb: His own body to emphasize the plea of God for "mercy instead of sacrifice."

Considering the long hours of meditation that preceded His courageous cleansing of the temple, one must assume that He had also carefully thought out and prepared a most convincing speech to justify His action. Nowhere could He find truer support than in the Scriptures themselves.

The "Covenant of Love" describes what might have been practically the same Scriptural references used by Jesus. Certainly His speech was most convincing, for apparently it rendered the temple priests helpless to contend. They could not deny Him without also denying the Scriptures.

"And all the people were astonished at His doctrine." (Mark 11:18) These words of Mark indicate that He had a great deal more to say on this occasion than the three lines attributed to Him by the evangelist. (Mark 11:17)

The reader might question several of the Old Testament references as interpreted in this Chapter of the "Covenant of Love." Verse 23 of this chapter reads: "Ye love sacrifice because ye love to eat flesh, but the Lord has no delight in you." Hosea 8:13 R.S.V. reads: "They love sacrifice, they sacrifice flesh and eat it . . ." Here the meaning is very clear *why* they love sacrifice. The word *love* as it is used here indicates pleasure, or anticipated sensual satisfaction.

Titus Flavius Clemens, one of the most learned of the early Christian fathers, wrote: "Sacrifices were invented by men to be pretext for eating flesh." [5] Here Clemens also agrees with the words of Hosea.

In Ezekiel 40:3-43, a "man of brass" appeared and stood in the gate. And the man said, "Behold with thine eyes and with thine ears all that I shall show you, Son of Man; and set thy heart upon it. Declare all that thou seest to the house of Israel."

The man of brass is interpreted in this 34th Chapter of the Covenant of Love as the brazen one, the false one, or as Satan himself. That this was the usual manner of interpreting a man of brass by Old Testament writers is verified by the following passage: "They are grievous slanderers: they are brass, they are corrupters." (Jer. 6:28)

One cannot doubt, then, that the man of brass referred to by Ezekiel was intended as a personification of Satan, corrupter of the souls of men. It will be recognized that after the evil one had finished gloating over the carnal devices of the temple, the text becomes garbled and confused by a contradictory passage which apparently rearranges the text to conform with the priestly code: to the glorification of the sacrifice in contradiction to the prophets' interpretation of the pleasure of Moses. This appears to be what was similarly referred to by Jeremiah and the Essenes when they accused the Scribes of making the law and the prophets into a lie. "The Priesthood the corruptors of the law, wanton abusers of beasts."* (Levi)

Jesus had read this line many times and it aroused his indignation against the Temple customs. He also taught from the Essene Scriptures which say: "Keep the commandments of the Lord and show mercy and to have compassion not only for men, but for the creatures also." **

Here it might again be emphasized, irrespective of the evangelists' apparent stress put upon the money changers as the object of the temple cleansing, that in denouncing the sacrifice, Jesus had "shown His hand" so to speak: the die had been cast and He was destined thereafter to play His "trump card" in the greatest mercy appeal that has ever been recorded in the history of humanity. From the time He first strode into the temple and made His final plea for "mercy instead of sacrifice," He was a marked man. It was now only a question of when and where the Roman authorities would find Him and condemn Him to death.

Josephus tells us that those who officiated in the divine services received sacrifices from Rome: "that the true beginning of our war with the Romans was," when Eliazar, son of Ananias the high priest, rejected the custom, and refused to accept the sacrifice of Caesar (Wars B.11,XVII, 2).

Therefore let it be made clear that when Jesus prophesied his death, he was possessed of the common knowledge that to interfere with, or to demonstrate against the temple ritual of sacrifice, was to commit treason against Caesar, as well as to blaspheme the Gods of Rome.

---

* Testament of Levy, part of Essene Scriptures.
** Zebulun Z:I, part of Essene Scriptures.

COMMENTARY

37 — Ye Are the City.
Prophetic Proof of the Nature of Jesus

According to a well known scholar whom I quote: "In 1897 Dr. Grenfell and Dr. Hunt began excavating at Oxyrhynchus; they discovered in a mound, among a number of other Greek papyri, the leaf of a papyrus codex containing . . . eight sayings of Jesus," apparently dating back to the First Century.

"In 1903 a fresh discovery of a similar character was unearthed at Oxyrhynchus. This papyrus was prefaced by an introduction as follows: "these are the wonderful words which Jesus the living Lord spoke to . . . and Thomas, and He said to them: 'Every one that harkens to these words shall never taste of death. Let not him who seeks (ever) cease until he finds, and when he finds he shall be astonished.' " [1]

"Practically the identical wording of this saying was recorded by Clement of Alexandria as being from the Gospel of the Hebrews," [2] a gospel which Jerome recognized as the original Aramaic Matthew.[3]

It is logical to assume, therefore, whereas this Oxyrhynchus papyrus saying has been identified as taken from the original Aramaic Matthew, that many of the other sayings contained therein are also of old Apostolic origin.

The saying, "Ye ask who are they that draw us to the Kingdom . . ." as explained by Jesus in Chapter 37 of the "Covenant of Love," is taken from these same Oxyrhynchus papyri. The author has presented a metaphysical interpretation of this allegory in a way he considers that Jesus might have explained it to His disciples. *

* For further reference on this see (Job. 12:7-10) also Essones, Foreword p. XVI.

314

In discussing the proof of the nature of Jesus as described in the prophecy of Isaiah, it seems that the Christian cannot question the "character emphasis" it refers to without also denying that the prophecy did come to pass, and that the Son of Man was of the root of Jesse and "the ensign which the Gentiles seek."

"The Rev. J. Todd Ferrier, in an article entitled, 'An Appeal to the Compassionate,' reveals how he was led to this same conclusion. 'How is it,' he asks, 'that the churches are so powerless to bring to earth the Kingdom of God? Is it because they must first become obedient unto the Heavenly Vision:" [4] the vision which prophesied the coming of the 'Humane Christ?'

"And the wolf shall dwell with the lamb, and the leopard shall lie down with the kid; and the calf and the young lion and the fatling together; there shall be neither harm nor hurt in all my Holy Mountain, for the earth shall be full of the knowledge of the Lord as the waters cover the sea."
(Isa. 11:1-10)

Is it possible that Christians do not believe the character of Jesus to have been as Isaiah described it? Surely this cannot be, for in every Christian heart is the realization that the very Presence of the Son of Man would cause the ax to fall from the hand of the knocker, and the knife from the grasp of the butcher, even as He would cause the wolf to lie down with the lamb. Certainly, as the prophecy indicates, "Those who attain full knowledge of the Lord shall neither harm, hurt, nor destroy one of God's creatures," for knowledge of Him is knowledge of His character even as Isaiah clearly interprets it.

"And all the animals will use those foods that are the products of the soil and become in turn peaceable and in harmony with one another and with man." [5] Thus does the wolf lie down with the lamb.

Again says Isaiah: "Behold a virgin shall conceive, a child shall be born, and they shall call his name Emanuel. Curds and honey shall he eat so he may know to refuse the evil and choose the good." [6] Certainly, to choose the good products of the soil for food so that he might exemplify in person the Lord whom the earth shall have full knowledge of as the waters cover the sea.

"Which thing is true in Him can now be true in you: because the darkness is past, and the true light now shineth" (John 2:8) in the "Covenant of Love."

COMMENTARY

38 — Jesus Prophesies the Sacrifice
of His Life.

The Nazarenes, also known as the Ebionites (the poor), used a gospel which St. Jerome had recognized as the original Aramaic Matthew (Authenticum Matthoei). "It was written in Aramaic words and Hebrew letters." (Hegasippus A.D. 160) In this gospel one of the objects of Jesus' coming was the abrogation of the sacrificial system. (Hoer. XXX 16) Thus, in Jesus one recognizes the concluding means wherein the combined protestations of all the prophets before Him were to be realized. (See footnotes)** As the Father in Heaven had so many times before voiced His displeasure through the prophets, denouncing the merciless pretenses of the temple priests and pleading for loving kindness instead of sacrifice, so likewise was His will to be demonstrated through the Son.

But the final act of the Son has a far greater ethical significance than merely abolishing the temple sacrifice, for as the Father had asked for mercy and loving kindness instead of sacrifice, so was He in principle denouncing the total practice of slaughtering animals because of the pain, torture, and merciless cruelty involved. How else can one interpret the word *mercy* in reference to the sacrifice? It is the animal's life that is sacrificed. Mercy is asked by God in consideration for His creatures. Mercy and loving kindness instead of pain, suffering, and death.

In Jesus, the pleading voice of "God in Heaven" spoke

** Footnotes: See Amos 4:4,5:21-24; Hosea 4:13, 5:6, 6:6, 8:13; Isa, 22:13-14, 1:11-15, 66:3, 22:13; Jer. 6:20, 7:21-23, 11:3-8; Ezek. 39:17-24; Mic. 6:6-8; Ps. 40:6-11, 51:16; Prov. 15:8, 21:27, 50: 8-13, 23:20.

317

through the voice of God in the flesh of man, and the greatest humane act in all history became a fact of record: supreme because it involved the giving up of His own body
to the same torture and pain suffered by the creatures He
sought to deliver.

This Jesus knew long before He went forward in His
final soul-stirring mission of mercy. Many times before He
had succored man from cares and pains, but now His boundless love and compassion reached out towards the innocent
creatures of His Father's kingdom, for they too knew pain
and suffering; they too were from the same life-giving
bosom of God.

It was a completely resigned and dedicated Jesus Who
informed His disciples that His hour was drawing near:
that He would not be with them much longer. For even as
the lamb of the Pharisees would be sacrificed at Passover,
so also would the Lamb of God be sacrificed. That Jesus had
foretold His death to His disciples indicates that He had
carefully planned a course of action, the consequences of
which would be inevitable. Well He knew that He would
sign His own death warrant the very moment that He dared
to speak against the gods of Rome, for in denouncing the
Pharisees' custom of slaying animals for sacrifice, He automatically denounced the temple rites of Rome. But Jesus
accepted His appointed destiny. Nowhere else in the Scriptures did Jesus so convincingly demonstrate that He and
the Father were one: that the concern of God was His concern: that God's love and mercy for all His creation was
His love and mercy for all creation. "Believe me that I am
in the Father and the Father in Me." (John 14:11)

"Think then," says the venerable Cardinal Newman, "of
your feelings at cruelty practiced upon brute animals, and
you will gain one sort of feeling which the history of Christ's
cross and passion ought to excite within you. And let me
add, this is in all cases one good use to which you may turn
any . . . wanton and unfeeling acts shown towards the . . .
animals; let them remind you, as a picture, of Christ's suf-

ferings. He who is higher than the Angels, deigned to humble Himself even to the state of the brute creation . . ." [1]

According to Exodus 12:5,6, the lamb shall be killed in the evening of the fourteenth day of the month in preparation for the paschal feast. It was in the evening on the fourteenth of Nisan, "the day of preparation" (John 19:14) that the flesh of Jesus was brutalized along with the flesh of a hundred thousand other "lambs of God."

"A man who has learned to hate the exploitation of animals and be a good neighbor to even the most unpopular species will have learned something of the Christian virtues of ungreediness, humility and charity. He will be disposed to see in the crucifixion a comradeship with the suffering that exists in nature. He will be ready to worship the Creator whose creatures he respects, and will be not far from the Kingdom of God." [2]

COMMENTARY

39 — The Love Supper
The Vindication of Judas

"Now before the feast of the Passover, when Jesus knew that His hour was come that He should depart out of this world . . ." Thus begins Chapter 13 of the Gospel of John. Here we not only recognize a contradiction of the synoptists, but also what is actually a correction of them. John reveals that the calling together by Jesus of His disciples in the Upper Room was not to indulge in the Passover feast,* but rather to gather with Him in a last spiritual communion — a Communion in which Jesus represented Himself as the Paschal Lamb, the Lamb of God.

The breaking of bread and the drinking of wine** (See Footnote) was a familiar custom which on this occasion Jesus made into a ceremonial commemorating the anticipation of His Own passing.

In placing the "love supper" on the night before the Passover, John not only corrects the synoptists, but also conforms the will of Jesus to the Nazarene doctrine that one of the purposes of the Son of Man was to abrogate the sacrifice.

The offering of Jesus Himself as the Paschal lamb provided the climax of a plan projected through the divine Spirit of the Cosmic Christ, persevered through the continuous admonitions of the prophets, and resolved in the mercy loving heart of the human Jesus.

Thus the Gospel of John, in revealing that the gathering for the Love Supper took place the night *prior* to the Passover, qualifies both the temple incident and the crucifixion

* Return to p. 44 — Prof. Kuhn's explanation.
** Footnote: "Wine" for this purpose was, according to Hebrew tradition, "prepared wine," that is, wine mixed with water.

320

as parts of a perfectly timed and divinely authorized plan: a plan that reached its climax in the most profound demonstration of humane ethics ever contributed to the moral and spiritual education of man. The sacrifice of Jesus, along with a hundred thousand lambs, exemplified in His Own gentle person the inhumanity of inflicting pain, suffering, and death on the other gentle creatures of God's Kingdom.

"The wrongs of others wound the Son of Man, and the stripes of others fall on his flesh.

The sin, and injustice and ignorance in the world are the nails in his hands and in his feet.

He is smitten with the pains of all creatures and his heart is pierced with their wounds.

There is no offense done that he suffers not, nor any wrong that he is not hurt thereby.

For his heart is in the breast of every creature, and his blood in the veins of all flesh.

For to know perfectly is to love perfectly and so to love is to be partaker in the pain of the beloved.

And inasmuch as a man loves and succors even the least of God's creatures he ministers unto the Lord.[1]"

(Anna Kingsford)

The Vindication of Judas

In every powerful melodrama there is always a character who betrays the confidence of another. A drama would not be complete without a villain, a traitor, or a deceiver who usually receives his just dues in the end.

Religious stories are no exception. The Old Testament is full of them; so are the ancient books and legends of every other religion. Satan is the criterion of this evil one, whether in song, story, or in the descriptive references of religious teachings.

The great story of the life of Jesus is unique and beautiful. It overflows with love and compassionate understanding. Unlike the trite characterization of even the most outstanding of literary masterpieces, the sublime story of the Son of Man stands alone. It does not need a villain or a

whipping boy to provide dramatic color. This idea grew
out of a misunderstanding which, although unique, is
clearly self evident. The story of Jesus is not a story of in-
trigue. It is a story of love and mercy, in which the principal character is not deceived or betrayed. On the contrary, He anticipates and plans for the day, the place, the
occasion, the hour, and the purpose of His death.

In the First Chapter of Acts, Peter is described as saying that the treachery of Judas was a part of the divine
plan that "this scripture must needs have been fulfilled."

The ambiguity of this sort of thinking is obvious. How
can a plan or an act be both divine and treacherous? Here,
as in the First Chapter of Genesis and numerous other
places in the Testaments, the means of "Divine Intelligence"
are again made to parallel the mechanisms and devices of
the human mind. The criterion of the *all good* can only be
rationalized as valid when it is set apart from any condition or circumstance pertaining directly or indirectly to the
category of evil. Hence, to propose that the treachery of
Judas was part of a divine plan would require the adulter-
ation of the *all good,* necessitating removal of the prefix
all. God consequently could no longer be acclaimed as
absolute.

It seems, therefore, that if one is to be logical in his thinking as well as steady in his faith, he must reject the concept
that Judas was evil, yet being evil was still eligible to par-
ticipate in a divine plan. The Covenant of Love rejects this
as unbecoming the true nature of God. It is not necessary
that Judas be made the scapegoat in order to have a divine
plan fulfilled.

The plan that began with the denouncing of the sacrifice
in the temple and attained its climax with the sacrifice on
Calvary originated in the mind of Jesus Himself; and as the
Christian firmly believes Jesus Himself was the Spirit of
God incarnate, then the plan was accordingly divinely conceived. Also accordingly, Judas, being an instrument in a
divine plan, must necessarily have been a most trusted and

sincere confidant of Jesus instead of the rascal the mis-understanding evangelists have pictured him to be.

The evidence in support of the vindication of Judas is overwhelming. In the first place, divine authority cannot be conscripted to do duty for evil; hence, the reverse of this statement must also be true. Secondly, it was not necessary for Judas to actually be a deceitful one even if it might have been necessary to represent him as such. Next, the fact that Judas was selected to be the treasurer of the Twelve, one who managed their economic necessities, indicates that Jesus recognized his particular trustworthiness. Certainly, as was later shown, Jesus could not have felt the same towards the others. He knew beforehand that Peter would deny Him thrice, and the loyalty of the rest of His disciples was clearly uncovered that night in the Garden of Geth-semane. Surely, Jesus was not entirely alone among His disciples. There must have been one whom He could count on in a crisis: one who would risk even his own neck for Him if necessary.

Even though the Four Gospels fail to recognize this, one might rightly assume that Judas was in fact the one among the disciples who had the complete confidence of Jesus. It appears, then, in accord with this confidence, that Judas carried out the secret instructions of Jesus even though he himself was made to assume the role of a traitor. Next, Judas was the last disciple to be in the Presence of Jesus before He was convicted. He was also the only one who im-mediately followed Him by also sacrificing his own life.

This Judas did, certainly not to hasten the time of his immersion in "hell fire," but rather to hasten his departure from this world that he might be with the Master in death, even as he had been in life.

Furthermore, according to the Gospel of John, Jesus said: "I know whom I have chosen that the Scriptures be fulfilled." Later on He said to Judas as He gave him some food to eat on his way, "That thou doest, do quickly."

Returning to the first saying, here Jesus freely admits

that He has chosen the one to assist in carrying out His plans, so "that the Scriptures may be fulfilled." Thus, when Jesus gave Judas a choice morsel of food and instructed him to "go quickly and do it," it is obvious that Judas was acting by reason of a pre-arranged pact and should not tarry.

One does not choose one's own betrayer. The very thought is paradoxical. To betray is to plan secretly for the conviction of another. The betrayer and the betrayed are at opposite poles. One does not know the plans of the other. The very act of the "betrayed" in choosing the course of action to be taken by the "betrayer" requires the existence of a previous agreement. This, as the evidence points out, was true between Jesus and His trusted disciple, Judas.

Also, it is apparent that time was the essence of Jesus' whole plan. The purging of the temple a few days before the Passover, the Garden of Gethsemane right outside the walls of Jerusalem, the trial before Pilate just six hours before the Passover—all were anticipated chronologically by Jesus.

It was necessary to the success of the plan for Him to be taken before Pilate no later than the sixth hour if He was to become Himself a suffering example as a victim of men's cruelty: a sympathetic companion to a hundred thousand other innocent creatures — a Lamb of God sacrificed along with other lambs created out of and as part of His ethical Kingdom.

It was growing late as Jesus and His disciples broke their last bread together. Judas was reminded that he must "go quickly" if he was to bargain with the Roman authorities and still have time to lead them to a prearranged rendez-vous before morning.

Plainly, if the time and place of arrest of Jesus were not prearranged, how could Judas have led the Roman centurions to the exact spot where Jesus awaited him?

Bear in mind that the Romans trusted no word of a Jew —and vice versa. If Judas had simply appeared before a

Roman officer, stating that he would lead the soldiers to
where Jesus had secluded Himself, they would never have
believed him. In fact, he would have been thrown out of
the place as a fool, for why would one Jew betray another to
a Roman?

On the other hand, if Judas in his superior knowledge approached the "powers that be" in a bargaining mood, he
would surely have gained the attention of his listeners.
Thirty pieces of silver as a reward would verify the integrity of the informer, and it goes without saying that his
neck would pay the forfeit of his failure to produce the Man
they sought after.

Judas, upon completing his trusted mission, returned
again to the office where he had previously bargained for
the thirty pieces of silver, and defiantly threw them to the
floor. Thus did the twelfth apostle vindicate his "guilt." Sorrowfully thereafter, he sought out a secluded place where
he breathed his last lament even as the cry of "It is finished," echoed from the lips of his Master and deepest love.

But only Judas and his merciful Master knew the anguish
that was his when he trustingly and dutifully carried out
the instructions of his Lord. A greater test because he could
confide in no one. He was honor-bound to secrecy. No one
was to know that Jesus Himself had planned out the sacrifice of His own life. The critics of His day would use this
against Him. They would say that He made Himself to conform to the prophesies. If Jesus was divine, then He Himself was the intervening means of fulfilling them.

The idea is not a new one; it has been suggested before
by various writers and is supported by historical evidence.

The Cainites, a Christian sect mentioned by Irenaeus
(A.D. 181-89) used a gospel that might have been written
before the Four Gospels, and this was attributed to Judas.
It described Judas as having possessed deeper knowledge
of the truth than the other disciples. This was mentioned
also by Epiphanius.

This conforms to the evidence that Judas held a trusted

position among the group and that he was indeed much closer to Jesus than the other eleven were even aware of. The traditional placing of Judas as the Twelfth Disciple might have actually awarded to him the place of honor he deserves. Numerically, his position parallels the twelfth sign of the Zodiac, which is Pisces.

This is the constellation in which, according to astronomers, the phenomenal star arrangement of Jupiter, Saturn, and Mercury took place around the year 6 to 4 B.C., the time when Jesus was born. The Greek word for Pisces (or fish) is *ixous* the component letters of which are the intials of Jesus Christ Son of God Saviour.

Thus does the Twelfth One stand redeemed, even by Jesus Himself Who said "The last shall be first." (Mark 10:3)

* * *

To those who believe, it is well to point out here that the vindication of Judas removes the most blighting of all evidences against the reliability of the many miracles attributed to Jesus. That is to say, whereas Judas was himself witness to the great works and wonders performed by Jesus, he would surely have been too deeply impressed to have dared even to think upon, let alone to have been the guiding genius of any device that did not have the blessings of the Master himself.

COMMENTARY

40 — The Agony of the Garden
Judas Concludes His Mission.
The Disciples Desert Jesus.

"Then He went out and His disciples followed Him to the Mount of Olives.

"He withdrew from them a little way and kneeled down to pray." (from Luke 22:39-41)

The agony in the Garden can best be understood as a deep compassionate concern for the inevitable suffering of all life; as a merciful hand reaching out toward the creatures in a thousand forests and upon a thousand hills; yes, toward a million homes and firesides, gathering together into itself all the heartaches, pains, and sufferings endured therein; also as a deep objective awareness of the sorrows and agonies awaiting all creatures, with an overflowing pity for the waywardness of human understanding.

Without the least concern for His own welfare, the agony of Jesus is more meaningfully explained as the frustration of an infinite LOVE, crying out solicitously for the salvation of all the living. That beautiful prophecy of Isaiah: "The wolf shall lie down with the lamb," must have brought tears of blood to His cheeks as He knelt beneath the symbolic branch of the Olive. "The leopard shall lie down with the kid, and no creature shall hurt nor destroy upon all my holy mountain, for the earth shall have full knowledge of the Lord as the waters cover the sea."

Had He Himself failed to fulfill this prophecy? Certainly in His own nature He was Himself the very essence of it, but He could only strive for peace and speak out against the evils of the world. He could not bring love, and mercy into the hearts of men if they were not ready to receive it; but

He could and would gather into His own heart all the pain and suffering their sins have caused, and as witness thereof pour the terrible total out through his own tortured flesh upon the cross.

"And when Jesus arose from His prayer and came to His disciples, He found them sleeping." (Luke 22:45) Here is illustrated the indifference of human nature, for this is a part of the complex behavior of man. Again, as the disciples flee and leave Jesus alone is illustrated the selfish side of man, the lack of fortitude to face adversity, or to become identified in defense of an ideal.

It has been said that the act of deserting Jesus in His final hour of need casts a veil of doubt over the reliability of the source data of the Gospels; that loyalty cannot be violated without casting a pall upon truth.

In the story the Gospels tell, one of the disciples betrayed Jesus and repented by taking his own life, while the others who deserted and denied Him lived to repent of their own breach of trust. Here the degree of the repentance of the one is proportionately far greater than the difference between the offenses. If the one did betray Jesus "that the prophecy be fulfilled," he acted as an instrument of destiny. But the breach of that trust exhibited by the others was not induced by Providence but through their own uncommitted choice. Here, then, the offense of the one is necessarily far less than that of the others whose actions were not so committed.

But now Judas returns from his errand of fulfillment. He approaches Jesus and kisses Him. To the writer, the kiss of Judas was wholly sincere. It was a last parting caress of farewell "until we meet again in paradise." No other disciple had this intimate privilege. Moreover, it is reasonable to assume that if the meeting of Jesus and Judas in the Garden of Gethsemane were not the result of a mutually planned rendezvous, Jesus would surely have repulsed Judas as He often had the Pharisees for a far lesser offense. Certainly there was no other reason for Judas to kiss Jesus.

To identify Him to His captors was unnecessary, for Jesus was no ordinary person who would need to be pointed out among a group of people. He stood out. Alone. Especially this night, since one of the soldiers had threatened His company with a drawn sword, causing them all to forsake Jesus and flee into the night.

This latter viewpoint needs some clarification:

Now in the first place, according to Mark, Jesus admonished his captors for coming out against him with swords and staves. Certainly he could not have made a point of their carrying weapons if his own follower had done likewise. Mark in 14:46, 47, 48 says: "they lay their hands on him and took him. And one of them that stood by drew a sword and cut off the ear of a servant of the high priest. And Jesus answered by saying to them, Are ye come with swords to take me?" The continuity of thought here implies that one of the Roman soldiers among those who laid hands on Jesus drew his sword and cut off the ear of the Jew nearest to him (which happened to be the servant of the high Priest) in order to dismay the Jews who accompanied Jesus. That this demonstration was successful is verified in the words: "And they all forsook Him and fled."

It should be remembered that the Roman constabularies had very little respect for an Israelite. A Roman soldier on police duty needed only a slight provocation to make a show of his authority especially at the expense of a Jew.

It is quite obvious that the striking off of an ear, as reported by Mark, describes just such an occasion. Only one of a soldier's calling, an expert in the art of swordsmanship, one whose precise aim and timing had been developed to an "nth degree" could have performed such a skillful act.

The following words which were partially overlooked in Mark but found their way into Matthew "Put up thy sword: for all that take the sword shall perish by the sword" were obviously addressed to the Roman soldier who had made the show of skill. They refer to those of a soldier's calling, to the "sons of war" rather than to those of a far less violent profession.

It is probable that the writer of Mark caused quite a little concern among the early Christians when he reported the disciples as deserting Jesus without even the slightest demonstration of loyalty. It seems that later the writer of Matthew either endeavored to compromise this report or he mistook the reference in Mark to mean that someone among Jesus' followers drew a sword, which would be quite natural in view of the report that a servant of the high Priest was the victim. In any case Matthew by putting the "Roman soldier's sword" in the hand of one of the disciples provided at least a suggestion of loyalty even though he also described them as fleeing.

Later the writer of Luke attempted to compromise both the reports of Mark and those of Matthew. He probably reasoned that one sword was not enough to encourage the followers of Jesus to stand their ground. In his gospel Luke produces two swords, which he probably reasoned would be "enough" to support the followers of Jesus. It seems therefore that when Luke reported Jesus as saying "it is enough," he unconsciously emphasized his own thinking. Being "enough" he saw no reason to portray the disciples as fleeing. The gospel of John later supported Luke and also had the disciples stand their ground. However in John the transition of the question "who drew the sword" finally came to an end in the person of Simon Peter. However, by the time the gospel of John was written, Peter was nowhere around to either reject or agree with the writer.

In the interest of justice, the records we have regarding the character of Peter do not in the least conform to the act described in the Fourth Gospel. Peter was an ascetic of a very high order — a man of peace. The carrying of a weapon of any kind would be entirely out of character with his way of life. Furthermore, if any companion of Jesus had drawn a sword to strike out in violent resistance, the Roman guards would have annihilated him. He would have been guilty of an armed assault against Roman law and order. It is altogether remote to concede that a Jew could have done such a thing and lived to see another day. Still the mistake began with the writer of Matthew putting the sword in the hand of a disciple of Jesus in the first place — instead of in the hand of a Roman soldier, where it belonged.

The words of Jesus as recorded in Matthew, "All they that take the sword shall perish with the sword," and again in Revelations, "If any man shall kill with the sword, with the sword must be he killed," emphasize the unalterable position of Jesus regarding the possession of a sword or swords. Certainly Jesus was Master of His Own company, for these words verify that He was. They also spell out the truth that the ethics of Jesus cannot be compromised by His followers to accommodate violence in any form, whether offensive or defensive.

COMMENTARY

41 — The Trial Before Pilate
An Apology to the Jews

"Then they led Jesus into the hall of judgment: and it was early; and they themselves went not into the judgment hall, lest they should be defiled; but that they might eat the Passover." (John 18:28)

This reference to the Passover emphasizes the words at the beginning of Chapter 13, where John testifies that the Feast of the Passover was not celebrated by Jesus and his disciples as suggested by the synoptists. "Now before the feast of the Passover when Jesus knew that His hour had come . . ." John continues with the usual ceremony as described in the synoptic version of the breaking of bread and the drinking of wine. Again, as Jesus is brought before Pilate, John testifies: "And it was the preparation of the Passover, and about the sixth hour: and he saith unto the Jews, "Behold your King." Here, for the third time, the Gospel of John corrects the three synoptic writers.*

If Jesus was to present Himself as the Paschal Lamb, it would be necessary for Him to be sacrificed the same day that the lives of the lambs were sacrificed. Time was here the essence of His example before men.

There could be only one accord, one climax that would identify the sacrifice of Jesus: The return of His Spirit to God in communion with the living essence of a hundred thousand lambs. How else could Jesus be exemplified as "The Lamb of God?"

The wrongful blaming of the Jews for the death of Jesus has been one of the most effective roadblocks ever placed in the highway leading to the brotherhood of man. It is not

* See Sacrifice Appendix p. 416.

only shameful, but completely illogical, for one to continue to hold that the Jews were responsible for the death of Jesus.

As all evidences of comparative beliefs seem to verify, Jesus and the Pharisees were more in agreement on religious issues than they were in disagreement. The only major point of opposition was the practice of animal sacrifice. Other variances were minor. Besides the Pharisees, there were also, in Jesus' time, more than four thousand other Jews (Essenes) who also disapproved of animal sacrifice. No doubt many of them before Jesus had disagreed with the Pharisees on this same issue. It was for this that they were "excluded from the Roman court of the temple." *

As for Jesus' declaring Himself to be the Messiah, the Jewish hierarchy would have been more amused than hostile at the audacity of anyone from Galilee making such a claim. The Jews, with very few exceptions, were far from being averse to the principles of Jesus. Even those who were annoyed by His jibes and His admonitions would not have felt justified in taking severe measures against Him. There were great multitudes of Jews who, although they dared not protest to the Romans, wept deeply as they followed Jesus to His crucifixion. Even the gospel of Luke openly admits the sincere affection the Jews had for Jesus. "And there followed Him a great company of people and of women who also bewailed and lamented Him." (Luke 23:27)

The trial and execution of Jesus was strictly a Roman responsibility. It was prompted by and carried out in accord with strict Roman ordinances which extended little leniency to a Jew. The Jews under Roman authority were tolerated only when they conformed to all the articles of strict obedience. To be involved in the slightest misdemeanor, even among themselves, could mean the lash or other harsh humiliating punishment.

During the Roman occupation of Judea, it was the custom of the time to mete out severe punishment to a Jew for an offense that would hardly warrant the arrest of a Roman citizen. One does not need other historical evidence to confirm this; verification is found where Paul is charged with disturbing the peace: "The chief captain brought him into the castle and bade that he should be examined by scourging, and as they bound him with thongs Paul said to the centurion that stood by, 'Is it lawful for you to scourge a man that is a Roman?' When the centurion heard that, he told the chief captain, saying, 'Take heed what you do to this man, he is a Roman,' . . . and the chief captain was afraid after he knew him to be a Roman and because he had bound him." (Acts 22: 24-29)

"The crucifixion of Jesus is explicable on one ground only: that he was sentenced to death and executed by Roman authority as a sower of sedition against Roman rule. A sentence by the Sanhedrin was imagined, and condemnation pronounced on the grounds that Jesus laid claim to be the Son of God. Jesus, as all four evangelists are compelled to admit, was condemned to death by Pilate on political grounds as 'King of the Jews,' that is, as a Messianic agitator who laid claim to some kind of royalty in Israel, which automatically made Him subversive of the imperial government. Historically, the case of Jesus is intelligible only if we admit from the outset that He was sentenced to death by Pilate alone, acting as representative of Roman authority." [1]

Crucifixion was strictly a Roman means of execution. Death by stoning was the method used by the Jews, and this was ordered by the Sanhedrin only upon conviction of blasphemy; i.e., for cursing or denying the existence of God, which Jesus did not do.

Up to the time of Jesus the Sanhedrin had not imposed a death sentence in over 200 years. In fact even if they had desired to do so they could not, for capital punishment was administered solely by Roman authority for crimes against imperial law or for insulting or belittling the pleasure of the Roman gods. The latter Jesus did when He denounced the practice of animal sacrifice.

In other words, sedition was not the only charge the Romans placed against Jesus. He had impugned as well the integrity of their gods. It has always been customary right up to the late centuries, for a religiously dominated state to punish, even with death, a so-called "heretic" or "schismatics." Long before and after the poisoning of Socrates in the Third Century B.C., and the horrible torture (death) of Dolcino in the Thirteenth Century A.D., men have murdered men in defense of a prostituted faith.

In pagan times it was an unpardonable offense to question the authorized customs of the gods. To denounce the sacrifice was to blaspheme the religious rituals of the governing state or empire. This Jesus did in a very decisive manner. The system and practice of animal sacrifice were all one to Him. The deed constituted a crime against God and nature whether practiced by the Pharisees or the Romans. Hence, His amounted to an international offense, for at that time the greater part of the world's religions practiced animal sacrifice, either to appease idols or otherwise to satisfy unseen gods or demons.

In condemning the practice of animal sacrifice, Jesus not only slurred the integrity of the Roman gods, but at the same time He disparaged a characteristic highly regarded by the Roman—his pride. This is evidenced in their vindictive treatment of Jesus. Nothing but retaliation for a wounded ego would have prompted the Romans to put a scarlet robe on Him, a crown of thorns on His head, and a reed in His hand: to spit on Him, and take the reed and smite Him in the face. They probably used even more humiliating devices than these before they scourged Him and sent Him on His way to be crucified.

Then they nailed a sign on the cross to show their contempt for the Messianic claims of Jesus: "Behold Him THE KING OF THE JEWS." These words which appear in all four gospels spell out examples of Roman vituperation, not Jewish judgment. The Romans cast lots for His garments, and it was the Romans that derided Him with slurring remarks, which probably went as follows: "If your

God is greater than the gods of Rome, call upon Him to bring you down from the cross. You claim that Your god loves mercy instead of sacrifice. Let Him now demonstrate His mercy."

All these things they said and did, to belittle Jesus so that Roman pride might be sustained.

Pilate, washing his hands, was apparently introduced later as a symbolic device to throw back the responsibility upon the Jews.

The efforts of the early heathen Christians were directed towards converting the Gentiles and to reach an accord with the Roman Empire. Hence it was necessary to reshape the new religion toward conforming to the free-living customs of the pagans. The Jewish Christians, who were the immediate followers of Jesus, practiced a far too disciplined way of life than could be compromised by the self-indulgent customs of the Gentiles. The Nazarene Jews abstained from sacrifice, the eating of flesh, and the drinking of wine. They also opposed the keeping of slaves.

It was in no little sense a guilt complex on the part of the Gentile Christians that set up defense mechanisms to cope with the extremely ethical practices of the Jewish Christians.

Early Christianity was a contest between Nazarene (or Essene) ethics and heathen mysticism. In due course the Christian Jews became known in the Gentile world as "heretics." Later, opposition of the so-called Jewish heretics grew into a religious opposition to the whole Jewish people. No more positive way could be devised to gain the confidence of a heathen candidate than to put the blame for the crucifixion of Jesus upon the Jews. The reaction to this was also favorable to the Roman powers that be, for it removed the stain from the hands of Imperial Rome — symbolized by Pilate washing his hands — and paved the way for later imperial recognition.

The Christians owe a debt to the Jews which all the combined conciliatory efforts put forth by the total Gentile community for centuries to come could never repay. It was the Jews who furnished the Gentiles with the foundation stones upon which to build a religion. Jews were the Chosen Ones who made the highway straight in the desert for the coming of the Christian God.

Almost totally unrecognized for this great contribution, the Jews have been made to suffer undue mortification, persecution, and death. They have been falsely accused by an unfortunate implication that was inconsistently made part of the Four Gospels. The voice of Jesus preached, "Love thy neighbor as thyself," but the early century "correctors" of the Gospels made a mockery of His words by smoothly planting therein seeds of hatred. For two thousand years the bitter fruit of resentment has tainted the lips and misshaped the hearts of many who call, "Christ, Christ," but fail miserably in their attempts to find Him.

"Mankind has not been saved by Christianity as Jesus said it could be, because our rulers, and churchmen . . . have eliminated all the saving elements from His gospel. And it can only fulfill its mission of salvation if its original teachings and practices are recovered and applied by those who have so long mistakenly been believing themselves to be Christians." [2]

BOOK THREE

Commentary

Chapter 1

1 *Harpers Bible Dictionary* by Madeleine and Lane Miller, Harper, N. Y.
* Translated by Gaster, *Dead Sea Scriptures*.
2 Alexander Pope from *Millennium Guild Literature*. 40 Central Park So., N. Y.
3 Ellen G. White, *Counsels on Diet and Foods*. Review and Herald Publishing Assn., Washington 12, D. C.
4 Joseph Krutch, *The Great Chain of Life*. (Houghton Mifflin Co., Boston. The Riverside Press, Cambridge)
5 Henry Stevens, *Recovery of Culture*. Harper, N. Y.
6 Roy Walker, *The Golden Feast*. (Macmillan Co., N. Y.)

7   Miami Herald, Miami, Fla., Aug. 28, 1960.
8   These illustrations appeared with an article by Hobart M. Van Deusen and Russell F. Peterson in *Natural History*, Oct. '58. American Museum of Natural History, N. Y.

Chapter 2

1   Love, the Organ of the animal's friend. Delhi 6, Delhi, India.

Chapter 3-4

1   Theodore H. Gaster, *Dead Sea Scriptures*. Doubleday & Company, N. Y.

Chapter 5

1 Martin A. Larson, *The Religion of the Occident*. Philosophical Library, N. Y.

Chapter 6-7

1   From St. Bonaventura, *Millennium Guild Literature*.
2   *Religious Foundations*, Edited by Rufus M. Jones. (The Macmillan Co., N. Y.)
3   C. W. Hume, M.C., B.S.C., *Status of Animals in the Christian Religion*. (Courier Printing Co., Ltd., Grove Hill Road, Tunbridge Wells, Kent, England)

Chapter 8

1   Martin A. Larson, *The Religion of the Occident*. (Philosophical Library, N. Y.)

Chapter 11

1   Daniel-Rops, *Jesus and His Times* (E. P. Dutton & Co., Inc., N. Y.)
2   Ellen G. White, *Counsels on Diet and Foods*. (Review and Herald Publishing Assn., Takoma Park, Washington, D. C.)
3   Millar Burrows, *The Dead Sea Scrolls*. (Viking Press, N. Y.)

Chapter 12

1   From Milton's Paradise Regained; excerpted from Roy Walker's book, *The Golden Feast*. (Macmillan Co.)

Chapter 15

1   Rev. Holmes-Gore, *These We Have Not Loved*. (C. W. Daniel Co., Ltd., Essex, England)
2   *Lost Books of the Bible*, World Publishing Co., N.Y., Cleve-
3   land, O.

Chapter 16

1   The Humane Society of the United States, Washington, D. C., *Facts About Your Meat*—a folder pleading for a humane method of slaughter.

Chapter 17

1   Jer. 7: 4-8-11. 5:31.
2   Jer. (8:8) (16:19) (7:21-22).
3   Amos 5:21,25.
4   Theodore H. Gaster, *The Dead Sea Scriptures*. (Doubleday & Co., N. Y.)
5
6
7   Selected from the Book of Hymns, *Dead Sea Scrolls*.

8, 9 Edgar J. Goodspeed, *Introduction to Apostolic Fathers.*
      (Harper, N. Y.)
10   Martin A. Larson, *The Religion of the Occident.* (Philosophical
     Library, N. Y.)

Chapter 18

1   Otto Pfleiderer, *Christian Origins.* Translated from the German
    by Daniel A. Huebsch, Ph.D. (B. W. Huebsch, N. W., 1906)
2   *The Gospel According to Thomas.* Harper, New York.

Chapter 21

1   Duncan Howlett, *The Essenes and Christianity.* (Harper).
2   Albert Schweitzer, *Man and God,* p. 339, by Victor Gollancz.
    (Houghton Mifflin Co., Boston, Mass.)
3   The Encyclopedia Britannica, 11th Ed. V. 12, p. 153.

Chapter 24

1   Science and Health with key to the Scriptures, p. 518—L. 13,
    by Mary Baker Eddy.
2   p. 550.

Chapter 25

1   Harpers Bible Dictionary. (p. 189)
2   Albert Schweitzer, *The Quest of the Historical Jesus.* (Mac-
    millan Co., N. Y.)
3   Ellen G. White, *Counsels on Diet and Foods.* Christian Home
    Library, Review and Herald Publishing Assn., Takoma Park,
    Washington, D. C.
4   Edmond Bordeaux Szekely, *The Essene Gospel of John.* Seventh
    Edition, C. W. Daniel Co. Ltd., London, England.

Chapter 26

1   From the exhortations of Father Zossima, Victor Gollancz,
    Man and God, p. 540. (Houghton Mifflin Co., Boston)
2   Contributed by Lois Ewing, wife of the author. Mrs. Ewing has
    given many years to the training of children. With love as her
    "medium" she has obtained remarkable results.

Chapter 29

1   From *A foreword to the gospel of the Holy Twelve* by Rev. Rich-
    ard Ouseley. (John M. Watkins Publishers, London) (1952)
2
3   *Manas,* Vol. X, No. 35, p. 8, Aug. 28, 1957. (Manas Publishing
    Co., Los Angeles, Cal.)

Chapter 30

1   Poem by M. Frida Hartley, *Wagners Essays and other writings.*
    (Millennium Guild, M. R. Freshel Founder)

Chapter 31

1   Albert Schweitzer, *The Mystery of the Kingdom of God.* (Mac-
    millan Co., N. Y.)
2

Chapter 32

1   Josephus.

Chapter 36

*   Taken in part from a translation by Gaster.
1 2 Ency. Brit. Vol. 23 p. 984.

3 Edgar J. Goodspeed, *The Apostolic Fathers*. (Chap. 2:4-10)
   Harper.
4 Otto Pfleiderer translated from the German by Daniel Huebsch,
   Ph.D. (B. W. Huebsch, N. Y. 1906) *Christian Origins*
5 Howard Williams, *Ethics of Diet*. From the second treatise the
   Instructor by Clemens A.D. 1-? 190. (Manchester Albert Broadbent, London, Richard James)

Chapter 37

1 Rev. George Milligan, D.D., D.C.L.
2 Rev. Adam Fyfe Findlay, M.A., D.D. *History of Christianity in
   the Light of Modern Knowledge*. (Harcourt, Brace & Co., N. Y.)
3 Hastings Encyclopedia on Religion and Ethics. Jerome ad. Matt:
   X1117.
4 Rev. V. A. Holmes-Gore, M.A. *These We Have That Loved*,
   C. W. Daniel Co. Ltd, Ashingdon Rochford, Essex.
5 Part of a saying of Jesus by the apostle John and reported by
   his pupil Papias.
6 Isaiah 7:14-15.

Chapter 38

* See Josephus on the Essenes.
1 Dom Ambrose Agius O.S.B. *Cruelty to Animals*, London Catholic
   Truth Society.
2 C. W. Hume, *The Status of Animals in the Christian Religion*,
   Courier Pub. Co., Ltd., Tunbridge Wells, Kent.

Chapter 39

1 Dr. George Seaver, *Schweitzer The Man and His Mind*, p. 298.

Chapter 41

1 Alfred Loisy, Origins of the New Testament, Macmillan Co.,
   N. Y.
2 Esme Wynne Tyson.
* Josephus Ant. B.XVIII,1,5).

BOOK FOUR

Chapter One

RECAPITULATION
and
Christian Response to the Ethics of
The Humane Christ

In reviewing the evidence as presented in the foregoing chapters of this work, it appears overwhelmingly to support the life and doctrine of the morally humane and spiritually ethical Christ. It might truthfully be said that, without the supporting evidence as set forth in the "Covenant of Love," the idea of a "Cosmic Christ" is completely without rational foundation; that is, were the ethics of the historical Jesus not to have extended beyond the relationship of man to his fellowman, they would have had no connection whatsoever with the universe.

Therefore, the re-discovery of the Humane Jesus, as revealed in the Covenant of Love,* returns to Christianity the long lost proof in principle of the Cosmic Christ as revealed in the Gospel of John. Christians everywhere should rejoice for in the recovery of the Ethical Jesus they can feel a great deal more secure in the sincere and uncompromised love of God.

Let us reconsider again, the evidence of proof of the Humane or "Cosmic Christ" in the prophecy of Isaiah 11:1-9. Here the trusting security of a vegetarian way of life illustrates the peaceful co-existence of all creatures who have attained the full knowledge of the nature of the Lord.

Next, Isaiah prophesies the coming of the L o r d Jesus. Here he symbolizes in the words, "curds and honey," the innocent diet through which the Son of Man's extreme powers of discrimination would be benefited. (Isa. 7: 14-15)

* See Love as a Universal Ethic p. 256.

342

The next Old Testament proof of the vegetarian way of life of the Son of Man is in the words of the Psalmist: "Do I eat the flesh of bulls or drink the blood of goats?" (Ps. 50: 12-13). Would the Son, therefore, eat from a table different from the Father's?

Next are the many Biblical references we have previously reviewed which reveal the blessings of a fleshless diet as well as the sordid consequences of flesh eating:* Of these, certainly Jesus was well aware because of his very nature as described by Isaiah.

Next are the many references of the prophets, not only as to flesh eating, but also for the redemption of the plight of animals, and the pleadings for mercy instead of sacrifice: It was their many pleadings and denunciations of the priestly code that in no small measure contributed to their own destruction. These exhortations by the prophets were well known to Jesus. His saying, "I have come to fulfill the prophets," (Matt. 5:17) is historically corroborated by the Nazarene doctrine that one of the purposes of the coming of Jesus was to abrogate the ritual of sacrifice.

Next the validation of the Sixth Commandment by Isaiah to include ALL creatures: Here Isaiah makes a man a murderer who kills an ox. Certainly Jesus would not have preached contrary to the teachings of His favorite prophet.

Next a review of the archaeological evidence as suggested in the Dead Sea Scrolls: Herein we find that they, (Essenes) even as Jeremiah, denounced the vain scribes and garblers of the law of Moses as it was interpreted by the priestly code. This, as their Psalms clearly indicate, involved the Pharisees' custom of sacrifice.

The Essenes, according to these scrolls, both abhorred the sacrifice and the eating of flesh. This is confirmed also by Philo, Josephus, Epiphanius, Porphyry, and even Jerome in the Fourth Century.

The closeness of Jesus and His Disciples to the customs

* I Kings 19: 5-8 Dan. 1: 14-17, Num. 11: 18-20, 31-34 Prov. 12: 10, 23: 20, 24: 11-13, 27: 25-27, 30:8. Amos 6:4 Hosea 8:13 Is. 22:13,14.

of these holy ones can hardly be doubted in face of all the evidence at hand.

Out of the Essenes came John the Baptist and his disciples. At least two, and probably more of these later became disciples of Jesus.

The Baptist, and quite obviously his disciples also, neither ate flesh nor drank wine.

Now as to other documentary evidence preserved by Irenaeus, Pliny, Epiphanius, Hegesippus, Clement of Alexandria, Jerome, Eusebius, and others, the Humane Christ is further supported. Herein, Peter, Matthew, Andrew, Thomas and James, the Lord's brother, are clearly described as abstaining from wine and the flesh of animals. Also herein, according to the report of Papias, the Evangelist John may be included as an abstainer. The evidence also indicates that both Bartholomew and Philip followed a similar way of life. None of the other disciples are mentioned. In fact, a very little is known about them, but it is almost certain that they also must have followed the same humane way of life as did Peter, Matthew, Thomas, and the others.

The documentary evidence referring to the Apostles and James, the Lord's brother, as abstaining from flesh meats, is further expanded upon by the Carmelite tradition to include the entire Holy family.

As the story which has never been officially denied by the Holy See asserts, Elias established a community of hermits on Mount Carmel which existed until the Christian era as a Jewish Carmelite Order to which belonged the sons of the prophets and the Essenes. Members of it were present at St. Peter's first sermon on Pentecost. They built a chapel on Mount Carmel in honor of the Blessed Mary who, as well as the Apostles, were members of the order.*

The pure humane way of life apparently practiced by the Holy family and the Apostles has been strictly adhered to down through the centuries. Today the Discalced Carmelites still remain faithful to the founding principles of the

* See Ency. Britt. 11, Ed. V. 5, p. 358.

order adhering strictly to the bloodless diet prescribed by God in the beginning (Gen. 1:29,30).

It was recorded by Jamblichus (A.D. 300) that Pythagoras spent some time in silent prayer in the sanctuary of Carmel.** Pythagoras and the Essenes, according to tradition, were closely related morally and spiritually which adds credence to the probability to their meeting together at Carmel.

The innocent and blood guiltless diet of both Pythagoras and the Essenes is also in complete accord with the "uncorrupted" portions of Elias' reported contact with the Divine Source. (Kings 17:12-6, 19:4-8)

Next is the historical evidence that the first Christians were the Jewish Christians. These were known as the Nazarenes, also called the Ebionites (the poor). Both Jesus and Paul were identified with them. They followed closely the ethics of the Cosmic Christ, the Humane Christ, holding it as a crime against God to kill any of His creatures. They neither ate flesh nor drank wine.

Further evidence of proof concerning the "Humane Christ" is emphasized by the early century Christian orders of the "Apostolic Brethren." It was their purpose to imitate as near as possible the way of life of Christ and His Apostles. They ate no flesh and drank no wine.

Next, according to historical evidence, of the seven First Century Christian sects, the "Paulinists" were the only ones who refused to abide by the humane diet. However, as it shall be pointed out in a later chapter, Paul himself appears to have remained faithful to the humane diet.

To cite further proof of the humane doctrine and diet as practiced by the Son of Man, the letter of Pliny to Trajan in the First Century refers to the Christians in Bithynia, where Peter preached, as meeting together and taking food but "ordinary and harmless food," that is to say, innocent or blood guiltless. One of the most convincing proofs preserved by Irenaeus in the fragment of Papias, the pupil of

** Catholic Dictionary.

John the Evangelist, is again repeated herein: "Papias related how the elders and John had heard the Lord teach that creation renewed and liberated shall yield an abundance of all kinds of food, seeds, grass, fruits, grains, and flour in corresponding proportion, and that all animals will use these foods and become in turn peaceful and in harmony with one another and with man." [1] (Condensed version) How well the character of these words harmonize with Isaiah's revelation that, "the wolf shall lie down with the lamb, and no one shall hurt or destroy, for all the earth shall have knowledge of the Lord." "Knowledge of the Lord" is therefore knowledge of His teachings, part of which appear in the above quotation. Here the Lord actually teaches that an anti-flesh diet is the efficacy of peace upon the world.

Another proof is that the dozen or more of the early sects comprising Christianity almost unanimously abstained from flesh eating, the Pauline branch excepted.

The great Christian Tatian who founded the Christian Church in Syria, wrote a book on the *true nature of Jesus Christ*.

Tatian and his followers believed it an offense to God to kill or to eat the flesh of animals. It is almost certain that if a copy of this work were to be discovered today, it would indeed reveal a similar Jesus as the one presented herein. It goes without saying that many of the early Church Fathers knew of the "Humane Jesus" and his doctrine, but because of the unfortunate position taken by the early Roman Church, they confined this knowledge to their own personal practices.

It was unlawful for any Christian, according to the doctrine of the early Roman Church, to refuse to eat flesh by reason that it was contrary to the pleasure of God to kill.

In consequence, those who still wished to follow the humane way of life compromised with the Church by interpreting their abstinences as merely a body subduing, or self mortifying measure instead of observing it as a Christian ethic.

Notwithstanding, however, at least four of the Fathers of the early Roman Church wrote extensively on the subject:

"The great figure in Latin Christianity was Tertullian, or Quintus Septimius Florens Tertullianus. He was born in Carthage about 155-60 A.D. Cyprian, the Bishop of Carthage, referred to him as the "Master," suggesting that Tertullian had firsthand access to the wisdom of Jesus himself." [2]

"This earliest of the Latin Christian authorities extant has a place in the history of anti-kreophagist literature on account of his strong protest against the general contempt for the teachings, or example, of the original founders of Christianity as to diet.

"In regard to the well known Pauline sentences, Tertullian supposes them to refer to certain teachers of abstinence who acted through vanity, not from a sense of right: — 'And even if he had handed over to you the keys of the slaughter house or butcher shop, in permitting you to eat all things, excepting sacrifices to idols, at least he has not made the kingdom of Heaven to consist in *butchery*: for, says he, eating and drinking is not the Kingdom of God, and food commends us not to him.' You are not to suppose it was said of vegetable, but of gross and luxurious food; since he adds, 'neither if we eat have we anything the more, nor if we eat not have we anything the less.' How unworthily too, do you press the example of Christ as having come 'eating and drinking' into the service of your lusts: he who pronounced not the full but the hungry and thirsty 'blessed,' who professed his work to be the completion of his Father's will, was wont to abstain—instructing them to labor for that 'meat' which lasts to eternal life, and enjoining in their common prayers petition not for gross food but for bread only." [3]

These words confirm Bishop Cyprian's reference that Tertullian had firsthand access to the wisdom of Jesus Christ. In regard to the "ethical," and the "spiritual," Tertullian continues: — "And if there be 'One' who prefers the works of justice, not, however, without sacrifice — that is to say, a spirit exercised by abstinence — it is surely that God to whom neither a gluttonous people nor priest was acceptable — Consistently do you men of flesh reject the things of the spirit. But if your prophets are complacent towards such persons, they are not my prophets. Why preach you not, 'Let us eat and drink, for tomorrow we die,'* just as we preach, 'Let us abstain, brothers and sisters, lest tomorrow perchance we die?" [4] "Whether or No, he proceeds, 'I have unreasonably explained the cause of the condemnation of the gross food by the deity, and of the obligation upon us, through the Divine will, (obedience to Christ) to renounce it, let us consult the common conscience of men, Nature herself will inform us whether, before gross eating and drinking, we were not of much more powerful intellect, of much more sensitive feeling, than when the entire domicile of men's interior has been stuffed with meats." [5]

"It was divinely proclaimed," continues Tertullian, 'Wine and strong liquor shall you not drink, you and your sons after you.' Now this prohibition of drink is essentially connected with the vegetable diet. Thus, where abstinence from wine is required by the deity, or is vowed by man, there, too, may be understood suppression of gross feeding, *for as is the eating, so is the drinking,** (qualis enim esus, talis et potus).* It is not consistent with truth that a man should sacrifice half of his stomach only to God — that he should be sober in drinking, but intemperate in eating. Your belly is your God, your liver is your temple, your paunch is your altar, the cook is your priest, and the fat steam is your Holy Spirit; the seasonings and the sauces are your chrisms, and your belchings are your prophesying. 'I ever,' continues Tertullian with bitter irony, 'recognize Esau, the hunter, as a man of taste (sapere) and as his were, so are your whole

---

* Tertullian refers here to Isa. 22: 13-14.
* See Prov. 23: 20-21 for support of Tertullian's statement.

skill and interest given to hunting and trapping — just like him, you come in 'from the field' of your licentious chase. Were I to offer you a mess of pottage (a thick broth or stew) you would, doubtless, straightaway sell your 'birthright.' It is in the cooking-pots that your love is unflamed —it is in the kitchen that your faith grows fervid — it is in the flesh dishes that all your hope lies hid — who is held in so much esteem with you as the frequent giver of dinners, as the sumptious entertainer, as the practiced toaster of healths? Let us openly and boldly vindicate our teaching. 'We are sure that they who are in the flesh cannot please God.' Not, surely meaning in the covering or substance of the flesh, but in the lust, the affection, and desire for it. Let wrestlers fatten themselves up, for them a mere corporeal ambition suffices. And yet even they become stronger by living on vegetable food. But other strength and vigor is our aim, as other contests are ours, who fight not against flesh and blood, but with faith and a strong mind. For the rest a grossly-feeding Christian is akin (necessarius) to lions and wolves rather than God." [6]

"Tertullian said, 'Our Lord Jesus called himself Truth and not habit.'

" 'For the Lord sent the Paraclete (Spirit) that, because human weakness could not grasp all at once, that discipline should be ordered gradually, Scripture explained, knowledge corrected and progress made toward the better.

" 'Not only novelty, but truth also disproves heresies. Whatever is thought contrary to truth is heresy, be it ever so old a habit.

"As everything in nature gradually develops to its maturity, so righteousness was, in the beginning, nature; it progressed through the Law and the Prophets to childhood, through the gospels it acquired the strength of youth and through the Spirit comes the development to maturity,' says Tertullian.

"Clement of Alexandria, contemporary of Tertullian declared, 'not the Bishop, but the genuine ecclesiastical gnostic who added philosophic knowledge to his faith, to be the true successor of the Apostles, the true presbyter and servant of divine will.' " [7]

This great Christian Father, Titus Flavius Clemens, was the founder of the famous Alexandrian school of Christian Theology. He succeeded Pantaenus (in 190).

His three great works are: *A Hortatory Discourse Addressed to the Greeks, The Instructor, and the Miscellanies.* Another work *On Abstinence or Fasting,* has, probably for quite obvious reasons, not come down to us.

"Though Clement, in his writings, unsparingly set forth the vagaries of the Greek philosophers, he referred to such philosophers as Plato, Socrates, and Pythagoras as speaking with divine inspiration. But the true teachings, he says, are to be found in the prophets and in the person of Jesus Christ." [8]

It is understandable why Clement referred to Plato, Socrates and Pythagoras as having been divinely inspired for they also taught and practiced the same "mercy towards the creatures" as is to be found in the prophets and in the person of Jesus Christ.

"It is far better," writes Clement, "to be happy than to have a devil dwelling in us: for happiness is found only in the practice of virtue. Accordingly, the Apostle Matthew lived upon hard shelled fruits, (seeds, grains and nuts) and vegetables without the use of flesh." [9] Here Clement refers to Matthew as an example of the 'good life' as taught by Jesus Christ, however, as the records illustrate, he could have said the same of James the Lord's brother, Peter, Thomas, Andrew and the others who walked with the Master. Also, and notwithstanding the questionable references to the contrary, Clement places, and rightfully so, the personal practices of St. Paul on the same high spiritual plane as those of the other Apostles. He writes:

"And if we would persuade any of our fellow-guests to virtue, we are all the more on this account to abstain from those dainty dishes and to exhibit ourselves as a bright pattern of virtue. 'It is good then neither to eat flesh nor to drink wine,' as both he (Paul) and the Pythagoreans acknowledge, for this is rather characteristic to a beast and the fumes arising from them, being dense, darken the soul . . . For a voice will whisper to him saying: 'Destroy not the work of God for the sake of Food.' 'Whether ye eat or drink, do all to the glory of God,' aiming after true frugality. 'For it is lawful for me to partake of all things, yet all things are not expedient.' 'For those that do all that is lawful, quickly fall into doing what is unlawful.' 'For just as righteousness is not attained by avarice, nor temperance by excess; so neither is the regimen of a Christian formed by indulgence; for the table of truth is far from lasciviousness. Nor are you in the midst of the repast, to exhibit yourselves hugging your food like wild beasts nor helping yourselves to a fullness of sauce, for man is not by nature a gravy eater, but a bread eater." [10]

"We must guard against those sorts of food which persuade us to eat when we are not hungry, bewitching the appetite (continues Clement), for is there not within a temperate simplicity, a wholesome variety of eatables — vegetables, roots, olives, herbs, milk, cheese, fruits, and all kinds of dry food? If any righteous man does not burden his soul by the eating of flesh, he has the advantage of a rational motive . . . Poleman in his work on *Life according to Nature,* seems clearly to affirm that animal food is unwholesome. If, as it is said, the animals are assigned to us it was not of them as food — but of them that do our work." [10a]

"The writings of St. Ioannes Chrysostom, the most eloquent of the Fathers, are voluminous. The style of the Greek orator, it must be noted, is necessarily but feebly represented in the literal English version:

" 'No streams of blood are among them (the Ascetics); no butchering and cutting of flesh: no dainty cookery; no heaviness of head. Nor are there horrible smells of flesh-meats among them, or disagreeable fumes from the kitchen

. . . With their repast of fruits and vegetables even angels from heaven, as they behold it, are delighted and pleased. For if over one sinner who repents they rejoice, over so many just men, imitating them, what will they not do?' [11] Here the venerable Christian Father points out that heaven rejoices with him who eats of innocent food, whose repentance spares God's creatures the pain of slaughter and the outraging of their tortured flesh, for what other reason would the angels rejoice?

" 'Wherein therefore,' continues St. Chrysostom, 'are we different from or superior to ants, if we compare ourselves with them? For as they care for the things of the body only, so also do we. And would it were for these alone! But alas! it is for things far worse. For not for necessary things only do we care, but also for things superfluous. Those animals pursue an innocent life while we follow after all covetousness. Nay, we do not so much as imitate the ways of ants. We follow the ways of wolves, the habits of tigers;* or, rather, we are worse even than they. To them nature has assigned that they should be thus fed, while God has honored us with rational speech and a sense of equity (knowing right from wrong). And yet we are become worse than the wild beasts. I say 'food' not 'luxury,' 'raiment,' not 'ornament.' Rather this frugality—to speak correctly—is, in the best sense, luxury. For consider, who should we say more truly feasted—he whose diet is herbs, and who is in sound health and suffering no uneasiness, or he who has a table of a Sybarite and is full of a thousand disorders? Clearly the former. Therefore, let us seek nothing more than these, if we would at once live luxuriously and healthfully.

"A man who lives in pleasure (i.e., in selfish luxury) is dead while he lives, for he lives only to his belly. In other senses he lives not. He sees not what he ought to see; he hears not what he ought to hear; he speaks not what he ought to speak . . . Look not at the superficial countenance,

---

* In the gospel of Thomas Jesus infers that the man who eats as a lion shall become as a lion. (Log. 5-8.)

but examine the interior, and you will see it full of deep dejection. If it were possible to bring the soul into view, and to behold it with our bodily eyes, that of the luxurious would seem depressed, mournful, miserable, and wasted with leanness. The more the body is pampered, the more the soul is hampered." [12]

Here St. Chrysostom suggests that not only the body is made corrupt by the eating of "superfluous meats," but the soul is corrupted or "hampered" also. Now the soul being a spiritual property, its welfare is in consequence affected only by spiritual and not by material conditions. Luxurious living is a material condition that is beholden to the spiritual only wherein a law of life or a law of God is violated. As harm, or hurt, or the acquiring of a thing by violence is contrary to God's law of love, the outraging of one of God's creatures, whether for food, clothing, or pleasure, is in consequence the soul-"hampering" component of luxurious living. Also, where luxurious living denies others the necessities of life, the soul is again hampered through selfishness, or lack of concern.

It appears, therefore, that selfishness, or lack of concern as applied here, are offenses against God's Law of Love which applies to the welfare of *all* life, *all* creatures. Being an offense against God, it is contrary to the first great commandment: "Love thy God with all thy mind, with all thy heart, and with all thy soul." Under such conditions luxurious—or what today is called "gracious living," does "hamper" the soul.

"Clemens Prudentius, the first Christian hymn writer, in one of his hymns exhorts his fellow Christians not to pollute their hands and hearts by the slaughter of innocent cows and sheep, and points to the variety of nourishing and pleasant foods obtainable without blood-shedding. As far as we are aware, Prudentius has had no successor as a writer of hymns in this sort of morality in the following fourteen centuries of Christianity." [13]

Origen was one of the greatest Christian scholars and

the most prolific Christian writer of antiquity. He was born in A.D. 184-85 and was destined to carry on where Pantaenus and Clement left off in the great school at Alexandria.

While Origen, like Clement before him, practiced abstinence from the flesh of animals, he, unlike Tertullian, Clement, and others among the Church Fathers, ascribed his motivations to conform to the face saving compromises of the "powers that be;" he expressed the otherwise "soul edifying" Christian ethic of abstinence as being a means of mortifying or subduing the body. He wrote: "We Christian leaders practice abstinence from the flesh of animals to subdue our bodies and treat them as slaves, and we wish to mortify our members upon earth." [14]

Anything that is natural is rational, and *vice versa*. Therefore, since we are dealing with the natural, the only two rational viewpoints pertaining to a vegetarian way of life are the ethical and the hygienic. The third attitude adopted by the Church is completely irrational and inconsistent. It has no logical significance. For example, it is both natural and rational to abstain from eating flesh in order to avoid causing pain, suffering, and death to God's innocent creatures. It is also both natural and rational to abstain because man is not by nature a flesh eater, and therefore is more healthy feeding upon a vegetable diet.

But on the other hand, it is neither natural nor rational to abstain from eating flesh as a means of subduing or mortifying the body. Certainly, a sincere Christian can hardly disagree that of the three motives for abstinence, the one fitting the nature of the Son of Man is undoubtedly the ethical, the humane, and the one that calls for mercy, compassion, and love uncompromised.

We recognize that Jesus fasted often, as did His disciples. Fasting is defined as either total or partial abstinence, or as abstaining from certain kinds of food. Fasting has for centuries been recognized as a means of cleansing the body of impurities.

In consequence, the spirit becomes more sensitive to

higher values, the reason truer, the intuition more recep-
tive, and the memory keener and more reliable. Thus one
becomes better equipped to follow through and to solve
problems. It was through His forty days and nights of fasting that Jesus was able to resolve his great inward conflicts
and see clearly His appointed destiny. It is most probable
that the fasting of Jesus in the wilderness was much the
same as that of John the Baptist who lived upon wild honey
and the bean of the "locust," or Carob, tree. However, this
kind of fasting, while it also was "meatless," did not subdue or make slaves of the body. It did not mortify, but instead, it glorified the body as the very temple of God.

"It already has been shown that the earliest Jewish
Christian communities, both in Palestine and elsewhere—
the immediate disciples of the Twelve—regarded abstinence
as one of the primary obligations of the new Faith; and that
the earliest traditions represent the foremost of them as
the strictest sort of vegetarians. If, then, we impartially review the history of the practice, the teaching, and the traditions of the first Christian authorities, it cannot but justly
provoke severe censure that the Orthodox Church, ignoring
the practice and highest ideal of the most sacred period of
its annals, has even within its own ecclesiastical order
deemed it consistent with its claim of being representative
of the Apostolic period to substitute very partial, and peri-
odic, for total and constant abstinence." [15] However, in spite
of the church's attitude, total abstinence from flesh eating
did afford certain spiritual remuneration to the Church
Fathers even as they fell short of reaching the heights attained by the Apostles.

Only in cases where the saints had placed the love of God
foremost in their relationships with His creatures of the
woods and meadows, was the spirit of the Master revealed
in its fullest.

"Many of the saints understood God's creatures, and together they shared the pattern of obedience to law and
praise of God that still leaves us wondering. The quickest

way to understand is surely to bring our own lives as closely as possible into line with the intention of the Giver of all life, animate and inanimate."* (Father Ambrose Agius)

The stories attributed to these Christian heroes are numerous and in support of the "humane doctrine" as being the criterion of abstinence, it might be well to consider a few of the more pertinent.

"As recorded in Montalembert's *Monks of the West* in *Vita Columbani*, the Chronicler Jonas, writing within twenty-five years of the death of St. Columban, relates that this saint spent long periods in solitary contemplation and communion with the wild creatures of the forest, and insisted on his monks living, like himself, on the fruits of the earth, mentioning herbs and pulses which would indicate that in making rules for his followers in regard to non-meat eating, he was moved by his love and regard for the rest of God's creation."**

A rather moving story is told of the hermit monk St. Giles. This holy man dwelt in a cave by the side of a clear spring, living upon herbs, nuts, and fruits of the forest. One day the King of France came hunting in the neighborhood. His dogs pursued a young deer which dashed into the cave of St. Giles, and as the dogs snapped at its heels, it took refuge in the arms of the holy man.

When the King and his followers witnessed this act of "Christly protection," they prostrated themselves before the good man and begged his forgiveness. St. Giles loved all of God's creatures and all the animals of the forest were his friends.

St. Francis was another of the outstanding Christian heroes because of his Christly compassion for the welfare of all of God's creatures.

" 'Dearly beloved!' he once began a sermon after a severe illness, 'I have to confess to God and you that . . . I have

---

* From the Ark Dec. 1956.
** By E. Eyre-Smith *The Ark, Bulletin of the Catholic Study Circle for Animal Welfare.*

eaten cakes made with lard.'

"St. Francis' gift of sympathy seems to have been wider even than St. Paul's, for we find no evidence in the great Apostle of a love for nature or for animals.

"During Christmas time 1223, Francis wished to persuade the Emperor to make a special law that men should provide well for the birds and the beasts, as well as for the poor, so that all might have occasion to rejoice in the Lord." [16]

No doubt he pleaded with the hunters to spare the woodland creatures and not to stalk them as a tiger stalks its prey.

"Francis' love of creatures was not simply the offspring of a soft sentimental disposition. It arose from that deep and abiding sense of the presence of God. To him all are from one Father and all are real kin. His dearest desire was to seek among the wise and simple, perfect and imperfect, the means to walk in the way of truth. To Francis love was the truest of all truths: hence, his deep sense of personal responsibility towards fellow creatures: the loving friend of all of God's creatures.

"Francis placed the chief hope of his redemption and the redress of a suffering humanity in the *literal* imitation of his Divine Master. He imitated the example of Christ as literally as it was in him to do so."[17]

Obviously, Francis believed that redemption was not vested in the acceptance of a name or a creed, but only in the actual living of the "Christ life," or "redemption through compassion."

The story of the conversion of Sir Hubert is another of those legends which have been handed down to inspire men toward recognition that, in Jesus Christ, ALL creatures are one in the love of God.

Sir Hubert was hunting in the forest when he came upon a beautiful stag standing in stately dignity before him. According to the story, just as Sir Hubert took careful aim, the cross upon which the compassionate blood of Jesus was shed in behalf of all of God's creatures appeared between the antlers of the stag. In reverent obedience the astonished hunter threw away his weapons and fell to his knees in penitent supplication.

Notwithstanding, however, later hunters have failed to understand the great ethical significance of this reported vision. Instead of obeying its pleading admonition as did Sir Hubert, they have made him their patron Saint and ask his blessing as they go forth to drench the forest with innocent blood.

"The blessed St. Andrew's food was herbs, olives, oil, and bread. He lived to be 105 years old." [18]

The Humane table of St. Gregory of Nizianzus is seen in the following excerpts of one of his poems. Herein one might suppose that Milton's "Temptation in the Wilderness" was influenced by this poem.

> Would a taste suit thy wishes
> Fragrant with sweet oils and dishes
> And the maddening wine-cups flame
> Joys for drinkers who love shame.
> Leaf or herb, or branch of vine
> Fearless to be drunk for wine.
> Spread a table there beneath thee
> Whose sweetness shall up-breath thee
> And which the dearest earth is giving
> Simple present to all the living
> When we have placed thee near it
> We will feed thee with glad spirit
> Wilt thou eat? Soft take the bread?
> Oaten cake if that bestead?
> Wilt thou drink of here doth bubble
> Water from a cup unspent.[19]

The Trappists or Cistercians and the Carmelites appear to uphold a similar attitude as did St. Francis, to imitate the example of Christ as literally as they know how. It might be said that through these devout followers of Jesus, the Catholic Church still maintains a very close connection with the "Humane Christ" and His Apostles.

Whether or not they follow the attitude of Origen or that of Francis as to vegetarian practices is not too important, for the fact remains that none of God's creatures are brutalized to supply them with food. Thus their souls are hampered neither by a corrupted temple (body) nor through compromising the purity of God's love for all His creation.

The great unselfish and uncompromised love of Jesus Christ for all of God's creatures is clearly evident in the following letter of Clement, Bishop of Rome, to the Corinthians (A.D. 88-97) : — "Perennial springs, created for enjoyment and health unfailing, offer their life giving breasts to man and to even the smallest of animals that they get together in harmony and peace. All things the Creator and Master of the universe ordered to be in peace and harmony in His kindness to all . . . to take refuge through our Lord Jesus Christ." [20]

This epistle of Clement very closely harmonizes in character with the report of Papias, pupil of John the Evangelist, wherein Jesus stresses the necessity of a vegetarian diet to bring about harmony among all creatures. (see p. 86) It also verifies the Humane Christ as so prophesied by Isaiah.

"In the early days of Christianity there was a record which was valued very much, in which the pure Christian and the Jewish ideas on this subject were debated. I refer to the Clementine Homilies, which date back to the middle of the Second Century. This record was founded on the preaching of Peter; and in it we have these words:

" 'The unnatural eating of flesh-meats is as polluting as the heathen worship of devils, with its sacrifices and its impure feasts, through participation in which a man becomes a fellow-eater with devils.' " [21]

And from the First Century gospel of Hermas is the following: "First of all it is an evil desire to covet another's wife; as also to desire the dainties of riches; and a multitude of superfluous meats, and drunkenness. Such lusting therefore is evil and pernicious. Whosoever therefore shall depart from all evil desires, shall live unto God; but they that are subject unto them shall die forever: For this evil lusting is deadly." (2 Hermas XII: 4,5,6)

Here the eating of flesh is, as a sin, comparable to the coveting of another's wife.

Father Zossima, a brother in the faith with St. Francis, said: "Love all God's creation. Love every leaf, every ray of God's light. Love the animals, love the plants, love everything. If you love everything, you will perceive the divine mystery in things. Once you perceive it you will begin to comprehend it better every day. And you will come at last to love the whole world with an all-embracing love. Love the animals: God has given them the rudiments of thought and joy untroubled. Do not trouble it, don't harass them, don't deprive them of their happiness, don't work against God's intent. Man, do not pride yourself on superiority to the animals: they are without sin,* and you with your greatness defile the earth by your appearance on it, and leave the traces of your foulness after you . . .

"My brother asked the birds to forgive him; that sounds senseless, but it is right; for all is like an ocean, all is flowing and blending; a touch in one place sets up movement at the other end of the earth. It may be senseless to beg forgiveness of the birds, but birds would be happier at your side — a little happier, anyway — and the children and all animals, if you were nobler than you are now. It's all like an ocean, I tell you. Then you would pray to the birds too, consumed by an all-embracing love, in a sort of transport, and pray that they too will forgive you your sin. Treasure this ecstasy, however senseless it may seem to men." [22]

"Life in any form is our perpetual responsibility. Its abuse degrades those who practice it; its rightful usage is a signal token of genuine manhood. If there be a superintending Justice, surely It takes account of the injuries and sufferings of helpless yet animate creation. Let us be per-

---

* The Herbivores (See Gen. 1:30).

fectly clear about the spirituality of the issue before us. We have abolished human bondage because it cursed those who imposed it almost more than those who endured it. It is now our bounden duty to abolish the brutal and ferocious oppression of those creatures of our common Father which share with man the mystery of life . . . this theme is nothing if not spiritual: an acid test of our relation to the Deity of love and compassion." [23]

Rev. Dr. S. Parkes Cadman

"Now what is it moves our very heart and sickens us so much at cruelty shown to poor brutes? I suppose this: first, that they have done us no harm; next, that they have no power whatever of resistance; it is the *cowardice and tyranny* of which they are the victims which make their sufferings so especially touching; . . . there is something so very dreadful, so satanic, in tormenting those who have never harmed us and who cannot defend themselves; who are utterly in our power." [24]

Cardinal Newman

"Animals are in our power in a peculiar sense; they are committed by God to our sovereignty, and we owe to them a considerate regard for their rights. No animal life can be treated as a THING. Willful disrespect of the sanctities of physical life in one sphere bears its fruit in other and higher spheres." [25]

Bishop Westcott

"At the heart of it, what is humane education? It is the teaching of the principles of all that is fundamental in religion, no matter what our creed. Indifference to the question of sect or church never asking whether the school be Catholic or Protestant, finding always common ground where all can stand." [26]

Dr. Francis H. Rosley

"The practice of kindness toward dumb creatures is a sign of development to the higher reaches of intelligence and sympathy. For, mark you, in every place there are those who are giving of their time and thought and energy to the work of protecting from cruelty and needless suffering the beasts of the field and streets. These are the people who make the earth clean and sweet and more like what God intended it should be." [27]   The Rev. George Laughton

"Think of the cruelty that meat eating involves, and its effect on those who inflict and those who behold it. How it destroys the tenderness with which we should regard these creatures of God!" [28]   Ellen G. White

"Tenderness accompanies all the might imparted by Spirit. The individuality created by God is not carnivorous, as witness the millennial estate pictured by Isaiah. (11:9) All of God's creatures, moving in the harmony of Science, are harmless, useful, indestructible. A realization of this grand verity was a source of strength to the ancient worthies. It supports Christian healing, and enables its possessor to emulate the example of Jesus. 'And God saw that it was good.' " [29]   Mary Baker Eddy

"If you want to pass from the consciousness of flesh into the consciousness of Spirit, you must withdraw your attention from the things of the flesh. You must recognize that there is but one universal life, one universal substance, one universal intelligence, and that every animal is contending for its life and is entitled to that life . . . But in the matter of animal slaughter, who countenances it or defends it after his eyes have been opened to the *unity of life?* Let us remember that the right kind of food will give our minds and our spirits opportunity to express that which is one with ideal life." [30]   Dr. Charles Filmore
Founder of Unity

A Benedictine Father of St. Mary's Priory in Newark, N.J. has recently been extraordinarily informed as to the truth of Genesis (1:29).

This righteous man, having passed through the greater part of fourscore years, became practically confined to the wheel chair with rheumatism and arthritis.

One day, as he came to the Lord in humble supplication, "The Holy Spirit descended upon him," according to his own testimony, and told him to "eat no more flesh meat."

Reverently obedient to divine council the good Father is now well along in the eighties. Fully recovered he rides many miles every day on a bicycle.

"John Wesley the father of Methodism, in his correspondence assigns his remarkable power of endurance, physical and mental, to his frugal and pure food.

"In 1747 he wrote to the Bishop of London: Thanks be to God! since the time I gave up the use of flesh-meats and wine I have been delivered from all physical ills." [31]

"Many of the great religious reformers have affirmed the dynamic value of a non-flesh diet for body, mind, and soul; yet, their followers repudiate their humane thoughts and acts. Even by the hosts who glory in his name, John Wesley, were he here today, would be considered an uncertain faddist. These words I write not to hurt the sensitive feelings of the religious hero's followers, but rather afresh to emphasize the fact, that when the laws of a higher type of manhood intercept those of the lower plane, there is a pause and a drawing back on the part of the majority. For what is true of the disciples of the Christ, is also true of most of the partisans of every great thinker." [32] (Rev. J. Todd Ferrier)

In the Encyclopedia of Religion and Ethics, Vol. XI pp. 618-20, we find the following comment: "The ethical argument, including our duty to the lower animals, the bearing of the example of Christ, and the question how far a non-flesh diet is a help to the higher life.

"Thus, if man recognizes the claims of animals to good treatment, it is futile to defend the slaughter of them because the results of the opposite line of conduct is not easy to foresee. This is the point at which religious consideration supplements ethical. If we believe that God has committed animals to us, we are bound to treat them kindly, even if the results were likely to be far more inconvenient than they possibly could be. Indeed, the experiencing of food shortage has taught us that all the difficulties supposed to be inherent in vegetarianism are faced without hesitation as soon as the situation is understood. In other words, professing followers of Christ ignore what is admittedly a divinely sanctioned claim, but recognize it as soon as ever 'provision for the flesh,' against which St. Paul (Rom. 13:14) and our Lord (Matt. 6:25) warn us, seems to be in question."

"There are three main reasons which prompt people to adopt a pure diet. Some do it for reasons of health. This is prudent. Others do it because it is humane. This is excellent. But the noblest of all are those who do it because they realize it is a religious essential since the pure life is absolutely necessary for the redemption of this planet. Indeed, we cannot hope to rid the world of war, disease, and a hundred other evils until we learn to show compassion to the creatures and refrain from taking their lives for food, clothing, or pleasure.

"The Church is powerless to free mankind from such evils as war, oppression and disease because it does nothing to stop man's oppression of victimizing living creatures. Men do not grasp that our cruelty to the creatures has its rebound. Every evil action, whether it be done to a man, a woman, a child, or an animal, will one day have its effect upon the transgressor. The rule that we reap what we sow is a Divine Law, from which there is no escape. God is ever merciful, but He is also righteous, and if cruel men and women will learn compassion in no other way, then they will have to learn through suffering, even if it means suffering the same tortures that they have themselves inflicted. God is perfect Love, and He is never vengeful or vindictive, but the Divine Law of mercy and compassion cannot be broken without bringing tremendous repercussions upon the transgressor.**

"When one thinks of the millions of creatures that are slaughtered, tortured, and hunted every year for the sake of food and clothing, or for so-called 'sport,' it is not the

** See p. 165.

least surprising that the world is in its present state. In this wonderful country* of ours we have made many great reforms, but there remains much to be done. We have improved the lot of children, of prisoners, and of the poor beyond all recognition in the last hundred years. We have done something to mitigate the cruelties inflicted upon the creatures. But though some of the worst forms of torture have been made illegal, the welter of animal blood is greater than ever, and their sufferings are still appalling. What we need is not a reform of existing evils, but a revolution in thought that will move Christians to show real compassion to all God's creatures. Many people claim to be lovers of animals who are very far from being so. *For a flesh-eater to claim to love animals is as if a cannibal expressed his devotion to the missionaries he consigns to the seething cauldron."* [33]

Those who long to be part of a world where all creatures can enjoy the love of true brotherhood, pray that the noble ones within the Church will once again take up the cause of the creatures where it was left off by those early Christians who lived the life of perfect love, compassion, and pity so beautifully manifested by the Master.

The Christian teaching that man is the only creature endowed with a living soul is contrary to Bible precedents. The story of Genesis, in the original Hebrew, states that "God said, let the earth bring forth the *living soul* (Nephesh Chayah) after its kind, the cattle, the beasts of the earth and the fish in the sea." In the King James version the words *Nephesh Chayah* or living soul have been made to read "living creature."

"In wisdom hast thou made them all:

"When thou sendest forth thy Spirit they are created" (Ps. 104:24,30)

"In whose hand is the soul of every living thing and the breath of all mankind." (Job 12:10)

"And every soul of man is according to number, similarly beasts will not perish, nor all souls of beasts which the Lord

* England.

created, till the great judgment, and they will accuse man
if he meet them ill." (The Book of the Secrets of Enoch 1st
Century)

"For the fate of man and beast are the same. They all
have the same breath, and man has no advantage over the
beast, for all is vanity. Who knows whether the spirit of
man goes upward and the spirit of the beast goes down to
the earth?" (Eccles. 3:19,21 R.S.V.)

Here the writer of Ecclesiastes infers quite clearly that
it is pure vanity to suppose that man holds a "spiritual"
advantage over the animal inhabitants of God's kingdom.
In fact the history of human morality, with but few exceptions, decisively contradicts any notion of human "spiritual"
supremacy, especially over the peace loving herbivores who
still maintain to this day a way of life born of the golden
age before the "fall."

"In general Christians hold it as a part of their belief
that in his primary conditions prior to what is termed 'The
Fall,' man was perfect. Now is it not a remarkable thing
that the story of man's beginnings as told in the poem of
creation should declare in favor of Humane diet? i.e., 'Behold we have given you every herb-bearing seed, which is
upon the face of the earth, and every tree, in which is the
fruit of a tree yielding seed: to you it shall be for meat.
And to every beast of the earth and to every fowl of the
air, and to everything that creepeth upon the earth wherein
there is a living soul, we have given every green herb; and
it was so. And the Elohim of God saw everything that they
had made, and behold it was very good.' (Gen. 1: 29, 30)

"There was certainly no 'Human Carnivora' then! When
did the human race become carnivorous? When the human
descent had reached a certain stage whose commentary
may be found in Gen. 6:1-9. Who were the Nephilim that
were abroad? Were they not the embodiments of giant
wrongs, the mighty animal forces let loose, the result of the
loss of soul intuition and divine inspiration through a gross
ministry of the flesh? As the outcome of this unhallowed

condition of life; we have the flood — which was of a moral and spiritual order, not simply physical; and after it we have such teaching as could only be the outcome of expediency to meet the low needs of the remnant of the race— Gen. 9: 2-6. 'And the fear of you and the dread of you shall be upon every beast of the earth, and upon every fowl of the air; with all wherein the ground teemeth; and all the fishes of the sea, into your hand are they delivered. Every moving thing that liveth shall be food for you. Here Carnivorism is an acknowledged fact in man and beast. Every moving thing was for food! What a fall there was there, from the first mortal world dominion of man to the brute-force here revealed! And even here we see the close connection between Carnivorism and drunkenness, a fact which should weigh with those who seriously face the temperance problem. For surely Genesis 9: 20-21 shows what Noah the Carnivorous could do." [34]

And then came the teachers and the prophets who denounced the drinking of wine, the eating of flesh, and the merciless practice of sacrifice. But man still gloried in his iniquities and avoided any opportunity to rise above his sinful life.

And then the Spirit of God came to earth in the flesh of One most favorable to His nature. As an example for all mankind to follow, Jesus demonstrated in His own humane way of life the means and the course by which mankind might once again arise to his sinless state before the great Fall.

This was truly a sincere and equitable revelation of a merciful, just, and generous God. Mankind had fallen to a state of almost complete indifference to humane ethics. His potential dignity had turned to vainglory on one hand and to an equal of the loathsome creatures that feast upon dead things, on the other. This he did through his own free will and choice.

Therefore, regardless of all the wishful thinking and vain demonstrations which delude the hopes of man, the only sure way he can ever regain the heights and so save himself from oblivion is through the same means he used to sink to his present state — his God-given free will and power of choice. Certainly, God did not give him his freedom of choice so he would become lost through its working. If man has used this power indiscriminately and thereby lowered himself to the brink of spiritual oblivion, then even as a loving father, with the welfare of His son at heart, would insist upon, man as the child of God must again use the same means to work his way back to complete redemption.

In Jesus Christ, His way of life and His teachings, as revealed in the "Covenant of Love," the Christian — in fact man of any creed, race, or color — can, during his own lifetime, reject the aimless life of the Fall. In its place he can take on the life as demonstrated by the "Humane Christ," thereby assuring, in fact instead of fancy, a realistic redemption and return to a spiritual Oneness with the Father.

Man must gain his own victory even as he succeeded to his own defeat. The power of choice and his awareness of right and wrong are his "God-given" means to achieve the goal he seeks.

It is a law of nature and a law of God that no one shall find peace and contentment nor spiritual security in a "thing" that is not earned through self denial and conscientious endeavor. The greater the "thing" to be gained the more sincere must be the effort put forth. That which can be had for the mere asking, let no one deceive you, is not worth the having. Have a care therefore, lest you be disillusioned into believing for yourself a "hereafter" that you have not earned in the "here and now."

*   *   *

"The best knowledge of the truly spiritual man comes through his intuition. His affection guides him more than his intellect. He is not a literalist though he may accept all the spiritual truths of historic religion as divinely inspired. He is not an iconoclast, though through the possession of a

scientific mind he may weigh all evidence. He is a disciple
of the 'Cosmic faith'—one who is caught up by the sub-
limity of Truth itself, wherever found, or by whomsoever
spoken. And being so, he will seek truth in the higher planes
of existence. Laws of expedience passed in the process of
national or religious evolution will not be high enough for
him to accept as the final standard of attainment, or even
to walk by. He will rather seek those laws written neither
on tablets of stone nor in hieroglyphics, but in the heart
where the Divine Love reigns. And where the Eternal Love
reigns, there can be no narrowness, exclusiveness, conceit,
grossness of living, and inhuman attitude towards the sentient creatures under him. The spiritual man is to become
one with the Divine. That is the end of all religion. And
when a man attains even a measure of Oneness with God,
he must also recognize his Oneness with all life. Such a
man rises into the conditions of the fourth dimension —
the state of sublime fellowship — the eternal regions of the
Cosmos — the plane where the great realities are things
celestial and not things of earth." [35]

BOOK FOUR

Chapter 1

1   Edgar J. Goodspeed. Abbreviated from a page of *The Apostolic
    Fathers.*
20 *Ibid.*
2   Edgar J. Goodspeed, *A History of Early Christian Literature.*
    (University of Chicago Press)
8   *Ibid.*
3   Howard Wiliams, Ethics of Diet. Manchester: Albert Broad-
    bent, London & Richard J. James, 1907)
4   *Ibid.*
5   *Ibid.*
6   *Ibid.*
9   *Ibid*
10a *Ibid.*
11 *Ibid.*
12 *Ibid.*

13 *Ibid.*
14 *Ibid.*
15 *Ibid.*
7   Otto Pfleiderer translated from the German by Daniel A. Huebsch, Ph.D. (New York, B. W. Huebsch, 1906) *Christian Origins.*
10 *A Treasury of Early Christianity,* edited by Anne Freiniautte. Viking Press, N. Y.
18 *Ibid.*
19 *Ibid.*
16 The Catholic Encyclopedia.
17 *Ibid.*
21 Rev. J. Todd Ferrier On Behalf of the Creatures. (The Order of the Cross, 10 DeVere Gardens, Kenington, London)
31 *Ibid.*
32 *Ibid.*
34, 35 *Ibid.*
22 Victor Gollancz, *Man and God,* p. 539. Houghton Mifflin Co., Boston.
23, 24, 25, 26, 27 *Wagner's Essays and other writings.* Millennium Guild Inc. M. R. L. Freshel Founder, 40 Central Park So., N Y.
29 Science and Health with key to the Scriptures, by Mary Baker Eddy, p. 514-L. 18, L. 28.
30 Dr. Charles Filmore, Introduction *Unity Cook Book,* Unity Center, Lee Summit, Mo.
33 Rev. V. A. Holmes-Gore, M.A. *These We Have Not Loved,* C. W. Daniel Co., Ltd., Essex, England.
28 Ellen G. White, *Counsels on Diet and Foods,* Herald Pub. Assn., Washington, D. C.

Chapter Two

THE VINDICATION OF ST. PAUL

As former references herein clearly indicate, the true Christian ethics, as practiced by the Nazarenes and the old Apostles, represented the very foundation of the Church of Jesus Christ. The first concern of these ethics was twofold, for it denounced both the merciless custom of sacrifice, and its co-practice of slaughtering animals for food: the next involved the repudiation of slavery, and the third was the renunciation of war and all other forms of violence.

When St. Paul made his zealous crusade to Christianize the Gentiles, he came face to face with the alternative of either compromising the disciplined ethics of the Apostolic Church in order to attract the heathen candidate, or failing completely in his efforts to make the world conscious of Jesus Christ. Choosing the first alternative, he attempted to reconcile the disciplined ethics of the pure Christian doctrine with the customs and practices of the Romans.

Now, as to the first ethic, the universal ethic: the cosmic ethic of Love unrestrained and uncompromised by limitations, the ethic that seeks to abrogate all harm and hurt in the world of life—and its antithesis, the slaughtering of animals for food, must have caused Paul no little concern and embarrassment, for one finds suggested in Romans and Corinthians where he endeavored to compromise the situation. While many of these references involve the eating of those things sacrificed to idols, others apply more directly to the practice of flesh eating as a basic issue, i.e., "Him that is weak in the faith receive ye: but not to doubtful disputations. For one believeth that he may eat all things: another who is weak eateth herbs." (Rom. 14: 1,2). However, in II Cor. 12:9 Paul quotes Jesus as saying "My

371

strength is made perfect in weakness." In the latter the word weakness means acquiescence to the will of God. In comparison, "He who is weak eateth herbs," eateth therefore in acquiescence to the will of God.

Again Paul says, "Let not him that eateth despise him that eateth not; and let not him which eateth not judge him that eateth."

It appears that while Paul offered this compromise to effect harmony in the Gentile Church, he himself conformed to the older Apostles. (See Clement of Alexandria, page 351) "I keep under my body and bring it into subjection; lest that by any means which I have preached to others, I myself should be a castaway."

"All things are lawful for me but I will not be brought under the power of any. All things are lawful unto me but all things edify not.

"Meats for the belly and the belly for meats, but God shall destroy both it and them. Know ye not that your bodies are the members of Christ? That it is the temple of the Holy Ghost. and ye are not your own? For ye are bought with a price: therefore glorify God in your body and in your spirit which is God's." (I Cor. 6: 12, 13, 15, 19, 20) "Be imitators of me, as I am of Christ." (I Cor. 11:1). Here it appears that Paul hoped later to reform those whom he had accepted into the fold through offering his own way of life as an example.

The writers of Acts represent Paul as being ordered by James and his council at Jerusalem to take four poor Nazarites along with him and go to the temple and finance a sacrifice to purify himself. (Acts 21:23)

The next day Paul carried out their directions according to Acts 21:26.

That this bit of writing is a later interpolation intended to confuse the issue in regards to the ascetic practices of Paul and the Jewish Christians is self evident.

In the first place we now know that the Jewish Christians not only opposed the sacrifice, but also abstained from the eating of flesh; that James and the other apostles were Nazarenes whose doctrine described one of the purposes of Jesus' coming was to abrogate the sacrifice. In fact, this same book of Acts has Stephen, who was a member of the Jewish Christians under James, himself denouncing the sacrifice. (Acts 7:42)

It is apparent, therefore, that the passage about Paul's offering in the Temple is either a later interpolation or the writer has confused a former incident in the life of Paul, when he was Pharisee, with his later activities. The Temple sacrifice was a Pharisiac, not a Christian practice. Any reference which described Paul as observing the rituals of the Pharisee must be considered therefore as antecedent to his higher enlightenment. Paul was referred to as a Nazarene (Acts 24:5). He was consequently identified with the immediate followers of Jesus, who, according to documented evidence, denounced both the sacrifice of animals and the eating of flesh as being an offense to God.

The next ethics of Jesus, which was first introduced into the world by His Essenic brethern, was the inalienable rights and privileges of all creatures to tread God's green earth in freedom: "He has sent me to proclaim liberty to the captives to set at liberty them that are bruised." (Luke 4:18)

Here the great disciple was again obliged to compromise the second ethic of freedom in order to gain the attention of the heathen candidates, that is, to acquaint them first with Jesus Christ, hoping that later they would find it more humane to modify their customs.

Paul, at this time, was no doubt under great stress and pain both in body and spirit, for in assuming the responsibility of accepting the Roman custom of slavery he was in consequence severely criticized and shunned by the Old Apostles, — for this, and not the trivial disagreement on circumcision, was he called an "Apostate."

"The Greek democracies had slavery; the great landed estates of the Roman Empire were worked by slaves. The lot of slaves was often unhappy, and public opinion condoned the use of the lash on them, the killing of them when their usefulness was past, and the selling of them at a low price when they became old." [1]

But Paul's sympathy was with the slaves. It was his hope that their owners' hearts would become softened upon receiving knowledge of Jesus Christ. No doubt many of the converts did free their slaves through becoming aware of the teachings of Jesus, but the greater part of them, while growing more sympathetic, retained their ownership.

In an unprejudiced recognition of the spiritual and moral integrity of Paul, one must admit that any references that favor slavery in the epistles attributed to him are deliberate interpolations, and not from the pen of the great Apostle. Paul's letter asking forgiveness of a brother Christian for a runaway slave whom he is returning, is evidence that he did not approve of the custom of slavery even though he did not oppose it as being absolutely taboo to Christian conversion.

Paul's attitude is clearly observed in his letter to Philemon. Here he expresses his hope and faith that the "Christ presence" would eventually bring about a reconciliation in the heart and soul of the slave owners.

"I thank God always when I remember you in my prayers, because I hear of your love and of the faith which you have towards the Lord Jesus and I pray that the sharing of your faith may promote the knowledge of all the good that is ours in Christ.

"Accordingly, though I am bold enough in Christ to command you to do what is required, yet for love's sake I prefer to appeal to you as an ambassador for Jesus Christ.— He, (the slave) was parted from you for a while that you might have him back, no longer as a slave, but as a beloved brother especially to me but even more to you in the flesh and in the Lord."

In representing himself as the ambassador of Christ, Paul, in this letter to Philemon, made it clear that the

Master Himself was sent "to proclaim" release to the captives and to set at liberty those who are oppressed." (Luke 4: 18 RSV). The word "oppressed" is translated in King James as "bruised." A slave is both oppressed by his master and bruised by his lash. The suffering servant of Isa. 53:7 is similarly oppressed and afflicted (or bruised). Jesus read in the synagogue from Isaiah where it was further written "and open the prisons to those who are bound." Any attempt, therefore, to interpret these sayings other than that they refer directly to slavery, is but a means of compromising the centuries-old guilt of the Christian doctrine.

The Church of past centuries has never considered slavery to be a moral evil. The Protestant churches of Virginia, South Carolina, and other southern states, actually passed resolutions in favor of the slave traffic* notwithstanding the fiendish cruelties, inhuman tortures, many suicides, and vile immoralities it embraced. It is doubtful if Paul would ever have used the psychology of "converting first and cleansing later" if he could have foreseen the future attitude of his followers. But this was Paul's "cross to bear." What must have been his inward struggle in discriminating between the ethical and the expedient! On one hand he was condemned for compromising the doctrine of Jesus, and on the other, he realized that in order to perpetuate in time the knowledge of Jesus throughout the world, he must necessarily approach the Heathens through mitigating instead of condemning their traditional customs. Thus one might recognize in St. Paul the "hand of providence" keeping the flame alive in the hearts of men until a time when humanity would itself remove the compromises suffered by his inspired wisdom, and rediscover the New Covenant of Jesus Christ as it was known to him and the other Twelve Apostles.

* "Slavery in America," from Chambers Tracts published in Edinburgh 1845.

The Covenant All But Abrogated

However, and notwithstanding, it was apparently through the compromises of Paul that the Church gradually became divided within itself. Those who insisted upon abiding by the three major ethics of the spirit of Jesus Christ either joined monastic orders within the jurisdiction of the Church or organized separate sects outside the Church. The latter were usually persecuted as heretics.

The main Church body, however, retained its viewpoint of ignoring the first two major ethics, thereby maintaining a worldly attitude concerned more with the political and numerical growth of the material church than it was with the development of its spiritual commitments.

Returning again to the discussion of Paul's compromises, it might be said that while Paul found it expedient to compromise the first two great ethics of the covenant, he could not possibly have done so with the third ethic, i.e., the ethic of "peaceful relationships." Upon this ethic the very life of the covenant depended. Without it the "Sermon on the Mount," in fact, the whole doctrine of Jesus, would become an empty shell: "Blessed are the peace makers" (the pacifists). "Blessed are the merciful, the pure in heart;" "Whosoever shall kill shall be in danger of the judgment;" "Resist not evil but whosoever shall smite thee turn the other cheek;" "Love your enemies and bless them that hate you;" "Forgive men their trespasses;" "No man can serve two masters;" "Judge not that ye be not judged;" "Love thy neighbor as thyself;" "He who lives by the sword dies by the sword," were the very foundation stones upon which Christianity was to be built. Without these sayings, Paul could never have convinced his followers that Jesus was the "Son of God."

But as the Church grew in numbers its political aspirations also became more evident. Under the Emperor Constantine the Great, who was converted in 312, Christianity became exalted into a State religion. Christianity thereafter began to turn towards the State for support. In so doing it severed its last remaining attachment as an organization to the peaceful entreaties of Jesus Christ, and became reconciled to war and the soldier's calling.

Thus began the unholy alliance between Church and State and Jesus Christ again became compromised by the "war god" of the Old Testament. In fact it might be said that here the New Covenant of Jesus Christ was in consequence all but abrogated. Here was compromised the third and last sublime ethic which the Spirit of God and the Son of Man had set forth as the criteria of the "good life:" as the only means to bring about peace and happiness for all creatures on earth. Proof of this is in the evidence that 90% of all the harm, hurt, sorrows, sufferings and pains of death which have continually plagued living creatures are brought about outside the scope and authority of the three basic ethics of Jesus Christ. Without these ethics no religion can ever maintain full allegiance to a God of love, mercy, justice and compassionate understanding.

However, in spite of its many centuries of allegiance to the "blood-letting God" of the Old Testament the Christian Church has come a long way towards the goal of spiritual fulfillment.

Slowly but surely, the God of love and mercy is overcoming the vengeful God of past centuries. Today in the cathedral, the church, the meeting house, and in the synagogue, the God of love is gradually taking hold of the hearts of men.

The religions of the world are becoming more understanding and more compassionate. There are hopes that this same attitude may extend towards peaceful relationships with the expanding ideologies of the world. Indeeed a wholehearted allegiance by the Christian churches to the three major ethics of the "Essene Christ" may eventually be brought about through our modern day awareness of a God of Love.

It has been said that the Mother Church, which has for centuries observed within its system the "Divine Formula" of Gen. 1: 29,30, is to lead the world towards the realization of the prophetic vision: that the Trappists, the Carmelites and other organizations within its jurisdiction maintain to-day the same simple purity of life as it was observed by Jesus and His Apostles; and that their practices need only be extended to, and be moderated by, family life to lead all creatures toward the realization of the "Kingdom."

This saying may indeed be prophetic for even now an organization which seems to have been inspired by the merciful heart of St. Columban comes forth out of the depths of Irish faith. It is known as the *Catholic Study Circle for Animal Welfare*. A bulletin called The Ark, published four-monthly by the group, is devoted to the "here and now" salvation of God's creatures. Both the humane and the health aspects of vegetarianism are supported by its contributors.

There is also a sincere and rapidly growing group of Christians known as Seventh Day Adventists who could also be the remnant to lead the world to the Kingdom upon earth.

They refuse to slaughter animals for food. In this they adhere to the ethics of the Cosmic Christ: to the love that knows pity even for the sparrow that falls to the ground.

Another Christian remnant whose members still follow the way of life demonstrated almost two thousand years ago by the Master is known as the Order of the Cross.

The Order is an informal Brotherhood and Fellowship having for its service in life the cultivation of the Spirit of Love towards all souls: helping the weak and defending the defenseless and oppressed; abstaining from hurting the creatures, eschewing bloodshed and flesh eating, and living upon the pure foods so abundantly provided by nature.

Here among this Brotherhood the spark of the divine vision is kept alive gradually increasing strength until it illuminates the dark passages of a wayward world consciousness and brings all souls together under the Heavenly guidance of the Coming Great Church.

We also find among the Tolstoyans, those that adhere to the humane doctrine: also some among the Unitarians, the

Bible Christians, the Salvation Army, as well as many of the
Jewish faith.

The frustrations akin to the flesh pots of "Kilbroth-
Hattaavah" are conscientiously avoided at Lee's Summit,
Missouri where the Unity School teaches Christianity as it
came sweet and pure from the heart of Jesus.

Unity believes that the time will come when man will
look back upon flesh eating as it now looks upon cannibalism.

"As man unfolds spiritually he more and more perceives
the necessity of fulfilling the divine law in every department
of his life. From experience and observation Unity believes
that somewhere along the way, as he developes spiritually,
man comes to question seriously the rightness of meat as
part of his diet.

"Man is naturally loath to take life, even though the idea
of killing animals for food has so long been sponsored by
the race that he feels it is right and proper to do so.

"However the Commandment, 'Thou shalt not kill,' considered in its fullest sense, includes the killing of animals*
... There is a kindred spirit in all living things** a love for
life. Any man who considers honestly the oneness of life
feels an aversion to eating meat: that is a reaction of his
mind towards anything so foreign to the idea of universal
life":[2] and we might add universal love. Here one realizes
in the teachings of Unity the Unity of created beings
wherein God, life and love represent a universal unity: a
synthesis of the Divine, the eternal and the "all good."

Thus the student at the Unity School is particularly
blessed with an atmosphere wherein his mind, body and
soul are, in effect, no longer alienated but are united in a
oneness of thought and activity. The teachings of Unity
parallel those of the "humane Christ' whose true spirit must
inevitably come forth to be realized in the heart and soul of
every man.

---

* See Isaiah 66:3.
** See Psalm 104:30   Job 12: ,7-10.

From behind the so-called "iron curtain" comes reports of humane activities which are indeed embarrassing to the Christian culture of the Western World. On page six of the February issue of LOVE, the Official Organ of the International Cultural Forum appears the following announcement: "Mr. Bogdanowicz has consented to represent the International Animals Charter in Poland and the Zbar Unitariani-ski Kongregacio, under the leadership of Marianus Lubecki, who is also a strong supporter of the Charter: for this religious body includes also the animals in its Unitarian creed of the unity of Life as, indeed we would wish to be the case of all religious organizations."

This report is indeed a challenge to the customs and practices of the so-called free Christian world: for the Animals Charter supports a sincere reverence for all life, i.e., the discontinuing of vivisection and the slaughter of animals either for sport, clothing, or for food.

But let us not forget the many other Christian forces at work, both within and without the orthodoxes, which are striving towards the moral and spiritual fulfillment of mankind.

Towards this realization, the "Covenant of Love" was written. It represents the devoted efforts of many minds who contributed in no small way to its development. May its contents inspire the reader to re-discover the true covenant of Jesus Christ as it was known and practiced by the Old Apostles.

Here, too, our Jewish brethren might be reminded that this was not a heathen or a Gentile religion. The true Christian movement was primarily Jewish. It represented the Highest point in moral ethics the Jews or any other people has ever attained. A return, therefore, by the Christian Church to the pure apostolic ethics would actually represent their re-conversion to the religion of the Jews as it was practiced by Jesus of Nazareth.

Here the brotherhood of Jew and Gentile is forever made

complete: sealed by the Spirit of the "Essene Christ" acting through God the Father.

Chapter 2

1 Kenneth Scott Latourette, *The History of Christianity*, Harper, N. Y.
2 From the Foreword of the Unity Cook Book, Unity School of Christianity, Lee's Summit, Mo.

Chapter Three

THE CATEGORIES AND
THE DOCTRINE OF
THE COVENANT OF LOVE

In the following evaluation of the Covenant of Love gospel, the doctrine of the life, death, and resurrection of the Cosmic Christ is re-examined. The various opinions expressed herein may be considered from a theological, metaphysical, symbolical, or philosophical point of view. It is the author's concern, however, to avoid, in his interpretation of the purpose of Jesus Christ, much of what appears to be illogical, inconsistent, and inequitable in the traditional point of view. If one fails to observe in the "Christ Principle" a highly ethical and humane tendency, as well as a dignified and equitable interpretation of a divine plan, then any connection of this concept to a great universal intelligence must necessarily be considered as remote.

Here it seems that the whole idea of God continges upon the individual's personal or conditioned interpretation which conforms either to customized beliefs or to the complexes of his own character. This is verified by the fact that the only way man can know the character of God is through the character of man; that is to say, through human experiences. Through these mediums man learns of peace, love, mercy, kindness, justice, honor, dignity, humility, etc. But also through these mediums, he learns of hate, vengeance, pride, deceit, envy, selfishness, violence, etc. In due recognition thereof, he places the former in a category he calls "The Good" and the latter in a category he calls "Immoral or Evil." These shall hereafter be referred to as the "first' and "second" categories.

Now when man extends his thoughts in the direction of

God, he usually characterizes Him through the use also of a third category. This brings forth thoughts expressed as Power, Majesty, Eternal, All Mighty, Omniscient, Omnipotent and the like. Through this category he recognizes, and rightfully so, that there does exist in the universe a power, an intelligence, a plane of life, or a factor of awareness far greater than his own.

However, in his characterization of this power, he draws upon the first two categories and proceeds to recognize the nature of his god accordingly. In other words, he selects the properties therefrom which best comply with his own individual temperament and feelings. These he mixes together and, through the aid of the third category, projects them to cosmic dimensions. Thus he presumes, and even plans, to obtain supernatural approval of behavior that sometimes even his own conscience rejects.

The "Tribal gods" of the Old Testament and the "war god" of David were characterized through a mixture of the three categories for they are characterized as vengeful, jealous, and even merciless, as well as trustworthy, just, and kind. Here the natures of these gods are illustrated to be as inconsistent as the natures of men.

Today, however, the Jewish fathers are drawing more heavily upon the first category in their growing awareness of God. Many of them have rejected completely the influences of the second category.

Even though Jesus of Nazareth, as described in the "Covenant of Love," exemplified without reservation all the virtues of the first category, the somewhat outmoded doctrine of the Old Christian Church still binds Christians to the influences of the second category in its characterization of God.

It is inconsistent to the nature of the first category, as well as derogatory to the integrity of God, for one to suppose that He would have planned a means of human salvation which could not bear up under both rational analysis as well as ethical criticism.

When the Christian says that God gave His only begotten Son to be sacrificed, he obviously draws upon the second category in describing God, for he contradicts the prophets who insisted upon mercy instead of sacrifice.

A clearer and more equitable interpretation of the "Father and Son" relationship would go a long way towards removing from the divine heritage any taint of the second category. However, the more enlightened definition of the "Son-Father relationship," which presents the Son as the materialization of the Father, or as the Spirit of God which is in all men* accentuating itself in the person of Jesus, tends to free the Christian doctrine from the influences of the second category. Thus, one finds the means through which to retain a highly ethical definition of the purpose of Jesus without also intimidating one's own honor and self respect as a man. Human dignity at its best reflects the dignity of God. In accord therewith, the honorable man tends to reject the thought that "Jesus Christ died for his sins, that he might attain everlasting life." In rejecting this thought, however, he does not necessarily reject Jesus Christ as the expression of God. *On the contrary, he may be a more sincere follower of Christ than those who place the saving of their own souls before His suffering on the cross.*

The idea of faith alone as the means of salvation resulted through the formulations of the Pauline doctrine by the early Roman Church. Whether this doctrine is from the pen of Paul is disputable. Scholars more or less agree that the original epistles were not all written by Paul and that much in his original letters have not come down to us unaltered.

With all due respect for the integrity of Paul, he was not one of the Twelve Apostles. To these only did Jesus unveil the inner secrets. Paul never knew Jesus in life. He never

* "I said ye are gods, The Kingdom of God is within."

walked and prayed with Him as he went from place to place, teaching the word of God.

On the other hand, we have the word of James which, in no small terms opposes the Pauline doctrine of "faith alone." The epistle of James is traditionally accepted as coming directly from James, the Lord's brother, copying and editing, notwithstanding.

Which are we to believe, then, as being closer to the doctrine of the Master Himself: Paul, the Pharisee, who never knew Jesus, or James, the Lord's own brother? Paul is reported as writing to the Romans: "And if by grace, then is it no more works: otherwise grace is no more grace: But if it be of works, then is it no more grace, otherwise work is no more work." One might take this to mean that faith and works mix like oil and water. Again, the epistle reads: "Moses writes that he who practices righteousness based on the law (the Decalogues) shall live by it. But the right answer based on faith says, 'Do not say in your heart, who will ascend to heaven?'" (Rom. 10: 5-6) This means: It is needless, even hopeless, to base your salvation upon the kind, merciful, just, and understanding voice that speaks within you. Base it rather, upon the faith that, even though your heart be as hard as stone, you will be saved if you confess with your lips and believe that God raised the Lord Jesus Christ from the dead.

As a contradiction of this doctrine an early century evangelist wrote: "They who never seek out the truth but only 'believe' are involved in the affairs of the heathen." (11-Hermas X:3)

However, as was suggested before: "Paul's teachings about faith and works had become greatly garbled" (Harpers Bible Dictionary), for Paul also demanded an active faith that showed itself in deeds. (Rom. 2: 13)

James, the Lord's brother, in the epistle attributed to him, says, "But wilt thou know, O vain man, that faith without works is dead? Be doers of the word, and not hearers only, deceiving yourselves. But he who looks into the perfect law, the law of liberty,** and perseveres, being no hearer that forgets, but a doer that acts, he shall be blessed in his doing. To whoever keeps the whole law, but fails in one point, has become guilty of all of it. For he who said, 'Do not commit adultery,' said also, 'Do not kill.' If you do not commit adultery but do kill,* you have become a transgressor of the law. So speak and so act as do those who are to be judged under the law of liberty. For judgment is without mercy to one who has shown no mercy; yet mercy triumphs over judgment.

"What doth it profit, my brethren, though a man say he hath faith, (believes that God raised the Lord Jesus from the dead) and have not works? Can faith save him? Yea, A man may say, 'Thou hast faith, and I have works: shew me my faith *by my works*. Who is wise and understanding among you? *By his good life* let him show his works in the meekness of wisdom: for the wisdom from above is first pure, then peaceable, gentle, open to reason, full of mercy and good fruits, without insincerity. And the harvest of righteousness is sown in peace by those who make peace."

Thus, do we have the word of the epistle of James, which was written before the epistle of Paul and before the canonized gospels. Its priority of authority therefore can hardly be doubted. Our present canonized Matthew, according to the early Church Fathers, was taken from an original Aramaic Gospel used by the "Nazarenes." The authenticity of the epistle of James is here again verified, for its remarkable similarity to Matthew reveals that it also harmonized with the original Aramaic gospel of Matthew, or the gospel of the Hebrews, used by those first Jewish Christians under the direction of the Old Apostles.

---

* One is reminded here again of God's word through the voice of His prophet Isaiah: "He who kills an ox is as if he kills a man."
** The perfect law, the law of liberty, stresses the freedom of man: a virtue he cannot possibly possess if both his moral honor and spiritual dignity be intimidated by accepting a gift of great value at the expense of the unmerciful suffering and death of his best friend.

Let the Christian candidate not be deluded then by any doctrine of salvation which compromises the epistle of James, the first authority on the way and the means as demonstrated through the spirit and works of Jesus Christ.

When James, in stressing the "criteria of works," said, "By his good life let him show his works," he emphasized the necessity of taking on, or the adapting of one's own way of life to, the way of life exemplified by Jesus, thereby providing the "necessary works" to insure the success of faith.

"Christ committed no sin, no guile was found on His lips. When He was reviled He did not revile in return: when He suffered He did not threaten, leaving you an example, that you should follow in His steps." (Peter 3: 21-23)

Here Peter also illustrates that acceptance of Jesus Christ involves a great deal more than the "confession of the mouth or a belief in the heart" as set forth in Romans 10:9. His thought is clear: The mere acknowledgment of the belief that Jesus died for one's sins is insufficient.

Jesus Christ, as the Spirit of God in man, was inspired that man might know the true character of the Eternal Being he worshipped. Thus, God offered a means through which man might save himself. In Jesus, God supplied the ideal example of perfect man. In Him He put the words, "Be like Me, for even as your Father in Heaven is perfect, you also can be perfect, for in Me doth He dwell even as He may dwell in you." Perfect and complete salvation is therefore in the paralleling of one's spiritual being with the Being of God. God, being Himself immortal, the bringing into harmony of the human spirit with the Spirit of God closes the circle, and everlasting life is assured.

Thus, in both the life and death of the immortalized Jesus, was represented the complete way to human salvation. One without the other is incomplete, for in the life is demonstrated the "works:" that is to say, love, mercy, humility, charity, honor, justice and everything of good report; while, in the death or rather in the resurrection, is the evidence that God concluded His lesson to mankind with a spiritual phenomenon demonstrating the completion of a sincere and truly earned salvation. As the Spirit of God in Jesus Christ exemplified a way of life, He also demonstrated in the resurrection the reward of that way of life. Again, in the living of the life, one witnesses the way, and in the resurrection, one witnesses the fruit of the way.

In this doctrine the responsibility for the merciless death of Jesus is separate and apart from the structure of salvation. The pure love and kindness of God remains unchallenged by human compromise, and the choice and manner of the death of Jesus becomes an earthly instead of a heavenly responsibility.

It was the human Jesus who chose to die that man in his remorse would seek atonement through resolving to give up his evil ways and follow in the ways of God. In so doing, the evil dies and the good begins a new life. Thus, is man born again as a child of God. Here again, the resurrection finds fulfillment through the works of man as exemplified by and through the works of Jesus. "I am the door; through Me do you find eternal life." When Jesus said, "I am the door," he did not mean "my death is the door." The words "I am" represent the individuality and the character of actual Being. It describes a timeless property: one that transcends all equivocations or contingencies involving death. The words, "I am the door," cannot mean other than *through my character, or through my way of life do you enter into the kingdom.*

"In this kind of faith no promises of reward are necessary. It is only necessary to understand that salvation from inevitable destruction lies in living a common life according to the Master's will. Whoever understands that, will not seek for confirmation but will save himself without exhortation.

"To the Disciples' request for a confirmation of their faith Christ says: 'When a workman returns from the field, his Master does not at once tell him to have dinner, but tells him to stall the cattle and serve him, and only then will the workman sit down to table and have dinner.' The workman does all this without considering himself ill-used, and does not boast or demand gratitude or reward, but knows that so it should be, and that he is but doing what is needful: that this is a necessary condition both of the service and of the true welfare of his life. This is the faith Christ teaches." [1]

According to the doctrine of the Covenant of Love, God in His great love and understanding realized that man had wandered far from the paths of righteousness; that even his heart had lost its awareness of the divine nature. In His infinite pity and concern. He caused His prophets to instruct and to reveal to them the love of the Heavenly Father for all His creation; but to little avail. The time had come therefore, for God to reveal His true nature so that man might learn firsthand the means through which he could rise above the sinful life that binds his spirit to the dark regions of despair.

The words on the first page of this chapter, "The only way man can know the character of God is through the character of man," seems to be in accord with the purpose of Jesus. "The word was made flesh to dwell among us." (John 1:14) Or, the divine Spirit materialized before the world so man might know the true character of his God. Here one becomes aware of the prime purpose of the coming of Jesus Christ. All the teachings and demonstrations pertaining to His life and death are necessarily contingent to this divine revelation. Thus, was man to know firsthand the God of peace instead of war; of love, mercy, and forgiveness instead of vengeance; of humble dignity instead of vanity and pretense; of humane kindness instead of harm, hurt or abuse; of moral righteousness and ethical judgment instead of compromise and inconsistency; of temperance and self-respect instead of greed and self-indulgence; of liberation instead of slavery; of hope instead of despair; and last but not least, of life instead of death.

In the life of Jesus came the great teachings of love, **mercy, peace, justice,** the brotherhood of **man** and **the** Fatherhood of God.

Through Him spoke the Divine Voice pleading for mercy instead of the cruel practice of animal sacrifice. Hundreds of times had the prophets and other holy men pleaded as it were of the voice of God to abrogate the sacrifice. Over twenty times in the Holy Scriptures alone it is inclusively written that man should kill neither his fellow man nor his fellow creature; neither should he feast upon their flesh (compromises of the priestly code and interpolations of false scribes notwithstanding).

"I have come to fulfill the prophets" said Jesus: (Matt. 5:17) and fulfill He did. Through the sacrifice of his own flesh and blood He demonstrated for all time to come God's opposition of the temple sacrifice, and the merciless practice of slaying His gentle creatures to satisfy the indulgence of men.

"According to John, the last supper took place on the evening before the Passover, and the crucifixion on the 14th of Nisan, the day of preparation while the paschal lambs were being killed for the Passover meal after sunset."* (Harpers Bible Dict. p. 343.) Thus, the dramatic denunciation of the temple sacrifice and the following crucifixion can be recognized chronologically as the sequences of a carefully laid plan.

In this doctrine, however, the death of Jesus has an ethical as well as a religious significance. As to the gospel of "death and resurrection," Jesus could have died or been put to death in one of a thousand other ways without altering the significance of the orthodox concept of salvation. However, in bringing about His own crucifixion through His merciful act of opposing the temple sacrifice, Jesus demonstrated the principle of "Redemption through Compassion." This gave an ethical meaning to His death which extended to cosmic proportions: that is, to the recognition of a universal law of love.

"Had the interpretation of the Life, the Fall, and the Redemption given by the Master been understood by Paul and those who followed Him, and had the churches been also

* See date of Crucifixion p. 416.

taught the same, there would have been a very different order of religious expression in the West today. The churches would have been truly Christian, for they would have understood Jesushood and Christhood; their message would have brought redeemed life into beautiful individual and social manifestation, for it would have taught a real redemption, and not a mythical one which after eighteen centuries, has left the West as pagan as it was in the last days of the Roman Empire." [2]

The immortal Richard Wagner wrote: "Among the poorest and most distant from the world appeared the Saviour, no more to teach redemption's path by precept, but example; His own flesh and blood He gave as last and highest expiation for all the sin of outpoured blood and slaughtered flesh." * [3]

No other point in the whole ethical system of Jesus supports so emphatically the fourth gospels doctrine of the Cosmic Christ as does His demands for mercy instead of the sacrifice of the paschal lambs. In fact, the idea of a Cosmic Christ must necessarily be based on an all inclusive love and mercy for all creatures and for life upon every planet of God's universe.

"Only a complete ethic has mystical significance. An ethical system which is concerned only with the attitude of man to his fellow man has no relationship with the universe." (Albert Schweitzer)

In His denunciation of the temple sacrifice, Jesus demonstrated that all creatures, even as man, await the salvation of God: "That no creature shall harm or destroy upon all my holy mountain, for the earth shall be filled with the knowledge of the Lord." (Isaiah)

Even as Isaiah had prophesied the true character of the Lord, so likewise must have been his full and complete nature. Therefore even as the prophetic vision was realized in Jesus Christ so also must it be realized in the heart of every man. To be "born again" is in consequence a realization

---

* Wagner shaped the legend of Parsifal's rise to kingship of the Holy Grail into a drama of *Redemption through Compassion*.

within one's own heart of the prophetic vision being brought to pass. It is to bring to witness one's own soul in harmony with the pure Spirit of Divinity instead of with a god-head pledged to concur with human customs and practices.

Thus in consequence the "second coming of Christ is realized as a rebirth within the individual consciousness of the Christ Spirit."

The Agony in the Garden

My soul is exceedingly sorrowful even unto death. (Matt. 26:8) The agony in the garden is here explained as the gathering together of all the pain and suffering in the world of life into the sorrowing heart of Jesus. Here Jesus is exemplified as feeling in an objective sense all the sufferings and despairs of men, and all the pitiful inner cries of the dumb creatures of God's kingdom. These being the inevitable result of violence, greed or error, they represent, in effect, the mistakes, the sins and the evils of men which Jesus carried to the cross.

The agony in the Garden demonstrates a divine principle whereby all life may be delivered from harm, hurt or abuse. The subjective awareness of pain, suffering and sorrow is a divine means of informing one that his fellow men, yea, even his fellow creatures, also feel pain, suffering and sorrow. This is a means of the "God within," of the "Christ consciousness," through which one becomes aware of feeling pain in an objective sense. Only when mankind recognizes this divine informant will he "break the bow and the sword and the battle out of the earth and make all the fowls of the heavens and the beasts of the field to lie down safely." (Hos. 2: 18)

In the crucifixion, Jesus carries in His heart all the sufferings of the world and pours them out through His own tortured flesh upon the cross in a soul stirring exposure of the sins of men.

Through this divine demonstration man is to become aware of his sinful ways. His heart is to be filled with remorse for all the sufferings he has caused and for which

Christ died. Thus does he seek atonement through accepting the uncompromised Spirit of Jesus Christ as the awakening within his own heart of love, peace, honor, dignity, and compassionate understanding towards all of God's creation.

In the death is the sacrificing (or the dedication) of one's self to the alleviation of pain and suffering and to the improvement of the moral and ethical relationships of life.

Thus, does one take on the Christ consciousness and become, even as the Son of Man, a child of God.

The Resurrection

In the resurrection is revealed the realization of the way to eternal life, or eventual attainment of the sublime plane of spiritual Oneness with the Father.

It symbolizes the fulfillment or compensation of a salvation, truly, honorably, and consistently earned. It is the final and complete sequence of a plan whereby each step is of equal importance to its successful conclusion; the Cosmic Christ character is the seed, the human Christ behavior is the blossom, and the Spiritual Christ resurrection is the fruit thereof. Thus, the Trinity becomes evident as "the means," "the way," and "the fulfillment."

The seed = the "means," the cause or, The Father.

The blossom = the way, the life or The Son.

The fruit = the "resurrection," or, the fulfillment in The Holy Spirit.

The logic of this system of salvation is that the fruit is a natural consequence of the seed and the blossom. If this were not so, all natural laws or all the principles or ordinances of God would be invalid.

Here, also, the law of liberty, referred to in the epistle of James, is uncompromised, and a follower of Jesus Christ retains his honor and dignity as a human being.

Finally, the Holy Spirit retains His Integrity as an equitable designer and planner of all things.

Thus is concluded the Doctrine of The Convenant of Love.

Chapter 3

The Doctrine of the Covenant of Love

1 Leo Tolstoy, Vol. 11, *A Confession*. (Oxford University Press, London—Humphrey—Milford)

2 Rev. J. Todd Ferrier, *The Logia or Sayings of the Master*. (Order of the Cross, 10 De Vere Gardens, Kensington, London)

3 From *The Essays of Richard Wagner*, (published by the Millennium Guild, N. Y.)

Chapter Four

CONCLUSION

And The Ethics of Reverence for Life

In conclusion, I humbly contribute the production of this book to the welfare of Christianity. May it stimulate a more responsible recognition of the "Christ example" in the hearts of those who praise his name.

My entire thought and efforts have been dedicated to the challenging task of recovering the lost Jesus of history: to strip him of the grave clothes of dogma and present his pure simple godliness of character before the bar of modern day judgment.

Will he again be stripped with the stinging lash of prejudiced tongues, and nailed to a rack constructed out of the worm wood of a dying world conscience? Will He be crucified even by those who call His name or will He be taken by the hand and invited to sit down and eat of our innocent table? Let us hope that He may, this time, survive his coming, i.e., survive it in the hearts of men as the uncompromised spirit of love, mercy and justice towards all of God's creation.

The Christian whose security of faith continges upon the extraordinary nature of Jesus should be filled with joy after reviewing the Convenant of Love doctrine of the humane Christ, for the "missing link" which for centuries has separated, ethically, the historical Jesus from the "Cosmic Christ" of the gospel of John has now been restored.

Also with the recovery of the humane Christ came the revealing, for the first time, of an actual proof that the Bible does contain certain prerequisites necessary to the welfare of both body and spirit. Here again both Christian and Jew alike should rejoice, for they can now be assured that wherever the "greater good" is found in the Scriptures, here also is the "will of God."

For my own part, I feel sure that it was mainly through my awareness of the universality of love which extends the Golden Rule to all realms of life that I was inspired to seek out and to recover this humane addition to our present knowledge of the ethical system of Jesus.

But here it should be stressed that merely abstaining from eating the flesh of animals does not in itself provide the "key to heaven." While this is a necessary asset to the complete spiritual unfoldment of the human potential, other means, as spoken of in the Sermon on the Mount, cannot be overlooked.

Ethics has many facets. *The pure and the good have* many doors that must be passed through before one is privileged to stand in the "Presence." However, in the ethics of "Reverence for life," as taught by the Master and as practiced in our own time by the apostle of Lambarene, is to be found the means of opening many of the otherwise unyielding doors leading to the realms of the most high. It is appropriate, therefore, to conclude this book as it began, with thoughts pertaining to Schweitzer's ethic of Reverence for life.

* * * *

The behavior of the human race reflects the habits and customs it has adopted. If one is inclined to disapprove of the terrible consequences resulting from these behaviors, it might be well to realize, it is not the human sensitivities that are delinquent, but rather the many customs and conventions that have for centuries confused the ethical responsibilities man owes to the whole of life.

The allegory of the fall of man does not incriminate the heart and soul of the individual, but it does illustrate the evil of certain practices and customs which for ages have challenged the inherent love and dignity of the human family.

To be completely human is to be humane. Funk and Wag-nalls dictionary defines the word *humane* as "having or showing tenderness, kindness, and compassion." It also presents this all-inclusive description: "The humane man will not needlessly inflict pain upon the meanest thing that lives."

In order to begin to understand the deep ethical signifi-cance of this statement, let us approach it both subjective-ly and objectively.

In the realm of the subjective, we know through experi-ence that we feel pain and that it causes within us various degrees of suffering. In apprehension thereof, we strive to avoid that thing which might be of harm or hurt to us. Now, if we hold closely to this realization while at the same time allowing our subjectivity to expand or carry over into the objective realm of consciousness, we soon become aware that other creatures feel pain as we do and, like us, also strive to avoid that which might be of harm or hurt to *them*.

Along with the full realization of this truth the humane man begins to feel a sense of unity with the whole of creation. He no longer separates himself from the universe, but becomes one with it in consciousness and spirit even as the atomic substance of his body are one with it. In a unified whole, no creature is separate and apart from any other creature; all are proportionately related—in mind, flesh, and spirit.

Space, then, instead of separating, binds all matter, energy, and their effects into a unified whole—a whole wherein the spirit of God embraces the harmony and order of natural law, the will to live of every creature, and the consciousness of every man.

Man is an individual, not as unique from other creatures, but rather, as an individual link in a chain of individuals making up the whole of life, the whole of God's kingdom.

The human mind—that is, the psychophysical being of man—parallels in its acquired nature all the mental or mind-like properties characteristic of every living thing upon this earth.

I am a living creature of a living world, in a living universe. The mind through which I think, recognize injustice, pain, sorrow, joy, and love, is of the same property through which you too recognize these things. It is also the same means, or same sense of awareness, through which every other creature feels pain and sorrow—loves, and wills to live.

Consideration for the rights and privileges of living things is "Reverence for Life." It is the unselfish respect for the great mysterious force we call *creation*. Reverence for life is based on a fundamental awareness of the good— of mercy, justice, and love. It comprises the basic evidence, the unadulterated identification, of ethics in its most vital form.

This is beautifully illustrated in the life and works of Albert Schweitzer, the greatest spiritual force in the world today.

"Ethics are boundless in their domain and limitless in their demands," says Schweitzer. They are concerned with all living things that come within our sphere. Only a complete ethic has mystical significance. An ethical system which is only concerned with the attitude of man to his fellowman and to his society cannot really be in harmony with a world view. It has no relationship with the universe.* To found an ethical world-view on ethics which are concerned only with our fellowman and human society is logically an impossibility. It is the fault of too narrow a conception of ethics that thought has so far been unable to present an ethical world-view in a way that carries conviction.[1]

"The important thing is that the truly religious or the sincerely ethical man can not avoid the knowledge that all life is sacred. "What we call love is in its essence reverence for life. All material and spiritual values are values

* Note reference to the Cosmic Christ, p. 8.

only in so far as they serve the maintenance of life at its highest level and the furtherance of life. A man is really ethical only when he obeys the constraint laid on him to help all life which he is able to succor, and when he goes out of his way to avoid injuring anything living."[2]

"However, in the practical application of the principle of Reverence for Life, ethical man is called upon from day to day, almost hour to hour, to exercise intelligence and discrimination. He finds himself the inhabitant of a world which is not ethical, which is utterly indifferent to ethics. No sooner do creative and life-conserving energies arise than destructive and death-dealing forces are at work among them."[3]

"The world offers us the horrible drama of will-to-live divided against itself," says Schweitzer. "One existence holds its own at the cost of another: one destroys the other."[4]

But when we speak of the will-to-live being divided against itself we assume nature herself to be guilty of unethical practice. How then can one adopt a reverential attitude towards a system which, characteristically, appears to be undeserving of homage? Certainly any form of existence which makes "murder" a necessity deserves only the meanest of respect.

While this point of view bears witness to the way of life of the cruel, merciless predators of the animal world, it seems to lose its sting when applied to the innocent peace loving victims of the horrible drama of blood.

Here the warmhearted side of human nature responds to the terrible injustice of it all and longs for understanding.

"As an ethical being," says Schweitzer, "man strives to escape whenever possible from the horrible law of being obliged to live at the cost of other life, and as one who has become enlightened and merciful to put a stop to this disunion of the will-to-live so far as the influence of his own existence reaches. He thirsts to be permitted to preserve his humanity and to be able to bring to other existences release from suffering."⁵

Thus the truly humane man takes cognizance of the evil within the will-to-live and strives to recover his true manhood.

"Admitting the fact of universal moral evil and the fall of man, ethical mysticism goes back to a prior state of grace from which man fell and reaffirms his original righteousness. Sin is not natural or indigenous to man. it is unnatural. What is called the "supernatural" is really the most truly natural."⁶

However, if sin is not natural to man it is also unnatural to the lesser creatures, in which case the evil in the whole of the will-to-live is not natural but rather "pseudonatural." In consequence, the truly natural is the ethical or the actual prototype of the "supernatural," in which case God and nature are one and the same.

Here the dualism of God and nature is both dissolved and retained as a unity to identify the "good" or the ethical as opposed to the evil tendencies within and throughout the whole of the will-to-live.

But suppose we test the worth of this hypothesis. For instance, along with and following Darwin's theory of natural selection came the doctrine of "survival of the fittest." Life in its struggle to exist was thought to be primarily subjective to this ruthless prerogative. Accordingly only those characters who had acquired the necessary means were fit to survive. In keeping with this doctrine the entire process of evolution continged upon the success of life in competition with life.

However, it seems that if this had been the only means available to insure the existence of life on this planet it would still be somewhere in the primordial slime struggling to discover the great secret leading to the most phenomenal of all miracles: the force capable of combining with space and time to change a tiny speck of protoplasm into a creature with the potential of a god.

It can therefore be assumed that the doctrine of "survival of the fittest," while stressing an obvious need, can only refer to a part, or to one side of the great process of organic evolution: a side which is necessarily the least effective to the success of life upon this earth. In the first place, the cold ruthless severity contained in the doctrine of "survival of the fittest" is void of even the slightest potential favorable to the development of ethics.

It is quite obvious, therefore, that another more fruitful tendency was destined to assert itself within the will-to-live. Here one may contemplate a point of reference on the tree of life where, to quote Schweitzer, "the will-to-live is divided against itself."

Contrary to the "devil take the hindmost" doctrine of ruthless competition, this other more constructive tendency is not indifferent to the rudiments of cooperation. It seeks accord with its environment and responds to the urgency of growth and development, not alone to effect a mere ephemeral success but rather as illustrating a progressive trend towards a greater more permanent goal: i.e., a point of perfection in space time.

Thus one may recognize a duality of purpose in the will-to-live, both of which, while being opposed to each other, must necessarily cooperate in order to accomplish either or both a temporal and a more permanent objective.

However, as both these tendencies are indigenous to living things they may be considered as representative of two separate conditions of existence: i.e., (a) the cooperative, progressive goal seeking characteristic which points towards perfection, and (b) the ruthless self-centered survival at any cost characteristic which points towards inevitable extinction.

It is clear which of these contains the ethical or constructive side of life and which the evil or destructive: which favors cooperation with, understanding of, and love for, another living being and which leans toward the exploitation of another life for its own gain.

Thus, if what is called supernatural is really the most truly natural and what is called "sin" or evil is unnatural then (a) is actually the truly natural and (b) is the unnatural or "pseudo-natural." The former therefore, is in perfect accord with the will of God in the will-to-live.

In consequence, one may describe the horrible drama of the will-to-live divided against itself as a war between (a) the creative, the organizing, and the cooperational will in nature and (b) the self-centered "pseudo-natural" urgencies of the animal's chosen way of life.

It is due to the former or (a) that life upon this planet has not only survived the urgencies of ruthless competition but has in the image of man attained the potential of a god.

The "cosmic" or the "nature will" in the will-to-live is the genius of creation, the catalyst of order, the perfector of cooperation and the incentive of the will-to-love. "The eternal Spirit meets us in nature as mysterious creative power," says Schweitzer. "In the will-to-live we experience it within us as volition which is both world-and life-affirming and ethical."[7] Thus one must admit that the will-to-live, even though it is, in varying degrees, divided against itself, deserves all the consideration and reverence that the higher endowments of mind are capable of extending.

"We are all part of everything living," continues Schweitzer. "We are born of other lives; we possess the capacities to bring still other lives into existence. In the same way if we look into a microscope we see cell producing cell. So nature compels us to recognize the fact of mutual dependence, each life necessarily helping the other lives which are linked with it. In the very fibres of our being, we bear within ourselves the fact of the solidarity of life. Our recognition of it expands with thought. Seeing its presence in ourselves, we realize how closely we are linked with others of our kind. We might stop here, but we cannot. Life demands that we see through to the solidarity of all life which we can in any degree recognize as having some similarity to the life that is in us."[8]

"All life in the world can be placed on a graduated scale, which extends from the most simple to the most complex. Today man gives himself the place of the most complex. This does not necessarily show that his life is the most valuable. On the contrary, science has shown that man could never have developed his complex form without the structure of the one-celled life that can only be seen by the aid of the microscope. It is doubtful whether man could exist today if his world was not filled with this simple life. All life is inter-dependent. The man of today first exists in the physical world as a very simple one-celled organism. The complexities of man are rooted in the mysterious deterministic development of this single cell."[9]

Man has come a long way through many eons of time and many phases of development. The human organism is still as inclusively a part of the goal seeking process of evolution as it was that momentous day it first stood erect on two feet. The development of the apprehensive or the "psychic" properties of living things has from the advent of the primordial organism progressed along with and somewhat in advance of the development of physical form. The more intense was the complexity of the "psychic know how" in living things the more successful became the adaptability of their physical structure.

What appears so obvious to us as the evolution of physical form might more truly be described as merely the effect or results of a "psychic know how"; i.e., a psycho-determined physical evolution. The will-to-live is witness to its own emergence as a psycho-physical entity. Without the will-to-live as the incentive, no electro-chemical synthesis of vital ingredients could ever have organized to support a tree of life upon this planet.

The will-to-live might be described as an exposition of a "psychic nature" wherein all organisms are individuals each struggling for security and each striving in accord with the measure of its volition to perfect itself.

This is ethical metaphysics brought into focus with knowledge science has become increasingly cognizant of.

In spite of the apparent apathy in the moral and spiritual attitude of modern man, history clearly indicates that human nature is becoming more ethical and more humane in behavior.

This is "natural selection" operating in the all embracing developmental category. Certainly the trend towards perfection which we, in our limited means observe more approvingly in the physical evolution of living forms must necessarily be all inclusive. Consequently it appears quite proper to propose that selection in nature has many phases one of which must be towards the ethical. Here it might be pointed out that those creatures who have consistently applied the doctrine of survival of the fittest to their way of life are gradually being overcome by a sort of selection which opposes the horrible drama of blood. The most voracious of all creatures, the giant reptiles, most of which were flesh eaters, have long since become extinct. Very few are the descendants today of the early peoples in various parts of the world who practiced cannibalism. Most of the great nations of American Indians who depended almost exclusively upon the hunt for sustenance are no longer with us. Gradually the great army of carnivores, mountain lions, badgers, wolves, coyotes, bears, birds of prey, etc. are dwindling in numbers and will soon become extinct. These are facts that can not be denied even though various arguments can be offered to explain them. These trends toward extinction are as much part of natural selection as were the many simple life forms which were discarded as unfit for the perfecting of evolution. They are in direct relation to the first law of organic nature which says that carnivorism is unalterably opposed to life as we know it. Animal life never could have been made possible upon this earth under a law that required each creature to eat its neighbor in order to survive. Such a law would be hopelessly inoperable for it would be equivalent to demanding that a snake swallow its own tail and consume itself for food.

This is the fallacy that underlines the voracious tendencies of "survival of the fittest" which has in the past and which will continue to play a losing part in life's courageous struggle to seek perfection.

Man, as a participant in the evolution of life, has taken over legally or illegally a large measure of control in nature. He has now reached a most precarious position on the great tree of life: his fruit can either ripen with enduring seed or it can fall to the ground in rot. Through his own choice he can continue on the road to extinction along with the other creatures who adhered too tenaciously to the fallacy of "survival of the fittest" or he can lend an ear to Albert Schweitzer's challenge to civilization, thereby insuring the survival, both of his own will-to-live and the will-to-live of all other life upon this planet. Let us hope that the courageous struggle within the will-to-live to seek perfection, rather than destruction, will prevail.

Reverence for life is therefore reverence for this courageous tendency within the will-to-live. It is a soul gratifying respect for the mysterious source which makes life possible. It is the realization that other creatures have certain rights and that they also have obligations and responsibilities, each relative to their own plane, phase, or methods of living, whether they be our kind of people or other kinds of people; or whether they be creatures that dwell in a palace, a mud hut, a nest of grass and clay, or a hole in the ground.

Life is a great system which, to the universe, is eternal or immortal. Man, as an ethical member of this system, is obliged to obey two basic rules: the first, the necessity of *living off of* lower forms of life, and the second, an obligation to *live for*, higher forms of life. One is a physical necessity and the other is a spiritual responsibility. A dividing point between the first and the second, or, between the lower and the higher planes of life—becomes immediately self evident through one's common awareness of pain. In consequence, harm, hurt, and suffering have an ethical significance through enabling the self to become aware of the same feelings in other creatures. Thus the *living for* in the promotion of life and in the will to spare, is a spirit-edifying responsibility, while the *living off of* is to one's immediate means of knowing, merely a physical necessity.

Here are presented the rudiments of a universal approach to ethics: to the veneration of a merciful God through a sincere reverence for all that lives.

Beginning in the lower rounds of life as consideration, and extending to the higher rounds of life as mercy and compassion, one discovers the true, pure and uncompromised significance of the word LOVE. Any religious philosophical or ethical system which excludes these provisions from its doctrine is in consequence guilty of an affront to the Author of Love.

"All deep philosophy, and all deep religion," says Schweitzer, "are ultimately a struggle for ethical mysticism and mystical ethics. Ethics are responsibility without limit towards all that lives." "Reverence for life engenders a new-found sensitivity which to conventional morality may well appear extravagant. All life is sacred to him. By going out of our way to rescue life, however apparently insignificant, he is paying a debt of honor to the Author of life, including his own." [10] "In this becoming one with all life he realizes the active becoming one with the primal Source of Being to which this life belongs."[11]

Religious dogmas can no longer survive the skepticism of thinking man without the support of a God whose very nature is opposed to violence in any form whatsoever. If religious teachers actually believe in a God of peace and loving kindness, a truly merciful creator, then they must at long last show proof of such belief in their way of life by being followers instead of pretenders.

Traditional religion is at the crossroads: it can either advance as a strong humanely ethical movement exhibiting a sincere desire to cooperate in its fullest capacity with a God of peace and loving kindness, or, it can lose its integrity as a force for the good in obedience to the vindictive blood letting God of Bible lore.

Only a soul searching motivation stimulated by a realistic approach to the ethics of "Reverence for Life" can save western religion from a mammonish expansion to spiritual oblivion.

The more extensively a religion expands its ethical foun dation the greater love will its structure support and the higher will its aspirations reach towards God.

As long as the various religions, both traditional and liberal, resist the abolition of the centuries old heathen or pagan custom of animal sacrifice, so long will they also resist the only love that can insure peace for all that lives.

So long as men prefer to dwell in the shadow of the shambles, so long, also will they fail to comprehend the meaning of an absolute ethic: for the lower a man carries his love, the higher he carries his ethics: and the higher a man carries his ethics the nearer he is to his God.

Conclusion

1   Charles R. Joy, *Albert Schweitzer, An Anthology*. Adam and Charles Black, London. Beacon Press, Boston.

2
4
5
8
11

3   Rev. George Seaver, *Albert Schweitzer, The Man and His Mind*, Harper & Brothers, N. Y.

6

7   Albert Schweitzer, *Civilization and Ethics*. Adam and Charles Black, London.

9   Georgia Ann Todd, *Essay on the Challenge of Albert Schweitzer*. Schweitzer Educational Foundation contest. Third place award January 14, 1960.

10 George Seaver, *Reverence for Life, an Interpretation*. Published by Friends of Albert Schweitzer, Dr. H. A. Jack, editor.

APPENDIX

The Healthiest of All

"The Bantic natives of South Africa who subsist on a shockingly 'insufficient' diet, last week were, by U.S. Medicine's admission 'men of mystery.' In spite of their meager meals, composed solely of cereals plus a few vegetables, the Bantic people appear to be the healthiest in the world.

"Physical endurance tests with what American nutritionists would call 'undernourished' Bantic boys and girls showed that 50 percent were in 'excellent' or 'superior' condition. Only about 5 percent of well-fed American children scored as high in similar tests.

"About 90 percent of the children were found to be free of dental caries whereas the reverse ratio is true of American children.

"The Bantic enjoys a low incidence of the serious diseases which, taken together, exact the highest toll of mortality from Western populations."[1]

High in the Himayalas, between Afghanistan and Tibet, in the mysterious land of Hunza, live a people who have long been declared to be the world's healthiest. The country's 25,000 inhabitants are taller and fairer of skin than their neighbors, and subsist almost entirely on fruits and nuts the year around.

Jean and Frank Shor—the latter now on the editorial staff of the National Geographic Magazine—made the trip to this little-known land several years ago.

During their stay Naar Shah, the Shor's guide, took them to his home and shared with them his family's simple fare. "We eat potatoes, some vegetables, and a little grain," he said, "but fruit and nuts are the most important."[2]

Frank Shor tells of the great physical endurance of these people compared with that of the other men (see National Geographic October 1953).

The Strength and Endurance of Vegetarians

One needs no reminder of the fact that the animals favored with the greatest strength, endurance and length of life are vegetarians.

Statistics indicate man is no exception to this rule.

According to our modern day reportings, two of the longest lived among men were vegetarian. Both of these men had attained almost a century and a half upon this earth.

"Even in view of their tremendous minority, vegetarians have in many instances demonstrated their superiority in the world of sports. Vegetarians are represented in national and international races winning the Berlin and Dresden walking match (125 m), the Carwardine Cup (100 m) and Dibble Shield (6 hours), cycling races (1901-1902), the Amateur Championship of England in racquets and in tennis (held by Mr. Eustace Miles for a series of years), the cycling championship of India (3 years), half mile running championship of Scotland (1896), world's amateur cycle records for all times from 4 hours to 13 hours, 100 miles championship Yorkshire Road Club." [3]

"Vegetarian athletes hold records and have achieved distinction in all kinds of athletics out of all proportion to their small numbers. They have been particularly successful where stamina and strength are necessary.

"Many have taken championships and broken records when well past middle age. At one time the Vegetarian Cycling & Athletic Club held as many as 40% of the national road records. Such achievements have exploded for all time the idea that flesh foods are necessary for physical fitness.

"Running

E. R. Voight

5 miles Olympic Championship (1908)

4 miles English Championship (1908 & 1909)

1 mile Open Championship (1910)

W. Kolemainen

Professional Marathon, 26 miles 385 yds. (1912) in World Record Time 2 hrs. 39⅕ scs. Holder of World Records for 25 and 26 miles.

H. Kolehmainen

Olympic Marathon (1920) in World Amateur Record Time. Holder of World Records for 5,000, 20,000 and 25,000 metres.

4 miles English Championship (1911) Olympic 8,000 metres Cross Country (1912).

E. Ouafi

Olympic Marathon (1928) ·

Paavo Nurmi

Olympic 10,000 metres and holder of many world records.

F. A. Knott

Broke Belgian 5,000 metres record (1908)

A. A. Robertson

Peak bagging record in Snowdonia (1952) lowering the record by 84 mins. (7 hrs. 24 mins.)

Eustace Thomas

At the age of 51 took the Lake District record in 1920.

"Walking

George Allen

Land's End to John o' Groats record averaging 60 miles per day (unbeaten since 1908)

S. Norwood

(At age of 66) walked 100 miles in
24 hour open path event.

G. R. J. Withers

London Railways 16 miles Championship held three years.

"Tennis

Eustace Miles

Won the English Championship 10
times. World Amateur Champion
at tennis and racquets and in 1900
won the American titles.

Hon. Neville Lytton

English Championships in 1911 and
1913.

Peter Freeman

Open Welsh Championship 1920,
Welsh local championship in 1920,
1921 and 1922. He also, with Sweet-
Escott, defeated Manual Alonso
(World Champion) and S. Slaquer.

"Boxing

Freddy Welsh

World's Light-Weight Championship
(not strictly vegetarian when not
in training).

Trevor King

Close to Australian Featherweight
title and extremely well developed.

"Wrestling

S. V. Bacon

Famous wrestler in addition to winning the Olympic Games Middleweight Championship in 1911, won
15 British National Championships, Lightweight, Welterweight,
Middleweight a n d Heavyweight

(an almost incredible perform-
ance). Four of the British won in
1924 were in his fortieth year and
he was one of five vegetarian
brothers who won wrestling championships, national and international too numerous to list.

"Weight Lifting

W. Harwood

For many years Heavy Weight Lifting Champion of the North of
England. Weighing only 168 lbs.
himself, he was one of the few
Englishmen who have lifted over
300 lbs. (1912)

"Swimming

Kenneth Wilson

Yorkshire One Mile Champion (1920)
at the age of 16. 500 yards Champion of Bradford. 100 yard Junior
Champion of Yorkshire (1919) in
record time.

Murray Rose

Young Australian 14 years old in
1953 hailed "as the best all rounder
Australia has ever produced."
Never beaten in school or State age
championships. Won two Gold
Medals at 1956 Olympic Games—
400 metres (Olympic Record), and
1500 metres free style.

Bill Pickering

Broke Channel Swim record in 1955
and plans at the time of writing to
be the first to swim both ways non-
stop.

"Cycling

Mr. Henry Light, who was Captain for 20 years of the Vegetarian Cycling and Athletic Club, made the following selection from hundreds of cycling achievements (in World Records & Championships by Vegetarian Athletes published by The Vegetarian Society in 1921)

F. H. Grubb broke the following unpaced out and home World's Road Records: 50 mls. in 2 hrs. 17 mins. 38 secs.; 100 miles in 4 hrs. 43 mins. 33 secs.; and 220½ miles in 12 hours. He also holds the English Unpaced Path Record for 1 hour, of 24 miles 1546 yards; and the London to Brighton and Back record of 104¾ miles in 5 hrs. 9 mins. 41 secs.— the most prized and hottest contested road record in the kingdom.

G. A. Olley won Tandem-paced Path Records from 6 hrs. to 12 hrs. (154 to 277 miles). Also the 1 mile and the 4 mile Unpaced Path Records (standing start) in 2 mins. 7⅘ secs., and 1 min. 34⅕ secs. respectively; and was England's Representative at the World's Championships at Copenhagen." [4]

*   *   *

"London March 20—A diet of vegetables and raw fruit is more nourishing to children than beefsteaks and dumplings, a woman physician reported.

"She serves two children's homes in London in which one or the other diet is used.

"Children at the home where the vegetable-fruit diet is eaten are well and have sound teeth and clear skins, the report said. But the children at the second home are frequently sick." [5]

Statistics today reveal that abstainers actually are a better insurance risk than meat eaters.

The Albert E. Priest & Co., Ltd. of London in co-operation with two other insurance companies are providing facilities whereby members of the various vegetarian bodies can obtain specially favorable rates of premium for all forms of insurance contracts.*

* From a letter addressed to the author Nov. 5, 1959 by the Priest Co. Ltd.

Need those who have been influenced by the hackneyed "animal protein" ideas of "Nineteenth Century medicine men," any longer bow to the propaganda of the meat institute.

Long life, cleanliness of body and majesty of spirit are indeed the products of one's power of choice, or, if you will, one's obedience to the "will of God."

Conscience as the Intermediary
Between the Ego and the
Spirit of God

There is an innate sense of right and wrong centered deep in the soul of every man. This is the "God within" striving through what is called "conscience" to lead man in the paths of love and peace. Conscience is a means of reminding the self that it is not being fair to the God within. Through the reprimands of conscience the ego takes on a feeling of guilt which generally leads to its submission to the inner sense of right and wrong or the "God within." A clear example of this process at work may be found in the following news item:

"Burbank, Calif. — The sizzling lamb chops which the Warner Bros. Commissary delivered to "The Burning Hills" for lunch while the troupe was locationing at the Warner Ranch were tasty and good, but they went untouched.

"It just so happened that all morning the company had been working with a flock of sheep for scenes in the Cinema Scope Warner-Color outside drama.

"Stars Tab Hunter and Natalie Wood, along with other members of the cast, and crew, took one look at the chops and at the nearby bleating sheep and immediately lost their appetites." [6]

The Greats of the Human Family

"Those who are inclined to think that vegetarianism is only practiced by a few cranks may be interested to know that it has been supported by such great moral and spiritual reformers as Jesus, Buddha, Confucius, Pythagoras, Philolaus, Apollinares of Tanya, Socrates, Plato, Empedokles, Asoka, Ovid, Diogenes, Porphyry, Iamblicus, Seneca, Plutarch, Musonius, Plotinus, Leonardo Da Vinci—all master spirits, men of giant intellects and divine souls, who sang and laboured to redeem their people from inhumane feeding and living, and lift them onto the plane of Celestial Being. Theirs was an inspiration worthy of the Christian teaching and ideal.

"And in addition to these great names there were many others to whom we cannot even make the slightest reference—a great army of Theologians, Philosophers, Historians, and Poets who have for physical, humane or moral reasons been abstainers from flesh foods. And if the writers quoted seem in the dim past of history, we have nearer our own times such notable thinkers and writers as Thomson, John Milton, Pope, Benjamin Franklin, Sir Isaac Newton, Swedenborg, Goldsmith, Paley, Shelley, John Wesley, Locke, Voltaire, Gleizes, Michelet, Struve, Rousseau, Schopenhauer, Newman, Richard Wagner, Tolstoy, Darwin, Gandhi, Booth, Thoreau and George Bernard Shaw. These are but a few of the many familiar names of men who were constrained to consider the rights of the sub-human races, and to abstain from having them killed for food." [7] Nor should one overlook the great women who have more or less devoted their lives to the moral and spiritual refining of humanity. To name a few: St. Theresa, Anna Kingsford, Emeral Freshel, Mary Ellen White, Dr. Annie Besant, Ella Wheeler Wilcox, the Duchess of Hamilton, Margaret Ford, Lindaf Hagerby, Mme. Blavatsky, Lotta Crabtree, Minnie Maddern Fiske, Pegeen Fitzgerald, Mary Kemmis, Florence Barker, Gloria Gasque, and many others. It also might be well to point out that Mary Baker Eddy, discoverer and founder of Christian Science, let it be known to her followers that in their higher illumination all gross attachments to a carnal existence would in consequence become remote. "The individuality created by God is not carnivorous, . . .

All of God's creatures moving in the harmony of science, are harmless, useful, indestructive. Tenderness accompanies all the might imparted by Spirit." [8]

"It is said that in nature everything preys upon something else and so man cannot be expected to do otherwise. This argument is absurd, because if we are to take nature as the guide to all our conduct we shall end by practicing cannibalism, rape and promiscuity of the sexes. For the purpose of discovering the right kind of conduct the 'proper study of mankind is man' and, we must add, not man as he is but as he was meant to be—a Godlike being." [9]

The Date of the Crucifixion

"St. John's Gospel distinctly implies that the Passover feast had not yet taken place and thus makes the crucifixion fall on the 14th. Early Christians are unanimous on this side; either the 14th is mentioned, or the crucifixion is made the antitype of the slaughter of the paschal lamb (and the Resurrection of the first fruits), in the following authorities anterior to A.D. 235: St. Paul, I Cor. V.7, XV, 20; Quartodecimans of Asia Minor, who observed the Christian Pascha on the "14th," no matter on what day of the week it fell: Claudius Appollinaris, Clement of Alexandria, Hippolytus, all three quoted in the *Paschal Chronicle;* Irenaeus (apparently) IV, X, 1 (XXI); Tertullian *adv* Judaeos, 8; Africanus, in Routh, *Rell.* Sacr. II. 297.

"The Crucifixion then should be placed rather on the 14th than on the 15th of Nisan." [10] The fourteenth of Nisan was the day of preparation, the day the lambs were slaughtered. The feast was on the 15th. On this day Jesus was lying in His tomb and could therefore not be among those who participated in the paschal supper.

Radiations and Diet

"We eat food when we are hungry, to satisfy an appetite which is both physical and psychic. Probably if we would give more consideration to the psychic potentialities involving appetite, we would enjoy a more heathful co-ordination of mind and body.

"The general notion that all foods are burnt up in the body, like fuel in a steam engine, doesn't encourage abstinence or selection of any sort.

"However, the human system is a great deal more complex than a steam engine.

"It is a reduction plant, capable of separating and processing the foods we eat and the air we breathe.

"In the human body, just as in the universe, natural law is the dominant factor. The same laws govern the forces of attraction and repulsion or the quality and behavior of various electro-magnetic and other radiations. Just as atomic substances are in effect reduced to probably the same radiations from which they generated in the universe, so the human body reduces food energy in part to radiations. In other words, the organic radiations which seem to emerge from the body may be the vital properties of the food we eat which have endured a complex process of reduction.

"It has been suggested in experiment that the hairlike portions of the chromosomes in the cell nucleus form a tiny oscillating mechanism. This mechanism might well be a partial means of expending the converted food energy or the effects of respiration in the form of radiations.

"It is entirely probable that the effectiveness of these radiations depends in part upon the temper and tone of the cell wall as a responding or reflecting surface. It might be that the secret of longevity involves the temper and tone of the cell planes or walls.

"But why, one might ask, does the human body radiate? Probably for the same reason that the earth radiates: to conclude a contact with outside forces vital to its orderly function.

"Body radiations might represent the only means through which a living being can maintain contact with various outside radiations vital to its existence.

"If food is the raw material which the body ultimately reduces to radiations, then a wholesome diet is most important to one's general well being.

"Such a diet must be both complementary and sympathetic to purer and more wholesome vibrations of mind, as well as the requirements of the physical system, i.e., the whole body is mind.

"Flesh foods do not contain in substance or principle either of these attributes.

"An animal carcass represents death in all its heinous sequences of suffering. How can it induce other than like effects when absorbed into a living system?

"For example, through the operation of various electronic laboratory equipment, a telecast has been recorded upon paper or plastic tape. In actual practice therefore all the horrors attending the sufferings, tortures, executions and deaths at a prison camp could be inscribed upon a narrow strip of paper.

"If such vibrations can be permanently recorded upon a strip of paper, does it not seem even more likely that the pain and suffering attending the slaughter of an animal are likewise indelibly fixed in its flesh? If vibrations of sound and light are compatible to transcription or reproduction, does it not seem reasonable that emotional vibrations are equally if not more susceptible to reproduction?

"Are not emotional responses usually effected through some outside stimulation which records certain events, upon or through the nervous system? If nerve responses are brought about through various electro-magnetic impulses, then it is reasonable to suppose that these impulses are capable of a similar influence upon the flesh, even as they are upon a piece of paper tape.

"Upon a paper tape such vibrations are reposed in a latent state even as are the emotional potentials they represent. They need only an electronic reproducing mechanism to bring about a re-enactment of the exact incident they involve.

"The animal body is an electronic mechanism far more

complex and infinitely more sensitive in its potentials than the mere workings of man's inventions. What limitation can one put upon the reacting potential of the animal system? Surely the dire emotional behavior of the human entity is not a natural but rather an acquired state: a state brought about in part through dietary extravagances.

"Flesh foods represent in substance and principle, not life, but the contradiction of it. It seems indeed most probable that the extreme emotional disturbances, the cringing terror and mental torture gripping the body of an animal leading up to its slaughter, leave in their wake certain vibrations or humors to contaminate its carcass. Certainly, the pain and suffering the flesh has endured can not be removed through processing. Dead flesh does not radiate. It cannot therefore favor a contact beneficial to the physical function of the human body. Most certainly, it cannot produce a sympathetic accord with radiations intrinsic to life and mind.

"Through experiments conducted at Duke University, it has been demonstrated that animal life even exceeds human capabilities in various extra sensory responses.

"*'The psi-in-animals or anpsi program as a whole has in fact, already grown into an active and fruitful branch of para-psychology.' *

"If animals are capable of extending or responding to certain radiations or vibrations of a special nature, it seems entirely possible that human thought may react to the influencing of these radiations. In a world inhabited by living things, man represents a distinct minority. All other life, including many of his own kind, fear and hate him.

"It seems that the human, or rather inhuman discharges of violent superiority, have all but established the vibratory nature of thought response, in the particular radiating plane of animal versus human consciousness.

"No wonder the human mind is impinged with such a

* New World of Mind, Dr. J. B. Rhine.

variety of acute emotional disturbances unknown to other primates. The chimpanzee and other anthropoids to which man is closely related as an earthly creature do not kill their fellow beings for food. They do not have cancer, polio and many other loathsome diseases common to their more intelligent brothers, and the animals he eats for food.

"We might ponder the thought that nature, acting through a certain protective tendency to insure the survival of an organism, deliberately infects the bodies of certain animals to make their flesh either repulsive or hazardous as a food.

"A good example is the ruvittus or oil fish whose flesh, if eaten, causes severe nausea and vomiting. Some insects, as well as animals, are also protected through selection by their inedible flesh.

"We know that nature is constantly striving to preserve the orderly regeneration of a species. The century-old practices of unsexing food animals and the consistent slaughter of lambs and calves before they can complete their natural cycle, must be contended by the same forces of nature which directed their evolution.

"It seems therefore, that the only means available for nature to correct the interference of man is to somehow inform him that the flesh he covets is unfit for food.

"Returning to the biological or physical process of the body functions, we find that the cell structure is constantly rebuilding, and that the refuse of former cells is being carried off as waste through perspiration and through the kidneys.

"This process is going on at all times, even in the most healthy animal.

"A roast beef or a steak is proportionally made up of new cells and the waste or refuse which would have in a matter of minutes been passed off through the kidneys of the living creature.

"Therefore, when man eats meat, his kidneys must do double duty—they must eliminate the waste products of both his own body cell structure, as well as proportionately, the waste of the cell structure of the animal he eats!

"It has been observed in a laboratory experiment that the melting point of pork fat can be raised 20 degrees by feeding a hog a diet of mutton fat.

"This seems to indicate that the properties of animal fat are transferred from one animal to another. A pork eater therefore, carries around as part of his carcass, slabs of swine fat. This rather distasteful observation cannot flatter the vaunted pride of man as a superior creature. Most certainly it cannot add much to the dignity he is capable of."[11]

It might also be pointed out that man is about the only animal whose dietary habits parallel those of the hyena and the carrion eating vultures in his consumption of dead, moldy, and putrefied flesh.

* * * *

In a report issued in Sept., 1948, by Maurice C. Keighley, secretary of the Vegetarian Society of Leeds, England, the contents of a letter from Dr. Szekely to Mrs. Sadie Stave, Associate Editor of the "American Vegetarian," is presented in part.

Dr. Szekely affirms that the manuscript, from which he translated and published parts, is from the disciple John. He writes: "My translation consists of the Aramaic and Ancient Slav texts which I compared and edited. The Aramaic text is in the library of the Vatican, "Biblioteca Apostolica Vaticana" under the care of Anselmo M. Albareda, Perfecto. The Ancient Slav Text was in the Royal Library of the Hapsburgs, now the property of the Austrian Government. If I recall correctly, its reference is 156-P. From my English translation Professor Werner Zimmerman translated it into German and published it from the same also into French and published it in Switzerland in 1946. There also appeared Spanish and Hungarian editions, all based upon my first translation of the Aramaic."

The writer has not seen the original manuscripts referred to by Dr. Szekely but their reported contents certainly do parallel the doctrines of the primitive Christians, the Essenes, Nazarenes, and the Ebionites, as well as those of many later Christian Sects.

If anyone wishes to satisfy his own doubts about the authenticity of these reports, he can check the references Dr. Szekely gives in his letter to Mrs. Stave.

Appendix

1 Newsweek, March 11, 1957.
2 See National Geographic Magazine, October, 1953. Taken from a reprint in Today's Foods, Autumn, 1958, Pacific Union Assn. of Seventh Day Adventists.
3 Encyclopedia Britannica, Vol. 27, p. 968.
4 Geoffrey L. Rudd, *Why Kill for Food.* The Vegetarian Society, Bank Square, Wilmslow Cheshire, England.
5 Los Angeles Times, March 21, 1955.
6 Miami Herald, Mon. September 3, 1956.
7 Paraphrased from On Behalf of the Creatures, by Rev. J. Todd Ferrier. (Order of the Cross, 10 De Vere Gardens, Kensington, London)
8 From Science and Health with key to the Scriptures by Mary Baker Eddy, p. 514—L 18 * L 28.
10 See Bible, *Encyclopedia Britannica.*
9 Rev. Holmes-Gore, M.A. *These We Have Not Loved.* The C. W. Daniel Co., Ltd., Ashingdon, Rochford, Essex.
11 Upton Clary Ewing, *Thresholds of Existence.* Philosophical Library, N. Y.

INDEX

Elizabeth 103, 106, 196
Elkesaites 88
Eloah 185
Elohim 185, 366
Emanuel 110, 316
Embryo 185
Emotional frustrations
 A cure for 262
Empedokles 164
Eneratites 35, 36, 85
Encyclopedia
—Brittanica 90, 217, 344
—Catholic 345
—Hastings 90, 262
—Religion & Ethics 90, 363
Enemies
—Love 124
—Revile 126
Enoch 55, 366
Enslin Morton Scott 27
Ephesus 50
Epiphanius 33, 34, 35, 187, 307,
 325, 343
Epistles of Paul 15, 16
—of James 16
—of John 16
—of Jude 16
—of Peter 16
—of Timothy 16
—of Titus 16
Equilibrium, State of 262
Esau, the hunter 348
Eschatolog (y) 42
—(ical) experience 2
Essenes 1, V, 34, 42, 44, 49, 78, 87,
 104, 116, 138, 177, 193, 237, 290
—Four thousand 333
—house open 72
—returned 179
Essenism 80
Essenic priesthood 198
Essenio-Christians 64
Essene Christ, 1, 23, 50, 56, 82
—documents 23
—prophecy 174
—Scriptures 161, 188
Ethics
—as Reverence for Life
 8, 398, 405, 406
—has many facets 396
—of Love 64, 280

—of Jesus 7
—Religion of Jesus 7
—Rudiments of, 406
—Universal 8
Ethical IX, 406
—metaphysics 403
—mysticism VII
—responsibility 7, 406
—Spirituality 7
—vs., Sensational 254, 278, 289
Eusebius 18, 21, 23, 33, 35, 36,
 82, 85, 344
Evangelists 92, 94
—not one an eye witness 15
Eve 161, 185
Evil, 118, 125, 126, 130
—interpreted 96
—unnatural 401
Evolution of life 403, 404, 405
Example XII, 2, 283, 387, 388
Eye Witness, not one is 15
Eyre-Smith E. 356
Ezekiel, made to conform
 to priestly code 112

—F—

Fables, cunning 5
Faith 152
—a discussion of 384, 388
—James on 385, 386
—that saves 283, 387
Fall, The 97, 165, 366, 390, 396,
 400
False
—Christs 48
—expositors V, 233
—doctrines 233
—hood 118
—hopes 283
—in principle 94
—Scribes 126, 228
Fast 109, 132, 134, 201, 206
—definition of 354, 355
Father
—Ambrose Agius 356
—Heavenly 117, 122, 128, 131,
 133,210
—of all creation 389
—Zossima 360
Ferrier Rev. J. Todd 363
Fig tree, to curse 129